MCSE Microsoft® Windows NT® Server Exam Guide,
Second Edition

Written by Emmett Dulaney

Contents at a Glance

A Division of Macmillan USA
201 W. 103rd Street
Indianapolis, Indiana 46290

MW01182095

MCSE Microsoft Windows NT Server Exam Guide, Second Edition

Copyright © 2000 by Que Corporation

International Standard Book Number: 0-7897-2264-x

Library of Congress Catalog Card Number: 99-65933

Printed in the United States of America

First Printing: **November 1999**

01   00   99   4   3   2   1

Trademarks

All terms mentioned in this book that are known to be trademarks or service marks have been appropriately capitalized. Que cannot attest to the accuracy of this information. Use of a term in this book should not be regarded as affecting the validity of any trademark or service mark.

Use of the Microsoft Approved Study Guide Logo on this product signifies that it has been independently reviewed and approved in complying with the following standards:

- Acceptable coverage of all content related to Microsoft exam number 70-067, entitled Implementing and Supporting Microsoft Windows NT.

- Sufficient performance-based exercises that relate closely to all required content.

- Technically accurate content, based on sampling of text.

Warning and Disclaimer

Credits

Publisher
Jim Minatel

Acquisitions Editor
Tracy Williams

Development Editors
Jill Hayden
Todd Brakke

Managing Editor
Lisa Wilson

Project Editor
Linda Seifert

Copy Editor
Fran Blauw

Indexer
Heather McNeill

Proofreader
Katherin Bidwell

Technical Editor
Bruce Ford

Team Coordinator
Vicki Harding

Software Development Specialist
Michael Hunter

Interior Designer
Ann Jones

Production
Dan Harris
Timothy Osborn

Composed in ***AGaramond*** and ***Futura*** by Que Corporation.

For Kristin, Evan, Spencer, and Karen.

Table of Contents

APPENDIXES

About the Author

Emmett Dulaney, MCSE, MCP+I, CNA, A+, Network+ is the Certification Corner columnist for Windows NT Systems Magazine and cofounder of D S Technical Solutions. A Windows NT/certification instructor for Indiana University/Purdue University of Fort Wayne, he is also the author of over a dozen titles on certification and Windows NT integration.

Acknowledgments

First and foremost, all credit should be given to Steve Kaczmarek—the author of the first edition of the book you are holding. Were it not for his expertise and prose in the beginning, this book would have never come to pass.

At Que, Jim Minatel, Tracy Williams, and Jill Hayden are owed an enormous amount of gratitude for making this edition possible. Rick Kughen, Todd Brakke, and Kezia Endsley are to be thanked for their skillful development edits, and Jim Cooper for overseeing the technical accuracy.

Lastly, thanks are due to Jeff Durham for helping manage the project from conception to submission.

Tell Us What You Think!

As the reader of this book, *you* are our most important critic and commentator. We value your opinion and want to know what we're doing right, what we could do better, what areas you'd like to see us publish in, and any other words of wisdom you're willing to pass our way.

As a Publisher for Que, I welcome your comments. You can fax, email, or write me directly to let me know what you did or didn't like about this book—as well as what we can do to make our books stronger.

Please note that I cannot help you with technical problems related to the topic of this book, and that due to the high volume of mail I receive, I might not be able to reply to every message.

When you write, please be sure to include this book's title and author as well as your name and phone or fax number. I will carefully review your comments and share them with the author and editors who worked on the book.

Fax: 317-581-4666

Email: certification@macmillanusa.com

Mail: Publisher
          Que
          201 West 103rd Street
          Indianapolis, IN 46290
          USA

Introduction

This book was written by Microsoft Certified Professionals for Microsoft Certified Professionals and MCP candidates. It is designed, in combination with your real-world experience, to prepare you to pass the Implementing and Supporting Microsoft Windows NT Server 4.0 exam (70-67), as well as to give you a background in performance monitoring, optimizing, system management, and troubleshooting in a Windows NT Server environment.

You should have a strong working knowledge of the following subjects before beginning a study of this product:

- **Windows 95:** It is strongly suggested that you be well acquainted with the look and feel of Windows 95, because this is also the interface used by Windows NT 4.0. Although Windows 98 is available as a product and a certification exam, the Server exam was written and released when Windows 95 was the newest non–NT client available. You therefore must know certain elements of Windows 95 for questions that can appear on this exam, but you need no knowledge of Windows 98.

- **Windows NT Server 4.0:** It is not the intention of this book to teach you Windows NT Server 4.0. Instead, this book builds on your existing knowledge of the product. Wherever it is appropriate, however, functions and procedures are reviewed.

- **Basic networking concepts:** Again, it is not the intention of this book to teach you how to network or to explain what networking is all about. Instead, you'll learn how you can use Windows NT Server 4.0 to create and manage a network environment.

As of this writing, the exams cost $100 each. The exam format changes regularly, and Microsoft is not required to announce a change. The most popular formats used are a 15-question adaptive exam, a 30-question shortened standard exam, and a 55-question standard exam. Each of these formats is discussed in the appendixes of this book, but regardless of the format, you are expected to know the product well—and the purpose of this book is to ensure that you do.

Depending on the certification you are pursuing (MCP, MCSE, and so on), you may have to take as many as seven exams, covering Microsoft operating systems, application programs, networking, and software development. Each test involves preparation, study, and for some of us, heavy doses of test anxiety. Is certification worth the trouble?

Microsoft has cosponsored research that provides some answers.

Exam Objectives

The Implementing and Supporting Microsoft Windows NT Server 4.0 certification exam measures your ability to implement, administer, and troubleshoot Windows NT Server 4.0 computer systems in a large, processing-intensive environment. It focuses on determining your skills in six major categories:

- Planning
- Installation and Configuration
- Managing Resources
- Connectivity
- Monitoring and Optimization
- Troubleshooting

The Implementing and Supporting Microsoft Windows NT Server 4.0 certification exam uses these categories to measure your abilities. Before taking this exam, you should be proficient in the job skills talked about in the following sections.

Planning

The Planning section tests your understanding of the hardware requirements of Windows NT Server 4.0. You'll also need a knowledge of general networking concepts.

Objectives for Planning

- Plan the disk drive configuration for various requirements, including
  - Choosing a file system
  - Choosing a fault-tolerance method

- Choose a protocol for various situations. Protocols include
  - TCP/IP (Transmission Control Protocol/Internet Protocol)
  - NWLink IPX/SPX (Internetworking Packet Exchange/Sequenced Packet Exchange) Compatible Transport Protocol
  - NetBEUI (Network BIOS Extended User Interface)

Installation and Configuration

The Installation and Configuration part of the Server exam tests you on virtually every possible component of Windows NT Server 4.0.

Objectives for Installation and Configuration

- Install Windows NT Server on Intel-based platforms.
- Install Windows NT Server to perform various server roles, such as
  - Primary domain controller
  - Backup domain controller
  - Member server
- Install Windows NT Server by using various methods, such as
  - CD-ROM
  - Over the network
  - Network Client Administrator
  - Express versus Custom
- Configure protocols and protocol bindings. Protocols include
  - TCP/IP
  - NWLink IPX/SPX Compatible Transport Protocol
  - NetBEUI
- Configure network adapters. Considerations include
  - Changing *interrupt request* (IRQ), IObase, and memory addresses
  - Configuring multiple adapters
- Configure Windows NT Server core services. Services include
  - Directory Replicator
  - License Manager
  - Other services

- Configure peripherals and devices, including
  - Communication devices
  - *Small computer system interface* (SCSI) devices
  - Tape device drivers
  - *Uninterruptible power supply* (UPS) devices and UPS service
  - Mouse drivers, display drivers, and keyboard drivers
- Configure hard disks to meet various requirements. Requirements include
  - Allocating disk space capacity
  - Providing redundancy
  - Improving performance
  - Providing security
  - Formatting
- Configure printers. Tasks include
  - Adding and configuring a printer
  - Implementing a printer pool
  - Setting print priorities
- Configure a Windows NT Server computer for various types of client computers, such as
  - Windows NT Workstation
  - Microsoft Windows® 95
  - Microsoft MS-DOS®–based

Managing Resources

The Managing Resources component concentrates on daily administration issues.

Objectives for Managing Resources

- Manage user and group accounts. Considerations include
  - Managing Windows NT groups
  - Managing Windows NT user rights
  - Administering account policies
  - Auditing changes to the user account database

- Create and manage policies and profiles for various situations. Policies and profiles include
  - Local user profiles
  - Roaming user profiles
  - System policies
- Administer remote servers from various types of client computers. Client computer types include
  - Windows 95
  - Windows NT Workstation
- Manage disk resources. Tasks include
  - Copying and moving files between file systems
  - Creating and sharing resources
  - Implementing permissions and security
  - Establishing file auditing

Connectivity

The Connectivity component of the Server certification exam concentrates on how to use the various interconnecting components of the TCP/IP protocol, *Remote Access Service* (RAS), and NetWare, among others.

Objectives for Connectivity

- Configure Windows NT Server for interoperability with NetWare servers by using various tools. Tools include
  - Gateway Services for NetWare
  - Migration Tool for NetWare
- Install and configure RAS. Configuration options include
  - Configuring RAS communications
  - Configuring RAS protocols
  - Configuring RAS security
  - Configuring Dial-Up Networking clients

Monitoring and Optimization

The Monitoring and Optimization component of the NT Server 4.0 Server certification exam focuses on performance issues.

Objectives for Monitoring and Optimization

- Monitor performance of various functions by using Performance Monitor. Functions include
  - Processor
  - Memory
  - Disk
  - Network
- Identify performance bottlenecks.

Troubleshooting

The Troubleshooting component of the certification exam includes a number of components running the entire gamut of troubleshooting.

Objectives for Troubleshooting

Choose the appropriate course of action to take in order to resolve

- Installation failures
- Boot failures
- Configuration errors
- Printer problems
- RAS problems
- Connectivity problems
- Resource access and permission problems
- Fault-tolerance failures. Fault-tolerance methods include
  - Tape backup
  - Mirroring
  - Stripe set with parity
  - Disk duplexing

Benefits for Your Organization

At companies participating in a 1994 Dataquest survey and many since then, a majority of corporate managers stated that certification is an important factor in the overall success of their companies because of these reasons:

- Certification increases customer satisfaction. Customers look for indications that their suppliers understand the industry and have the ability to respond to their technical problems. Having Microsoft Certified Professionals on staff reassures customers; it tells them that your employees have used and mastered Microsoft products.
- Certification maximizes training investment. The certification process specifically identifies skills that an employee is lacking or areas where additional training is needed. By so doing, it validates training and eliminates the costs and loss of productivity associated with unnecessary training. In addition, certification records enable a company to verify an employee's technical knowledge and track retention of skills over time.

Microsoft maintains current case studies on the benefits of certification at `http://www.microsoft.com/train_cert`.

Benefits Up Close and Personal

Microsoft also cites a number of benefits for the certified individual:

- Industry recognition of expertise, enhanced by Microsoft's promotion of the Certified Professional community to the industry and potential clients
- Access to technical information directly from Microsoft
- A complimentary one-year subscription to *Microsoft Certified Professional Magazine*
- Microsoft Certified Professional logos and other materials to publicize MCP status to colleagues and clients
- Invitations to Microsoft conferences and technical training sessions, plus a special-events program newsletter from the MCP program

Additional benefits, depending on the certification, include the following:

- Microsoft TechNet or Microsoft Developer Network membership or discounts
- A one-year subscription to the Microsoft Beta Evaluation program, providing up to 12 monthly CD-ROMs containing beta software for upcoming Microsoft software products
- Eligibility to join the Network Professional Association, a worldwide independent association of computer professionals

Some intangible benefits of certification are

- Enhanced marketability with current or potential employers and customers, along with an increase in earnings potential
- Methodology for objectively assessing current skills, individual strengths, and specific areas where training is required

How Does This Book Fit In?

One of the challenges that has always faced the would-be Microsoft Certified Professional is deciding how to best prepare for an examination. In doing so, there are always conflicting goals, such as how to prepare for the exam as quickly as possible and yet still learn how to do the work that passing the exam qualifies you to do.

Our goal for this book is to make your studying job easier by filtering through the reams of Windows NT 4.0 technical material. Through the chapters and lab exercises, this book presents only the information you actually need to know to pass the Windows NT 4.0 certification exam (plus a little bit extra). Other information we think is important for you to have available while you're working has been relegated to the appendixes, sidebars, and notes.

How to Study with This Book

This book is designed to be used in a variety of ways. Instead of locking you into one particular method of studying, forcing you to read through sections you're already intimately familiar with, or tying you to your computer, we've made it possible for you to read the chapters at one time and do the labs at another. We've also made it easy for you to decide whether you need to read a chapter by giving you a pre-chapter quiz, a list of the topics and skills covered at the beginning of each chapter, and a description of how the chapter relates to previous material.

Labs are arranged topically so that you can use them to explore the areas and concepts of Windows NT 4.0 that are new to you, or that you need reinforcement in. We've also decided not to mix the labs with the text of the chapter, because nothing is more frustrating than not being able to continue reading a chapter because your child is doing his homework on the computer, and you can't use it until the weekend.

The chapters are written in a modular fashion, so you don't necessarily have to read all the chapters preceding a certain chapter to be able to follow that particular chapter's discussion. The prerequisites for each chapter specify the knowledge you need to have to successfully comprehend the current chapter's contents. Frequently, subsequent chapters build on material presented in previous chapters. For example, Chapter 2, "Understanding Microsoft Windows NT 4.0 ," explains the features and functions offered by the network operating system. Without a thorough understanding of the implications of this concept, the rest of the material presented in the book will be less than satisfying.

Don't skip the lab exercises, either. You certainly can practice what you read on your PC while you are reading. Some of the knowledge and skills you need to pass the Windows NT 4.0 MCP exam can be acquired only by working with Windows NT 4.0. Lots of practice and the lab exercises help you acquire these skills.

The Chapter Notes companion booklet that accompanies this book condenses the information in each chapter into bullets and lists. Use the Chapter Notes to

- Review pertinent facts before reading each chapter.
- Study key concepts after reading each chapter.
- Review right before taking the actual exam.

Note that the Chapter Notes booklet is a companion to this text and is not intended to be a standalone entity. Only the Exam Guide gives you all the information you need to pass the exam.

How This Book Is Organized

The book contains 17 chapters. Each chapter has information relating to a common subject or theme that is an important piece of the overall picture.

- Chapter 1, "Microsoft Certified Professional Program," gives you an overview of the Microsoft Certified Professional program, what certifications are available to you, and where Windows NT 4.0 and this book fit in.
- Chapter 2, "Understanding Microsoft Windows NT 4.0," provides an overview of the network operating system and the features it includes.

- Chapter 3, "Windows NT Server 4.0 Setup," explores how Windows NT is installed in the Intel environment.

- Chapter 4, "Configuring Windows NT Server 4.0," explores configuration settings, both basic and advanced.

- Chapter 5, "Managing Users and Groups," discusses users, groups, and profiles.

- Chapter 6, "Security and Permissions," explores security and access control lists. It also covers shares and setting permissions on shares.

- Chapter 7, "Managing Disk Resources," discusses the *file allocation table* (FAT) versus *New Technology File System* (NTFS), and the different partitioning options that NT supports.

- Chapter 8, "Performance Monitor," examines how to use the Performance Monitor to evaluate performance and tune the server.

- Chapter 9, "Disk Management and Fault Tolerance," discusses *redundant array of inexpensive/independent disks* (RAID) levels available in Windows NT Server.

- Chapter 10, "Managing Printers in the Domain," examines the printing process and how to add a printer, including information on printer spooling and setting priorities.

- Chapter 11, "Windows NT 4.0 Architecture and Boot Sequence," dives into the guts of NT, discussing the difference between user and kernel modes.

- Chapter 12, "Windows NT Networking Services," examines the basic structure of network connectivity and how browsing works.

- Chapter 13, "TCP/IP and Windows NT," shows you how to configure *Dynamic Host Configuration Protocol* (DHCP), *Windows Internet Name Service* (WINS), and *Domain Name Service* (DNS) for Windows NT in a TCP/IP environment.

- Chapter 14, "Novell NetWare Connectivity Tools," examines how Windows NT interacts with NetWare all the way from coexistence to migration.

- Chapter 15, "Network Client Configuration and Support," discusses how to make client computers interact on the NT domain.

- Chapter 16, "Remote Access Server," explains how to set up RAS for NetBEUI, IPX, and TCP/IP.

- Chapter 17, "Network Monitor," examines stop errors and using the kernel debugger.

Appendixes include a glossary, lab exercises, and references to other resources. As mentioned earlier, you can do the lab exercises at your own pace, when you want to—you're not tied down to the computer for every chapter. Any dependencies among the labs are noted at the beginning of each lab. Also, most of the labs assume that you have completed the very first lab, which takes you through the initial configuration of the computers.

All the Windows NT Server 4.0 exam objectives are covered in the text of the chapters and the lab exercises. Information in sidebars gives you history, extends the topic, expounds on a related procedure, or provides other details. It is useful information but not primary exam material.

Finally, each appendix in this book provides you with additional advice, resources, and information that can be helpful to you as you prepare and take the Implementing and Supporting NT Server 4.0 Certified Professional exam, and later as you work as a Windows NT 4.0 Certified Professional:

- Appendix A, "Glossary," provides you with definitions of terms that you need to be familiar with as a Windows NT 4.0 MCP.
- Appendix B, "Certification Process," provides an overview of the certification process.
- Appendix C, "Testing Tips" gives you tips and pointers for maximizing your performance when you take the certification exam.
- Appendix D, "Alternate Resources," presents a list of reading resources, Web sites, and other items that can help you prepare for the certification exam.
- Appendix E, "Using the CD-ROM," gives you the basics of how to install and use the CD-ROM included with this book.

Special Features of This Book

Many features in this book make it easier to read and make the information more accessible. The following sections describe those features.

Chapter Overview

Each chapter begins with an overview of the material covered in that chapter. The chapter topics are described in the context of material already covered and material coming up. Also, any prerequisite information you need to fully appreciate the contents of a chapter is presented.

Key Concepts

Key concepts present particularly significant information about a Windows NT function or concept. Count on this material being on the test. Here's an example of a key concept:

Key Concept

When you share a resource in Windows NT, the default is to provide everyone with complete access to the resource. If you want additional security, you must add it yourself by restricting access with permissions.

Underlined Hotkeys or Mnemonics

Hotkeys in this book are underlined as they appear onscreen. In Windows, many menus, commands, buttons, and other options have these hotkeys. To use a hotkey shortcut, press Alt and the key for the underlined character. To choose the Properties button, for example, press Alt and then R. You should not study for the MCP exam by using the hotkeys, however. Windows is a mouse-centric environment, and you will be expected to know how to navigate it using the mouse—clicking, right-clicking, and dragging and dropping.

Shortcut Key Combinations

In this book, shortcut key combinations are joined with plus signs (+). For example, Ctrl+V means to hold down the Ctrl key while you press the V key.

Menu Commands

Instructions for choosing menu commands have this form:

Choose File, New.

This example means that you should open the File menu and choose New, which in this case, opens a new file.

This book also has the following typeface enhancements to indicate special text:

Typeface	Description
Italic	Italics indicate new terms and variables in commands or addresses.
Boldface	Bold indicates text you type.
Computer type	This typeface is used for onscreen messages, commands (such as DOS copy or UNIX commands), and Internet addresses and other locators in the online world.
My Filename.doc	Filenames and folders are set in a mixture of upper- and lowercase characters, just as they appear in Windows NT 4.0.

CHAPTER PREREQUISITE

This chapter has no prerequisites—just a desire to become a Microsoft Certified Professional.

Microsoft Certified Professional Program

─ WHILE YOU READ ─

1. An MCP is any individual who has passed a current exam in any Microsoft Professional track, with one exception. What is the exception?

2. True or false: The MCSE is a widely respected certification, because it focuses on one aspect of computing.

3. Which certification instructionally and technically qualifies you to deliver Microsoft Official Curriculum through Microsoft authorized education sites?

4. To maintain certification, a Microsoft Certified Trainer is required to pass the exam for a new product within how many months of the exam's release?

5. An MCP+I is an MCP who has specialized in _____ technologies.

As Microsoft products take an increasing share of the marketplace, the demand for trained personnel grows, and the number of certifications follows suit. As of July 1999, the team of Microsoft Certified Professionals increased to more than 376,000 product specialists, more than 159,000 engineers, and more than 23,000 solution developers. There were also more than 20,000 certified trainers of Microsoft products.

There is every indication that these numbers will continue to grow, given Microsoft's commitment to its products and to the certification program, as well as the continued market interest in these products and in those certified to administer them. The best place to look for changes is Microsoft's Web site at `www.microsoft.com/train_cert`.

This chapter covers the Microsoft Certified Professional Program and describes each certification in more detail. Microsoft certifications include the following:

- Microsoft Certified Professional (MCP)
- Microsoft Certified Professional + Internet (MCP+I)
- Microsoft Certified Professional + Site Builder
- Microsoft Certified Systems Engineer (MCSE)
- Microsoft Certified System Engineer + Internet (MCSE+I)
- Microsoft Certified Database Administrator (MCDBA)
- Microsoft Certified Solutions Developer (MCSD)
- Microsoft Certified Trainer (MCT)

Exploring Available Certifications

When Microsoft started certifying people to install and support its products, only one certification was available: the *Microsoft Certified Professional* (MCP). As time went on, employers and prospective customers of consulting firms demanded more specialized certifications. Several certifications now are available from Microsoft, as described in the following sections.

Microsoft Certified Professional (MCP)

As of October 1998, an MCP is any individual who has passed a current exam in any Microsoft Professional track, with one exception: Networking Essentials (exam 70-058). If you take only the exam for which this book is written, you will become an MCP in Windows NT.

Microsoft Certified Professional + Internet (MCP+I)

An MCP+I is an MCP who has specialized in Internet-related technologies. To become certified as such, you must take three exams:

- Implementing and Supporting Microsoft Windows NT Server 4.0 (exam 70-067)
- Internetworking with Microsoft TCP/IP on Microsoft Windows NT 4.0 (exam 70-059)
- Implementing and Supporting Microsoft Internet Information Server 4.0 (exam 70-087)

As of this writing, exam 70-087 can be replaced by exam 70-077 (Implementing and Supporting Internet Information Server 3.0 and Microsoft Index Server 1.1), but the latter exam is scheduled to retire.

Microsoft Certified Professional + Site Builder

One of the newest certifications, this one requires passing two exams out of the following three possibilities:

- Designing and Implementing Web Sites with Microsoft® FrontPage® 98 (exam 70-055)
- Designing and Implementing Commerce Solutions with Microsoft® Site Server 3.0, Commerce Edition (exam 70-057)
- Designing and Implementing Web Solutions with Microsoft® Visual InterDev™ 6.0 (exam 70-152)

Microsoft Certified Systems Engineers (MCSE)

Microsoft Certified Systems Engineers are qualified to plan, implement, maintain, and support information systems based on Microsoft Windows NT and the BackOffice family of client/server software. The MCSE is a widely respected certification, because it does not focus on just one aspect of computing, such as networking. Instead, the MCSE has demonstrated skills and abilities with the full range of software, from client operating systems to server operating systems to client/server applications. Currently, there are two tracks to MCSE certification, and both require you to pass six exams. These are the exams required within the NT 4.0 track:

- Implementing and Supporting Microsoft® Windows NT Server 4.0 (exam 70-067).
- Implementing and Supporting Microsoft® Windows NT Server 4.0 in the Enterprise (exam 70-068).

- Networking Essentials (exam 70-058).
- Choice of a client exam. Choices include Windows NT Workstation 4.0 (70-073), Windows 95 (exam 70-064), and Windows 98 (exam 70-098).
- Two electives of the candidate's choosing from a large list of valid options. You can find an up-to-date list at http://www.microsoft.com/train_cert.

The Networking Essentials exam requirement is waived for those candidates who are also Novell *Certified NetWare Engineers* (CNE) or Banyan *Certified Banyan Engineers* (CBE).

Microsoft Certified Systems Engineer + Internet (MCSE+I)

An expansion of the MCSE certification, with a specialty in Internet technology, this certification has the following requirements:

- Implementing and Supporting Microsoft® Windows NT Server 4.0 (exam 70-067).
- Implementing and Supporting Microsoft® Windows NT Server 4.0 in the Enterprise (exam 70-068).
- Networking Essentials (exam 70-058).
- Internetworking with Microsoft® TCP/IP on Microsoft® Windows NT 4.0 (exam 70-059).
- Choice of a client exam. Choices include Windows NT Workstation 4.0 (70-073), Windows 95 (exam 70-064), and Windows 98 (exam 70-098).
- Implementing and Supporting Microsoft® Internet Information Server 4.0 (exam 70-087) or exam 70-077 (Implementing and Supporting Microsoft® Internet Information Server 3.0 and Microsoft® Index Server 1.1).
- Either exam 70-079 (Implementing and Supporting Microsoft Internet Explorer 4.0 by Using the Internet Explorer Administration Kit) or exam 70-080 (Implementing and Supporting Microsoft® Internet Explorer 5.0 by Using the Microsoft® Internet Explorer Administration Kit).
- Two electives of the candidate's choosing from a list that has been narrowed to include only SQL, Site Server, Exchange, Proxy Server, and *Systems Network Architecture* (SNA).

Microsoft Certified Database Administrator (MCDBA)

To become certified as a Database Administrator, you must pass five exams:

- Implementing and Supporting Microsoft® Windows NT Server 4.0 (exam 70-067)
- Implementing and Supporting Microsoft® Windows NT Server 4.0 in the Enterprise (exam 70-068)
- Administering Microsoft® SQL Server™ 7.0 (exam 70-028)
- Designing and Implementing Databases with Microsoft® SQL Server™ 7.0 (exam 70-029)
- An elective in a number of categories, including more SQL, Visual C++, TCP/IP, *Internet Information Server* (IIS), Visual Basic, or Visual FoxPro

Microsoft Certified Solution Developers (MCSD)

Microsoft Certified Solution Developers are qualified to design and develop custom business solutions with Microsoft development tools, platforms, and technologies such as Microsoft BackOffice and Microsoft Office. MCSD candidates are required to demonstrate a full understanding of 32-bit architecture, *Distributed Component Object Model* (DCOM), Visual Studio, and other related topics. Requirements include passing four exams:

- Analyzing Requirements and Defining Solution Architectures (exam 70-100)
- An exam in designing desktop applications in Visual C++, Visual FoxPro, or Visual Basic
- An exam in designing distributed applications in Visual C++, Visual FoxPro, or Visual Basic
- An elective from a number of programming categories

Microsoft Certified Trainers (MCT)

Microsoft Certified Trainers are instructionally and technically qualified to deliver Microsoft Official Curriculum through Microsoft authorized education sites. These sites consist of Microsoft *Certified Technical Education Centers* (CTECs), including companies such as Productivity Point International, which specializes in offering technical and application training to corporate clients, and *Authorized Academic Training Partners* (AATPs), which represents educational institutions that offer certified classes for continuing education. In order for a trainer to be certified by Microsoft as an MCT, that trainer also must have attended and completed—or, in some cases, studied—each certified class that he or she expects to teach.

Understanding the Exam Requirements

The exams are computer-administered tests that measure your ability to implement and administer Microsoft products or systems; troubleshoot problems with installation, operation, or customization; and provide technical support to users. The exams do more than test your ability to define terminology and recite facts. Product knowledge is an important foundation for superior job performance, but definitions and feature lists are just the beginning. In the real world, you need hands-on skills and the ability to apply your knowledge—to understand confusing situations, solve thorny problems, optimize solutions to minimize downtime, and maximize current and future productivity.

To develop exams that test for the correct competence factors, Microsoft follows an eight-phase exam-development process:

1. In the first phase, experts analyze the tasks that make up the job being tested. This job-analysis phase identifies the knowledge, skills, and abilities related specifically to the performance area to be certified.

2. The next phase develops objectives by building on the framework provided by the job analysis. This means translating the job-function tasks into specific and measurable units of knowledge, skills, and abilities. The resulting list of objectives (the objective domain) is the basis for developing certification exams and training materials.

3. Selected contributors rate the objectives developed in the previous phase. The reviewers are technology professionals who are currently performing the applicable job function. After the objectives are prioritized and weighted based on the contributors' input, the objectives become the blueprint for the exam items.

4. During the fourth phase, exam items are reviewed and revised to ensure that they are technically accurate, clear, unambiguous, plausible, free of cultural bias, and not misleading or tricky. Items also are evaluated to confirm that they test for high-level, useful knowledge instead of obscure or trivial facts.

5. During alpha review, technical and job-function experts review each item for technical accuracy, reach a consensus on all technical issues, and edit the reviewed items for clarity of expression.

6. The next step is the beta exam. Beta exam participants take the test to gauge its effectiveness. Microsoft performs a statistical analysis based on the responses of the beta participants—including information about difficulty and relevance—to verify the validity of the exam items and to determine which items are used in the final certification exam.

7. When the statistical analysis is complete, the items are distributed into multiple parallel forms, or versions, of the final certification exam—usually within six to eight weeks of the beta exam.

During this phase, a group of job-function experts determines the cut, or minimum passing score, for the exam. (The cut score differs from exam to exam, because it is based on an item-by-item determination of the percentage of candidates who answered the item correctly.)

If you participate in a beta exam, you may take it at a cost that is lower than the cost of the final certification exam (typically by half), but it should not be taken lightly. Beta exams actually contain the entire pool of possible questions, about 30 percent of which are dropped after the beta. The remaining questions are divided into the different forms of the final exam. If you decide to take a beta exam, you should review and study as seriously as you would for a final certification exam. Passing a beta exam counts as passing the final exam—you receive full credit for passing a beta exam.

Also, because you will be answering all the questions that will be used for the exam, expect a beta to take significantly longer than the final exam.

8. The final phase—Exam Live!—is administered by Sylvan Prometric or *Virtual University Enterprise* (VUE)—independent testing companies. The exams always are available at Sylvan Prometric testing centers worldwide. You can schedule an exam by calling 800-755-EXAM or going to www.2test.com. To register with VUE worldwide, visit its Web site at www.vue.com or call 888-837-8616.

Windows NT 3.51 Track to the MCSE Certification

As of this writing, the NT 3.51 track is still valid for MCSE certification but is scheduled to retire with the release of Windows 2000. The exams required follow:

- Implementing and Supporting Microsoft Windows NT Server 3.51 (exam 70-043)
- Implementing and Supporting Microsoft Windows NT Workstation 3.51 (exam 70-042)
- Networking Essentials (exam 70-058)
- A valid client exam
- Two electives chosen by the candidate from a large list. You can find up-to-date lists at http://www.microsoft.com/train_cert.

As with the MCSE track under 4.0, exam 70-058 (Networking Essentials) is waived for those who are similarly certified by another vendor.

Continuing Certification Requirements

After you gain an MCP certification, such as the Microsoft Certified Systems Engineer certification, your work isn't over. Microsoft requires you to maintain your certification by updating your exam credits as new products are released and old ones are retired.

A Microsoft Certified Trainer is required to pass the exam for a new product within three months of the exam's release. For example, the Windows NT Server 4.0 exam (70-67) and Enterprise Exam (70-68) were released in December of 1996. All MCTs were required to pass these exams by March 31, 1997, or lose certification to teach the Windows NT 4.0 Core Technologies course.

Holders of the other MCP certifications (MCSD, MCSE) are required to replace an exam that gives them qualifying credit within six months to a year of the withdrawal of that exam. For example, the Windows for Workgroups 3.10 exam was one of the original electives for the MCSE certification. When it was withdrawn, MCSEs had six months to replace it with another elective exam, such as the TCP/IP exam.

After you become a certified trainer, you begin receiving monthly updates regarding the tests and courses that have become obsolete, as well as the introduction of new courses, tests, and certification requirements via Microsoft's *Education Forum* newsletter. You also can find updates by browsing Microsoft's Web site at `www.microsoft.com/train_cert`.

QUESTIONS AND ANSWERS

1. An MCP is any individual who has passed a current exam in any Microsoft Professional track, with one exception. What is the exception?

   A: Networking Essentials (exam 70-058)

2. True or false: The MCSE is a widely respected certification, because it focuses on one aspect of computing.

   A: False. The MCSE has demonstrated skills and abilities with the full range of software, from client operating systems to server operating systems to client/server applications.

3. Which certification instructionally and technically qualifies you to deliver Microsoft Official Curriculum through Microsoft authorized education sites?

   A: *Microsoft Certified Trainer* (MCT)

4. To maintain certification, a Microsoft Certified Trainer is required to pass the exam for a new product within how many months of the exam's release?

   A: Three

5. An MCP+I is an MCP who has specialized in _____ technologies.

   A: Internet-related

CHAPTER PREREQUISITE

Readers should be familiar with the basic operation of Windows 3.x or Windows 95. This book provides a brief overview of the new Windows NT 4.0 user interface, but it is essential that readers have a strong working knowledge of basic networking concepts and terms.

Understanding Microsoft Windows NT 4.0

WHILE YOU READ

1. The type of multitasking employed by Windows NT Server 4.0 is _____.

2. True or false: NT supported *High-Performance File System* (HPFS) through all versions until 4.0.

3. The maximum number of remote dial-in sessions supported by NT Workstation is _____.

4. The number of NT Servers needed to implement the workgroup model is _____.

5. Trust relationships allow an individual to log on to a portion of the enterprise and access resources elsewhere. This is known as _____.

Before beginning a detailed discussion of Microsoft Windows NT 4.0 Server, this chapter provides an overview of the NT product line so that you will gain a clear understanding of what is included and how you can use it in an organization. This chapter then covers the features and functionality of Microsoft Windows NT 4.0 Server.

Exploring Windows NT 4.0's New Features

Microsoft Windows NT is a 32-bit operating system designed to provide fast and efficient performance for power computer users, such as software developers, *computer-aided design* (CAD) programmers, and design engineers. Figure 2.1 shows a glimpse of the features common to both Windows NT Workstation and Windows NT Server (versions 3.51 and 4.0, respectively). Because NT provides better performance for existing 16-bit applications (both MS-DOS and Windows), as well as 32-bit applications developed specifically for the operating system, NT is found increasingly on the desks of business users.

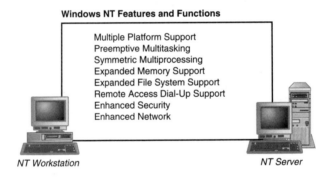

Windows NT Features and Functions

Multiple Platform Support
Preemptive Multitasking
Symmetric Multiprocessing
Expanded Memory Support
Expanded File System Support
Remote Access Dial-Up Support
Enhanced Security
Enhanced Network

NT Workstation   *NT Server*

Figure 2.1
These features are common to both Windows NT Workstation and Windows NT Server.

These performance enhancements include the following:

- Multiple platform support
- Preemptive multitasking
- Expanded processing support
- Expanded memory support
- Expanded file system support
- Remote access dial-up support
- Enhanced security
- Network and communications support

Multiple Platform Support

Microsoft Windows NT is engineered to run on several hardware platforms. The *Hardware Abstraction Layer* (HAL) component of the NT architecture isolates platform-specific information for the operating system—for example, how to interact with a *reduced instruction set computer* (RISC)-based processor as opposed to an Intel x86 processor. This architecture makes NT a highly portable system. Only a few pieces of code, such as the HAL, need to be recompiled. NT supports Intel x86 and Pentium-based computers, as well as RISC-based computers, such as MIPS R4000, DEC Alpha AXP, and PowerPC. Future support will be limited to Intel and Alpha machines.

Preemptive Multitasking

All processes in NT are given at least one thread of operation. A *thread* represents a piece of code related to a process. Loading a file, for example, may require several threads to carry out the process—in other words, locating the file on disk, allocating RAM for the file, moving it into that allocated memory space, and so on. Many processes and applications written for Windows and NT have multiple threads associated with them.

NT can treat each thread of a process independently of the others, providing a greater degree of control over the overall performance of the system. Each thread also is given a processing priority based on its function. For example, an operating system process, such as memory allocation, receives a higher priority for its threads than a file-save process.

 Key Concept

The smallest denominator a process can be divided into is a thread. Windows NT's capability to process threads independently instead of successively enables most processes to complete much faster.

Each thread is given a specific amount of time with the processor. This sometimes is called *time slicing*. Higher-priority threads are processed ahead of lower-priority threads. All the threads of one priority are processed first before those of the next priority, and so on. This process is called *preemptive multitasking*. In addition, certain threads, primarily those that are system related, are processed in the protected mode of the processor (known as ring 0) and thus are protected from other processes and crashes.

Other threads—those related to application functions such as file printing—run in the unprotected mode of the processor. This means that, although they may be given their own memory space, other poorly written applications (and their threads) might try to butt in and cause what generally is referred to as a *General Protection* or *GP fault.* Microsoft has taken several precautions to ensure that this does not happen in NT. These threads, and the precautions Microsoft has installed in NT, are discussed in more detail later in this book. Supporting both multitasking and multithreading gives applications excellent processing support and protection against system hang-ups and crashes.

Expanded Processing Support

Microsoft Windows NT provides symmetric multiprocessing with support for *original equipment manufacturer* (OEM) implementations of up to 32 processors. Every process that runs under NT has at least one thread of operation or programming code associated with it. A process might be *user-generated,* such as the writing of a file to disk or printing a document, or *system-generated,* such as validating a user logon or providing read access to a file.

Symmetric multiprocessing enables the NT operating system to load balance process threads across all available processors in the computer, as opposed to *asymmetric multiprocessing,* in which the operating system takes control of one processor and directs application threads to other available processors.

Expanded Memory Support

Windows NT supports computers with up to 4GB of RAM and theoretic file or partition sizes of up to 16 exabytes (although this number varies, depending on the type of hardware you have). An *exabyte* is 1 billion gigabytes. You might consider that to be a theoretical number, and to a certain extent, it is. However, it was not that long ago that *management information systems* (MIS) departments debated the wisdom of purchasing 10MB disk drives for their users' computers because they felt the drives would never be filled up.

Expanded File System Support

Windows NT provides support for the MS-DOS *file allocation table* (FAT) file system, as well as its own *New Technology File System* (NTFS). Previous versions of NT also supported OS/2's HPFS.

Key Concept

NT 4.0 no longer provides support for the HPFS used by OS/2. Support for HPFS has been in all versions of NT prior to 4.0.

Just as NT can run in two file systems (NTFS and FAT), OS/2 can do likewise (HPFS and FAT). If you are running OS/2 in FAT, migration to NT is simple.

NTFS provides a high level of security in the form of file- and directory-level permissions similar to those found in other network operating systems, such as the trustee rights used in Novell NetWare. NTFS also provides *transaction tracking* to help recover data in the event of system failure, as well as *sector sparing,* which identifies potentially bad disk storage space and moves data to good storage. NTFS also provides data compression implemented as a file or directory property. For more information on NTFS, see Chapter 7, "Managing Disk Resources."

Enhanced Security

Security begins with NT's `WINLOGON` and `NETLOGON` processes, which authenticate user access to a computer, workgroup, or enterprise by validating the username and password, and assigning each user with a security identifier. In addition to this mandatory logon, NT offers share-level resource control, security auditing functions, and file- and directory-level permissions (in NTFS partitions).

Network and Communications Support

Windows NT is designed to provide several internetworking options. The NetBEUI, NWLINK (IPX/SPX), TCP/IP, AppleTalk, and DLC protocols are all supported and included. NT also is supported on Novell NetWare networks, Microsoft LAN Manager, IBM LAN Server and SNA networks, Banyan VINES, and DEC PATHWORKS.

Through *Remote Access Service* (RAS), NT offers a secure dial-up option for clients and servers. RAS clients can remotely access any shared network resource to which they have been given access through RAS's gateway functions, such as shared folders and printers.

In an NT network, valid workstation clients include Microsoft Windows NT Workstations and Servers, Windows 3.x, MS-DOS, Windows for Workgroups, Windows 95, OS/2, Novell NetWare (client/server), and Macintosh.

Choosing Windows NT Workstation or Server

The difference in choosing when to use NT Workstation or NT Server is not necessarily the difference between desktop and enterprise computing. Both NT Workstation and NT Server provide the capability to make resources available on the network and thus act as a "server." For that matter, an NT Server can be made part of a workgroup of NT Workstations to act as the resource server for that workgroup. Choosing between NT Workstation and NT Server really comes down to the features specific to each product and the type of network model that will be implemented. The following sections discuss the differences between NT Workstation and NT Server.

Microsoft Windows NT Workstation

Microsoft Windows NT Workstation is designed for so-called power users, such as developers or CAD designers, but increasingly is becoming the desktop operating system of choice for end-user business computing because of its robust feature set, as described in the preceding section. In addition to those features and functions common to both NT Workstation and NT Server, NT Workstation offers the following specific characteristics (see Fig. 2.2):

- Unlimited outbound peer-to-peer connections.
- Ten inbound client connections for resource access.
- It can be either a RAS client or server, but it supports only one remote dial-in session.
- Retail installation supports two processors for symmetric multiprocessing.
- Acts as an import server for Directory Replication Services.

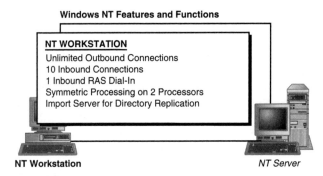

Figure 2.2
Windows NT Workstation features and functions.

Microsoft Windows NT Server

Windows NT Server is designed to provide file, print, and application service support within a given network model. Figure 2.3 lists specific characteristics of NT Server. Although NT Server also can be used as a desktop system, it is engineered to provide optimum performance when providing network services—for example, by optimizing memory differently for application servers than it does for domain controllers.

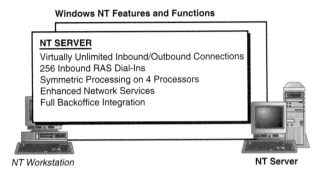

Figure 2.3
Windows NT Server features and functions.

In addition to the features and functions described previously, NT Server offers the following capabilities:

- Allows as many inbound connections to resources as there are valid client licenses (virtually unlimited).

- Supports as many as 256 remote dial-in RAS sessions.

- Retail installation supports as many as four processors for symmetric multi-processing.

- Provides a full set of services for application and network support, such as the following:

    - Services for Macintosh to enable client support for Macintosh computers.

    - Gateway Service for NetWare to enable NT clients to access Novell NetWare file and print resources.

    - Directory Replication Service for copying directory structures and files from a source NT Server computer to a target NT Server or Workstation computer.

- Provides full integration into the Microsoft BackOffice suite, including *Systems Management Server* (SMS), *Systems Network Architecture* (SNA) Server, SQL Server, and Microsoft Exchange Server.

The Microsoft Windows NT Server product can be installed as a server that provides only network-accessible resources or as a domain controller that additionally provides centralized administration of user accounts and resource access. These concepts are reviewed later in this chapter.

CH
2

New Features and Functions in Windows NT 4.0

This newest version of Windows NT continues Microsoft's commitment to reliable, performance-driven, network-ready operating systems by combining the power, features, and functions of the NT operating system with the object-oriented Windows 95 user interface. Enhanced features and functions common to both NT 4.0 Workstation and Server follow:

- Windows 95–like user interface
- Windows Explorer
- Hardware profiles
- Enhanced dial-up networking support
- NetWare Directory Services (NDS)–aware client services for Novell NetWare 4.x
- Integrated Windows Messaging Engine
- Internet Explorer 2.0
- Web services

Windows 95 User Interface

All the basic features of Microsoft's Windows 95 interface have been integrated into Windows NT 4.0, including updated or enhanced system utilities, such as the Performance Monitor (called the System Monitor in Windows 95), as well as additional utilities, such as Windows Explorer, Network Neighborhood, Briefcase, desktop shortcuts, Microsoft Network support, and the Recycle Bin.

Windows Explorer

This feature of the interface replaces the File Manager utility. Windows Explorer provides excellent browsing capabilities for the management of drives, directories, files, and network connections. Explorer presents users' data-access information as a hierarchy of drives, desktop, network connections, folders, and files. The browsing capabilities of Explorer offer not only browsing of file and directory names, but also of data strings within files. Throughout this book and its labs, you will use Windows Explorer to access files and folders, set permissions, create and manage shared folders, and so on.

File Manager

Although Windows Explorer replaces the File Manager utility by default, File Manager still is available and can be launched by users.

Users can run File Manager by following these simple steps:

1. Choose Start from the taskbar.
2. Choose Run from the Start menu.
3. Type the File Manager filename `winfile.exe`.
4. Click OK.

Microsoft recommends using File Manager only until you become comfortable with Windows Explorer. File Manager still is made available only for transitional purposes.

Hardware Profiles

Perhaps one of the most useful enhancements to Windows NT 4.0 is the support for multiple hardware profiles. First introduced in Windows 95, this feature enables you to create hardware profiles to fit various computing needs. The most common example of using hardware profiles is with portable computers. You can create separate profiles to support the portable computer when it is in use by itself, and for when it is positioned in a docking station.

Key Concept

Plug and Play is a feature of Windows 95 that is much appreciated. Note that, although the Plug and Play service has been included with Windows NT 4.0, *hot Plug and Play* (the capability of the operating system to recognize a configuration change on-the-fly and implement it) will not be fully supported until the next major release of Windows NT. Windows NT 4.0 does recognize some hardware changes when it restarts, however. Additional memory or a new hard disk, for example, are detected by NT the next time you boot up.

Enhanced Dial-Up Networking Support

The RAS Client service now is installed as Dial-Up Networking. In addition, NT 4.0 provides the Dial-Up Networking Monitor for monitoring user connections and devices, as well as Remote Access Admin for monitoring remote user access to a RAS Server.

NT 4.0 also offers *universal modem* (Unimodem) driver support, which provides communications technology for fax applications, the Microsoft Exchange client, the Microsoft Network (MSN), and Internet Explorer.

NT 4.0 offers *Telephony Application Programming Interface* (TAPI) 2.0 as well, which provides access to the signaling for setting up calls and managing them, as well as preserving existing media stream functionality to manipulate the information carried over the connection that TAPI establishes. This feature allows applications to not only dial and transfer calls, but also to support fax, desktop conferencing, and applications that use the telephone set dial pad to access voice-prompted menus.

NDS-Aware Client Service for Novell NetWare 4.x

Microsoft provides an enhanced version of its *Client Services for NetWare* (CSNW) with NT 4.0, which supplies compatibility with Novell NetWare servers (versions 3.x and later) running *NetWare Directory Services* (NDS). This feature enables users to view NetWare-shared resources that are organized in a hierarchical tree format.

Integrated Microsoft Windows Messaging

Microsoft Windows Messaging is Microsoft's newest electronic mail product. Windows Messaging has been included with NT 4.0, which enables users to send and receive mail, embed objects in mail messages, and integrate mail functionality into Microsoft applications.

Internet Explorer 2.0

Microsoft's Internet Explorer 2.0 is included with NT 4.0 to provide users access to the Internet. However, Microsoft now offers Internet Explorer 5.0 through its various Internet sites (www.microsoft.com, for example). Watch for Microsoft to continue to enhance this product and make upgrades widely (and cheaply) available.

 Key Concept

Internet Explorer requires that *Transmission Control Protocol/Internet Protocol* (TCP/IP) be installed and a connection made to the Internet.

Web Publishing

Microsoft includes Web publishing services in NT 4.0 that enable you to develop, publish, and manage Web pages, as well as *File Transfer Protocol* (FTP) and Gopher services for your company's intranet or for smaller peer-to-peer networks. With NT 4.0 Server, Microsoft provides Internet Information Services designed for heavy intranet and Internet use. With NT 4.0 Workstation, Microsoft provides *Peer Web Services* (PWS) for smaller workgroup-based Web publishing.

Integrated Network Monitor Agent

NT 4.0 includes a full version of the Network Monitor utility, which is included with Microsoft's Systems Management Server BackOffice product. Network Monitor provides a full range of network-analysis tools for tracking and interpreting network traffic, frames, and so on.

Last, But Certainly Not Least

Of all the features offered with NT 4.0, one feature particularly will give you the most productivity. It also is an example of enhancements made to NT's Open GL and direct-draw video support. This is, of course, PINBALL! Yes, a new game has been added to NT 4.0, and it is quite an addition. As mentioned, it takes full advantage of changes to NT's architecture and enhancements for video support. Try it out!

In addition to these features that NT 4.0 Workstation and Server share, Windows NT 4.0 Server offers the following list of specific features and functions:

- Microsoft *Internet Information Server* (IIS)
- *Domain name server* (DNS) and enhanced support
- *Windows Internet Naming Service* (WINS) name resolution service
- Integrated support for multiprotocol routing
- Enhanced support for *Bootstrap Protocol* (BOOTP) and *Dynamic Host Configuration Protocol* (DHCP) routing
- Remote reboot support for Windows 95 clients
- New remote server administration tools for Windows 95 clients
- Installation wizards for most utility program installations

Distinguishing a Workgroup from a Domain

Two distinct types of networking are supported by Windows NT: *workgroup computing* and the *domain model.* As you plan your network, you need to distinguish between these two types and decide which model best meets your networking needs. The next section compares these two models.

Workgroup Model

The workgroup model of networking is more commonly referred to as the *peer-to-peer model.* In this model, all computers participate in a networking group. All the computers can make resources available to members of the workgroup and can access other computers' resources. In other words, each computer acts as both a workstation and a server.

Computers using Windows NT, Windows 95, and Windows for Workgroups have the capability to participate in a workgroup network model, as Figure 2.4 shows. In fact, both Windows NT Workstations and Windows NT Servers can be members of a workgroup. However, only Windows NT Server offers the added capability of providing user-level security for network resources.

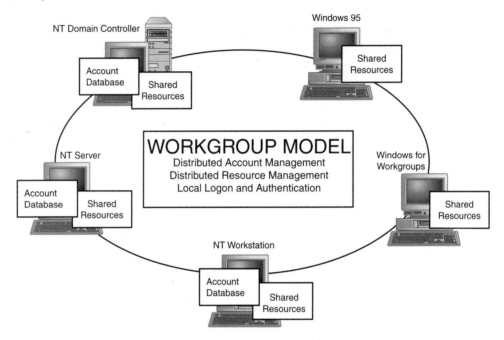

Figure 2.4
An example of the workgroup network model.

Key Concept

Windows 95 can provide user-level network resource security by using an NT (Server or Workstation) or Novell Server. However, this capability requires that one or the other be present on the network.

On computers using Windows NT, access to resources is provided by authenticating the inbound user at the resource computer. Each Windows NT computer participating in a workgroup must maintain a list of users who will be accessing the resources on that computer.

Potentially, this method means that each computer will have at least as many user accounts as participating members in the workgroup. Account administration in a workgroup thus is considered to be distributed, as is resource administration. In other words, the responsibility for maintaining the integrity of user accounts and resource access generally falls to the owner of the computer. A workgroup model, then, might be construed to have limited security potential.

The workgroup model works quite well within smaller networks where the number of users requiring access to workgroup resources is small and easily managed. This number has been suggested to be between 10 and 20 computers/users. As mentioned before, a Windows NT Server can participate in a workgroup. If a larger number of computers or users is required within a workgroup model (more than 20), the more heavily used resources might be located in a Windows NT Server participating in the workgroup. This setup can help simplify the management of large groups of users accessing resources. Nevertheless, the main characteristics of this network model are distributed account management, distributed resource management, and limited security.

Domain Model

The domain model of networking, also known as the *enterprise model,* was introduced by Microsoft as a response to the management challenges presented by the growing workgroup model.

Unlike the workgroup model, the domain model maintains a centralized database of user and group account information (see Fig. 2.5). Resource access is provided by permitting access to users and groups that are members of the domain, and thus appear in the domain's account database. Recall that in the workgroup model, each computer maintains its own account database, which is used for managing resource access at that computer. In the domain model, by virtue of their participation in the domain, the resources use the same central account database for managing user access. Resource managers also enjoy a higher level of security for their resources.

 Key Concept

> In most cases, a workgroup can be created by taking machines that already exist and adding cards and cables to them. A domain is more expensive than a workgroup because it requires the addition of a dedicated server as well.

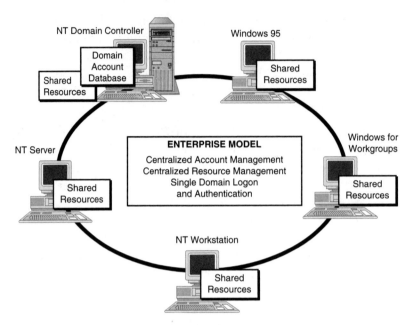

Figure 2.5
An example of the domain network model. The domain model answers what Microsoft refers to as the "enterprise challenge."

Organizing an Enterprise Network

When planning a large *wide-area network* (WAN) for an organization (hereafter referred to as an *enterprise),* Microsoft advocates implementing a structure that answers the following challenges:

- A single network logon account for the user, regardless of the user's location or domain affiliation
- Centralized account administration
- Easy user access to network resources, regardless of the location of the user or the resource in the enterprise
- The focus of network resource administration in the hands of the resource owner or administrator
- Synchronization of account and security information across the enterprise

The structure should be capable of supporting enterprise networks of varying sizes, with servers, computers, and users in a variety of geographic locations. The structure also should support, and in some cases use, a variety of network architectures, protocols, and platforms to provide a completely flexible and open architecture.

Microsoft responds to this challenge with its Directory Services solution. Windows NT's Directory Services provides a domain model of enterprise computing that centralizes account information and management into a single domain account database, while placing the network resource management focus on the owner/administrator of the resource.

You can think of a domain as a logical grouping of computers in a Microsoft network. A domain controller establishes the domain's identity and is used to maintain the database of user, group, and computer accounts for that domain. In addition to the domain controller, a Windows NT domain can include member servers and workstation computers. A member server might be a Windows NT 4.0 Server configured as an application server, a database server, a RAS server, a print server, or a file server. Workstation computers might run Windows NT Workstation 4.0, Windows 95, Windows for Workgroups 3.11, MS-DOS, Apple Macintosh System 7, or LanMan 2.2c for DOS or OS/2.

All of the computers that identify themselves as belonging to a particular domain are part of the same logical grouping. As such, those computers have access to the account database on the domain's domain controller for authenticating users as they log on, and for creating *access control lists* (ACLs) for securing network resources stored on those computers. An enterprise may consist of one domain, or several domains, following one of the domain models suggested by Microsoft. See the following section, "Types of Domain Models," later in this chapter, for more information on these models.

For example, a domain might be centered around the organizational hierarchy and reflect its departmental structure. Perhaps the MIS department has assumed all responsibility for maintaining user and group accounts, while placing resource management within each department. Possibly, the enterprise is organized according to regional areas, such as the West, Midwest, and East domains. The domain structure might even be global in nature, reflecting the enterprise's international presence. Windows NT's Directory Services provides a fit for each of these structures because Windows NT domains are logical groupings of computers; therefore, they are extremely flexible. Although the physical layout of your network may affect the type of domain model that you choose to establish, domains simply don't care what the network topology looks like.

Single Network Logon

The concept of a single network logon is really quite simple: Provide the user with a single logon account that can be used to access the network from anywhere within the enterprise. An account executive based in Chicago should be able to fly to her company's office in London, use her same account to log on to the network at any computer in the London office, and access the same resources she has access to when in Chicago.

Windows NT 4.0 Directory Services is designed to provide just that capability by combining the domain model of networking with a security relationship called a *trust*. Briefly, a trust relationship enables users from one Windows NT domain to be granted access permissions to the network resources in a second Windows NT domain.

Assume that a trust exists between the London and Chicago domains. If the account executive's account is maintained in the Chicago domain, she still can log on to the company network at any computer in the London domain. Directory Services enables the account executive's logon request to be passed through the trust and back to the Chicago domain for authentication (see Figure 2.6). This process of passing the logon request back through the trust to the account domain is called *passthrough authentication*. After her account is validated, she can access any resource in the enterprise to which she has been given permission. Note that she needs only one logon account and password to access the network and its resources. Her physical location is not important, nor is the location of the resources.

TRUST RELATIONSHIPS

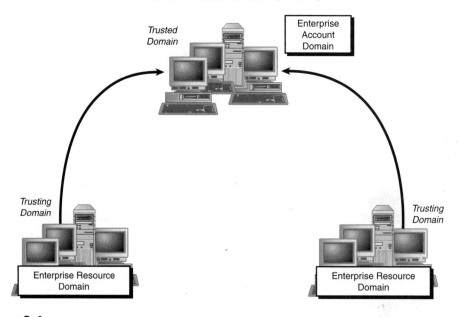

Figure 2.6
UserX's logon information is passed through the trust relationship to be authenticated in the appropriate domain, as depicted here.

Key Concept

Single network logon is a tremendous benefit to users and requires administrators to establish trust relationships between domains.

Centralized Account Administration

Recall that in a workgroup model, account administration tends to be decentralized to the desktop of each member of the workgroup. Each user might maintain his own workstation's account database, making it difficult to establish or maintain consistency or security.

By contrast, in a domain model, accounts are centralized on a specific domain server called the *domain controller*. The domain controller for the domain establishes the domain's identity in the enterprise. In fact, a domain is established by the installation of a *primary domain controller* (PDC). The PDC maintains the master account database for the domain. The PDC also can authenticate users on the network (or log on users), but its primary function is to maintain the domain's account database.

Although a domain can contain only one PDC for managing accounts and authenticating users, the domain can include one or more *backup domain controllers* (BDCs). The BDC receives a copy of the master account database maintained on the PDC. Its primary function is to authenticate users who are trying to log on to the network.

Windows NT 4.0 includes two utilities that can be used to manage user, group, and Windows NT computer accounts: User Manager for Domains and Server Manager.

See Chapter 5, "Managing Users and Groups," for an in-depth discussion of User Manager for Domains.

User Manager for Domains enables an administrator to manage the account database from any computer in the enterprise that supports the utility. This computer can be any Windows NT Workstation or Server, of course, but it also can be a Windows 95 or Windows for Workgroups 3.11 computer by using available add-on server-management tools.

Key Concept

User Manager for Domains is an administrative tool used to add users and groups to a domain on an NT Server. A similar tool—User Manager—exists only on NT Workstation and is used to add users and groups to the local machine.

Similarly, Server Manager enables the administrator to use Directory Services to remotely view and administer domains, workgroups, and computers. For example, administrators can use Server Manager on their Windows NT 4.0 Workstation desktops to start and stop services on a Windows NT 4.0 Server, or to synchronize account databases among domain controllers in a domain.

Network Resource Access

Through a combination of single logon accounts, centralized administration, and trust relationships, users easily can access any resource they have been given permission to use, from anywhere in the enterprise. Take another look at the example of the account executive in Chicago.

The account executive has an account in the Chicago domain that she uses to log on to the company's network. She regularly accesses a SQL database of client information that is located on a member server in the Chicago domain, and to which she has been given access permission. She frequently visits the company's London office, which has its own domain and its own SQL database. There is also a trust relationship between the Chicago and London domains.

As previously discussed, when she sits down at a computer in the London domain, she still can log on to the network by using her same logon account and password, just as if she were sitting at her computer in Chicago. Also, because of the trust relationship and passthrough authentication, she still can access the SQL database on the member server in the Chicago domain (see Fig. 2.7). The entire access process is transparent to her—as it should be for every user in the enterprise.

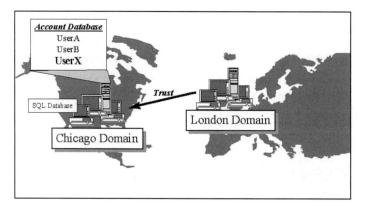

Figure 2.7
When UserX logs on, whether in Chicago or in London, she has access to any resources to which her account has been given permission, such as the SQL database.

This concept can be taken a step further by giving resources their own domain. This means that, in most organizations, each department, unit, project team, and so on, usually has its own set of resources that it wants to manage. Human Resources manages the company's Employee Handbook in Lotus Notes and maintains a SQL database of employee performance reviews, resumes, and other confidential information. Finance manages the company's budget spreadsheets, including the investment options for the retirement fund.

Each department wants to securely manage its own resources, ensuring that only authorized persons have access and that the level of access is controlled. But the department does not want to deal with day-to-day account management, such as forgotten passwords, locked-out accounts, new users, users changing group memberships, and so on. In a large organization, the number of resources and resource managers may make a single large domain impractical.

In this particular scenario, each department could be given its own domain for the purpose of managing its own resources, as Figure 2.8 shows. Account management still would be maintained in the account domain. By establishing trust relationships between each resource domain and the account domain, the resource managers can use the account domain's account database to create ACLs for each of their resources. Users still can log on to the network with the same single logon account and password, and they may access any resource to which they are given access permission. Everyone uses the same account database, yet account and resource management is centralized where it should be—with the appropriate account and resource managers. This setup is called a *master domain model.*

Once again, Windows NT Directory Services provides a flexible set of options for resource management that can fit the needs of most enterprise models.

Synchronization of Account and Security Information

As previously pointed out, a domain is established by the installation of a *primary domain controller* (PDC). As with all security objects in Windows NT, such as user and group accounts, trust relationships, and computer accounts, the creation of a PDC establishes a *security identifier* (SID) for the domain that is used for any security-related function, such as establishing trust relationships, implementing *backup domain controllers* (BDCs), and bringing about account synchronization.

Creating a domain controller is an implementation of Windows NT Server 4.0. Besides establishing the existence of the domain, the primary role of the PDC is to maintain the account database for the domain, hereafter called the *master account database.* If the PDC is the only domain controller created for the domain, it also will serve as the validation server to authenticate users' requests to log on to the network.

CH 2

TRUST RELATIONSHIPS

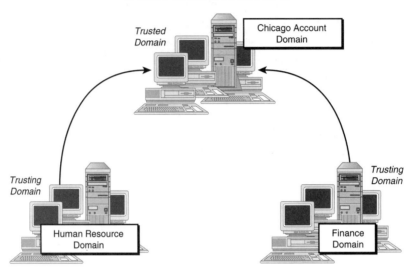

Figure 2.8
The trust relationship between each resource domain and the account domain enables resource managers to use one central account database to secure access to their resources.

In most networks, however, in addition to the PDC, one or more BDCs are created for the domain. The primary role of the BDC is to authenticate users' logon requests. To do so, it must receive a copy of the master account database from the PDC for that domain. In fact, when the BDC is created, you must tell it to join a specific domain as a BDC. A security relationship is established between the PDC and the BDC, and they share the same account database. The relationship between these domain controllers is so integral that any local group created on the PDC is considered local to all the domain controllers for the domain.

 Key Concept

Any change that is made to the account database for the domain affects only the master copy maintained by the PDC. Changes are never directly registered on a BDC. BDCs receive only the copies of the changes made to the master account database, according to a regular schedule.

If you are using User Manager for Domains on your London desk's Windows NT 4.0 Workstation, and the PDC for the domain you are administering is located in Chicago (accessible through a dedicated line), your change requests will be sent through the connection to the PDC in Chicago, even though you may have one or more BDCs located locally in London.

This process is easy to test. Shut down your PDC temporarily. Then try to use User Manager for Domains to add a new user account. User Manager for Domains will display a blank screen. It can't open the master account database because the PDC is not currently active. However, as long as a BDC is available on the network, the users will continue to be able to log on successfully and access any resource they have permission to access, provided the resource is not on the PDC that is down. Note that if you try this test, be sure that you restart your PDC. By doing this, the BDC will assume the duties of the PDC and hence be promoted to the PDC during an election until the original PDC is brought back up online and forces an election.

As stated earlier, the BDC receives a copy of the master account database and any changes made to it, according to a regular schedule. At regular intervals, every five minutes by default, the PDC checks the master account database for changes. When it detects a change, it sends a notification to the BDCs in the domain. This notification interval is called a *pulse* and can be modified in the PDC's Registry. You can find more information about setting this and other Registry values related to synchronization in Chapter 4, "Configuring Windows NT Server 4.0."

When the BDC receives a pulse from the PDC, it copies the changes from the PDC. In networking terms, this process is called a *pull operation,* because the BDC copies the changes instead of having the PDC send them. Until the BDC receives the changes, however, its copy of the master account database still contains "old" information.

Consider the following scenario. The administrator in London has added three new user accounts for three new employees who have joined the London office. The administrator uses User Manager for Domains to add the accounts, and these changes, as you already know, are registered in the master account database on the PDC in Chicago. You also know that, by default, it will take up to five minutes for the PDC to note the change and "pulse" the BDCs, including the BDC in London. Add the extra time it takes for the BDC to copy the changes. Depending on the amount of other network traffic, the BDC may not get the changes immediately. In fact, if the new employees are particularly motivated to get on to the network to start working, and they try to log on before the changes reach the BDC in London, they won't be able to log on because the BDC still will have the old information, which doesn't include the new employees.

The Server Manager utility includes two functions related to the synchronization process. The administrator can force a synchronization to take place at any time between the PDC and any specific BDC, or between the PDC and all the BDCs. If the PDC is down, access to the master account database is unavailable and synchronization cannot take place. The administrator in London can use Server Manager to have the London BDC synchronize with the Chicago PDC as soon as the new user accounts are created. Then the new employees can log on as soon as they want.

A domain may have no BDCs or several BDCs. The number and location of these BDCs likely will be determined by the number and location of the users in the enterprise, as well as by network performance and traffic concerns. For example, if the domain consists of 1,000 users who all are located in the same building, with little or no routing taking place, then the domain might consist of the PDC and perhaps one or two BDCs. On the other hand, if your network consists of the same 1,000 users dispersed in 10 regional offices, connected by various WAN connections (RAS, T1, 56K, and so on), your domain then might consist of the PDC and one BDC located at each regional office. Number and placement of BDCs are more likely driven by issues of performance than by the number of users.

However you plan for your BDCs, the synchronization process ensures that the master account database maintained on the PDC is kept up to date on each of the BDCs, enabling your users to log on to the network from wherever they are located in the enterprise.

Types of Domain Models

There are four types of enterprise domain models. As a general rule, you do not need to know these thoroughly for the Server exam (you are tested heavily on them in the Enterprise exam), but you should be familiar with them:

- Single domain model
- Master domain model
- Multiple master domain model
- Complete trust model

Single Domain Model

In the single domain model, there are no trust relationships. All users and all resources are contained in one enterprise domain. Figure 2.9 illustrates a single domain model.

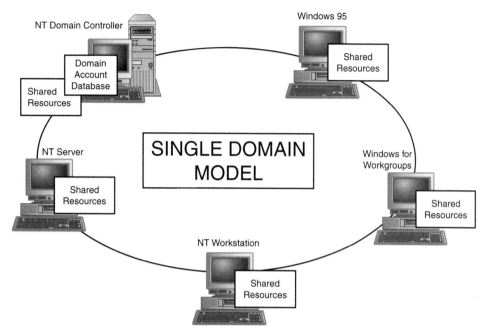

Figure 2.9
A single domain model.

The single domain model is common for small businesses, or in situations where the computers do not participate in a larger WAN environment.

Master Domain Model

In this model, one domain maintains the account database, and one or more domains administer resources (see Fig. 2.10). The account database contains all the users, groups, and NT computer accounts that are members of, or participate in, this domain. Resource domains generally do not contain lists of users and groups. Instead, they identify who can use their resources by obtaining the list of users and groups from the account domain through the creation of a trust relationship between the resource and account domains.

The master domain model is common in organizations where resources belong to various departments, and those departments maintain authority over access to their own resources. They do not need to maintain user accounts—just access to their resources. They maintain access by populating their resource ACLs with users from the account domain's database.

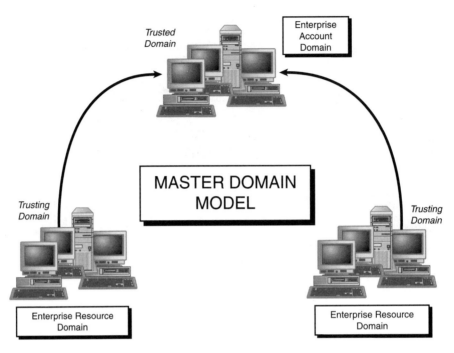

Figure 2.10
The master domain model—centralized account database management.

Multiple Master Domain Model

The multiple master domain model is similar to the master domain model. The difference is that, in the multiple master domain model, the account database may be distributed between two or more account domains. This may be a result of the way users are distributed through a WAN, the size of the databases, the type of server computers, and so on. Figure 2.11 illustrates a multiple master domain model with its trust relationships.

In the multiple master domain model, each resource domain trusts each account domain. In addition, the account domains trust each other. In this way, any resource manager can provide resource access to any account domain user.

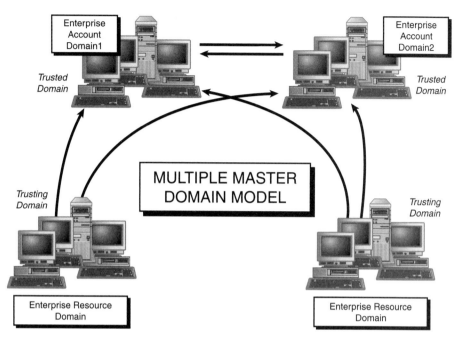

Figure 2.11
The multiple master domain model—distributed account management.

Complete Trust Model

The complete trust model is perhaps the simplest model to describe, although it provides perhaps the least amount of security (see Fig. 2.12). In this model, every domain trusts every other domain, and every domain maintains a copy of its own account database. Resource administrators can provide resource access to users from any other domain. However, resource access is potentially only as secure as the "worst" administrator. This is not to say that this model has not been implemented successfully in several large organizations. This model does require a greater degree of control in order to remain secure, however.

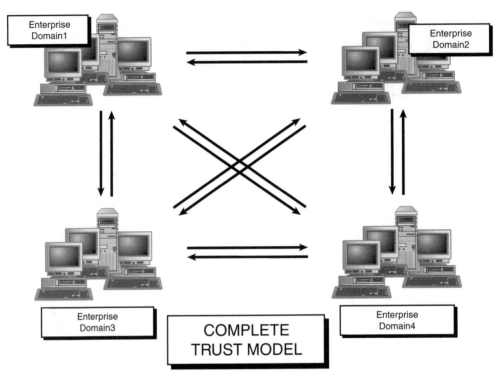

Figure 2.12
The complete trust model—domain-based account management.

Which Model Is Best?

Choose your networking model according to the number of users and the type, frequency, and so on of the resources the network will provide. Networks with relatively small numbers of users who are accessing specific resources on specific computers easily are accommodated and administered by the workgroup model. Recall that, in this model, both account administration and resource management are distributed to each member of the workgroup. Each computer maintains its own accounts database. As the workgroup grows, the number of users in each computer's database grows proportionately.

Networks with large numbers of users who require a single point of logon, centralized account administration, and centralized resource management benefit from the enterprise model. The type of domain model you choose for the enterprise depends on how the users and resources are distributed in your organization.

Summary

This chapter provided an overview of Windows NT Server 4.0. It introduced you to concepts that are expanded on in greater detail in later chapters.

The next chapter discusses the system requirements for Windows NT 4.0 and the installation procedures.

QUESTIONS AND ANSWERS

1. The type of multitasking employed by Windows NT Server 4.0 is _____.

   A: Preemptive. The processor is preemptively kept from being hogged by a runaway process. The older form of multitasking is cooperative.

2. True or false: NT supported HPFS through all versions until 4.0.

   A: True. NT 3.51 and all earlier versions supported HPFS. With NT Server 4.0, only FAT and NTFS file systems are supported.

3. The maximum number of remote dial-in sessions supported by NT Workstation is _____.

   A: One. NT Server supports 256.

4. The number of NT Servers needed to implement the workgroup model is _____.

   A: Zero. No NT Servers are needed to implement the workgroup model, although they may participate in such if they are configured as member servers. At least one NT Server is needed to create an enterprise/domain model.

5. Trust relationships allow an individual to log on to a portion of the enterprise and access resources elsewhere. This capability is known as _____.

   A: Single logon.

PRACTICE TEST

1. Which of the following are characteristics of NTFS? Choose three.
   a. Transaction tracking
   b. File- and directory-level permissions
   c. Auto-defragmentation of files
   d. Data compression

Answer a is correct. NTFS supports transaction tracking. Answer b is correct. NTFS supports file-level and directory-level permissions. Answer c is not correct, because NT does not include a defragmentation utility. **Answer d is correct. NTFS supports data compression.**

  2. Choose two features of Windows NT Server 4.0.

    a. Windows 95 interface

    b. Peer Web Services

    c. Plug and Play

    d. Hardware profiles

Answer a is correct, because the `Explorer.exe` shell used in Windows 95 also is used in Windows NT Server. Answer b is incorrect, because *Peer Web Services* (PWS) runs on NT Workstation, whereas IIS runs on NT Server. Answer c is incorrect, because NT Server 4.0 does not include Plug and Play. **Answer d is correct—hardware profiles and user profiles are employed.**

  3. Which of the following characteristics best apply to a workgroup network model? Choose two.

    a. A workgroup network model provides a high level of security for resource access.

    b. The workgroup model is best applied to smaller (fewer than 20) workstation groups.

    c. A workgroup model is identified by its domain controller.

    d. Each Windows NT computer participating in a workgroup must maintain a list of users who will be accessing the resources on that computer.

Answer a is incorrect, because only share-level security is possible, and it is inferior to user level (which cannot be present in a workgroup). **Answer b is correct. The workstation model is intended for smaller networks.** Answer c is incorrect, because the presence of a domain controller creates a domain (enterprise) and not a workgroup. **Answer d is correct. Every NT computer participating in a network must have as users those who access resources on it.**

  4. Which of the following characteristics best apply to a domain network model? Choose two.

    a. Resource access is provided by permitting access to users and groups that are members of the domain.

    b. User and group accounts are maintained on each workstation that is a member of the domain.

    c. A domain network model provides a relatively low level of resource security.

    d. Resource and account management is centralized.

Answer a is correct. Resource access is provided by permitting access to users and groups that are members of the domain. Answer b is incorrect, because user and group accounts are maintained on the domain controller. Answer c is incorrect, because the domain offers user-level security, which is superior to the share-level security offered in workgroups. **Answer d is correct. Resource and account management is centralized in the domain model.**

5. When planning a large WAN for an enterprise, Microsoft advocates implementing a structure that supports the following characteristics: (Choose all that apply.)

    a. Single network logon, regardless of location or domain affiliation.

    b. Easy user access to network resources, regardless of the location of the user or the resource in the enterprise.

    c. Decentralized account and resource administration.

    d. Synchronization of account and security information across the enterprise.

Answer a is correct. Microsoft strongly advocates the use of single logon. Answer b is correct. Microsoft strives for every user to have access to resources that should be available to them, regardless of where they log on from. Answer c is incorrect, because Microsoft encourages centralized administration. **Answer d is correct. Microsoft advocates synchronization across the enterprise.**

CH
2

CHAPTER PREREQUISITE

You should be familiar with the basic workings of your computer system, particularly how to boot it, its current operating system, and the basics of BIOS, memory, hard disks, CPU types, serial and parallel ports, network adapters, video adapters, and the mouse.

Windows NT Server 4.0 Setup

WHILE YOU READ

1. The three roles that an NT Server can be installed as are
   _____, _____, and _____.

2. The executable used to install NT on a system currently running
   Windows 95 is _____.

3. True or false: Windows NT Server 4.0 can be dual-booted with NT
   Workstation 4.0.

4. The two modes of client licensing are _____ and _____.

5. The temporary directory where files are copied to during installation
   is _____.

Preparing to Install Windows NT 4.0 Server

The installation of the Windows NT 4.0 server actually is pretty straightforward and relatively painless. However, you'll need to collect some information ahead of time to make installation even smoother. Before you begin your installation of Windows NT 4.0, do some detective work. You need to ask yourself two questions:

1. What is the system configuration of the computer on which I am installing NT 4.0?

2. What kind of an installation am I implementing?

System configuration includes such information as the make and model of the computer, the *basic input/output system* (BIOS) type and date, bus architecture, video card and monitor, network adapter, modem, memory, processor type, disk controller and drive, sound card, and so on. System configuration also includes the current operating system, installed applications, available disk space, and so on.

Beyond choosing from among the Typical and Custom options, you also need to know in which kind of network model, if any, the computer will be participating, the location of the installation files, the number of blank, formatted disks you need to have ready, and so on. A more exhaustive checklist is presented later in this chapter.

It sounds like a lot of detective work. But, if you think about it, you probably know the answer to most of these questions right off the top of your head. NT does an excellent job of detecting most of this information for you. What you should be most concerned with here is discovering the nuances of a specific configuration that can throw a speed bump into the installation process. If you have MS-DOS 5.0 or higher installed on your system, for example, you might use the Microsoft Diagnostics utility to provide some of the more subtle details, such as interrupt and *direct memory access* (DMA) settings. After you have installed NT Server a few times in your own organization, you will begin to understand and appreciate the nuances your particular computer and network configurations bring to the installation process.

Windows NT 4.0 Server System Requirements

Table 3.1 outlines the basic hardware requirements for a successful installation of Windows NT 4.0 Server.

Table 3.1   NT 4.0 Server Hardware Requirements

Component	Description
CPU	32-bit Intel 486/25 or higher, Intel Pentium, Pentium Pro, or supported RISC-based processors such as MIPS, Digital Alpha AXP, and Power PC.
Disk	120MB free disk space required for NT system file partition (149MB for RISC-based computers).
	Cluster size also is important. Microsoft recommends that a Windows NT Server with 32KB clusters have at least 200MB of free space.
Memory	12MB RAM minimum required; 32MB strongly suggested (16MB for RISC-based computers).
Video	Display adapter with VGA resolution or higher.
Drives	CD-ROM drive and 3 1/2-inch disk drive if installing locally. CD-ROM required for RISC installs.
Network	One or more supported adapter cards if a member of a network or if installing over the network.
File system	A *file allocation table* (FAT) or *New Technology File System* (NTFS) partition on an Intel-based computer; a minimum 2MB required FAT partition on RISC-based computers.

CH
3

The most important characteristic of the computer's configuration, and the one you should pay the closest attention to, is the hardware's compatibility with the Windows NT 4.0 Server. For most organizations, the compatibility of the hardware probably is not a big issue. However, if one piece of hardware is incompatible, expect your installation to have problems. In fact, if you have a hardware failure during installation, your first thought should be *incompatible hardware,* probably followed by some sort of stress-reducing phraseology.

Microsoft works very closely with most major hardware manufacturers to ensure the compatibility of its products with Windows NT. To this end, Microsoft regularly publishes and updates a *hardware compatibility list* (HCL). If you have any doubt at all about the compatibility of the hardware, consult this list. Pay particularly close attention to network adapters, *small computer system interface* (SCSI) adapters and drives, especially CD-ROM drives, video drivers, and sound and game cards. For example, video-driver support has changed significantly with NT 4.0, rendering earlier-version drivers inoperative. Also, do not take for granted that, just because your computer model is BrandName TurboX and it appears on the HCL, all the internal components (especially those just mentioned) also are supported. It is reasonable to assume that all internal components are supported. However, if your installation fails because of a hardware problem, check the failed component against the HCL as your first troubleshooting step.

Key Concept

You always should consult the HCL before making any attempt to install NT on a machine. Not only can this save you time and aggravation, but it is a required prerequisite as far as the exam is concerned.

You can access the HCL in several ways. If you subscribe to Microsoft TechNet or the Microsoft Developers Network, you will find a copy of the HCL there by searching for `Hardware Compatibility List`. You also can find the most up-to-date versions by accessing Microsoft's Web site at `http://www.microsoft.com/ntserver/nts/techdetails/default.asp`

or Microsoft's FTP server at `ftp://microsoft.com/bussys/winnt/winnt_docs/hcl`

The second most important consideration is third-party devices and drivers. Once again, Microsoft provides a tremendous list of support drivers for most major third-party products. Even though Microsoft provides most of the drivers you need, if there is any doubt, be sure to have an NT-compatible driver available just in case. You generally can obtain these relatively easily from the device manufacturer.

If you are installing the Windows NT 4.0 Server as part of a major rollout within your organization, you should consider performing a test installation on sample computer configurations from within your organization. At the very least, perform test installations on computers that can be identified as "iffy" in regard to their compatibility.

Choosing a Server Role

You must choose from three server roles before installing NT Server:

- *Primary domain controller* (**PDC**): Contains the master copy of the directory database (which contains information on user accounts) for the domain. Only one PDC can exist per domain, and the PDC must be the first machine installed.

- *Backup domain controller* (**BDC**): Helps the primary domain controller. The PDC copies the directory database to the backup controller(s). The BDC can authenticate users just as the PDC can. If the PDC fails, the BDC is promoted to a PDC. However, if a BDC is promoted, any changes made to the directory database since the last time it was copied from the old PDC are lost. A domain can have more than one BDC.

- **Member or standalone server:** A standalone server is a Windows NT Server machine that doesn't participate in the system of domain controllers of the domain. A standalone server can provide all Windows NT Server functions (file service, print service, Internet service, or whatever), but it doesn't maintain a copy of a domain accounts database and cannot authenticate domain users.

  A standalone server can be part of a domain or a workgroup. Standalone servers that are parts of domains are called *member servers;* these are useful because keeping a file or print server free from the overhead of authenticating users often proves cost-effective. You cannot change a standalone server into a domain controller after installing it. Your only option under such circumstances is to reinstall Windows NT and change the server type to domain controller during the installation process.

After you install a PDC or BDC into a domain, it must remain in that domain unless you reinstall Windows NT, because you can't change the *security identifier* (SID) for the domain after setting it during installation. You can change the name of a domain, however; change the domain name first on the PDC and then on the other network machines. Windows NT simply maps the new domain name with the old SID for the domain.

Key Concept

During the installation, you choose a role the server will fulfill within the domain. In most cases, changing that role requires reinstalling the operating system, so the choice you make here is crucial.

Using the Preparation Checklist

After collecting the computer's hardware information, ensuring its compatibility with Windows NT 4.0 Server, and making sure that it meets the minimum installation requirements, you need to know some additional information before executing the setup process. For future reference, use this checklist as a guide for preparation. With the exception of the first four items, this list is the information that is requested during the setup process:

- Read all NT documentation files.
- Assess system requirements. (Refer to Table 3.1.)
- Assess hardware compatibility. Verify by consulting the HCL.
- Gather device driver and configuration data:

Video	Display type, adapter, and chipset type
Network	Card type, *interrupt request* (IRQ), I/O address, DMA, connector, and so on
SCSI controller	Adapter and chipset type, IRQ, bus type
Sound/Media	IRQ, I/O address, DMA
I/O ports	IRQ, I/O address, DMA
Modems	Port, IRQ, I/O address, modem type

- Back up your current configuration and data files.
- Determine which type of initial setup will be performed. (You may need three blank, formatted disks before running Setup.)
- Determine the location of the source files for performing this installation. (Are they on CD-ROM or on a shared network location?)
- Determine on which partition the NT system files will be installed.
- Determine which file system you will install.
- Determine whether you will create an Emergency Repair Disk. (If so, you need one blank disk available before running Setup.)
- Identify your installation CD key.
- Decide on a unique computer name for your computer.
- Determine which workgroup or domain name the computer will join.
- Identify network connection data: IP addresses, *Internetworking Packet Exchange* (IPX) card numbers, and so on.
- Identify in which time zone the computer is located.

Key Concept

More than 90 text files contain additional information specific to individual devices, such as network cards and video drivers. You can find these files by browsing for .TXT files in the subdirectories for your specific platform. On an Intel computer, for example, look in the I386 platform directory on your NT 4.0 installation CD-ROM under the DRVLIB.NIC subdirectory for a subdirectory with your network card's name, and in that directory, look for and read the files with a .TXT extension.

Certain other files warrant close examination. In the platform directory, I386 for example, look for SETUP.TXT. It contains general information regarding devices and drivers that are used and required during installation. Three compressed files also contain release-specific information: readme.wr_, printer.wr_, and network.wr_. You can expand and read these files with the Windows Write program or the Windows 95 WordPad program. From a DOS prompt, switch to the platform directory and enter the command by using the following syntax:

```
expand file.wr_ c:\target directory\file.wri
```

If you've created a directory called readme on the C: drive, for example, expand the network.wr_ file there by typing

```
expand network.wr_ c:\readme\network.wri
```

Executing the NT 4.0 Server Startup Process

So far, this chapter has concentrated on preinstallation detective work and preparation. Now take a look at the actual setup process and the five major phases that occur:

1. The setup begins in what is referred to as *DOS* or *text mode*. If you have installed Windows before, this blue text screen format will look familiar. During this mode, several screens appear, asking for various pieces of information about the computer configuration for the NT 4.0 Server. These screens include

   - A menu of startup options
   - Detection and configuration of storage devices, such as SCSI drives
   - Initial hardware verification
   - Choice of the installation disk partition
   - Choice of the file system for the installation partition
   - Installation directory name

2. This information is used to reboot the computer and load a miniversion of NT 4.0. This is a 32-bit multithreaded kernel that enhances and supports the setup process.

3. As the computer reboots, NT hardware detection takes place. This event discovers and initializes hardware devices for use by NT. These devices include

   - SCSI adapters
   - Video adapter
   - Mouse and keyboard
   - Disk drives
   - CD-ROM drive(s)
   - COM and parallel ports
   - Memory configuration
   - Bus adapter

4. A GUI interface is installed, and the NT 4.0 Setup Wizard appears. The wizard walks you through the rest of the installation process, asking for information such as

   - Personal information
   - Unique computer name
   - Network card information
   - Network configuration information, such as protocols
   - Workgroup or domain membership
   - Whether to create an Emergency Repair Disk
   - Time zone
   - Video display setup

5. Finally, any additional support files are copied to the NT system directory, configuration information is saved in the NT registry, and the setup process completes and restarts the computer.

The following sections discuss each of these phases in more detail by walking through an actual installation of Windows NT 4.0 Server. Read through the process carefully, and then try it yourself in the lab.

Key Concept

The setup process is essentially the same for Intel-based and *reduced instruction set computer* (RISC)-based computers.

Beginning Setup

The setup process begins by locating the installation files. If you intend to install NT locally, you will need, at the very minimum, a compatible CD-ROM drive and, optionally, a 3 1/2-inch disk drive. If you are installing NT over the network, which will largely be the case in most organizations, you will need to have an active network connection and at least read access to the location of the installation files.

It's interesting to note that you don't have to have your installation files on an existing NT computer, and you don't need to be running the Microsoft network. Indeed, you can load the installation files on a Novell NetWare server, and the computer that is going to have NT installed can be running the NetWare client software. You can initiate the setup process as long as the NT computer-to-be can access a network drive.

The first phase of the setup process, by default, requires the creation of three startup disks. NT copies all the basic boot-configuration information, as well as the mini–NT kernel, to these disks and then uses them to start the process. If you are installing NT locally and have the original setup disks and CD-ROM, you probably have a set of startup disks in the NT box. You can use these or let NT create a new set for you. If your computer does not have a compatible CD-ROM drive, you need to use these disks to begin the setup process.

Key Concept

According to Microsoft's technical documentation for Windows NT 4.0 Server, if the *Basic Input/Output System* (BIOS) of your computer supports the El Torito Bootable CD-ROM (no emulation mode) format, you can begin Setup from the NT CD-ROM directly and let NT prompt you to create the startup disks. However, problems have been reported with various compatible CD-ROM drives that may require you to use the packaged setup disks to begin setup.

Generally, if you are installing NT over the network, you will not have access to the disks that come in the box, and you will need NT to create them for you.

CH

3

Another purpose of the startup disks is to provide a means of starting NT for repair or recovery purposes if you cannot later boot. If you intend to create and keep current an Emergency Repair Disk, you can use this disk only if you first boot by using the Startup disks.

It is not essential that you create these disks during the startup process, however. You can save some time by performing a diskless installation of NT. This is particularly useful when performing an over-the-network installation or rolling out NT on a large scale.

The NT Setup executable on the Intel platform is named WINNT.EXE. If you are installing NT for the first time on a computer, you use this executable. If you already have a copy of NT installed on the computer (for example, NT 3.51 Server) and intend to upgrade to NT 4.0 or install a new copy of NT 4.0, you can use an alternative executable called WINNT32.EXE. This is a 32-bit version of the Setup program and will run with increased performance.

WINNT.EXE and WINNT32.EXE offer a variety of setup option switches that give you more control over how the installation proceeds. The syntax for using either executable follows:

```
[WINNT|WINNT32] [/S:sourcepath] [/T:tempdrive] [/I:inffile] ➡
[/O or /OX] [/F] [/C] [/B] [/U[:scriptfile]] [/R or /RX:directory]
```

Table 3.2 outlines these switches.

Table 3.2 WINNT.EXE Option Switches

Switch	Explanation
/B	Performs setup without creating startup disks. Instead, it creates a temporary directory on the hard disk with the most free space, called WIN_NT.~BK. This requires an additional 4MB to 5MB of free disk space above the 114MB installation minimum.
/OX	Creates the three installation Startup disks. Note that with this switch, you can create these disks at any time.
/S:	Specifies the full drive or network path of the NT sourcepath installation files.
/U[:script]	Used with /S, it provides an unattended installation by skipping the screen that asks for the installation file location. When used with an optional script file, Setup does not prompt the installer for any information during setup.
/T:tempdrive	Enables you to specify the location of the temporary files. If not specified, NT chooses a drive for you.
/I:inffile	Specifies the filename of the setup information file. The default file is DOSNET.INF.

Switch	Explanation
/C	Skips the free-space check on the Startup disks. This can save a little time.
/F	Skips file verification as the files are copied to the Startup disks. This can save a little more time.
/R	Specifies an optional directory to be installed.
/RX	Specifies an optional directory to be copied.
/UDF	A *uniqueness database file* (UDF) lets you tailor an unattended installation to the specific attributes of specific machines. The UDF contains different sections, each identified with a string called a *uniqueness ID*. Each section contains machine-specific information for a single computer or a group of computers. You then can use a single answer file for all the network installations and reference machine-specific information by providing the uniqueness ID with the /UDF switch.

You now are ready to start the setup process. As stated at the beginning of this section, Setup begins by locating the installation files. Follow these steps:

1. If you have access to your CD-ROM drive on your computer, switch to the CD-ROM drive and locate the directory that pertains to your system type (I386, MIPS, ALPHA, PPC). Or connect to the network location of the installation files by using your DOS client-connection software.

   If you do not have access to your CD-ROM drive, try booting from the Startup disk provided in the NT 4.0 Server box.

2. Type **WINNT** with any desired option switches. The text mode phase of the setup process then initiates.

Key Concept

If you are installing NT 4.0 Server from an existing installation of NT, simply choose Run from the File menu in Program Manager or File Manager and enter **WINNT32**, followed by any desired option switches.

Setting Up NT 4.0 Server on RISC-Based Systems

On RISC-based systems, the setup process begins a little differently. Remember that on RISC-based computers, you must have a minimum 2MB FAT partition created before proceeding with NT Setup. This partition holds the two hardware-specific NT boot files:

OSLOADER.EXE and HAL.DLL. If you do not have a FAT partition, you must run the
ARCINST.EXE utility located on the NT Installation CD-ROM in the platform subdirectory.
When you boot your computer, choose Run a Program from the *advanced RISC computer*
(ARC) menu and enter the path to the ARCINSTALL.EXE utility.

After the utility starts, choose Configure System Partition and follow the screens. The rest
of the setup proceeds generally as described in this book.

Text-Mode Phase

Recall that the DOS or text mode phase of Setup has the following six basic events:

- A menu of startup options
- Detection and configuration of storage devices, such as SCSI drives
- Initial hardware verification
- Choice of the installation disk partition
- Choice of the file system for the installation partition
- Installation directory name

This section explores these events in more detail.

Startup Menu

The first screen that appears welcomes you to the Setup process and presents four ways to
proceed:

- To learn more about NT Setup before continuing, press F1.
- To set up Windows NT now, press Enter.
- To repair a damaged Windows NT 4.0 installation, press R.
- To quit Setup without installing Windows NT, press F3.

These are fairly straightforward options, and they are mirrored in the white status bar,
along with their keyboard shortcuts, at the bottom of the screen.

Key Concept

On all Setup screens, a useful Help dialog box is available by pressing F1. Also,
you can exit Setup at any time by pressing F3.

Of these four options, the one that may raise a question is the third option, repairing a damaged installation of NT. This is the option you use with the Emergency Repair Disk to restore configuration information. The Emergency Repair Disk contains data from the NT Registry (more about that later).

Mass Storage Device Configuration

The next step in the setup process is the detection of mass storage devices, such as CD-ROMs, SCSI adapters, and so on. The detected devices are displayed onscreen. *Integrated Device Electronics* (IDE) and *Enhanced Small Device Interface* (ESDI) drives also are detected, but they generally are not displayed in the list.

If you have a device installed that is not shown onscreen, you can choose to add it by pressing S. Otherwise, press Enter to continue with Setup. Of course, you always can add the additional devices after Setup has completed from the NT Control Panel. If you do press S, be sure to have your Drivers disk available.

License Agreement

Setup presents you with a multipage license agreement. This is the standard type of software agreement Microsoft displays, warning you to install a valid copy of NT and not a borrowed copy from somebody else. You will need to page down through the license screens to accept the agreement and to get to the next step of the installation.

Verifying Hardware

The setup process next displays the basic list of hardware and software components that it detected, including these:

- Computer
- Display
- Keyboard
- Keyboard layout
- Pointing device

If the list matches what you have installed on the computer, press Enter. If you need to make a change, use the up or down arrow to highlight the component that needs to be changed, press Enter, and then choose the appropriate item from the list.

CH
3

Partition Configuration

The next screen involves choosing the disk partition on which the Windows NT system files will be installed. This is referred to as the *system partition.* The system partition can be an existing formatted or unformatted partition, or it can be an area of free space on the hard drive. Setup displays the partitions and free space it detects on all physical disks. Use your up and down arrows to select the partition or free space where you want to install NT.

If you select an area of free space, you need to press C to create the partition. A new screen appears, telling you how large the partition can be and asking you for the size you want. Enter your choice for the size of the partition and press Enter. NT creates the partition for you, returns you to the Partition Configuration screen, and displays the new partition in the list. Select the new partition and press Enter to continue.

If you are using an existing partition as the NT system partition, select it and press Enter.

You also can select and delete partitions from this screen. This capability is useful if you need to free up some space and then create a larger partition for NT.

 Key Concept

Be certain that at least 120MB of free space is available on the selected partition. This is a minimum value; more free space will help performance. You will need space for a pagefile for virtual memory management, for example. Recall that the default initial size for a pagefile is 12 plus the amount of physical RAM installed on your computer for NT Workstation, and equal to only the amount of RAM installed on your computer for NT Server.

Do not install NT on a compressed partition. Disable compression before Setup begins.

If the partition is mirrored, disable mirroring before Setup begins.

If any partition is labeled as Windows NT Fault Tolerance, do not delete these partitions, because they represent stripe sets, volume sets, and mirrors that, if deleted, could result in significant loss of data.

Formatting the Partition

The boot partition contains all the NT system drivers, hardware configuration, security information, the Registry, and so on. There is also a primary or boot partition into which NT copies its boot files. The next screen enables you to choose with which file system—FAT or NTFS—you want to format the proposed system partition. If you select the wrong partition, just press Esc to return to the previous screen.

Your choice of file system depends on several factors. The following is a list of considerations for choosing NTFS:

- NTFS supports NT file and directory permissions security and access auditing; FAT supports only the read-only, system, hidden, and archive attributes.
- NTFS supports transaction tracking and sector sparing for data recovery; FAT does not.
- NTFS supports partition sizes of up to 16EB and file sizes of 4GB to 64GB, depending on cluster sizes. FAT supports a maximum file size of 4GB and is inefficient for partition sizes greater than 250MB.
- NTFS provides file and directory compression implemented as a property; FAT does not.
- NTFS is recognized only by NT on that computer. FAT is recognized by NT, MS-DOS, and OS/2.

If you are installing NT on a new computer and do not also intend to run MS-DOS or Windows 95 on that computer (called *dual booting),* then simply create the partition and format it as NTFS or FAT.

If you do intend to dual boot with MS-DOS or Windows 95, be sure that it is installed already and that the boot partition already is formatted as FAT. If you install NT on the boot partition, NT modifies the *master boot record* (MBR) with its boot information and maintains a boot pointer to the MS-DOS system files. If you install NT first, format the partition as FAT, and then install MS-DOS, the MBR will be altered, and you will not be able to boot NT successfully.

Key Concept

NTFS can be used on RISC-based computers. However, NT requires at least one FAT system partition of 2MB as a minimum size for its boot file information. Create this partition, as well as another system partition of appropriate size, for NTFS by following your RISC-based computer's documentation.

Key Concept

Windows NT and OS/2 can coexist on the same computer. If you have installed OS/2 and MS-DOS on the computer and use the OS/2 boot command to switch between operating systems, NT configures its bootup to dual boot between itself and whichever of the other two operating systems you had running when you installed NT.

...continues

...continued

Because NT 4.0 no longer supports the *High-Performance File System* (HPFS) file system, if you intend to keep OS/2 on HPFS, you must install NT in another partition. Similarly, if you are using the OS/2 Boot Manager, the NT installation process disables it upon completion. You must re-enable it by marking the Boot Manager partition as the active partition by using NT's Disk Administrator utility. If, after working in OS/2, you choose to boot to NT, use OS/2's Boot Manager to mark the NT partition as active and then reboot the computer.

Key Concept

Both NT 4.0 Workstation and Server may be installed on the same computer, and even different versions of either flavor of NT. The Setup program detects the existence of another installation of NT, Windows 95, Windows for Workgroups, or Windows 3.1 and displays that installation's system directory as an upgrade directory for your current installation. Simply press N for New Directory, as offered onscreen, to install this version of NT in a different directory. The Setup program keeps the other version(s) intact and installs this version in its own directory. Setup also modifies the boot menu to display this new version at the top of the boot menu and as the default bootup operating system.

Installation Directory

Setup next asks for the name and location of the NT system files. NT displays the path and default name of the directory for you on the selected partition. The default directory name is WINNT. You may change the name to whatever you want, but it is recommended that you keep the name recognizable, such as WINNT40, especially if you have other versions of Windows or NT on the computer.

If you do have an existing version of Windows, Windows 95, or NT on the selected partition, Setup detects that and displays that directory as the installation choice. Setup assumes that you want to upgrade the existing operating system.

Final Screens

The next screen of the text-mode phase informs you that Setup will examine the disk for corruption. It offers two types of exams: basic and exhaustive. The basic exam, initiated by pressing Esc, is best used on new partitions that do not already have data stored. The exhaustive exam, initiated by pressing Enter, runs slightly longer, depending on the size of the partition and the amount of data stored. Even though the exhaustive exam does take a little extra time, it is highly recommended if you are installing Windows NT 4.0 Server on an existing partition with existing data.

After you make your selection, Setup displays a dialog box showing the status of the process as it copies files to the new NT system directory.

After the files are copied and the directory structure is created, Setup informs you that the text-mode portion is completed and that you should press Enter to restart the computer. At this point, you can press Enter or, if it is getting late, you can just turn off your computer. Actually, it often is suggested that you do power off the computer and then power it back on to reset all the hardware devices, particularly network cards, for NT.

Restart, Lock, and Load!

When the computer reboots, if you watch very closely, you will see the NT boot menu appear briefly with a choice for NT installation. This is the default and will start automatically. If you are quick with your fingers, you can press the up- or down-arrow key to disable the default time and boot to MS-DOS or Windows 95. There will be a menu entry for either MS-DOS or Windows 95, depending on which operating system has been installed. Otherwise, just let NT take over.

It is during this phase that NT loads its 32-bit multithreaded kernel, which enhances and supports the setup process. As the computer reboots, NT hardware detection takes place. This event discovers and initializes hardware devices for use by NT, such as SCSI adapters, video adapter, mouse and keyboard drivers, CD-ROM drives, COM and parallel ports, memory configuration, and bus adapter.

You next see what will become a familiar set of bootup screens. The first screen is a black screen that loads system drivers (white consecutive dots), followed by the infamous blue screen—infamous because it is here that you see screen dumps related to unsuccessful boots of NT. Most of the time, however, this screen simply outlines the progress of various boot tasks. If you have chosen to format or convert a partition to NTFS, you will see messages to that effect as conversion takes place. Also, NT reboots the system once again for the file system to be recognized and to take effect.

After this process is complete, NT loads the GUI portion of Setup, which is called the Windows NT Setup Wizard.

Windows NT Setup Wizard

The Setup Wizard is a much streamlined and intuitive interface for gathering information pertinent to the configuration of NT on the computer. Essentially, the Setup Wizard asks you configuration option questions in several Windows GUI dialog boxes. After you make your selections and provide the appropriate information, the wizard loads the necessary drivers, updates the Registry, and completes the installation.

CH
3

Key Concept

Each Setup Wizard dialog box has Back, Next, and Help buttons to make it easy to move back and forth between the screens and to reselect options before committing yourself.

The very first screen you see outlines the standard Microsoft license agreement. You must choose OK to indicate your consent to this agreement before continuing with Setup.

The next dialog box outlines how the wizard will proceed. There are three parts to the Setup Wizard:

- Gathering information about your computer
- Installing Windows NT Networking
- Finishing setup

Gathering Information About Your Computer

The Setup Options dialog box in Workstation offers four installation options: Typical, Portable, Compact, and Custom. Table 3.3 highlights which components are installed by default for each Setup option. In Server, these choices are not present, and there is no Express option (although it appears as one of the exam objectives).

Table 3.3   Default Components Installed By Each Setup Option

Component	Typical	Portable	Compact	Custom
Accessibility options	Yes	Yes	No	Selectable
Accessories	Yes	Yes	No	Selectable
Communication options	Yes	Yes	No	Selectable
Games	No	No	No	Selectable
Windows Messaging	No	No	No	Selectable
Multimedia	Yes	Yes	No	Selectable

The Typical and Custom options are very much the same as the Express and Custom options that most users have encountered when installing Windows and most Windows applications. The two setup options new to NT 4.0 are the Portable and Compact options.

Typical setup is the default, as well as the recommended option. It installs all optional Windows components, including Microsoft Exchange and, of course, the games. It asks few questions and automatically configures component settings.

Custom, on the other hand, gives you the most control over the installation and configuration of options.

The next two dialog boxes prompt you for a username and company name for registration purposes, as well as a product identification number or CD key. You usually can find the number on the CD-ROM case or in your *NT Installation Manual.* In some organizations, depending on the type of installation being performed, you may not need this number because your organization has negotiated a companywide license for distributing the software. You must enter something in both these dialog boxes to proceed to the next dialog box.

The next dialog box asks you to specify a licensing mode. You have two options:

- **Per-server license:** Clients are licensed to a particular server, and the number of concurrent connections to the server cannot exceed the maximum specified in the license. When the maximum number of concurrent connections is reached, Windows NT returns an error to a connecting user and prohibits access. An administrator still can connect after the maximum is reached, however.

- **Per-seat license:** Clients are free to use any server they want, and an unlimited number of clients can connect to a server.

If you can't decide which mode to select, choose Per Server mode. You have a one-time chance to convert the per-server license to a per-seat license by using the Control Panel Licensing application.

The next dialog box asks for the computer name. This is the name that NT uses to identify this computer internally and for network and remote communication. It must be a unique name if the computer will be a member of a workgroup or domain. This name can contain up to 15 characters.

 Key Concept

Although a computer name may contain spaces, it is not recommended. In a large network, users connecting to computers can become confused as to the presence or absence of spaces in a name. In fact, in a large corporate network, a standard naming convention for computer, workgroup, and domain names greatly simplifies the configuration and maintenance of your network.

On the next screen, you must specify whether the computer is a primary domain controller, a backup domain controller, or a standalone server. These server-type options were discussed earlier in this chapter.

The next screen references the administrator account and asks for a password for that account. The administrator account is a built-in account that NT creates for managing the configuration of the computer, including security and account information. The name of the administrator account is ADMINISTRATOR, and the password can be up to 14 characters. You need to enter the password twice—once to confirm it.

 Key Concept

Passwords in NT are case sensitive, so be sure that you type yours correctly and then remember it! If you forget your password during the course of installation, you will not be able to access NT.

You may have read or heard that certain Pentium-based computers have a faulty floating-point module. In very specific circumstances, this sometimes can produce inaccurate results when dividing certain values. If Setup has detected that your computer has such a problem, the next screen gives you the option to disable the module and let NT perform the math. This results in a decrease in performance for floating-point operations. However, if your applications rely heavily on floating-point arithmetic, such as complex Excel macros, you may prefer to choose Yes for this option.

The next screen involves the option of creating an *Emergency Repair Disk* (ERD). The ERD contains setup information relevant to this installation of NT, including the location of source files and computer configuration and security information from the Registry. You can use the ERD to replace corrupted or missing boot files, recover account information, and restore NT to the master boot record of the computer boot partition if it has been modified. To use the ERD, you must have a startup disk with which to boot and then choose R for Repair from the startup menu.

If you choose to create an ERD, be sure to have a blank disk handy, and choose Yes.

 Key Concept

If you choose not to create an ERD at this time, you always can create one later. NT provides a command-prompt command called RDISK.EXE, which you use to create a new ERD and to update an existing disk.

Depending on the type of installation you choose at the start of the wizard, you may see a dialog box that lets you choose which optional components to install. You may choose one of two options: Most Common or Show a List.

If you choose Most Common, Setup continues to the next portion of the Setup Wizard process. If you choose Show a List, you see a new dialog box with a list of options. This is the same dialog box you see when selecting optional components in Windows 95.

The truly fine thing about this dialog box is the way it presents you with component information. You will see a list of five or six main components. Most of these actually are component areas that are composed of a list of component items from which you can choose. As you select each main component, a description box to the right explains what functionality each provides, as well as how many of the component items have been selected for installation. If you click the Details button, another dialog box appears with a checklist of component items. You may select or deselect these items and then return to the main dialog box. As you select items, the description screen notes how many items you selected, such as 12 of 14 items selected. You also see just how much additional disk space is required for the items in question.

After you click Next, the wizard takes you to part 2 of its setup process: Installing Windows NT Networking.

Installing Windows NT Networking

The next few dialog boxes involve the configuration of network-related functions and components. Your first choice is to indicate whether you are implementing network features at all and, if so, whether you will be wired to the network through a local interface, such as a network card, whether you have remote access to the network through a modem connection, or both.

If you choose Wired to the Network, the next dialog box prompts you to detect and install the network card. Choose Start Search to begin Setup's detection process. The dialog box displays a list of all detected network cards. You can choose to configure any combination of cards by enabling or disabling their check boxes.

If Setup cannot detect the card or you have a Drivers disk available, you can install the card from your disk by choosing Select from List and then clicking the Have Disk button.

CH
3

Key Concept

Remember to check the HCL to be sure that your network card is supported by NT. (See the "Using the Preparation Checklist" section earlier in this chapter.)

You can install additional cards or change card settings later from NT's Control Panel.

The Setup Wizard, most likely, will next display a configuration option dialog box for the specific card(s) you selected. This dialog box, or series of dialog boxes, asks for the correct IRQ, I/O base port address, and memory buffer address settings, as well as any other card-specific settings, such as onboard transceivers, thin versus thick coax, and so on.

Key Concept

NT displays the manufacturer's proposed or factory settings in these dialog boxes. Because some cards are software-configurable, the actual settings on the cards may not match the manufacturer's settings. To avoid conflicts, especially the failure of NT to initialize the card and network settings on your computer, be sure to know your card settings ahead of time. (See the "Using the Preparation Checklist" section earlier in this chapter.)

The next dialog box asks for network protocol choices. By default, NT selects *Transmission Control Protocol/Internet Protocol* (TCP/IP) and NWLINK IPX/SPX as your protocol. However, you may select any combination of TCP/IP, NWLINK (NT's 32-bit implementation of IPX/SPX), and *Network BIOS Extended User Interface* (NetBEUI). You may add other protocols—such as AppleTalk, DLC, and Point-to-Point Tunneling—by choosing Select from List.

The next step is to select the Network Services that are appropriate for your computer. By default, five services are installed with NT networking and cannot be deselected: Computer Browser, RPC Configuration, NetBIOS Interface, Workstation, and Server. Again, you can install additional services—such as Client Service for NetWare, Microsoft Internet Information Services, Remote Access Services, and so on—by selecting Select from Disk or by choosing Have Disk. Network services are discussed in Chapter 12, "Windows NT Networking Services."

At this point, you have made all appropriate choices, and the wizard gives you a choice to continue and install the network components or to go back and alter your selections. Click Back to make changes and Next to continue.

The next dialog box displays the network bindings. Think of bindings as being the network "paths" that determine how services, protocols, and adapters interact to effect network communications. You can adjust the bindings by changing their order, enabling them, or disabling them. NT has selected the optimum bindings based on your network component settings. If you need to adjust the bindings later, you can do so from NT's Control Panel. A further discussion of bindings appears in Chapter 12.

Each card you install may require protocol-specific information. If you choose TCP/IP, for example, you need to specify a local address, router information, *Windows Internet Name Service* (WINS) address information, and so on, or specify *Dynamic Host Configuration Protocol* (DHCP) configuration. These dialog boxes then are displayed as the wizard completes the setup of network components.

Key Concept

If you began your installation as an over-the-network type, and you did not power off your computer after the text mode, you may see a message stating that NT cannot verify the card settings and asking whether it should use them anyway. The answer you should choose is Yes!—use the settings. The reason for this message is that, in a warm boot such as the one NT performs after the text-mode setup, all device settings, particularly network card settings, are not reset. Thus NT is detecting that those settings are already in use. A cold boot, on the other hand, involves powering off the computer. This, of course, resets all device settings, including the network card settings that triggered the message in the first place.

If NT is unable to initiate network communication, you have the option to go back and check your settings or to continue without configuring the network.

After you click Next, the wizard takes you to part 3 of its setup process: Finishing Setup.

Finishing Setup

There are just two more dialog boxes to consider before the Setup Wizard completes the installation. The first dialog box displays the Date and Time utility. Adjust the settings to reflect the time zone of the computer and to ensure that the system time is correct.

Key Concept

Several interprocess mechanisms, as well as certain applications and Microsoft BackOffice products, rely on time stamps and time synchronization among computers. Inaccurate time zones or time values can result in process failures and, in some cases, an incomplete processing of data.

Finally, the Display Properties dialog box appears. This dialog box enables you to configure your video display by changing settings such as pixel resolution, color palette, refresh frequency, and font size, as well as by changing your video driver information. Before you complete this screen, choose Test to see whether you actually can read your display with the settings you chose. After testing, you can click OK.

A status box appears, showing the progress of files copied from the temporary directory (WIN_NT.~LS). When this process is complete, the wizard asks you to remove any floppy disks and to press the Restart button to reboot the computer. As before, at this point you can safely turn off your computer.

If you let the computer restart and have chosen a dual-boot configuration for your installation, you see NT's boot loader menu. Your new installation of Windows NT 4.0 Server is first on the list, and it is the default operating system unless you choose the other operating system option within 30 seconds. If you choose NT, it loads with all the options you chose and presents you with the Welcome screen.

Troubleshooting Installation and Setup

If you have carefully read this chapter, you will have relatively little problem, if any, with your installation of Windows NT 4.0 Server. In fact, installing NT 4.0 rarely is troublesome if you have done your detective work. It is designed to detect and configure as much on its own as possible. Nevertheless, this section runs through a couple of tips, suggestions, and reminders, beginning with the Preparation Checklist, just in case you encounter problems:

- Read all NT documentation files.
- Assess system requirements. (Refer to Table 3.1.)
- Assess hardware compatibility. Verify by consulting the HCL.
- Gather device-driver and configuration data:

Video	Display type, adapter, and chipset type
Network	Card type, IRQ, I/O address, DMA, connector, and so on
SCSI controller	Adapter and chipset type, IRQ, bus type
Sound/Media	IRQ, I/O address, DMA
I/O Ports	IRQ, I/O address, DMA
Modems	Port, IRQ, I/O address, modem type

- Back up your current configuration and data files.
- Determine which type of initial setup will be performed. (You may need three blank, formatted disks before running Setup.)

- Determine the location of the source files for performing this installation. (Are they on CD-ROM or on a shared network location?)
- Determine on which partition the NT system files will be installed.
- Determine which file system you will install.
- Determine whether you will create an Emergency Repair Disk. (If so, you need one blank disk available before running Setup.)
- Identify your installation CD key.
- Decide on a unique computer name for your computer.
- Identify network connection data: IP addresses, IPX card numbers, and so on.
- Identify in which time zone the computer is located.

Perhaps most critical to a successful installation of NT 4.0 Server is the compatibility of your computer's hardware. Here are two reminders:

- Be sure that your computer meets the minimum requirements necessary for installing and running NT 4.0 Server.
- Be sure that you have checked all hardware components in your computer against the HCL for NT 4.0 Server.

These two actions will significantly increase your success rate.

Next, become familiar with the hardware settings for installed devices, particularly network cards. These settings include not only IRQ, DMA, I/O address, and connector data, but also network protocol settings such as IP address, DNS location, router address, DHCP information, IPX card address, and so on.

Finally, follow a naming convention for your computers and workgroups that ensures uniqueness, recognizability, and ease of maintenance. If you are becoming a member of a domain, be sure that your computer already has a computer account in the domain you are joining (as well as a user account for you).

Occasionally, you may encounter unusual errors relating to your hard drive. If installation fails because of disk-related problems, explore these areas:

- Is the hard disk supported (on the HCL)?
- Do you have a valid boot sector available on the disk? Recall that, especially for RISC-based systems, NT requires a minimum 2MB FAT system partition.
- Are your SCSI drives being detected correctly by NT? You may need to check physical settings, such as termination.

CH

3

- Check for viruses in the *master boot record* (MBR). If there is a virus that alters the MBR before, during, or after installation, NT will not be able to boot successfully. A likely message you may receive is Bad or missing NTLDR.

- When NT reboots to start the GUI Setup Wizard, if it fails, usually with the message: Bad or missing NTOSKRNL, it could be because of a missed detection of the SCSI drive. Boot to DOS and use the DOS Editor to modify the BOOT.INI file. This read-only system file is created by NT during installation and is used to display the boot menu. It is stored in the root directory of the system partition. Use the DOS ATTRIB command to turn off the read-only (R) and system (S) attributes before editing the file. Change all references of scsi for this installation to multi. Also, check that the partition numbers listed in the BOOT.INI file for Windows NT match the partition number of the NT system file directory. Be sure to save your changes and set the attributes back.

The syntax for using the DOS ATTRIB command to turn off attributes follows:

```
ATTRIB -R -S BOOT.INI
```

Set the attributes back by typing

```
ATTRIB +S +R BOOT.INI
```

NT counts partitions, starting with 0, as listed here:

- Hidden system partitions.
- The first primary partition on each drive.
- Additional primary partitions on each drive.
- Logical partitions on each drive.

So, if the physical disk has a hidden system partition (such as a Compaq BIOS partition), a C: drive primary partition, and a D: drive logical partition, and you are installing NT on the D: drive, you are installing NT on partition 2 (hidden: 0, C: -1, D: -2).

Using NTHQ to Troubleshoot

NT also supplies a troubleshooting utility that may be of use for both NT 4.0 Workstation and Server in discovering how NT is detecting your hardware configuration. This utility is called NTHQ and is located in the \SUPPORT\HQTOOL directory on the installation CD-ROM.

To use this utility, boot to DOS, place a blank disk in the A: drive, switch to the directory on the CD-ROM, and run MAKEDISK.BAT. This process creates a bootable disk that you can use to run NTHQ. Reboot the computer with this disk and follow the directions.

NTHQ creates an onscreen report that you can save to a log file on disk and print. It performs a hardware detection on the computer similar to that performed by NT during Setup, and you can use it to determine your hardware settings and, specifically, which ones are causing Setup to fail. It includes data about the motherboard, such as I/O, DMA, and IRQ settings for *Complementary Metal-Oxide Semiconductor* (CMOS), memory access controller, COM and printer ports, and plug-and-play BIOS; data about the network card, video, and storage devices; and a summary of all device configuration settings. It also shows what is questionable regarding the HCL.

Key Concept

NTHQ prepares a text file report of the identified hardware in the system. You can compare this list to the HCL before beginning the installation to make certain there will be no incompatibilities when NT is installed.

NTHQ Sample Report

Here is an example of the kinds of data NTHQ captures and reports:

```
Hardware Detection Tool For Windows NT 4.0

Master Boot Sector Virus Protection Check
Hard Disk Boot Sector Protection: Off.
No problem to write to MBR

ISA Plug and Play Add-in cards detection Summary Report

No ISA Plug and Play cards found in the system
ISA PnP Detection: Complete

EISA Add-in card detection Summary Report
Scan Range: Slot 0 - 16
Slot 0: EISA System Board
EISA Bus Detected: No
EISA Detection: Complete

Legacy Detection Summary Report

System Information
Device: System board
Can't locate Computername
Machine Type: IBM PC/AT
```

```
Machine Model: fc
Machine Revision: 00
Microprocessor: Pentium
Conventional memory: 655360
Available memory: 32 MB
BIOS Name: Phoenix
BIOS Version:
BIOS Date: 06/12/96
Bus Type: ISA


Enumerate all IDE devices

IDE Devices Detection Summary Report
Primary Channel: master drive detected
Model Number: TOSHIBA MK2720FC
Firmware Revision: S1.16 J
Serial Number: 66D70208
Type of Drive: Fixed Drive
Disk Transfer Rate: >10Mbs
Number of Cylinders: 2633
Number of Heads: 16
Number of Sectors Per Track: 63
Number of unformatted bytes per sector Per Track: 639
LBA Support: Yes
DMA Support: Yes
PIO Transfer Cycle Time Mode 2
DMA Transfer Cycle Time Mode 2


IDE/ATAPI: Complete

=============End of Detection Report============
Adapter Description: Cirrus Logic VGA
Listed in Hardware Compatibility List: Yes

Adapter Description: Creative Labs Sound Blaster 16 or AWE-32
Adapter Device ID: *PNPB003
Listed in Hardware Compatibility List: Not found-check the latest HCL

Adapter Description: Gameport Joystick
Adapter Device ID: *PNPB02F
Listed in Hardware Compatibility List: Not found-check the latest HCL

Adapter Description: Unknown Cirrus Logic chipset, report!
Adapter Device ID: 12021013
Listed in Hardware Compatibility List: Not found-check the latest HCL
```

Performing an Unattended Setup of Windows NT 4.0 Server

It is possible to automate the setup process to provide some or all of the information needed during setup and thus request little or no additional user input. This can be especially helpful when installing a large number of computers with similar configurations, such as those with the same domain name, monitor settings, network card drivers and setting, and so on.

Five basic steps are involved in implementing an unattended setup of NT 4.0 Server:

- Create a distribution server by placing the Windows NT 4.0 Server installation files for the appropriate computer platform in a shared directory on a file server.
- Create an answer file that supplies information common to all the computers being installed.
- Create a uniqueness data file that supplies information specific to each computer's installation.
- Provide access to the installation files on the distribution server for the computers that are being installed.
- Run NT Setup, referencing the location of the setup files, answer files, and uniqueness data files.

This section discusses each of these steps in more detail.

Create a Distribution Server

It is relatively simple to copy the installation files to a shared directory on a file server. Simply identify which Windows NT server you want to use. This should be a server that the target computers will be able to access easily, preferably a server on the same subnet, and one that is not already being used to capacity by other applications or processes. It also should have its own CD-ROM or be able to access a CD-ROM drive.

Next, create an installation folder on that server. Into that folder, copy the installation files for the target computers' hardware platform from the appropriate platform directory on the NT 4.0 Server installation CD-ROM (i386, MIPS, ALPHA, or PPC). You can use the MD-DOS xcopy command with the /s switch (to copy all subdirectories) from a command prompt, or use Windows Explorer.

Finally, share the newly created directory.

Create an Answer File

You use answer files (unattend.txt) to supply setup information that is common to all the computers using that file. The kind of information common to the computers includes network settings, such as card driver, interrupts, DMA protocols to be installed, services to be installed, which workgroup or domain the computers are joining, modem types, and the organization name. Here is a copy of the sample unattend.txt file for an Intel-based computer located on the NT 4.0 Server CD-ROM. Each platform directory contains its own version of this file.

```
; Microsoft Windows NT Workstation Version 4.0 and
; Windows NT Server Version 4.0
; (c) 1994 - 1996 Microsoft Corporation. All rights reserved.
;
; Sample Unattended Setup Answer File
;
; This file contains information about how to automate the installation
; or upgrade of Windows NT Workstation and Windows NT Server so the
; Setup program runs without requiring user input.
;
; For information on how to use this file, read the appropriate sections
; of the Windows NT 4.0 Resource Kit.

[Unattended]
OemPreinstall = no
ConfirmHardware = no
NtUpgrade = no
Win31Upgrade = no
TargetPath = WINNT
OverwriteOemFilesOnUpgrade = no

[UserData]
FullName = "Your User Name"
OrgName = "Your Organization Name"
ComputerName = COMPUTER_NAME

[GuiUnattended]
TimeZone = "(GMT-08:00) Pacific Time (US & Canada); Tijuana"

[Display]
ConfigureAtLogon = 0
BitsPerPel = 16
XResolution = 640
YResolution = 480
```

```
VRefresh = 70
AutoConfirm = 1

[Network]
Attend = yes
DetectAdapters = ""
InstallProtocols = ProtocolsSection
JoinDomain = Domain_To_Join

[ProtocolsSection]
TC = TCParameters

[TCParameters]
DHCP = yes
```

As you can see, this text file looks very much like a Windows .INI file. You can create this text file simply by copying and modifying the sample file, creating your own file by using any text editor, or running the Setup Manager utility, also located on the Windows NT 4.0 installation CD-ROM. Although the file usually is called unattend.txt, you can give it any legal filename, as long as you refer to it correctly when running Setup. The Setup Manager utility provides a graphical interface for creating and modifying the unattend.txt file(s). You can find a complete treatment of the unattend.txt file and information on using Setup Manager in Appendix A, "Answer Files and UDFs," of the Windows NT Workstation Resource Kit Version 4.0 (a recommended companion to this Exam Guide).

After you create this file, you should place it in the same location as the Windows NT 4.0 installation source files on the distribution server.

Create a Uniqueness Data File

The unattend.txt file creates a setup data file that contains information common to all the computers being installed. However, this will not completely automate the process when installing more than one computer. Recall that each computer's computer name must be unique, for example. That sort of information cannot be supplied in the unattend.txt file alone.

You can create a *uniqueness data file* (UDF) to supply the more detailed and machine-specific information required to more fully automate the setup process. The UDF file identifies specific sections that should be merged into the answer file. Here is a sample UDF file:

```
; This section lists all unique ids that are supported by this database.
; The left hand side is a unique id, which can be any string but
```

```
; must not contain the asterisk (*), space, comma, or equals character.
; The right hand side is a list of sections, each of which should match the name
; of a section in unattend.txt. See below.
;
id1 = section1,section2
id2 = section1,section3,section4


[section1]
; This is a section whose name should match the name of a section in unattend.txt.
; Each line in this section is written into the same section in unattend.txt,
; via the profile APIs. A line here thus replaces a line in unattend.txt with the
; same left hand side. (If a matching line does not exist in unattend.txt, the line will
; be added.) A line that just has a left hand side and does not have a value will delete
; the same line in unattend.txt.
;
; To make this section specific to a particular unique id, precede its name with id:.
; This allows specification of different sections in this file that map to the same
; section in unattend.txt. See below.
;
key1 = value
key2 = value


[id2:section2]
; This section is merged into [section2] in unattend.txt for unique id2.
;
key5 = value
```

The sections contained in the UDF are the same sections used in the unattend.txt file. A section's entries in the UDF are merged into the corresponding section in the unattend.txt file. The unique ID referred to in the sample represents an ID that you assign for each computer you are installing. By assigning a unique ID to each section, you can create copies of the same section, each of which modifies the installation slightly from computer to computer. The [UserData] section, for example, can provide a different username and computer name for each subsequent computer installation by creating multiple copies of the [UserData] section, modifying each accordingly, and assigning each a different unique ID corresponding to that computer.

Suppose that you are installing three computers. Each should have a unique computer name: ComputerA, ComputerB, and ComputerC. You assign each computer a unique ID: ID1, ID2, and ID3. The attend.txt section that modifies the computer name is [UserData]. The UDF then looks like this:

```
ID1=[UserData]
ID2=[UserData]
ID3=[UserData]
[ID1:UserData]
Computername=ComputerA
[ID2:UserData]
Computername=ComputerB
[ID3:UserData]
Computername=ComputerC
```

You can find a complete treatment of the UDF files in Appendix A of the Windows NT Workstation Resource Kit Version 4.0.

Connect to the Distribution Server

The computers on which NT 4.0 Server will be installed must be able to connect to and access the shared folder containing the installation, answer, and UDF files. This generally is accomplished by installing the DOS Network Client 3.0 software on the computer if there is no other means of connecting to the distribution server, such as through Windows for Workgroups network connectivity options, Windows 95, or an existing installation of Windows NT Workstation.

After a network connection is established, you can use a simple net command at a command prompt to access the installation source files:

```
 net use d: \\distribution_server\ shared_ folder
```

This net command maps a logical drive letter on your computer to the shared folder on the distribution server. Switching to that drive letter at a command prompt, or through File Manager or Windows Explorer, effectively points you to the files in the shared folder. If the NT 4.0 installation files have been installed in a shared folder called INSTALL on a distribution server called SOURCE1, for example, connect to the folder by typing this command at a command prompt:

```
 net use E: \\SOURCE1\INSTALL
```

The E: drive now is mapped to the NT 4.0 source file directory on the distribution server.

Run Setup

The final step is to run NT Setup by referring to the source directory, answer files, and UDFs you created. You do this by using several of the boot switches that were outlined in Table 3.2. After you map a drive to the shared folder containing the NT 4.0 installation files on the distribution server, switch to that drive. At a command prompt, enter the following command syntax:

```
winnt /u:answer_filename /s:source_drive /UDF:ID[,UDF_filename]
```

Suppose that you have created an answer file called unattend.txt that contains common setup information for your computers, as well as a uniqueness data file called unique.txt that contains specific setup instructions for each computer. Each computer is identified by a unique ID, following the convention ID1, ID2, and so on. At the first computer, corresponding to ID1, you map a drive (E:, for example) to the distribution server. At a command prompt, enter the following command:

```
winnt /u:unattend.txt /s:e: /UDF:ID1[,unique.txt]
```

At the next computer, you would do the same thing, changing the ID reference to one appropriate to that computer, and so on, until you complete your installation.

Key Concept

During an unattended installation, you can place the command to map the drive and the Setup command together in a batch file, along with any other batch commands you want to include, such as one that disconnects from the mapped drive.

Network Client Administrator

If you choose to do an over-the-network installation, you can use Microsoft's *Systems Management Server* (SMS) to do so, or create the boot files needed to begin the installation from the Network Client Administrator utility. This utility creates a single Startup disk that is installed in the target machine. The files for the Startup disk must come from the CLIENTS directory of the CD-ROM, or the files must have been copied to a shared drive elsewhere.

You have some liberty in selecting the operating system for the client and the hard drive format. If you have appropriate software client licenses, Network Client Administrator also can make the Startup disk for NT Server (3.x or 4.0), NT Workstation (3.x, 4.0), or Windows for Workgroups (3.11). It is your responsibility to have a client license for the operating system you choose; Network Client Administrator does not prompt you for one.

You must specify a computer name that is unique for every machine on the network. This often means you must create a Startup disk for every client. Additionally, you must select the protocol and username on the server that the client will use to retrieve the files. It is imperative that the username you specify have adequate permissions to retrieve the files from the source.

An MS-DOS system disk (format /s) is required by Network Client Administrator to create the Startup disk. If you do not have a disk formatted as a system disk, you cannot continue from this point.

The target machine starts, reads the boot disk, and then gets the files over the network from the CD-ROM (or other locale) on the source machine. One potential problem lies in the network adapter cards being configured according to their default settings. If the networking component of the client does not come up properly, verify the appropriate network adapter card configuration.

Summary

This chapter discussed in detail the installation and setup process for Windows NT 4.0 Server. You can install NT on a number of platforms and dual boot with a number of different operating systems. The next chapter, "Configuring Windows NT Server 4.0," helps you become familiar with the new interface and explores how to modify the configuration.

```
┌─ QUESTIONS AND ANSWERS ──────────────────
```

1. The three roles that an NT Server can be installed as are _____, _____, and _____.

A: *Primary domain controller* (PDC), *backup domain controller* (BDC), and member server/standalone server.

2. The executable used to install NT on a system currently running Windows 95 is _____.

A: WINNT.EXE. The cousin to this utility is WINNT32.EXE, and it is used only when installing over a previous version of NT.

3. True or false: Windows NT Server 4.0 can be dual booted with Windows NT Workstation 4.0.

A: True. As long as you use a different directory to install to, Windows NT Server 4.0 can be dual booted with NT Workstation 4.0.

4. The two modes of client licensing are _____ and _____.

A: Per server (concurrent use) and per seat.

...continues

...continued

> **5.** The temporary directory where files are copied to during installation is
> _____.
>
> A:WIN_NT.~LS If the installation finished without failure, the directory is removed upon completion.

PRACTICE TEST

1. You are planning to roll out Windows NT Server 4.0 to a division that has the following computer configurations. On which computers can you install Windows NT Server 4.0 successfully?

   a. Three 386/25, 150MB free space, 8MB RAM, VGA, Windows 3.1

   b. Two 386/33, 120MB free space, 16MB RAM, VGA, Windows for Workgroups

   c. Five 486/66DX, 200MB free space, 16MB RAM, Super VGA, Windows for Workgroups

   d. Two Pentium/120, 100MB free space, 16MB RAM, Super VGA, Windows NT 3.51

Answer a is incorrect, because a 486/25 is required with at least 12MB RAM. Answer b is incorrect, because a 486/25 is required. **Answer c is correct. A 486/25 with at least 12MB of RAM and 120MB free space is needed.** Answer d is incorrect, because at least 120MB of free space is required.

2. Which of the following dialog boxes appear during the text mode of the Setup process? Choose three.

   a. Detection and Configuration of Storage Devices

   b. Initial Hardware Verification

   c. Request for Network Card Settings

   d. Choice of File System for the System Partition

Answer a is correct. The detection and configuration of storage devices is done during the text-mode phase. Answer b is correct. The initial hardware verification is done during the text-mode phase. Answer c is incorrect. The request for network card settings appears much later in the process after the text-mode phase. **Answer d is correct. You must choose the file system for the system partition during the text-mode phase.**

3. Which of the following dialog boxes appear as part of the Setup Wizard? Choose three.

    a. Personal Information

    b. Detection and Configuration of Storage Devices

    c. Request for Network Card Settings

    d. Video Display Setup

Answer a is correct. Personal information is requested by the Setup Wizard. Answer b is incorrect. The detection and configuration of storage devices are performed in the text-mode phase prior to the wizard. **Answer c is correct. Network card settings are requested by the Setup Wizard. Answer d is correct. The video display setup ID is performed by the Setup Wizard.**

4. Which of the following switches enables you to install Windows NT without creating the three Startup disks?

    a. WINNT /B

    b. WINNT /S

    c. WINNT /OX

    d. WINNT /T:c

Answer a is correct. The /B switch tells NT to skip Startup disks. Answer b is incorrect. You use the /S switch to specify the source path. Answer c is incorrect. You use the /OX switch to make the Startup disks. Answer d is incorrect; this switch specifies a location in which to place the temporary files.

5. On a RISC-based computer, which of the following statements is true regarding Windows NT installation?

    a. You execute setup from the CD-ROM or over the network by typing WINNT32 and any optional switches.

    b. You must have a 2MB FAT minimum system partition before starting setup.

    c. You execute setup only from a CD-ROM by running WINNT /ARC.

    d. You run SETUPLDR from the I386 subdirectory on the CD-ROM.

Answer a is incorrect. You must use WINNT if coming from anything other than a previous version of NT. **Answer b is correct. You must have a 2MB FAT minimum system partition on RISC before starting setup.** Answer c is incorrect; /ARC is not a valid parameter. Answer d is incorrect. There is no SETUPLDR executable, and the I386 path is used only for Intel.

CH

3

6. You have begun the setup process and have been queried for mass storage devices. Setup presents you with a blank list of devices, but you know that you have a 1.2GB IDE drive installed.

   a. IDE devices are detected but generally not displayed in the list.

   b. Windows NT has incorrectly identified your devices. Press F3 to exit setup and double-check your drive configuration.

   c. Press s to add the drive configuration to the list.

   d. Exit setup and run NTHQ to verify hardware detection.

Answer a is correct. IDE devices are detected but generally not displayed in the list. Answer b is incorrect, because everything has worked properly. Answer c is incorrect. The search will not look for IDE. Answer d is incorrect, because everything has worked properly.

7. True or false: You must preconfigure your installation drive before starting setup.

   a. True

   b. False

Answer a is incorrect. You do not need to preconfigure the drive. **Answer b is correct. You do not need to preconfigure the drive.**

8. During the text-mode phase, Windows NT displays a dialog box that shows you two drive partitions and 600MB free space on one drive. You would like to install Windows NT on the free space, but you want to use only 200MB. What should you do?

   a. Preconfigure the free space before starting setup.

   b. Select the free space during setup, but you cannot change its size.

   c. Select the free space and press Enter.

   d. Select the free space and choose C to create the new partition. Then select the new partition and continue with the installation.

Answer a is incorrect. You do not need to preconfigure the space. Answer b is incorrect; you can change the size. Answer c is incorrect; this choice does not allow you to change the size. **Answer d is correct. To perform this operation, select the free space and choose C to create the new partition. Then select the new partition and continue with the installation.**

9. Which of the following statements does *not* apply to NTFS?

    a. NTFS supports file and directory permissions security and access auditing.

    b. NTFS supports transaction tracking and sector sparing for data recovery.

    c. NTFS supports file and partition sizes of up to 4GB.

    d. NTFS provides file and directory compression.

Answer a is incorrect (it *does* apply). NTFS does support file and directory permissions, security, and access auditing. Answer b is incorrect (it *does* apply). NTFS supports transaction tracking and sector sparing. **Answer c is correct (it does *not* apply), because FAT is limited to 4GB. NTFS can support 16EB.** Answer d is incorrect (it *does* apply). NTFS supports compression at the file and directory levels.

10. You are installing Windows NT on a computer that also must support and boot OS/2. Which statement is true?

    a. Windows NT supports OS/2's HPFS, so there are no problems installing the Windows NT system files in the same partition as OS/2.

    b. Windows NT 4.0 no longer supports HPFS, so you must install Windows NT in another partition. When Windows NT restarts the system, you can use the OS/2 Boot Manager to manage both partitions.

    c. Windows NT 4.0 no longer supports HPFS, so you must install Windows NT in another partition. When Windows NT restarts the system, it disables the OS/2 Boot Manager, but you can re-enable it by marking the Boot Manager partition as active while in Windows NT and restarting the computer.

    d. Windows NT and OS/2 cannot coexist on the same computer.

Answer a is incorrect (false), because HPFS is no longer supported. Answer b is incorrect (false), because you cannot use the Boot Manager. **Answer c is correct (true). Windows NT stopped the support for HFPS as of version 4.0.** Answer d is incorrect (false). The two operating systems can exist on the same machine in a dual-boot environment.

CH
3

CHAPTER PREREQUISITE

The only prerequisites you should have for this chapter is a familiarity with the Control Panel and other utilities that affect entries in the Windows NT Registry.

Configuring Windows NT Server 4.0

WHILE YOU READ

1. You can make many Registry setting changes in applets located in the _____.

2. You can save different hardware configurations in separate _____.

3. The two Registry Editors included with Windows NT Server 4.0 are _____ and _____.

4. The administrative tool that enables you to display licensing information for the network is the _____.

5. The five tabs of the Display Properties dialog box are _____, _____, _____, _____, and, _____.

NT provides several utilities to help you configure and customize Windows NT. This chapter introduces you to these utilities and the Registry.

Personalizing Your Desktop Environment

One of the first things most users want to do when they get Windows, Windows 95, or, now, Windows NT 4.0, is to personalize their desktop. Usually, the first thing they change is the default color set, or the desktop background becomes a picture of the grandkids. Everyone likes to have control over their working space.

NT 4.0 Server offers several ways to customize your desktop environment. The next section tells you how to use the Display Properties dialog box to customize your desktop.

Display Properties

You can access the Display Properties dialog box by right-clicking anywhere in the desktop background. Then choose Properties to bring up a screen similar to the screen shown in Figure 4.1.

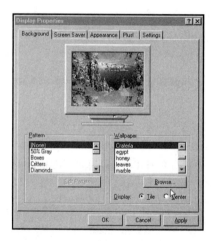

Figure 4.1
A new wallpaper bitmap has been chosen to replace the default background in this Display Properties dialog box.

The Display Properties dialog box has five tabs, each corresponding to one or more of the most popular changes users like to make to customize their computers: Background, Screen Saver, Appearance, Plus!, and Settings. A nice addition to this and many other dialog boxes is the Apply button. You can click this button to apply a change without having to close the dialog box.

You can use the Background tab to change the desktop wallpaper and pattern. These are the same types of changes you may have made in Windows when using the Desktop applet in the Control Panel. A wallpaper display can be any bitmap image, and you can store it anywhere on your computer. The Browse button helps you easily move from the default \WINNT directory to find the bitmap you want to use as your wallpaper pattern.

Screen savers were first introduced to protect monitors from "burning in" an image of what's onscreen. Screen savers display a moving image after a designated time of mouse and keyboard inactivity. Screen savers also can be fun to look at. Most new monitors today are designed to prevent burn-in.

Because it conforms to the Open GL standard (direct draw to the screen, 3D graphics support, and so on), Windows NT 4.0 supports some pretty cool screen savers. Among the new screen savers included in NT Server is the 3D maze, which displays a three-dimensional maze and then proceeds to maneuver you through it.

Most of the screen savers have additional customization options that you can access by clicking the Settings button. You also can designate the period of inactivity before the image kicks in, preview it in full-screen mode, and *password protect* it (which means that you have to know the password before you can release the screen saver and display your regular screen). Screen savers can use a lot of processor time, though, which can be wasteful because you won't be looking at the screen of the server very much, anyway. Setting the screen saver option to the password box or a blank screen is the best option for serious servers (as opposed to test servers).

By using the Appearance tab, you can change color schemes and set the color, size, and in some cases, the font settings for individual items, such as icons.

The Plus! tab gives you the option of using different icons for some of your desktop objects, as well as the choice of refining visual settings. A visually impaired person might want to use large icons, for example. If you have a high-resolution monitor, you can direct NT to smooth the edges of screen fonts and display icons using the full color range available.

You can use the Settings tab to make changes to the monitor settings. You can modify the display type, screen resolution, refresh frequency, color palette, and font size. Before you apply a change, you might want to click the Test button to preview the screen and be sure that it is viewable.

CH

4

Exploring the Control Panel

If you have worked with previous versions of Windows, you most likely have spent some time in the Control Panel. The Control Panel offers a variety of applets you can use to modify your system configuration. Microsoft has reworked most of the Control Panel applets in NT 4.0 to give you a much greater degree of detail when making your selections.

You can open the Control Panel in a variety of ways (see Fig. 4.2). You usually will open it from the Settings option on the Start menu. However, you also can access it by going to My Computer, Windows Explorer or by creating a shortcut to it or any of its applets on your desktop. The Control Panel contains 25 applets.

Figure 4.2
You can find many useful utilities in the NT 4.0 Server Control Panel.

Key Concept

As you add applications or NT services to your computer, additional applets are likely to be added to the Control Panel.

Whenever you need to change a system parameter, your first stop should be the Control Panel. Here is a list of the applets provided in the Control Panel:

- **Accessibility Options:** New to NT 4.0, this applet is designed for people with visual, hearing, or movement challenges. It offers several modifications, including making the keyboard easier to use, visualizing computer sounds, and enabling you to use the keyboard to control the mouse.

- **Add/Remove Programs:** Lets you install and remove Windows NT components, such as games and accessories. It also provides a built-in procedure to automatically install or uninstall applications from disk or CD-ROM. If the application being installed is set up by using a `Setup.exe` or `Install.exe`, Add/Remove Programs records the setup process, displays the application in its list of installed applications, and lets you remove the application by using its Uninstall Wizard.

- **MS-DOS Console:** Often confused with the MS-DOS prompt, which you access through the Start menu. MS-DOS Console lets you modify how a DOS window appears on the desktop. You can alter screen colors, window size, font style and size, cursor size, and the command history buffer.

- **Date/Time:** Modifies the computer's internal date and time values. There really is nothing remarkable here except that the screens are far more graphic and easy to use than ever before. Date/Time even shows you which part of the world your time zone covers.

- **Devices:** Shows you all the device drivers detected and installed by NT, as well as which devices are currently running. It lets you start, stop, and configure startup types for device drivers.

- **Display:** Produces exactly the same Display Properties dialog box that was discussed earlier. This is just another place to access it.

- **Fonts:** Lets you view fonts installed on your system, add new fonts, and remove fonts that no longer are needed. You also can choose to display only TrueType fonts in applications.

- **Internet:** This applet is installed in the Control Panel if you have installed Internet Explorer. It lets you set the proxy server on your network through which you access the Internet. The proxy server is usually the firewall that is used to filter which users on your network can access the Internet and which users from the Internet can access your network.

- **Keyboard:** Allows you to adjust the delay and repeat rates of your keyboard and enables you to change the keyboard type. Keyboard also lets you specify alternative-language keyboards if you want to include foreign language symbol sets.

- **Modems:** Displays the properties of any modems installed on your computer. From here, you can add and remove modems and modify modem settings. Choosing <u>A</u>dd starts the Install Modem Wizard. This wizard walks you through the detection, selection, and connection of your system's modem.

CH
4

■ **Mouse:** Lets you customize many characteristics of your mouse device. You can switch button use for left-handed persons, modify the double-click speed (test it on the jack-in-the-box!), and change the pointer speed. There is also a tab for changing the various mouse pointers, where you'll find interesting visual representations for the select, wait, working, and other pointers (see Fig. 4.3). Clicking Browse displays all the neat pointer files that NT supplies, including the infamous animated cursors. Look for the files with an .ANI extension. You can preview them before you apply them.

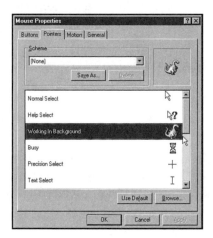

Figure 4.3
The Browse button displays a list of mouse pointer files you can use to customize the pointers. Notice how the mouse pointer for Working in Background has changed from the default hourglass with an arrow to a dinosaur.

■ **Multimedia:** Provides configuration options for audio, video, *musical instrument digital interface* (MIDI), CD music, and any other multimedia-related devices. This is where you add items such as a sound card.

■ **Network:** Identifies the computer; its relationship to the rest of the network; and all service, protocol, adapter, and bindings settings. You also can access this applet by selecting the properties for Network Neighborhood. This is where the majority of your network configuration takes place.

■ **PC Card (PCMCIA):** Tells you whether you have PC Card support on your computer, which cards are currently in use, and the resources those cards are using.

■ **Ports:** Lets you add, modify, and delete parameters for your computer's COM ports. For example, if you add a new COM port adapter card to your computer, or you connect a serial printer to an existing port, you may want to configure it for a certain speed and parity.

■ **Printers:** Replaces Print Manager and displays icons related to each printer installed on your computer or connected through the network. From this applet, you can manage the printing devices and print jobs. There is also an Add Printer Wizard that walks you through the process of installing, configuring, and sharing your printing device. You also can access this applet from the taskbar by choosing Start, Settings, Printers.

■ **Regional Settings:** Displays current settings for number symbols, currency formats, date and time values, and input locales based on world regions. This applet used to be called International and has been greatly enhanced.

■ **SCSI Adapters:** Displays SCSI adapters and drivers that have been installed on your computer and their resource settings (I/O, interrupt, and so on).

■ **Server:** Offers statistics relating to the server-based activities of your computer. Shows which network users currently are connected, which shared resources are being used and by whom, and any replication settings that have been configured. The Server applet also lets you set administrative alerts that deliver system message pop-ups to a specified user or computer.

■ **Services:** Displays a list of all the services that have been installed on your computer and their current running status. NT services are functions or applications that are loaded as part of NT Executive. Thus, these services run as part of the operating system instead of as a background or *terminate-and-stay-resident* (TSR) program.

As Figure 4.4 shows, the Services applet also gives you the capability to start and stop services, and to modify their startup configuration.

You also can set services based on hardware profiles so that only certain services run, depending on the specific hardware installation. For example, a laptop that is not connected remotely to a network while the user is on the road may have certain network-related services turned off. This makes additional resources available to other applications. When the laptop is docked at the user's desk at a station that is wired to the network, those network services then are turned on again.

■ **Sounds:** Lets you assign different types of sounds to system and application events, such as warnings, opening a program, doing what you shouldn't, and so on.

CH

4

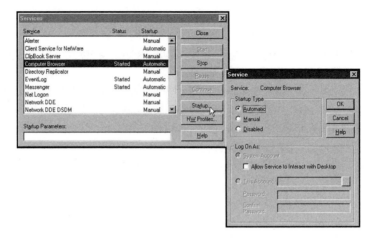

Figure 4.4
The Services dialog box shows the status of several NT services running on this computer, as well as the Service dialog box for one of the services, which you display by clicking Startup.

- ■ **System:** Enables you to define the default operating system at boot time, set recovery options for Stop errors, determine which hardware profiles to use during startup, view and delete user profiles stored on your computer, view and define environmental variables, modify application performance, and configure and customize pagefile parameters.
- ■ **Tape Devices:** Lets you view, add, or delete tape devices and their driver settings installed on your computer.
- ■ **Telephony:** Opens the Dialing Properties dialog box, which lets you view, add, or remove telephony drivers; and modify dialing parameters, such as pressing 9 to get an outside line or disabling call waiting. You can create a different set of dialing parameters for various situations or locations. Dialing out through your modem at work may require no additional settings, for example, whereas dialing out from a hotel room may require dialing one or more numbers in sequence to access a local or long-distance line.
- ■ **UPS:** Lets you set configuration parameters for your uninterruptible power supply connected to the computer. Parameters include setting interface voltages for power failure and low-battery signals, specifying a command file to be executed when the UPS is activated, and setting other UPS-specific characteristics, such as expected battery life.

Your Control Panel will have additional utilities to help you manage the specific hardware and software installed on your system.

Exploring the Administrative Tools

The Administrative Tools group contains utilities that are specific to your installation of NT 4.0 Workstation or NT 4.0 Server.

The following tools are installed on the Windows NT 4.0 Server:

- **Backup utility:** Gives you considerable control over what data you want to back up and to where you want to back it up. This utility also controls the restore process. You can back up entire disks or directories, or specific files, including the Registry. The Backup utility keeps summary logs indicating what was backed up or restored, when it was backed up or restored, and any files that it determined were corrupt.

- **Disk Administrator:** Can best be described as a much improved FDISK utility with a GUI interface. From the Disk Administrator, you easily can create and format disk partitions, create volume sets and extended volumes, and create stripe sets. On the Server version, you also can enable software fault tolerance (also known as *redundant array of inexpensive/independent disks* or *RAID),* such as striping with parity and mirrored disk partitions.

- **Event Viewer:** A great troubleshooting utility. It records system events, such as services that failed to start or devices that could not be initialized. When various audit functions are enabled in NT, Event Viewer provides logs that record the audit information and display it for your review.

- **License Manager:** Tracks software licenses throughout an enterprise. License information is collected from all primary domain controllers in your organization to a central database. You can view summaries of all per-seat licenses and per-server licenses in use. You also can view use patterns.

- **Network Client Administrator:** Enables you to install or update client workstations. You can use the Client Administrator to install any of the client files contained on the NT Server 4.0 CD-ROM.

- **Performance Monitor:** This tool still receives rave reviews from NT administrators for the sheer amount of system performance data that can be charted, saved, and reviewed. You use this utility to help determine performance bottlenecks on your system, processor use, server access, and so on. Performance Monitor is covered in more detail, along with Event Viewer, in Chapter 8, "Performance Monitor."

- **Remote Access Administrator:** After *Remote Access Service* (RAS) is installed and configured on your computer, the Remote Access Administrator utility offers you management functions for your RAS client, such as defining which users can access your computer through a dial-in connection, who is currently connected, which ports are in use, and whether the service is running.

CH

4

■ **Server Manager:** You can use this tool to administer both local and remote computers. You can view a list of users connected to another computer, view shared resources, enable/disable alerts, manage directory replication, and send messages to users. You also can add or remove computers from a domain, promote backup domain controllers, and synchronize servers in a domain with the primary domain controller.

■ **System Policy Editor:** Enables an administrator to control what users can do on client machines. You can restrict access to various portions of the machine. You can prevent Windows 95 users from launching the DOS shell, for example.

■ **User Manager for Domains:** You create and manage user and group accounts through User Manager. Password policy information, location of user profiles and logon scripts, users' functional rights, and user-access auditing are all configured through User Manager. This utility is covered in greater detail in Chapter 6, "Security and Permissions."

■ **Windows NT Diagnostics:** An enhanced and GUI version of Microsoft's MS-DOS–based *Microsoft Diagnostics* (MSD). This utility gives detailed information culled directly from the NT Registry relating to the system, display, disk drives, memory and pagefile use, network statistics, environment variable values, resources in use and their settings, and services installed and their state. This version actually provides a far greater level of detail than previous NT versions. You can even print out the information screens.

Creating and Managing Hardware Profiles

Hardware profiles offer a way for you to create and maintain different hardware configurations—including which services and devices are initialized—for different computing scenarios. The most common use for hardware profiles is with laptop computers that sometimes are placed in a docking station. While portable, the user can use the laptop's modem to dial in to the company network. When docked, that user can access the network through the network card installed in the docking station.

These are two methods of connecting to the network that are used in two different scenarios, so they require different hardware. You certainly can maintain the same profile for both scenarios. When users are portable, however, they are likely to receive event or system messages relating to the "missing" network card. Likewise, if the docking station disables the modem in users' laptops, they may receive similar messages when the computer is docked. If you maintain two hardware profiles, you can customize which device is activated during which scenario.

Creating a Hardware Profile

To create a hardware profile, you first must access the System Properties dialog box (see Fig. 4.5). You can open the System Properties dialog box in one of two ways:

- Right-click My Computer on the desktop and then choose P̲roperties.
- Open the Control Panel and start the System applet.

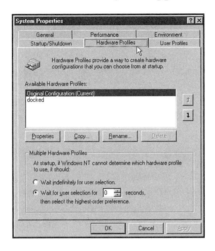

Figure 4.5
The System Properties dialog box with the Hardware Profiles tab selected.

After the System Properties dialog box is displayed, follow these steps to create a new hardware profile:

1. Select the Hardware Profiles tab.
2. Choose an existing or original profile from the Available Hardware Profiles list box and click C̲opy.
3. Enter the name of the new profile and click OK.
4. Use the arrow buttons to the right of the profile list to determine the order preference of the profiles. This list determines the order NT uses to load the profiles during system startup.
5. Click the P̲roperties button to indicate whether the computer is a portable, its docking state, and whether this profile should disable all network functions (see Fig. 4.6).

CH

4

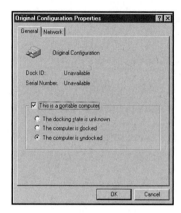

Figure 4.6
This hardware profile has been designated as a portable computer that is undocked.

6. Specify what NT should do during startup. If you want NT to display a list of profiles at startup, select Wait Indefinitely for User Selection. NT does not continue with the startup operation until a profile selection is made. Profiles are displayed after you are prompted to press the spacebar for the Last Known Good configuration.

   If you want to set a timeout value for selecting a profile before NT selects the first profile in the list, select Wait for User Selection for xx Seconds, Then Select the Highest-Order Preference. If you set the timeout value to 0, NT simply boots with the highest-order profile on startup. Pressing the spacebar when prompted for the Last Known Good configuration redisplays the profile list.

After you create the hardware profile, you need to identify which services and devices to enable and disable for each profile. You do this through the Services and Devices applets in the Control Panel.

To define a specific service or device to the hardware profile, follow these steps:

1. From the Services or Devices applet's dialog box, select the service or device you want to define from the list.

2. Click the HW Profiles button to display the dialog box shown in Figure 4.7.

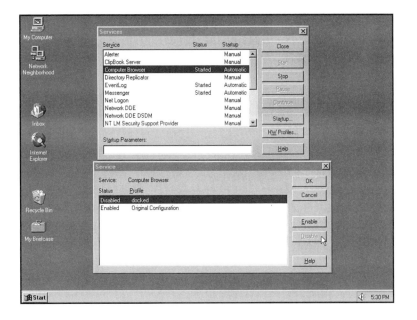

Figure 4.7
In this example, the Computer Browser Service, which normally is enabled, has been set to Disabled for the profile called Docked.

3. Select the profile you are modifying from the list.

4. Click Enable or Disable to turn the service or device on or off, respectively, for that profile.

5. Click OK and close the Services or Devices applet.

When you start NT and choose your hardware profile, the services and devices start as you configured them.

Examining the Windows NT 4.0 Server Registry

The Windows NT 4.0 Registry is perhaps the single most important element of the NT operating system architecture. The Registry is an encrypted database of configuration and environment information relating to the successful booting of NT 4.0. Think of this file as being the DOS AUTOEXEC.BAT and CONFIG.SYS files rolled into one—and then some.

The Registry is central to the operation of Windows NT 4.0. Driver information, services, hardware profile information, security objects and their permissions, and account information are all stored in the Registry. Microsoft considers the Registry to be so integral a part of Windows NT that it strongly discourages you from making changes to it.

In fact, the Control Panel, Administrative Tools group, and various properties sheets give you all the utilities you need to modify and customize your installation of Windows NT 4.0 for normal maintenance. All these utilities modify one or more Registry entries. Therefore, there are only limited and very specific reasons for you to make changes to the Registry directly.

Key Concept

A good rule of thumb for modifying the Registry: If there is a utility that can do the modification, use the utility! If you make substantial changes to the Registry that result in problems during bootup or execution, Microsoft will disallow your support call.

The Registry has several advantages over the older system:

- **Centralized:** Instead of PROGMAN.INI, CPANEL.INI, and a host of other such files for your applications, Windows NT stores all its configuration data in the Registry. As a result, all Windows NT components and Windows NT–based applications can easily find information about any other aspect of the computer. In addition, the Registry supports remote administration: An administrator, sitting at his or her own workstation, can alter another computer's configuration by remotely editing its Registry.

- **Structured:** The Registry can contain subsections within sections, something that was impossible with INI files. The result is a much more orderly, logical record.

- **Flexible:** INI files contained ASCII text. The Registry can contain text as well, but it also can hold binary and hexadecimal values. It can even hold executable code or entire text files. The Registry also contains preferences and restrictions for individual users—something that INI files never have done. This provides a configuration database that stores not only computer-specific information, but also user-specific information.

- **Secure:** You can protect the Registry just like any object in Windows NT. You can define an access control list for any Registry key, and a special set of permissions exists specifically for dealing with the Registry.

When viewed from this perspective, you might wonder how users survived without the Registry. However, the Registry has its drawbacks:

- **Cryptic:** Unlike INI files, the assumption with many parts of the Registry seems to be *Humans just don't go here.* It isn't always easy to determine why certain entries are present or how to effectively configure them.

■ **Sprawling:** Imagine all the INI files on an average Windows 3.x–based computer merged into a single file, with some additional hardware information as well. The Registry begins its life big, and it only gets bigger.

■ **Dangerous:** If you make a mistake when editing an INI file, or if you aren't sure about the potential effect of a change, you always can exit the text editor without saving the file. Even a fatal change to an INI file can be fixed by booting to MS-DOS and using a text editor to alter the problematic file. Not so with the Registry: Direct changes to the Registry often are dynamic and potentially irreversible.

That said, there are specific instances when you have to modify the Registry directly. These cases usually have to do with the absence of a utility to make a necessary change, or for troubleshooting purposes. Some of the more common changes are discussed in the next section, "Using the Registry to Configure Windows NT 4.0 Server."

Navigating with the Registry Editor

You can access the Registry by starting the Registry Editor utility with one of these methods:

■ Open Windows Explorer and select the SYSTEM32 folder under the Windows NT system folder (usually called WINNT or WINNT40). Double-click the file REGEDT32.EXE.

■ Choose Run from the Start menu. In the Open combo box, type **REGEDT32.EXE**. Then click OK.

If you are going to access the Registry often, you can create a shortcut to REGEDT32.EXE on your desktop.

Key Concept

Windows NT Server 4.0 ships with two Registry Editors. The first, Regedt32.exe, has been with Windows NT since version 4.0. The second, Regedit.exe, is a Windows 95 tool that was included with NT as of version 4.0.

Because there is *much* more power and strength in Regedt32.exe, that is the tool this book references. The majority of operations also could be done with Regedit.exe, but they are a subset of what Regedt32.exe can do.

Also, throughout the remainder of this book, the Windows NT system directory is referred to as WINNT40.

CH

4

The Registry Editor displays the five main windows, called *subtrees,* of the Windows NT 4.0 Registry for the local computer (see Fig. 4.8).

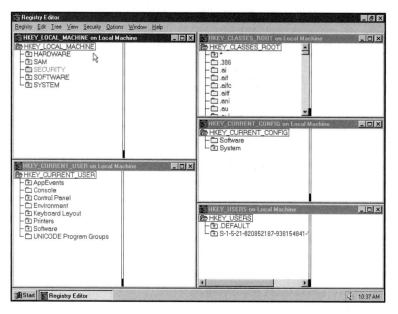

Figure 4.8
The five subtrees of the Windows NT Registry, tiled for better viewing.

Here are the five subtrees:

- HKEY_LOCAL_MACHINE
- HKEY_CURRENT_CONFIG
- HKEY_USERS
- HKEY_CURRENT_USERS
- HKEY_CLASSES_ROOT

By default, only those users with administrator access can make modifications to the Registry. Other users can only view the information contained there. I recommend setting the View option to Read Only, even for administrators. This guards against any accidental modifications that can lead to serious boot and operation problems. Enable it by choosing Read Only Mode from the Options menu in the Registry Editor.

Choose Options, Font to change the font style and size to facilitate viewing. Choose Confirm on Delete to guard against accidental deletions.

At first glance, these windows look a lot like File Manager or Windows Explorer, and in fact, you can navigate them in much the same way. The left pane of each subtree window displays the keys pertinent to that subtree. As you select each key, the parameters and values assigned to that key appear in the right pane. You can think of a key as being a more sophisticated INI file.

You may recall that an INI file consists of section headings, each section containing one or more parameters unique to that section, and each parameter having an appropriate value or values assigned to it (see Fig. 4.9). The values can be text strings, filenames, or simple yes or no or 1 or 0 values.

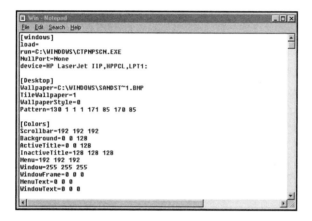

Figure 4.9
A Windows INI file. Notice the section headings in square brackets. Each section has at least one parameter. The values assigned to each parameter represent what the parameter "expects."

A Registry key is quite similar to an INI file. Think of a Registry key as a "nested" INI file (see Fig. 4.10). A key can consist of parameters with assigned values, or it can consist of one or more subkeys, each with its own parameters.

HKEY_LOCAL_MACHINE contains all the system configuration data needed to boot and run the operating system successfully. This data includes services that need to be run, device drivers, hardware profiles (including which hardware is currently loaded), logon parameters, and so on. HKEY_LOCAL_MACHINE is composed of five primary keys called *hives,* each of which can contain subtrees that are several folders deep (refer to Fig. 4.10). Each of the hives relates to a corresponding Registry file saved in the WINNT40 \SYSTEM32\CONFIG directory, except for the Hardware hive, which is built when the computer is booted. The Hardware hive is more properly referred to as a *key.*

CH
4

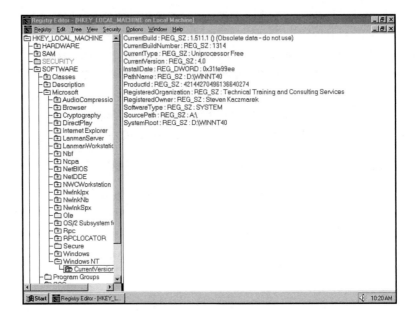

Figure 4.10
An NT Registry key can go several levels deep before finally displaying parameter values.

The five HKEY_LOCAL_MACHINE hives follow:

- HARDWARE (properly called a *key)*
- SOFTWARE
- SYSTEM
- SAM
- SECURITY

The HARDWARE hive, or key, contains data related to detected hardware devices installed on your computer.

Key Concept

The HARDWARE key is built during the startup process and, as such, is called a *volatile key*. This information is not written down anywhere or stored permanently on the system. Instead, NT detects this information each time it boots.

The HARDWARE key includes such information as the processor type and power, keyboard class, port information, SCSI adapter information, drive data, video, and memory. This information is stored primarily as binary data, and because it is built during startup, it is useless to modify. The Windows NT Diagnostics utility is the best tool to use to view this data.

The SAM and SECURITY hives contain security-related information. SAM stands for *Security Account Manager* and, as you may suspect, contains user and group account information, as well as workgroup or domain membership information. The SECURITY hive contains *Local Security Account* (LSA) policy information, such as specific user rights assigned to user and group accounts.

Neither of these hives nor their subtrees are viewable. It is part of Microsoft's security policy to hide this information, even from the system administrator. Even if you could look at this information, it probably would not make a lot of sense or give you any insight into violating account information.

Unlike the HARDWARE key, SAM and SECURITY are written to files on the hard drive. Each has a Registry and log file associated with it—SAM and SAM.LOG, and SECURITY and SECURITY.LOG, respectively. You can find these hives in the WINNT40\SYSTEM32\CONFIG subdirectory on the NT system partition.

The SOFTWARE hive consists of computer-specific software installed on your computer, as opposed to user-specific settings. This information includes manufacturer and version, installed driver files, descriptive and default information for NT-specific services and functions (such as the browser, NetDDE, and NT version information), and the WINLOGON service. This hive also has two files associated with it that are located in the WINNT40\ SYSTEM32\CONFIG subdirectory: SOFTWARE and SOFTWARE.LOG.

Whereas the SOFTWARE hive contains more descriptive information regarding the installation of applications, drivers, and so on on your computer, the SYSTEM hive provides configuration and parameter settings necessary for NT to boot successfully and correctly maintain your computer's configuration. A quick look at the subtrees below SYSTEM shows at least three control set entries (see Fig. 4.11).

These control set entries are used to control the startup process, indicating which services should load, which drivers to load and initialize, and so on. Any changes you make to existing driver settings, or any new drivers you install and configure, are added to a control set in the SYSTEM hive. Its corresponding files in the WINNT40\SYSTEM32\CONFIG subdirectory are SYSTEM and SYSTEM.ALT.

CH
4

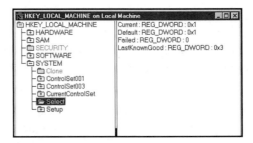

Figure 4.11

HKEY_LOCAL_MACHINE with the SYSTEM hive expanded to show the boot control sets.

HKEY_CURRENT_CONFIG is a new subtree added to Windows NT 4.0. It is a subset of HKEY_LOCAL_MACHINE and reflects only the current software and system modifications made during the current session, as well as the current startup settings. This is useful for isolating data specific to a hardware profile from other data stored in the Registry.

HKEY_CLASSES_ROOT will look familiar to administrators of previous versions of Windows. It represents *object linking and embedding* (OLE) and file association data that is specific to file extensions. This is information that was stored in Windows' REG.DAT file. This subtree is also a subset of HKEY_LOCAL_MACHINE and is located there under the SOFTWARE hive.

HKEY_USERS consists of two subkeys related to user settings. DEFAULT contains system default settings that are used when the Logon screen is first displayed. The second entry represents the user who is currently logged on to the system. The long alphanumeric value you see is the user's *security identifier* (SID).

HKEY_CURRENT_USER represents a subset of HKEY_USERS and points back to the settings of the current user (the SID entry in HKEY_USERS).

Using the Registry to Configure Windows NT 4.0 Server

This section introduces you to the method for looking up keys and making changes to them. It also points out some specific modifications you can accomplish only by changing the Registry.

Let me begin by stating the not so obvious. As you navigate through the Registry and select various keys, you may or may not see parameter values displayed in the windows. If no parameters are displayed, it does not necessarily mean that there are no values present. It may simply mean that NT is using the default values for that entry.

If you select the HKEY_CURRENT_USER\CONTROL PANEL\CURSORS subkey, for example, and you have made no changes to your mouse pointers, you will see no entries here. However, it is obvious that you do, in fact, have default mouse pointers displayed on your screen. In this case, NT does use parameter values—the default values.

Key Concept

Here is the general rule of thumb: If the Registry does not display parameter values when you select a subkey, assume that NT is using the defaults for that subkey, and realize that the default for some parameters is to have no values loaded at all.

As an example of NT using the default values, consider the choice of the cursor pointer. A user has selected the peeling banana to replace the hourglass "wait" cursor and wants to change it to the running horse. Also, this user wants to change the application-starting cursor (the hourglass with an arrow) to the lumbering dinosaur. You can simply and easily do this by using the Mouse applet in the Control Panel, but you feel particularly bold today.

You need to know three areas of information before you modify this particular entry, and in general, change any Registry entry:

- Which Registry entry you are going to change, what subkey or subkeys are involved (yes, there might be more than one!), and where those subkeys are located.
- Which parameter needs to be added, modified, or deleted to make your change effective.
- What value needs to be assigned to the parameter, and its type.

First, determining what is the subkey and where it is located is not always easy. If the change you are making modifies the way the system operates (new device driver, changing the video display, adding a new hardware profile), the subkeys to make this change most likely are located below HKEY_LOCAL_MACHINE, in the SYSTEM hive, under one of the controlset entries. If the change you are making affects the working environment of a particular user (desktop wallpaper, cursors, colors, window properties), those subkeys most likely are located below HKEY_USERS in the current user's subkey, identified by the user's SID.

Sometimes the subkeys that need to be modified are easy to identify, such as CURSORS. Sometimes they are not easily identifiable. Who could know intuitively that the HKEY_LOCAL_MACHINE\SYSTEM\CURRENTCONTROLSET\SERVICES\CE2NDIS31 entry refers to the driver settings for the Credit Card Ethernet Adapter installed on a particular laptop? So how do you find out? Sometimes your documentation tells you. Most times, however, you find the subkeys only by exploration, trial, and error. But remember, Microsoft recommends that you not make configuration changes through the Registry directly, especially when a utility can do it for you. In the case of the network adapter just mentioned, you don't really need to know where its configuration values are stored in the Registry, because you can configure it through the Network applet in the Control Panel or by using the Properties dialog box from Network Neighborhood.

Key Concept

There is a great difference in the types of Find operations the two Registry Editors can perform. Regedt32's Find only works with key entries, whereas Regedit's works with key entries and values.

Getting back to the example, because changing the cursor is a user environment change, you know you can find the subkey in the HKEY_USERS subtree, under the user's SID entry. You also can select the HKEY_CURRENT_USER subtree, because it points to the same location in the Registry.

From there, because you are modifying cursors, you want to look for a subkey called CURSORS. Because cursors are modified through the Control Panel, it is a pretty safe bet that you will find a CURSORS subkey below the CONTROL PANEL subkey. You now know the location and the subkey to modify: HKEY_CURRENT_USER\CONTROL PANEL\CURSORS.

The second thing you should know is which parameter needs to be added, modified, or deleted to make your change effective.

Once again, finding out which parameter value to change is difficult, unless someone gives you the parameter and value to enter. In this example, the parameter corresponding to the working hourglass is called WAIT, and the parameter corresponding to the application-start hourglass with an arrow is called APPSTARTING.

Finally, you need to know what value needs to be assigned to the parameter, and its type.

By now, you probably get the idea. Again, in this example, the filenames that correspond to the various cursors have a .CUR or .ANI extension. You can find these listed in the WINNT40\SYSTEM32 subdirectory. Recall that the WAIT cursor needs to change from the banana (BANANA.ANI) to the running horse (HORSE.ANI), and that the APPSTARTING cursor needs to be the lumbering dinosaur (DINOSAUR.ANI).

You can apply one of five data types to a parameter value. Again, you usually know which one to use—because it is obvious, because someone told you, or because you took the time to read the manual. Table 4.1 lists the value types and a brief description of each.

Table 4.1 Parameter Value Data Types

Data Type	Expects
REG_SZ	One text string data value
REG_DWORD	One hexadecimal string of one to eight digits
REG_BINARY	One string of hexadecimal digits, each pair of which is considered a byte value
REG_EXPAND_SZ	One text string value that contains a replaceable parameter, such as %USERNAME% or %SYSTEMROOT%
REG_MULTI_SZ	Multiple string values separated by a NULL character

In the cursor example, cursors can be associated with only one filename (a text string). Therefore, your parameter value will have a data type of REG_SZ, and its value will be the filename. Now you can modify the Registry. Just follow these steps:

1. Open the Registry Editor. From the <u>O</u>ptions menu, deselect <u>R</u>ead Only Mode, if it is selected.

2. Maximize the HKEY_CURRENT_USER subtree window to make it easier to work with.

3. Expand the CONTROL PANEL key.

4. Highlight the CURSORS key. In the right pane, because the WAIT cursor has been modified once already, there is an entry called WAIT, of data type REG_SZ, and value BANANA.ANI.

5. Double-click the parameter entry (WAIT) to display the String Editor (see Fig. 4.12).

6. Enter the new parameter value (D:\WINNT40\SYSTEM32\HORSE.ANI).

7. To add a new parameter and value, choose <u>E</u>dit, Add <u>V</u>alue from the Registry Editor menu bar.

8. In the Add Value dialog box, enter the value name (APPSTARTING) and choose the appropriate data type (REG_SZ). Then click OK (see Fig. 4.13).

9. In the String Editor dialog box, enter the appropriate parameter value (D:\WINNT40\SYSTEM32\DINOSAUR.ANI) and click OK.

10. Reselect <u>R</u>ead Only Mode from the <u>O</u>ptions menu, and then close the Registry Editor.

The change does not take effect immediately.

CH

4

Figure 4.12
The WAIT cursor currently has the value BANANA.ANI. Double-click it to display the String
Editor and change the value to HORSE.ANI.

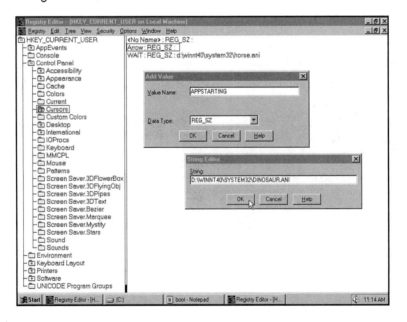

Figure 4.13
Choose Edit, Add Value to add the new cursor parameter APPSTARTING, with a data type
of REG_SZ, and click OK. In the String Editor, type DINOSAUR.ANI.

Key Concept

In general, if you make a user-environment change, the user has to log off and log back on before the change takes effect. In general, if you make a system change, you must shut down the computer and restart it before the change takes effect.

Parameter names are not case sensitive. Because these names can be quite lengthy, however, Microsoft uses proper case (the first letter of each word is capitalized) when displaying these values to make them easier to read.

If you misspell a parameter name, the result may be that NT simply ignores it, or the misspelling may result in a service stopping altogether. This also is true with parameter values. If in doubt, look up the spelling in the Windows NT Resource Kit, or test it first. Before testing, back up your original Registry, or at the very least, save the original subkey.

The following sections cover some other modifications you can make to the Registry when a utility does not exist.

Legal Notices

Legal notices are dialog boxes that pop up before a user can log on; they usually indicate who is authorized to access that computer. You generally see these boxes while logging on to enterprise networks. You can change these dialog boxes in the Registry by modifying the following subkey and parameter values:

```
HKEY_LOCAL_MACHINE\SOFTWARE\MICROSOFT\WINDOWS NT\CURRENT VERSION\WINLOGON\
LegalNoticeCaption and LegalNoticeText.
```

LegalNoticeCaption modifies the title bar of the dialog box that appears during logon, and LegalNoticeText is the text that appears in the dialog box.

For example, modify LegalNoticeCaption to display Legal Notice for Computer SDK. Modify LegalNoticeText to display Unauthorized users will be shot on sight!

To see this change, log off and log back on.

Logon Usernames

By default, NT records in the Registry the name of the last user who logged on to a system (along with the workgroup or domain that the user logged on to). You can view this information in the following entries:

```
HKEY_LOCAL_MACHINE\SOFTWARE\MICROSOFT\WINDOWS NT\CURRENT VERSION\WINLOGON\
DefaultUserName and DefaultDomainName
```

CH
4

For added security, you can hide the display of the last user who logged on so that no one can try guessing the password to get on to the system. As you know, users tend to use passwords that are easily guessed. If a potential hacker also must guess the username, it makes the computer less desirable to hack into (kind of like putting the Club on your steering wheel). If you would rather not display the last user who logged on to a computer, you need to add the following parameter name and value:

```
HKEY_LOCAL_MACHINE\SOFTWARE\MICROSOFT\WINDOWS NT\CURRENT VERSION\WINLOGON\
DontDisplayLastUserName
```

DontDisplayLastUserName expects a data type of REG_SZ and a value of 1 (Yes, don't display the last username) or 0 (No, do display the last username). This is an example of a parameter that does not appear in the right pane, but its default value is loaded by the Registry.

The System Policy Editor

Windows NT 4.0 Server includes a configuration-management utility called the System Policy Editor. It is intended to be used to manage server-based workstation and user policies—that is, configuration information that is stored on a logon server (domain controller) and downloaded to the user's workstation when the user logs on to the network. Most of the Registry changes discussed so far in this chapter can be made more safely through the System Policy Editor. Also, the configuration is assured to "follow" the user and thus be consistent and standard.

In Figure 4.14, for example, a system policy has been created for user SDKACZ. Note that, simply by pointing and clicking through a variety of intuitive screens, the user's access and environment can be fixed. In this example, the user's capability to modify the screen is reduced, a wallpaper has been selected, and the Run and Settings folders have been removed. This policy affects the user wherever SDKACZ logs on.

Similarly, you can establish a system policy by workstation name, thus regulating a user's environment and access by workstation. You can disable the last username from displaying, for example, or modify the legal notice dialog box—again, simply by pointing and clicking in the appropriate check box. These settings then affect every user who logs on to this specific workstation.

The workstation and user policies are saved in a file called NTCONFIG.POL and stored in the WINNT40\SYSTEM32\REPL\IMPORT\SCRIPTS subdirectory of each domain controller. This directory also is known by the share name NETLOGON.

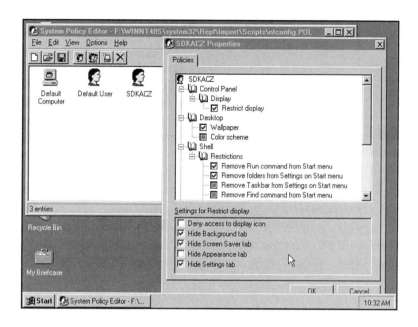

Figure 4.14
A System Policy Editor screen from NT 4.0 Server.

Changing the Default Startup Screen

The default startup screen is the Ctrl+Alt+Del screen that appears when you log off or boot NT. You can change how this screen looks by modifying entries in the DEFAULT sub-key of HKEY_USERS. If you have created a company logo called XYZ.BMP that you want all your computers to display during startup, for example, you need to modify the default desktop wallpaper. Access the following Registry entry:

```
HKEY_USERS\DEFAULT\DESKTOP\Wallpaper
```

Next, you need to change the Wallpaper entry from (DEFAULT) to XYZ.BMP. The change takes effect when you log off, and the logo appears in the center of your desktop.

If you want your bitmap to be tiled, change the TileWallpaper value in the same subkey from 0 to 1.

Through a little experimentation, you will find other changes you can make to the cursor using the Registry. For example, try changing the cursor pointers!

Accessing the Registry Remotely

A computer's Registry may have been modified, either through a utility or directly, and now the computer is not functioning quite as it should. The Registry Editor provides a facility for accessing the computer's Registry remotely. If you have an administrator account on your computer that matches one on the other machine (including password), you can access the other computer's Registry. Just follow these steps:

1. Open your Registry Editor.
2. Choose Registry, Select Computer.
3. In the Select Computer dialog box, enter the name of the computer, or select it from the browse list, and then click OK.
4. The Registry Editor displays the HKEY_LOCAL_MACHINE and HKEY_USERS subtrees from that computer. The title bar of each window displays the remote computer's name.
5. When you finish working with the remote Registry, make sure the remote Registry window is highlighted and choose Registry, Close.

If you do not close the remote Registry windows, they reappear on your computer the next time you start the Registry Editor.

Windows NT Core Services

A *service* is a built-in application that provides support for other applications or other components of the operating system. Windows NT includes dozens of services, each performing a highly specialized function. Many of Windows NT's services support NT's networking capabilities.

Here are some examples of Windows NT services:

- *Windows Internet Name Service* (WINS), which maps *Internet Protocol* (IP) addresses to *Network Basic Input/Output System* (NetBIOS) names.
- UPS service, which interacts with an uninterruptible power supply system to prevent your system from abruptly shutting down.
- Server Service, which accepts I/O requests from the network and routes the requested resources back to the client.
- Workstation Service, which accepts I/O requests from the local system and redirects the requests to the appropriate computer on the network.

Services are background processes that perform specific functions in Windows NT. Typically, services don't interact with the user interface in any way (including appearing in the Task List), so users shouldn't be aware of their existence. Think of a Windows NT service as the equivalent of a UNIX daemon, or if you are more comfortable with NetWare, the equivalent of a *NetWare Loadable Module* (NLM).

This section takes a closer look at some important Windows NT services and how to configure them.

The Services Application

The Control Panel Services application manages the services on your system.

The Services application writes directly to the following key, where configuration data for Windows NT services is maintained:

```
HKEY_LOCAL_MACHINE\SYSTEM\CurrentControlSet\Control\Services
```

Double-click the Services icon in the Control Panel to open the Services dialog box (see Fig. 4.15). This dialog box lists the services on your system, as well as the status (whether or not the service is started) and the startup type. The Startup column tells you whether the service will start automatically or manually, or whether it is disabled. Automatic services start at the very end of the boot process, after the Welcome: Press Ctrl+Alt+Del to Log On window appears. (Because services are Win32 programs, they require a fully functional operating system before they can be opened.) Manual services start after you select the service in the Services dialog box and click the Start button.

CH

4

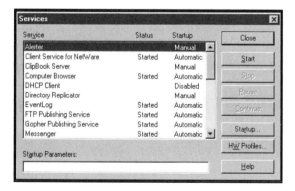

Figure 4.15
The Control Panel Services application.

Note that the Services dialog box includes buttons that stop a service, pause a service, or continue a service that has been paused. Pausing a service causes the service to continue handling the processes it is currently serving but to not take on any new clients. The Server Service is required to run on a server before it can accept connections from a client, for example. Stopping the Server Service causes all connections to be dropped immediately, but pausing the service preserves existing connections while rejecting new connection attempts.

Key Concept

Pausing a service does not release the resources it may have been using. Stopping a service, however, releases whatever resources the service may have been using.

To enable a service for a given hardware profile, click the H<u>W</u> Profiles button in the Services dialog box, select a profile, and click Close.

Double-click a service to open a configuration dialog box—called the Service dialog box, as opposed to the Services dialog box—that enables you to configure a startup type and define a logon account for the service.

The logon account defines a security context for the service. Because services are Win32 programs, they must run under the protection of a user account. The problem is, services continue to execute even when nobody is logged on to the computer, so the administrator must configure the service to use a specific user account. Here are two options:

- **System Account:** An internal account, called SYSTEM, can be used by the operating system or by the service. This method isn't recommended, however, because you can't fine-tune rights and permissions without possibly affecting the performance and stability of the operating system and other services that may use this account.

- **This Account:** You may designate any user account from your account database here. You should create a separate account for each service for which you want to configure rights and permissions.

Network Services

The Services tab of the Control Panel Network application lets you add, configure, and remove services that support network functions. Clicking the <u>A</u>dd button opens the Select Network Service dialog box, which provides a list of available Windows NT network services. Select a service and click OK to add the service to your configuration. Or, click the <u>H</u>ave Disk button if you are attempting to install a new service from a disk.

Server

Some of the services in the Network Services list are configurable through the Network application, and some are not. Select a service and click the Properties button to open a configuration dialog box for the service (if there is one). Figure 4.16 shows the configuration dialog box for the Server service.

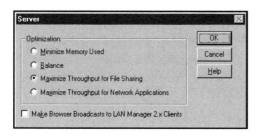

Figure 4.16
The Server dialog box.

Many of the network components you'll read about elsewhere in this book (DHCP, WINS, DNS, RAS, and Gateway Services for NetWare) are actually services that, although they often are configured elsewhere, still can be added, started, stopped, and managed through the Network Services tab and the Control Panel Services application. For the most part, anything you do on the network occurs through some form of network service.

The following sections examine some important topics related to Windows NT services:

- Directory replication
- Client license management
- The browser process

Directory Replication

Directory replication is a facility that lets you configure Windows NT Servers to automatically transmit updated versions of important files and directories to other computers on the network.

The purpose of directory replication is to simplify the task of distributing updates for logon scripts, system policy files, Help files, phone lists, and other important files. The network administrator updates the file(s) on a single server (called the *export server),* and the export server automatically distributes the file(s) to other network servers or even to network workstations. The computer receiving the update is called the *import computer.* A Windows NT Server, a Windows NT Workstation, or a LAN Manager OS/2 server can act as an import computer.

CH
4

Directory replication is performed by the Directory Replicator Service. You can start and stop the Directory Replicator Service from the Control Panel Services application. The parameters for the Directory Replicator Service are located in this Registry key:

```
HKEY_LOCAL_MACHINE\SYSTEM\CurrentControlSet\Services\Replicator\Parameters
```

Key Concept

Most of the parameters in the Registry key
`HKEY_LOCAL_MACHINE\SYSTEM\CurrentControlSet\Services\Replicator\Parameters`
can be configured within Server Manager (described later in this chapter). Two important exceptions are

- **Interval:** A REG_WORD value that defines how often an export server checks for updates. The range is from 1 to 60 minutes, and the default is 5 minutes.

- **GuardTime:** A REG_WORD value that defines how long a directory must be stable before its files can be replicated. The range is 0 to one-half of the Interval value. The default is 2 minutes. See the next section, "Configuring the Export Computer," for a discussion of the Wait Until Stabilized check box.

The export directory on the export server holds the files and directories that are replicated across the network. The default export directory is

```
\<winnt_root>\System32\Repl\Export
```

For each group of files set for replication, create a subdirectory in the export directory. When the Directory Replicator Service starts, NT shares the export directory with the share name Repl$.

Each import computer has a directory called the import directory, and the default directory is

```
\<winnt_root>\System32\Repl\Import
```

The Directory Replicator Service copies files from the export server's export directory to the import directories of the import computers. In addition to copying files, the Directory Replicator Service creates any necessary subdirectories in the import directory so that after each replication, the directory structure of the import directory matches the export directory's directory structure.

The Directory Replicator Service follows this process:

1. The export server periodically checks the export directory for changes and, if changes have occurred, sends update notices to the import computers.
2. The import computer receives the update notices and calls the export computer.
3. The import computer reads the export directory on the export server and copies any new or changed files from the export directory to its own import directory.

The following sections describe how to set up the export and import computers for directory replications.

Configuring the Export Computer

To set up the export server for directory replication follow these steps:

1. Double-click the Control Panel Services application to start the Directory Replicator Service.
2. Create a new account for the Directory Replicator Service. The Directory Replicator account must be a member of the Backup Operator group or the Replicator group for the domain. When you set up the new account, be sure to enable the Password Never Expires check box and disable the User Must Change Password at Next Logon check box. Also, make sure the account has logon privileges for all hours.
3. Start the Server Manager application in the Administrative Tools program group (see Fig. 4.17). Server Manager is a tool for managing network servers and workstations from a single location.

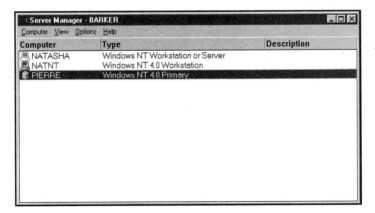

Figure 4.17
The Server Manager main screen.

CH
4

4. In the Server Manager, double-click the export server to open the Server Properties dialog box (see Fig. 4.18).

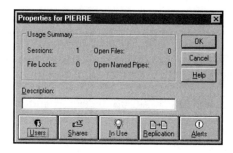

Figure 4.18
The Server Properties dialog box.

5. Click the Replication button to open the Directory Replication dialog box (see Fig. 4.19).

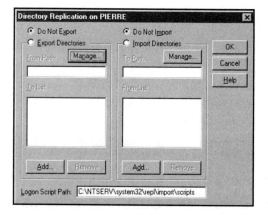

Figure 4.19
The Directory Replication dialog box.

Key Concept

A Windows NT Server can serve as an export server, an import computer, or both. A Windows NT Workstation can serve as an import server only.

6. In the Directory Replication dialog box, select the Export Directories option. The default path to the export directory appears in the From Path box. Click the Add button to open the Select Domain dialog box (see Fig. 4.20). Click a domain to select it. Double-click a domain to display the computers within that domain (see Fig. 4.21). If you select a whole domain, all import servers in the domain receive the replicated data. If you choose a specific computer, only that computer receives the replicated data. You can choose any combination of domains and specific computers.

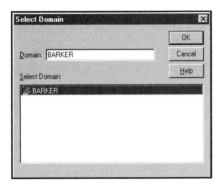

Figure 4.20
The Select Domain dialog box.

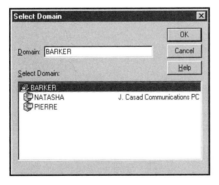

Figure 4.21
The Select Domain dialog box displays specific computers in the domain.

CH
4

7. Click the Manage button to open the Manage Exported Directories dialog box (see Fig. 4.22). Subdirectories within the export directory appear in the Sub-Directory list. You can add or remove subdirectories from the list by clicking the Add or Remove button. Note the check boxes at the bottom of the screen. Enabling the Wait Until Stabilized check box tells the Directory Replicator Service to wait at least two minutes after any change to the selected subdirectory tree before exporting. Enabling the Entire Subtree check box tells the Directory Replicator Service to export all subdirectories below the selected subdirectory. The Add Lock button lets you lock the subdirectory so that it can't be exported. More than one user can lock a subdirectory. (Consequently, a subdirectory can have more than one lock.) To remove a lock, click the Remove Lock button.

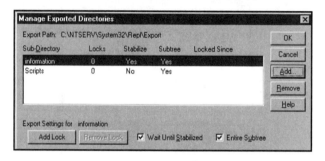

Figure 4.22
The Manage Exported Directories dialog box.

8. Click OK in the Manage Exported Directories dialog box, the Directory Replication dialog box, and the Server Properties dialog box.

Configuring the Import Computer

To set up the import computer for directory replication, follow these steps:

1. Double-click the Services icon in the Control Panel. Select the Directory Replicator Service and click the Startup button to open the Service dialog box (see Fig. 4.23).

2. In the Startup Type frame, select the Automatic radio button. Select the This Account radio button and enter a username and password for the replicator account you created on the export server.

Figure 4.23
The Service dialog box.

 Key Concept

If the import computer and the export server aren't part of the same domain or a trusting domain, you must create a replication user account on the import computer and give that account permission to access the Repl$ share on the export server. Enter this account and password in the Service dialog box in Step 2.

3. Start Server Manager, select the computer you're now configuring, and click the Replication button in the Properties dialog box. The Directory Replication dialog box appears. This time, you're concerned with the import side (the right side) of the dialog box, but the configuration steps are similar to steps for configuring the export side. The default import directory appears in the To Path box. Click the Add button to add a domain or a specific export server (see Step 6 in the preceding section). Click the Manage button to open the Manage Imported Directories dialog box, which lets you manage the import directories (see Fig. 4.24).

4. In the Manage Imported Directories dialog box, click Add or Remove to add or remove a subdirectory from the list. Click Add Lock to add a lock to the subdirectory (see the preceding section).

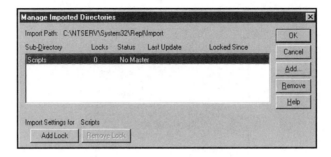

Figure 4.24
The Manage Imported Directories dialog box.

Troubleshooting Directory Replication

The Status parameter in the Manage Exported Directories and the Manage Imported Directories dialog boxes gives the status of the directory replication for a subdirectory. The possible values follow:

- **OK:** The export server is sending regular updates, and the import directory matches the export directory.

- **No Master:** The import computer isn't receiving updates, which means the export server may not be running, or the Directory Replicator Service on the export server may not be running.

- **No Sync:** The import directory has received updates, but the data in the updates isn't what it should be, which means there could be an export server malfunction, a communication problem, open files on either the import or the export computer, or a problem with the import computer's access permissions.

- **(Blank):** Replication has never occurred. The cause could be improper configuration on either the import or the export computer.

When the Directory Replication Service generates an error, check Event Viewer to learn what you can about the cause.

Microsoft recommends the following solutions for some common replication errors:

- **Access Denied:** The Directory Replicator Service might not be configured to log on to a specific account. Check Event Viewer. Check the Startup dialog box in the Control Panel Services application to see whether an account is specified, and use User Manager for Domains to check the permissions for the logon account.

- **Exporting to Specific Computers:** Designate specific export servers for each import server and specific import computers for each export server. If you just choose a domain in the dialog box opened by clicking the Add button in the Directory Replication dialog box, every domain computer receives replicated data, and every import computer receives updates from every export server in the domain.

- **Replication over a WAN link:** When transmitting replication data across a wide-area network link, specify the computer name instead of just the domain name after you click the Add button in the Directory Replication dialog box.

- **Logon Scripts for Member Servers and Workstations:** NT Workstations and noncontroller NT Servers must use the default logon script directory:

```
C:\<winnt_root>\System32\Repl\Import\Scripts
```

Windows NT Client Licenses

Microsoft requires that every client accessing a resource on a computer running Windows NT Server have a *Client Access License* (CAL). The CAL is separate from the license for the client's operating system. Your Windows 95 or Windows NT Workstation doesn't include an implied permission to access resources on a Windows NT Server; to access NT Server resources, you must have a CAL.

Microsoft provides two options for purchasing CALs:

- **Per-server mode:** CALs are assigned to each server. Suppose that a Windows NT Server is licensed for 10 simultaneous client connections. No more than 10 clients will be able to access the server at one time—additional clients will not be able to connect.

- **Per-seat mode:** CALs are assigned to each client machine. You purchase a CAL for every client computer on the network. If the total number of simultaneous connections on all Windows NT Servers exceeds the number of per-seat licenses, a client still can connect.

Microsoft allows a one-time switch from per-server to per-seat licensing mode. If you aren't sure which option to choose, you can choose per-server mode and change later to per-seat mode if you determine that per-seat mode is more cost-effective.

CH

4

If your network has only one server, Microsoft recommends that you choose per-server licensing mode. If you have more than one server on your network, Microsoft suggests the following formulas:

A = Number of servers

B = Number of simultaneous connections to each server

C = Total number of seats (clients) accessing computers

If A * B < C, use per-server licensing.
Number of CALs = A * B

If A * B > C, use per-seat licensing.
Number of CALs = C

Windows NT Server includes the following tools for managing client licenses:

■ Licensing Application
■ License Manager

The following sections describe these Windows NT license-managing tools.

Licensing Application

The Control Panel Licensing Application opens the Choose Licensing Mode dialog box (see Fig. 4.25). This dialog box lets you add or remove client licenses or switch from per-server to per-seat licensing mode.

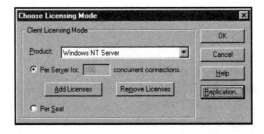

Figure 4.25
The Choose Licensing Mode dialog box.

Clicking the Replication button opens the Replication Configuration dialog box (see Fig. 4.26). This dialog box lets you configure license replication.

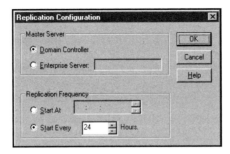

Figure 4.26
The Replication Configuration dialog box.

License replication is a convenient feature that lets individual servers send their licensing information to a master server. The master server creates and updates a database of licensing information for the entire network. This method provides a single, central location for licensing information.

License Manager

License Manager, a tool in the Administrative Tools program group, displays licensing information for the network (see Fig. 4.27). You can maintain a history of client licenses, examine your network's per-server and per-seat licenses by product, and browse for client license information on particular network clients. You also can monitor server use by per-seat clients, and even revoke a client's permission to access a server.

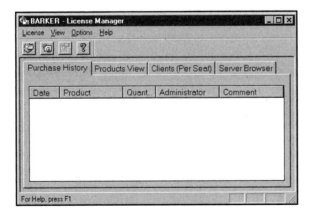

Figure 4.27
The License Manager window.

CH
4

You also can use License Manager to add or edit license groups. A *license group* is a group of users mapped to a group of per-seat licenses. License groups are a means of tracking per-seat license use in situations where an organization has more users than computers (or in some cases, more computers than users). For example, a retail outlet may have 10 employees sharing three per-seat licensed computers.

Computer Browser Service

One of the most important network services is the Computer Browser Service. The Computer Browser Service oversees a hierarchy of computers that serve as browsers for the network. A *browser* is a computer that maintains a central list of network servers. (In this case, a *server* is any computer that makes resources available to the network.) That list then becomes available to clients who are browsing the network looking for remote computers, printers, and other resources. The list that appears when you open the Network Neighborhood application, for example, comes from a network browser list.

The advantage of the browser process is that it allows a small number of network computers to maintain browse lists for the whole network, thereby minimizing network traffic and eliminating duplication of efforts. (The alternative would be for all computers to constantly poll the network in order to maintain their own lists.) Before the browser process can function efficiently, however, it must be highly organized so that clients know where to find a list and contingencies can take effect when a browser fails.

In a Windows NT domain, each computer assumes one of five browser roles:

- **Master browser:** Each workgroup or domain subnet must have a master browser. At startup, all computers running the Server Service (regardless of whether they have resources available for the network) register themselves with the master browser. The master browser compiles a list of available servers on the workgroup or subnet and forwards the list to the domain master browser. Master browsers then receive a complete browse list for the entire domain from the domain master browser.

- **Domain master browser:** The domain master browser requests subnet browse lists from the master browsers and merges the subnet browse lists into a master browse list for the entire domain. It also forwards the domain browse list back to the master browsers. The *primary domain controller* (PDC) serves as the domain master browser for a Windows NT domain.

- **Backup browser:** The backup browser gets a copy of the browse list from the master browser (on the subnet) and distributes the browse list to subnet clients who request it. If the master browser fails, a backup browser can serve as the master browser for the subnet.

- **Potential browser:** A potential browser is a computer that isn't presently serving as a browser but can become a browser at the request of the master browser or as a result of a browser election (described later in this section).
- **Non-browser:** A non-browser is a computer that cannot serve as a browser.

The first time a client computer attempts to access the network, it obtains a list of backup browsers for the subnet or workgroup from the master browser. It then asks a backup browser for a copy of the browse list.

If a master browser fails, a new master browser is chosen automatically in what is known as a *browser election.* A browser election can occur if a client or backup browser cannot access the master browser. A browser election isn't exactly an election; it's really more of a contest. The browsers and potential browsers rank themselves according to a number of criteria, and the machine with the highest ranking becomes the new master browser.

Here are some of the criteria used in a browser election:

- **Operating system:** Windows NT Server gets a higher score than Windows NT Workstation, which gets a higher score than Windows 95.
- **Version:** Windows NT Server 4 gets a higher score than Windows NT Server 3.51, and so on.
- **Present browser role:** A backup browser scores higher than a potential browser.

You can configure a Windows NT computer to always, never, or sometimes participate in browser elections by using the `MaintainServerList` parameter in the Registry key:

```
HKEY_Local_Machine\System\CurrentControlSet\Services\Browsr\Parameters
```

The possible values follow:

- **Yes:** Always attempt to become a browser in browser elections (default for Windows NT Server domain controllers).
- **No:** Never attempt to become a browser in browser elections.
- **Auto:** The Auto setting classifies the computer as a potential browser (default for Windows NT Workstations and Windows NT Servers that aren't acting as domain controllers).

To make other domains available to the browser service, select the browser service on the Network application's Services tab and click the Properties button. The Browser configuration dialog box appears. Enter a domain name in the box on the left and click the Add button; then click OK.

CH

4

Configuring Peripherals and Devices

The Control Panel includes several applications that help you install and configure peripherals and devices. You should be familiar with how to use these applications to install drivers and configure peripherals and hardware. The following sections examine these applications:

- Devices
- Multimedia
- Ports
- UPS
- SCSI
- Tape devices
- PC card
- Modems
- Keyboard
- Mouse
- Display

You should be familiar with how to use these applications for installing and configuring peripherals and devices.

Devices

The Devices application (SRVMGR.CPL) writes to HKEY_LOCAL_MACHINE\SYSTEM\CurrentControlSet\Services. You can start, stop, or disable device drivers in this Control Panel applet (see Fig. 4.28).

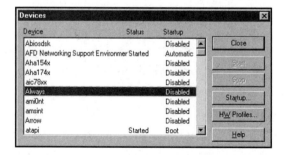

Figure 4.28
The Devices application.

The three columns in the Control Panel Devices main display area are labeled Device, Status, and Startup. The Device column identifies the name of the device driver as it appears in the Registry. The Status column displays Started if the driver is active; otherwise, it appears blank. The Startup column denotes when each driver is configured to initialize.

To set the Startup value, select the device driver you want to modify and click the Startup button. The Device dialog box appears, as shown in Figure 4.29.

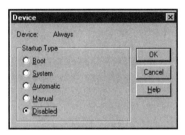

Figure 4.29
The Device dialog box.

Choose one of the following startup types:

- **Boot:** These devices start first, as soon as the kernel is loaded and initialized. (See Chapter 11, "Windows NT 4.0 Architecture and Boot Sequence," for more details about the boot process.) These devices have a start value of 0 in the Registry. Atdisk, the hard disk driver, is an example of a boot device.

- **System:** These devices start after the boot devices and after the HKEY_LOCAL_MACHINE subtree has begun to be built. These devices have a start value of 1 in the Registry. The video driver is a system device.

- **Automatic:** These devices start late in the boot process, after the Registry is almost entirely built, just before the Winlogon screen appears. These devices have a start value of 2 in the Registry. Serial, the serial port driver, is an automatic device.

- **Manual:** These devices are never started without administrator intervention. They may be started manually through the Control Panel Devices menu. These devices have a start value of 3 in the Registry.

- **Disabled:** These devices cannot be started at all unless their startup type is changed to something other than Disabled. These devices have a start value of 4 in the Registry. File system drivers are disabled by default (although file system recognizers are started with the system devices; if any file systems are recognized, the startup type of the file system drivers is changed to System as well).

CH
4

To start a device that isn't active, select the device and click the $\underline{S}$tart button. If the $\underline{S}$tart button is grayed out, the device is already started or disabled.

To stop a device that's active, select the device and click the S$\underline{t}$op button. A grayed-out S$\underline{t}$op button indicates that the device already is inactive.

To enable or disable a device for a given hardware profile, select the device, click H$\underline{W}$ Profiles, click $\underline{E}$nable or $\underline{D}$isable to change to the desired status, and click OK. You learn more about hardware profiles later in this chapter.

Multimedia

The Multimedia application (MMSYS.CPL) writes to HKEY_LOCAL_MACHINE\SYSTEM\ CurrentControlSet\Services. Multimedia device drivers are added and configured from this Control Panel applet. The Multimedia application also provides settings for CD music, audio, video, and MIDI.

Ports

The Ports application (PORTS.CPL) writes directly to the following key:

```
HKEY_LOCAL_MACHINE\SYSTEM\CurrentControlSet\Services\Serial
```

This Control Panel interface lists only the serial ports that are available but not in use as serial ports. In other words, if a mouse is connected to your COM1 port, COM1 doesn't show up in the Control Panel Ports dialog box. All serial ports, regardless of whether they appear in Control Panel Ports, are logged in the Registry under the following key:

```
HKEY_LOCAL_MACHINE\HARDWARE\Description\System\<multifunction_adapter>\ 0\
➡SerialController\<COM_port_number>
```

The Settings button displays values for the port's baud rate, data bits, parity, stop bits, and flow control.

If you need an additional port for use under Windows NT, click the Add button. You may assign a different COM port number, specify a base I/O port address or IRQ, or enable a first in–first out (FIFO) buffer for that port (see Fig. 4.30).

To remove a port, simply select it and click the Delete button.

UPS

The UPS application (UPS.CPL) writes to the following key:

```
HKEY_LOCAL_MACHINE\SYSTEM\CurrentControlSet\Services\UPS
```

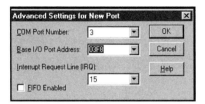

Figure 4.30
Adding a new port using the Ports application's Add button.

If your computer is equipped with an *uninterruptible power supply* (UPS), Windows NT can be configured to communicate with it. The specific voltages requested in the UPS Configuration area depend on the UPS manufacturer and model. You may need to consult with your vendor to get these values. Armed with the correct information, Windows NT can recognize the following:

■ **Power failure signal:** The point when an event is logged and the Server Service paused. No new connections to this server can be made, but existing connections still function.

■ **Low battery signal at least 2 minutes before shutdown:** As the name implies, Windows NT recognizes when the UPS battery is about to be exhausted.

■ **Remote UPS Shutdown:** Signals Windows NT that the UPS is shutting down.

The Execute Command File option enables an administrator to specify a batch or executable file that runs immediately preceding a shutdown. The program has 30 seconds before the system shuts down. The program cannot open a dialog box, because that would require an attendant user.

If no Low Battery Signal is configured, the administrator can enter the Expected Battery Life and the Battery Recharge Time Per Minute of Run Time options in the lower left corner of the dialog box.

After the initial PowerOut alert is raised (the power failure signal is received), Windows NT waits until the Time Between Power Failure and Initial Warning Message interval elapses, and then sends an alert to all interactive and connected users. Windows NT continues to send these alerts every time the Delay Between Warning Messages interval elapses.

If the UPS is about to run out of steam, the system shuts down safely. If power is restored, users are notified, an event is logged, and the Server Service resumes.

CH
4

SCSI Adapters

This application is one of the great misnomers in Windows NT. As it suggests, this application opens the SCSI Adapter Setup dialog box, which you use to install SCSI adapter drivers. However, you also use this dialog box to install and remove IDE CD-ROM drivers as well as drivers for CD-ROM drives that use proprietary interfaces, such as Mitsumi or Panasonic drives. The dialog box should refer to both SCSI adapters and CD-ROM drives; currently the interface is completely counterintuitive.

To add a SCSI adapter or CD-ROM device driver, follow these procedures:

1. Double-click the SCSI Adapters applet icon in the Control Panel.
2. In the SCSI Adapter Setup dialog box, select the Drivers tab and click the Add button.
3. Select the driver from the list of available drivers in the Install Driver dialog box. If your driver isn't listed but you have a disk from the manufacturer with a Windows NT driver, click the Have Disk button.
4. Click OK. You must point Windows NT toward the original installation files (or the disk that contains the driver) and restart the computer in order for the new driver to initialize.

To remove a SCSI adapter or CD-ROM device driver, follow these steps:

1. Select the Drivers tab in the SCSI Adapters dialog box.
2. Select the driver you want to remove.
3. Click the Remove button.

Tape Devices

Almost identical to the SCSI Adapter Setup dialog box in both appearance and function, the Tape Devices dialog box enables you to install and remove tape drives for use with a Windows NT Backup program.

To add a tape drive device driver, use these steps:

1. Double-click the Tape Devices icon in the Control Panel.
2. Select the Drivers tab.
3. Click the Add button.

4. Select the driver from the list of available drivers. If your driver isn't listed but you have a disk from the manufacturer with a Windows NT Driver, click the <u>H</u>ave Disk button.

5. Click OK. You must point Windows NT toward the original installation files (or the disk that contains the driver) and restart the computer in order for the new driver to initialize.

To remove a tape drive device driver, use these steps:

1. Select the driver from the list of installed drivers on the Drivers tab of the Tape Devices dialog box.

2. Click the Remove button.

PC Card (PCMCIA)

The PC Card application helps you install and configure PCMCIA device drivers. Select a PC card and click <u>P</u>roperties. Select the Drivers tab, and then click <u>A</u>dd, <u>R</u>emove, or <u>C</u>onfigure as necessary.

A red X next to a device in the PC card list indicates that NT doesn't support the device.

Modems

The Modems application enables you to add or remove a modem. You can ask NT to detect your modem, or you can select a modem from a list.

To add a modem, follow these steps:

1. Double-click the Modems application icon in the Control Panel.

2. Click <u>A</u>dd in the Modems Properties dialog box (see Fig. 4.31).

3. In the Install New Modem dialog box, click <u>N</u>ext if you want NT to try to detect your modem (see Fig. 4.32). If you want to select your modem from a list, or if you're providing software for a modem not listed, enable the Don't Detect My Modem; I will Select It from a List check box and then click <u>N</u>ext.

4. Select a manufacturer and a model, and click <u>N</u>ext. Or click the <u>H</u>ave Disk button if you're installing software for a modem not shown on the list.

5. Select a port for the modem, or select <u>A</u>ll Ports. Click <u>N</u>ext.

CH
4

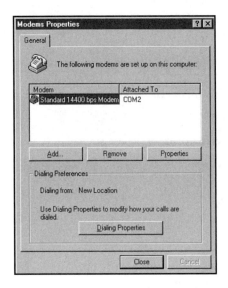

Figure 4.31
The Modems Properties dialog box.

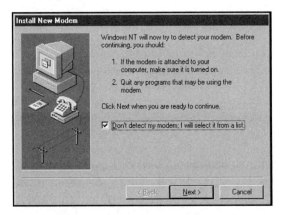

Figure 4.32
The Install New Modem dialog box.

Select a modem in the Modems list and click Properties to change the parameters for that modem. A new dialog box opens, with two tabs: General and Connection. The General tab enables you to set the port number and the maximum speed. The Connection tab enables you to define some connection preferences, such as the data bits, stop bits, and parity. Click Advanced for additional settings.

You can click the Dialing Properties button in the Modems Properties dialog box to access the My Locations tab, which is also in the Telephony application. The My Locations tab enables you to set the dialing characteristics for the modem. If you have a portable computer, you can define additional locations and configure a complete set of dialing properties for each location. If you sometimes travel to a certain hotel in Paris, for example, you can define a location called Paris and specify the dialing properties you want to use for the Paris hotel. The next time you're in Paris, you only have to change the location setting in the I Am Dialing From drop-down list box at the top of the My Locations tab. The other settings automatically change to the settings you defined for Paris.

To add a new location, follow these steps:

1. Click the New button at the top of the My Locations tab. (NT announces that a new location has been created.)

2. The new location has the name New Location (followed by a number if you already have a location called New Location). Click the name and change it if you want to give your location a different name. (NT might not let you erase the old name completely until you add your new name. Add the new name and then backspace over the old text if necessary.)

3. Change any dialing properties and click OK. The new properties will apply to your new location.

Keyboard

The Keyboard application opens the Keyboard Properties dialog box, which enables you to set the keyboard repeat rate, the repeat delay, the cursor blink rate, and the keyboard layout properties. The keyboard driver appears on the General tab in the Keyboard Type text box (see Fig. 4.33). To select a new driver, click the Change button. The Select Device dialog box appears (see Fig. 4.34). The Show All Devices option button displays a list of available drivers in the Models list. Choose the keyboard model that matches your hardware. If your keyboard comes with its own installation disk for a model that isn't in the list, click the Have Disk button.

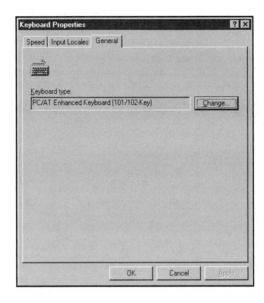

Figure 4.33
The Keyboard Properties dialog box.

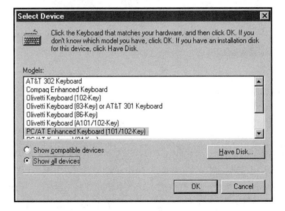

Figure 4.34
The Select Device dialog box.

Mouse

The values for this applet control the mouse speed, sensitivity, and left- and right-hand settings for the mouse buttons. The one new setting added to this dialog box's Win3.x predecessor is the Snap to Default option on the Motion tab, which instantly positions the pointer over the default button in the active dialog box. On the Pointers tab, you can select a pointer type. The General tab lets you install a new mouse driver. The procedure for selecting a mouse driver is similar to the procedure for selecting a keyboard driver (described in the preceding section).

Display

The Display application configures the values in the following key, including the video driver, screen resolution, color depth, and refresh rate:

```
HKEY_LOCAL_MACHINE\SYSTEM\CurrentControlSet\Services\<video_driver>\Device0\
```

The five tabs of the Display Properties dialog box, shown in Figure 4.35, follow:

- **Background:** Defines the wallpaper for the desktop.
- **Screen Saver:** Defines the screen saver for the desktop.
- **Appearance:** Defines window properties.
- **Plus!:** The Visual Enhancements tab from the Microsoft Plus! package for Windows 95 lets you configure the desktop to use large icons or stretch the wallpaper to fit the screen.
- **Settings:** Defines desktop colors, refresh frequency, and other screen-related settings.

CH
4

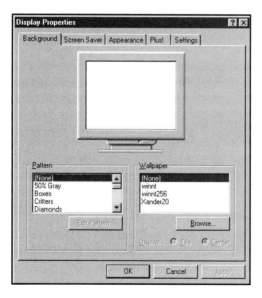

Figure 4.35
The Display Properties dialog box.

The Settings tab includes a Test button. You always should test new display settings before making changes permanent. Although Windows NT can detect the capabilities of your video card, it can't do the same with your monitor. Testing these settings before applying them ensures that both video card and monitor can support the new settings.

Key Concept

If you have specified the VGA Mode option on the boot loader menu, Windows NT boots using the standard VGA driver at a resolution of 640×480 pixels.

Follow these steps to change the video display adapter:

1. Start the Control Panel Display application and select the Settings tab in the Display Properties dialog box (see Fig. 4.36).

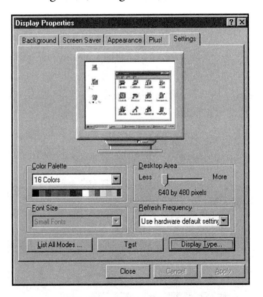

Figure 4.36
The Display Properties Settings tab.

2. Click the Display Type button. The Display Type dialog box appears (see Fig. 4.37).

Figure 4.37
The Display Type dialog box.

3. Click the <u>C</u>hange button in the Adapter Type frame. The Change Display dialog box appears (see Fig. 4.38). Select an adapter from the list and click OK. Or, if you have a manufacturer's installation disk, click <u>H</u>ave Disk.

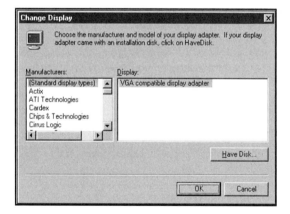

CH
4

Figure 4.38
The Change Display dialog box.

Summary

This chapter explored how to configure your NT installation, reviewed the Control Panel applets, and examined the Registry. These all are configurations of the computer and environment settings.

Another way to configure, or administer, your computer is to create and manage user accounts. Chapter 5, "Managing Users and Groups," covers the creation and management of user accounts in detail.

QUESTIONS AND ANSWERS

1. You can make many Registry setting changes in applets located in the _____.

    A: Control Panel.

2. You can save different hardware configurations in separate _____.

    A: Hardware profiles.

3. The two Registry Editors included with Windows NT Server 4.0 are _____ and _____.

    A: Regedt32.exe (which has been with NT since day one) and Regedit.exe (which is new to NT 4.0).

4. The administrative tool that enables you to display licensing information for the network is the _____.

    A: License Manager. The License Application (available from the Control Panel) serves a different purpose.

5. The five tabs of the Display Properties dialog box are _____, _____, _____, _____, and _____.

    A: Background, Screen Saver, Appearance, Plus!, and Settings.

PRACTICE TEST

1. Fred wants to modify his desktop wallpaper, screen saver, and screen colors. How can he get to the dialog box to change these settings?
    a. Double-click the Display icon in the Control Panel.
    b. Right-click the desktop and choose Properties.
    c. Right-click My Computer and choose Properties, Display.
    d. Choose Start, Programs, Display.

Answer a is correct. Fred can access the dialog box by double-clicking the Display applet in the Control Panel. Answer b is correct. Fred can right-click in the desktop and choose Properties to bring up the dialog box. Answer c is incorrect. There is no Display option after choosing Properties. Answer d is incorrect. There is no Display option after choosing Programs.

2. Which three of the following four features are a part of the Services applet in the Control Panel?
   a. Running status
   b. Load order
   c. Hardware profile assignments
   d. Startup options

Answer a is correct. You can use the Services applet to view/change the running status of services. Answer b is correct. You can use the Services applet to view/change the load order. Answer c is incorrect. You cannot configure the load order from the Services applet. **Answer d is correct. You can use the Services applet to view/change startup options for services.**

3. Which Control Panel applet can you use to create and manage accounts?
   a. Disk Administrator
   b. User Manager
   c. Accessibility Options
   d. There is no Control Panel applet that enables you to do this.

Answer a is incorrect. Disk Administrator (used to administer hard drives) is not a Control Panel applet. Answer b is incorrect. User Manager (a Workstation tool) is not a Control Panel applet. Answer c is incorrect. You use the Accessibility options to configure the system for users with disabilities. **Answer d is correct. User Manager for Domains is an administrative tool—not a Control Panel applet—that enables you to perform these functions.**

4. Janice is a hearing-impaired account manager who has asked whether Windows NT provides any options appropriate for her. What can you do to help?
   a. In the Control Panel, double-click the Sounds applet. Then increase the volume for system sounds.
   b. Double-click the My Computer icon. Right-click in the My Computer window, and choose Properties from the pop-up menu that appears. Then select the Accessibility tab to set Sound options.
   c. Double-click the Accessibility Options applet in the Control Panel. Then set the Sound options.
   d. Windows NT does not provide options for physically challenged persons.

CH
4

Answer a is incorrect. You use the Accessibility Options applet to configure the system for use by those with disabilities. Answer b is incorrect. You use the Accessibility Options applet to configure the system for use by those with disabilities. **Answer c is correct. Double-clicking Accessibility Options in the Control Panel and setting the Sound options is the proper response.** Answer d is incorrect; NT *does* provide options for physically challenged persons.

5. Antonio frequently travels for the company and accesses the network on his laptop via modem while on the road. When Antonio is at the office, he docks his laptop at his workstation and uses the network card in the docking station to access the network. How can you facilitate the boot process between these two hardware configurations?

   a. Hardware profiles are a feature of Windows 95, not Windows NT 4.0.

   b. Create a hardware profile for each configuration—docked and undocked—and set a default timeout value for the most frequently used configuration.

   c. Modify the BOOT.INI file and include a boot menu choice for a second hardware configuration using the \PROFILE:filename boot switch.

   d. Double-click the Services applet in the Control Panel. Then click the H<u>W</u> Profiles button in the Services dialog box and create a new profile.

Answer a is incorrect. Hardware profiles *are* a feature of NT Server. **Answer b is correct. Creating a hardware profile for each configuration will allow Antonio to switch between docked and undocked. Setting a default timeout value for the most frequently used configuration will keep him from having to make a selection at each boot.** Answer c is incorrect. The BOOT.INI file does not enable you to switch profiles (only operating systems). Answer d is incorrect. The Services applet does not perform this function.

6. Martha wants to modify her mouse pointers. What is the most appropriate procedure for doing this?

   a. Double-click the Mouse applet in the Control Panel. Then, on the Pointers tab of the Mouse dialog box, select the pointers.

   b. Right-click the desktop, choose P<u>r</u>operties, and select the Settings tab of the Display Properties dialog box.

   c. Start the Registry Editor, select HKEY_CURRENT_USER, and modify the CURSORS subkey.

   d. Start the Registry Editor, select HKEY_LOCAL_MACHINE, and modify the System\CurrentControlSet subkey.

Answer a is correct. You configure mouse pointers by double-clicking the Mouse applet in the Control Panel and then using the Pointers tab. Answer b is incorrect. This only brings up display properties and not mouse properties. Answer c is incorrect. This does not take you to the correct location. Answer d is incorrect, because it is not the most appropriate answer.

7. Which of the following hives in HKEY_LOCAL_MACHINE have corresponding directory files in the Windows NT system directory?

    a. SYSTEM

    b. SOFTWARE

    c. HARDWARE

    d. SECURITY

Answer a is correct. The SYSTEM file is located in the Config directory. Answer b is correct. The SOFTWARE file is located in the Config directory. Answer c is incorrect. The values held in HARDWARE are built dynamically at each boot. **Answer d is correct. The SECURITY file is located in the Config directory.**

8. Fran needs to add the company's logo to the default Windows NT bootup screen. From which Registry subtree(s) can she make this modification?

    a. HKEY_LOCAL_MACHINE

    b. HKEY_CURRENT_USER

    c. HKEY_USERS

    d. Fran can make this change only through Control Panel, Service, Startup.

Answer a is incorrect. Fran can find this information in HKEY_USERS. Answer b is incorrect. Fran can find this information in HKEY_USERS. **Answer c is correct. HKEY_USERS holds the bootup screen.** Answer d is incorrect. Fran can change this value in the Registry.

9. Which of the following boot files is essential to the boot phase of the boot process?

    a. NTLDR

    b. NTDETECT.COM

    c. NTOSKRNL.EXE

    d. BOOT.INI

Answer a is correct. NTLDR is crucial to the boot process and begins it. Answer b is incorrect. NTDETECT.COM is not essential to the boot phase. The system will boot without the detection, but not without NTLDR. Answer c is incorrect. NTOSKRNL.EXE is not essential to the boot phase. The system cannot boot at all in the absence of NTLDR. Answer d is incorrect. BOOT.INI is read by NTLDR. If NTLDR is not present, there will be no boot (or reading of BOOT.INI) at all.

CH

4

10. Which Control Panel applet displays current settings for number symbols?

    a. Regional Settings

    b. Numbers

    c. System

    d. Services

Answer a is correct. Regional Settings displays current settings for number symbols, currency formats, date and time values, and input locales based on world regions. Answer b is incorrect. There is no such applet. Answer c is incorrect. Although System shows a great deal of system information, it does not enable you to see or change number symbols. Answer d is incorrect. Services enables you to change the running services and does not interact with number symbols.

CHAPTER PREREQUISITE

Although this chapter reviews the basic concepts regarding the creation and management of user and group accounts, it is considered a prerequisite for this book that you already have performed this type of administrative function.

Managing Users and Groups

WHILE YOU READ

1. The two default user accounts created during an installation of the operating system are _____ and _____.

2. The three default global accounts created are _____, _____, and _____.

3. The syntax `\\servername\sharename\path` is known as _____.

4. The tool used for creating new users is _____.

5. The feature that maintains a history of passwords and does not allow a user to use the same password twice in a row is known as _____.

Understanding User and Group Accounts

The first screen you see after booting Windows NT and pressing Ctrl+Alt+Del is the Logon Security dialog box. Here, you must enter your username and password to gain access to the domain through network authentication—for example, the NETLOGON process.

You therefore should consider the user account as the first and foremost security object for access to your local and network resources.

Each user and group account that is created in the domain is unique to that Windows NT domain and, as such, has a unique *security identifier* (SID) associated with it. All references that Windows NT makes to any account, especially those dealing with security access and permissions, are linked to the SID.

If you delete the user account and re-create it by using exactly the same information, Windows NT creates a new SID for that user, and all security access and permissions have to be reestablished. The account information is stored in the *Security Account Manager* (SAM) database, which is part of the Windows NT 4.0 Registry— HKEY_LOCAL_MACHINE\SAM.

If the account is a *local account* (in other words, an account that someone uses to log on to a specific workstation), the account is included in the SAM database of that workstation's Registry. If the account is a *network account* (meaning an account that is used to log on to the enterprise network from any given workstation), the account is included in the SAM database of the *primary domain controller* (PDC) for the account domain of the enterprise.

Default User Accounts

When you first install Windows NT Server 4.0, two default accounts are created for you: the Guest and Administrator accounts. You cannot delete either of these accounts. For this reason, you must take care to preserve the integrity of these accounts.

The Guest account provides the least amount of access for the user and is, in fact, disabled by default on both Windows NT Workstation and Server to prevent inadvertent access to resources. It is strongly recommended that you assign a password to this account (preferably something other than password) and, for additional security, rename the account. This account automatically is made a member of the default domain global group Domain Guests.

The Administrator account, as you might expect, provides the greatest amount of access and complete functional rights to the domain. Because Windows NT creates this account by default, it also is the first account with which a user has to log on to the domain controller. In most organizations, this account is used to perform almost every administrative task in the domain. Therefore, it is strongly recommended that this account be password protected (again, with a unique and memorable password), and for additional security, it also should be renamed.

After all, if you were a hacker trying to break in with Administrative access, the first account name you would try would be Administrator, and then perhaps Supervisor or Admin or XYZadmin, in which XYZ is your company name. If this has exhausted your choices for alternative administrator account names, good! With Internet access especially prevalent, enterprise security has become an extremely significant and sensitive issue.

Another suggestion that Microsoft makes is to create a separate user account for specific functional access. For example, Windows NT provides a default group that is local to the domain controllers called Account Operators. Members of this group are given just enough functional access to be able to successfully manage user and group accounts for the domain. The administrator might identify a user or users who have the responsibility of managing accounts or create a specific user account for that purpose and add them to the Account Operators group for the domain. The user then would use his or her account or the specific user account to access the domain and manage accounts. This security eliminates a potential security hole—for example, being logged on as Administrator and leaving for lunch without locking the workstation or logging out. This situation may not be quite so significant when the intruder is logged on as a local administrator, but it becomes far more disconcerting when the intruder is logged on to a domain as a network administrator.

Default Group Accounts

When you install Windows NT Server 4.0, eight default local groups are created for you:

- Administrators
- Server Operators
- Users
- Account Operators
- Guests
- Print Operators
- BackUp Operators
- Replicator

CH
5

These groups are considered local groups because they are used to provide a certain level of functional access for that domain. Because the domain controllers share the same account database, a local group created on the PDC is considered local to all the domain controllers.

Windows NT also creates three global default groups:

- Domain Administrators
- Domain Users
- Domain Guests

You can use a global group account, like a global user account, anywhere in the domain or through a trust relationship to a trusting domain to manage user access to network resources. As with local groups, global groups created on a PDC are considered global to all the domain controllers for that domain.

Windows NT also creates and manages four groups—called *internal* or *system groups*—to place a user for accessing resources:

- Everyone
- Interactive
- Network
- Creator Owner

Everyone, of course means just that. Every user who logs on to the workstation or accesses a resource on the workstation or a server locally or remotely becomes a member of the internal group Everyone. It is interesting to note that Windows NT's philosophy for securing resources is not to secure them at all. By default, the group Everyone has full access to resources. It is up to the administrator to restrict that access and add security.

Everyone, when applied to Directory Services, means everyone within and outside of the enterprise. A user from one domain can access a resource on another domain if that user has a valid account in the other domain and if no trust relationship exists. This happens through passthrough authentication between the domains. That user then becomes a member of the Everyone group on the other domain.

There is a subtle distinction between the Everyone group and the Domain Users global group. Although Everyone always means absolutely everyone who accesses that domain, Domain Users means only those users from the domain. If you recall that Windows NT's default permission for network resources is Everyone with Full Control, replacing Everyone with Domain Users now subtly changes the access from absolutely everyone to only users from the domain.

Interactive represents to Windows NT the user who has logged on at the computer itself and accesses resources on that computer. This also is referred to as *logging on locally.*

Network represents to Windows NT any user who has connected to a network resource from another computer remotely.

Creator Owner represents the user who is the owner or has taken ownership of a resource. You can use this group to assign file access only to the owner of a file, for example. Although Everyone may have read access to files in a directory, Creator Owner will have full access; thus, although other users can read a file, only the owner of the file can make changes to it.

The Windows NT operating system fixes the membership of these internal groups, and they cannot be altered. If you create a file, for example, you are the owner of that file, and Windows NT places you in the Creator Owner group for that file.

Group Management in Domains

Microsoft's group strategy for domains recommends that domain users be grouped into as many global groups as is appropriate. Local resource managers then should create local groups to maintain access to the resources. The global groups then are used as members of the local groups. Whichever domain users are members of, the global group will get whatever level of access was given to the local group. Although this may seem to be a bit of overmanagement at first, in large networks with hundreds or thousands of users, this strategy makes a great deal of sense and actually can facilitate user management and resource access.

Extending this concept to the trust relationship follows naturally. Because the trust gives a resource administrator access to the account database of a trusted domain, the resource administrators can use the global groups created in the trusted domain as members of the local groups they create to manage access to their resources. If you want the administrators of the trusted domain to also administer the domain controllers or resource servers in the trusting domain, for example, you should make the Domain Administrator global group from the trusted domain a member of the local Administrators groups of the PDC and resource servers for the trusting domain.

Planning for New User Accounts

Part of setting up new user accounts—or group accounts, for that matter, especially on a domain controller—involves some planning. Here are six basic areas to consider before creating new accounts:

- Account naming conventions
- Dealing with passwords
- Group membership

CH
5

- Profile information
- Logon hours (when logon is possible)
- Which workstations the user can log on from

Naming Conventions

The choice of username determines how the user is identified on the network. In all lists of users and groups, the account names are displayed alphabetically, so the choice of username can be significant. If your naming convention is `FirstnameLastinitial`, for example, your usernames for the following users will look like this:

User	Username
Luke Smith	LukeS
Henry Sage	HenryS
Jerry T. Holmes	JerryTH

Now what if you have several `LukeS`s or `HenryS`s? In a large corporation, it is not uncommon to have 20 or 30 persons with the same first name. Looking through a list of users with the same first name and only a couple of letters from the last name could become not only confusing but irritating as well.

A more effective convention might be `LastnameFirstInitial`, like this:

User	Username
Luke Smith	SmithL
Henry Sage	SageH
Jerry T. Holmes	HolmesJT

With this convention, finding the appropriate user in a list is easier. Many organizations already have a network ID naming convention in place, and it may be perfectly acceptable to follow that.

Usernames must be unique with Windows NT's Directory Services. Therefore, your naming convention must plan for duplicate names. Henry Sage and Herbert Sage, for example, both have the username `SageH` according to the second convention example. So perhaps you could alter the convention to include middle initials in the event of a duplication (such as `SageHA` and `SageHB`) or include extra letters from the first name until uniqueness is achieved (such as `SageHen` and `SageHer`). Usernames are not case sensitive and can contain up to 20 characters, including spaces. Usernames cannot contain the following characters, though:

```
"  /  \  {  }  :  ;  |  =  ,  +  *  ?  <  >
```

You also might consider creating user accounts based on function rather than the user's name. If the role of administrative assistant is assigned from a pool of employees, for example, it may make more sense to create an account called AdminAsst or FrontDesk. This method ensures that the assistant of the day has access to everything to which that person should have access; it also minimizes your administrative setup for that person.

Password Considerations

Besides the obvious consideration that requiring a password provides the greater level of security, there are some other things to think about. One of these is who controls the password.

When you create a user account, you have three password-related options to determine:

- **User Must Change Password at Next Logon:** Enables you to set a blank or dummy password for the user. When the user logs on for the first time, Windows NT requires the user to change the password.
- **User Cannot Change Password:** Gives the administrator the most control. This option is particularly useful for temporary employees or the administrative assistant pool account.
- **Password Never Expires:** Ensures that users will not need to change their passwords, even if the overall password policy requires that users change their passwords after a set period of time has elapsed. This option is useful for the types of accounts just mentioned or for service accounts.

It is important to set company policy and educate users on the importance of protecting the integrity of their accounts by using unique and unguessable passwords. Among the most common choices for passwords are children's names, pets' names, favorite sports teams, and team players. Try to avoid the obvious association when choosing a password.

Passwords are case sensitive and can contain up to 14 characters. Network administrators generally suggest that you require a minimum password length of eight characters, using alphanumeric characters and a combination of upper- and lowercase letters. For example, I might use as my password a combination of my initials and the last four digits of my Social Security number—two things I am not likely to forget but are not obvious to anyone else. Thus, my password might be SDK4532, or it might be sdk4532, SdK4532, 4532sdK, 45sdk32, or—oh well, you get the idea.

Group Membership

The easiest way to manage large numbers of users is to group them logically, functionally, departmentally, and so on. Creating local groups for local resource access control is the most common reason for creating groups on the resource computers. As already discussed, local group membership consists primarily of domain global groups, although in specific instances, it may include domain global users as well.

Determining User Profile Information

The reference to user profiles on a Windows NT Server usually refers to a file of environment settings that is stored on a specific computer and downloaded to the Windows NT–based computer from which the user is logging on. The location of the logon script and personal folder also might be on a remote computer rather than on the local workstation, which is especially useful if the user moves around a lot (such as a pool of administrative assistants).

It is helpful, but not necessary, to determine ahead of time where you will keep this information and how much of this information you will use. Will you need a user profile stored on a server for every user or only for administrative assistants? Does everyone need a logon script? Should personal files be stored on the local workstation or on a central computer? (Again, this setup is useful for users who move around.)

Later in this chapter, you'll find more thorough discussions of user profile files and logon scripts, as well as another related utility called the System Policy Editor.

Home Directory

The home directory is a place in which the user can routinely save data files. This place is usually a folder (directory) that has been created on a centrally located server in the domain, although in small workgroups, the directory actually may be on the user's local workstation or not identified at all.

The advantage of placing the home directory on a centrally located server somewhere in the domain is primarily that of security. By using *New Technology File System* (NTFS) permissions, you can secure the users' folders quite nicely, so that only they (and whoever they determine) can have access to those folders. In addition, you then can include these folders in regular server data backups, thus ensuring the availability of the files in the event of accidental deletion, corruption, or system crashes.

In the Home Directory section of the User Environment Profile dialog box (accessed by viewing the Properties of the user account and choosing Profile), you have two choices:

- Local Path
- Connect To

The first option represents the drive and path to an existing home directory folder, such as C:\USERS, in which you can create the user's own profile folder. The other option represents a *Universal Naming Convention* (UNC) path that identifies the name of the server that contains an existing home directory share and a logical drive letter to assign to it that the user can use for saving files in applications, searching, exploring with the Windows Explorer, and so on.

Key Concept

A UNC name is very much like a DOS path—it represents the path through the network to a network resource. In this case, the network resource is a directory that has been shared for the creation of the home directory folder for the user. UNC names take the following form:

```
\\servername\sharename\path
```

Here, servername is the name of the server computer that contains the folder, sharename is the name of the directory that has been made available for use as a resource (shared), and path is an optional path to a subdirectory or specific file.

When entering the home directory location, you can specify the name of the folder explicitly or use an environmental parameter to create and name it for you. If you use the variable %USERNAME%, for example, Windows NT creates a directory using the username value as the directory name. This is particularly useful when you use a template for creating large numbers of users. Recall that when you create a new user account by copying an existing account, the user environment profile information also is copied. Using %USERNAME% enables you to create individual user home folders by using each user's username as the directory name. Table 5.1 lists the environment variables that Windows NT 4.0 can use.

CH
5

Table 5.1 Additional Environment Variables for Home Directories and Logon Scripts	
Variable	*Returns*
%HOMEDIR%	Logical mapping to the shared folder that contains the user's home directory
%HOMEDRIVE%	Logical drive mapped to the home directory share
%HOMEPATH%	Pathname of the user's home directory folder
%HOMESHARE%	Share name of the folder that contains the user's home directory folder
%OS%	Operating system of the user's computer

…continues

Table 5.1 continued	
Variable	*Returns*
%PROCESSOR_ARCHITECTURE%	Processor's base architecture, such as Intel or MIPS, of the user's computer
%PROCESSOR_LEVEL%	Processor type, such as 486, of the user's computer
%USERDOMAIN%	Name of the enterprise account domain in which the user is validating
%USERNAME%	User's logon ID (username)

Logon Scripts

If you have had any dealings with networks before, you have encountered a *logon script*. Logon scripts are simply files that contain a set of network commands that must be executed in a particular order. Often, as is the case with Novell NetWare, logon scripts have a specific command language and structure that should be used. In the case of Windows NT, logon scripts are simply batch files that support all the Windows NT command-line commands, or in some cases, an executable file.

Here is an example of a Windows NT logon script called LOGON.BAT:

```
@echo Welcome to the NT Network!
@echo off
Pause
Net use p:\\server5\database
Net use r:\\server4\budget
Net time \\server1 /set /y
```

The two net use commands map drives to existing network resource shares. The net time command synchronizes the system time on the current computer with the system time of the server specified.

The name of the logon script is arbitrary. Windows NT does provide a place for storing logon scripts. In a domain setting, they usually are placed in the WINNT\SYSTEM32\REPL\IMPORT\SCRIPTS folder on a domain controller. The scripts then are copied to WINNT\SYSTEM32\REPL\EXPORT\SCRIPTS so that they are replicated to all other domain controllers. Because the user uses any available domain controller to gain access to the network, it makes sense that the logon scripts be stored on all the domain controllers in the domain.

The advantage of storing the logon scripts on a domain controller is that, through Directory Replication, the scripts can be distributed to all the domain controllers in the network. Because a user may authenticate at any one of the domain controllers, this method provides a convenient way to ensure that the logon scripts are always available.

Also, it provides the administrator with one central storage place for the scripts, which makes maintaining them easier.

Windows NT assumes that you will store the logon script file in the WINNT\SYSTEM32\REPL\ IMPORT\SCRIPTS folder on the domain controller server. Because of this assumption, it is not necessary to use a UNC name when specifying the location of the logon script in the User Properties Environment Profile dialog box. In fact, after you have distributed the logon scripts to all the appropriate domain controllers, you just need to enter the file-name in the Logon Script Name text box. (Refer to Table 5.1 for more Windows NT environment variables.)

Understanding User Manager for Domains

You create and manage domain user and group accounts by using an administrative tool called User Manager for Domains (called just User Manager if you are not using domains). You also create and maintain account policies with this utility, as well as assign functional user rights, enable security auditing, and establish trust relationships. *Functional rights* define what functions a user can perform at a Windows NT computer. For example, shutting down the computer, changing the system time, formatting the hard drive, and installing device drivers are all functional rights.

User Manager for Domains acts as the database manager for user and group accounts stored on the SAM database (see Fig. 5.1).

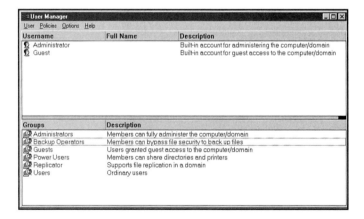

CH

5

Figure 5.1
User Manager displays the account database showing all user and group accounts. Here you see the two default users and six default local groups.

User Manager has four menus:

- **User:** Enables you to create and modify user and group accounts; copy, delete, rename, and change properties of user accounts; and change the domain focus for remote management of other domain databases
- **Policies:** Enables you to set account policies, assign functional user rights, enable security auditing, and establish trust relationships
- **Options:** Lets you enable/disable confirmation and save settings, set display fonts for User Manager, and specify a low-speed setting for use when administering a domain database across a slow connection, such as a 56Kbps *wide-area network* (WAN) line
- **Help:** Displays the Windows NT help files specific to User Manager

Creating a New User

Choosing New User from the User menu displays the New User dialog box shown in Figure 5.2. Table 5.2 explains this fairly intuitive screen.

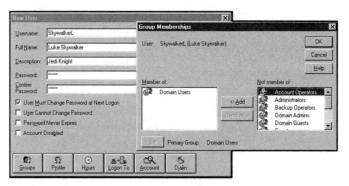

Figure 5.2
You select options in the New User dialog box; the Group Memberships dialog box shows the default membership in the Domain Users global group.

Table 5.2 New User Dialog Box Options	
Option	Description
Username	The logon ID you have chosen for the user. Recall that this name must be unique in the database (or in the enterprise when creating the account on a domain controller) and can be up to 20 characters, including spaces. The name cannot include these characters: " / \ [ ] : ;	= , + * ? < >

Option	Description
Full Name	The user's full name. As with usernames, it is recommended that you determine a convention for entering this name (such as Luke Robert Smith), because Windows NT uses the full name as an alternative user account sort order.
Description	A simple description of the account or user, such as Admin Assistant Account or Project Manager.
Password	The password is case sensitive and can contain up to 14 characters. Recall the discussion of password integrity earlier in the section "Password Considerations."
Confirm Password	You must confirm the password here before Windows NT can create the account.
User Must Change Password at Next Logon	Forces users to change their password the next time they log on.
User Cannot Change Password	Prevents users from being able to change their password. As mentioned earlier, this setting is useful for accounts for which the password should remain the same, such as temporary employee accounts.
Password Never Expires	Prevents the password from expiring and overrides both the Maximum Password Age option set in the Account Policy, as well as the User Must Change Password at Next Logon option.
Account Disabled	Prevents the use of the account. This option is a useful setting for users who are on vacation or extended leave, or whose accounts otherwise should not be available for logging on to the network. It is always more appropriate to disable an account if there is any possibility of the user returning. Remember that deleting a user account also deletes the user's SID, and thus removes all previous network resource access for that user.
Account Locked Out	Displays when the Account Lockout account policy is enabled. When a user exceeds the number of allowed incorrect logons, this option is enabled by the operating system and can be disabled only by an administrator or account operator.
Groups	Displays the Group Memberships dialog box, which shows you the user's group membership and enables you to modify the group membership.
Profile	Displays the User Environment Profile dialog box, from which you can reference a server-based profile, define a logon script, and identify a home folder (directory).

CH
5

…continues

Table 5.2   continued

Option	Description
Hours	Displays the Logon Hours dialog box, which you can use to determine what times of the day the user can log on to the network. This option is useful for shift employees or for backup times.
Logon To	Displays the Logon Workstations dialog box, which enables you to identify by computer name the computers at which this account can log on to the network. You can identify up to eight workstations.
Account	Displays the Account Information dialog box, in which you can specify an expiration date for the account and identify whether the account is a global domain account (default) or one for a user from another untrusted domain who needs occasional access to your domain.
Dialin	Displays the Dial-In Information dialog box, which you use to grant permission to use Dial-Up Networking to the user account and set Call Back options.

As you can see, creating user accounts is a fairly straightforward process. By double-clicking the account name in the User Manager window or highlighting the username and choosing <u>U</u>ser, <u>P</u>roperties, you can view these settings for each user and modify them as appropriate.

Creating a Local or Global Group

The process of creating a local or global group is even more straightforward in the Local Group Properties dialog box. Table 5.3 describes the options available in the Local Group and Global Group Properties dialog boxes.

Table 5.3   Global Group Properties Dialog Box Options

Option	Global or Local	Description
<u>G</u>roup Name	Both	The name you have chosen for the local group. The name can have up to 256 characters, except the backslash (\), which would be somewhat confusing in display lists of groups. Group names, unlike usernames, cannot be renamed. You can copy a group name, however, and preserve its member list for the copied group.
<u>D</u>escription	Both	Enables you to enter a simple description of the group, such as Administrative Assistants or Project Managers.
Show Full Names	Local Only	Displays the full name associated with each user account displayed in the Members list box.

Option	Global or Local	Description
Members	Both	Displays all the current user accounts (or domain user and global group accounts) that are members of this local group.
Not Members	Global Only	Displays the users from the domain whom you can add to the group member list.
Add	Local Only	Displays the Add Users and Groups dialog box. You use this dialog box to select user accounts from your domain's user and global group accounts database on the PDC or from the accounts database from a trusted domain. Select the trusted domain that has the desired accounts from the List Names From the user list box, click the user you want to add to the group in the Names list box, click Add, and click OK. Click the Search button to look for an account among all possible account databases. If you have selected a global group in the Names list box, use Members to display the members of that global group. You can select multiple accounts at one time by Ctrl+clicking the additional accounts.
		Clicking Add in the New Global Group dialog box adds the users you selected in the Not Members list to the Members list.
Remove	Both	Deletes the account selected in the Members list, thus removing it from group membership.

To prepopulate a group before you create the group, select all the usernames you want in the group from the User Manager Username screen by Ctrl+clicking the additional accounts. Then create the group. The Members list box displays any user account that was highlighted before the group was created.

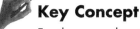

Key Concept

For the exam, know the primary membership difference between local and global groups. Local groups can contain user accounts from the local account database, global user and global group accounts from the domain database of the domain of which the server is a member, and global user and global group accounts from the domain database of a trusted domain. Global groups can contain only user accounts from their own domain database.

CH
5

Renaming, Copying, and Deleting Accounts

Recall from the discussion of the default Administrator and Guest accounts that for a higher level of security, you can rename these accounts. Renaming an account does not affect the account's SID in any way: It makes it relatively easy to change a username without affecting any of that user's access—whether it be changing the Administrator account to enhance its security or reflecting a name change because of marriage or the Witness Protection Program. Simply highlight the username in User Manager for Domains, choose User, Rename, and type the new username in the box provided. You cannot rename group names.

Key Concept

If you choose to delete an account, remember that the account's SID also will be deleted, and all resource access and user rights will be lost. This means that even if you re-create the account exactly as it was before, the SAM database generates a new SID for the account, and you have to reestablish resource access and user rights for that account.

To delete the account, highlight it and press Del on the keyboard, or choose User, Delete. Windows NT warns you that the SID will be lost. Choose OK, and the account is deleted.

Key Concept

You cannot delete built-in user or group accounts—global or otherwise.

The User, Copy command is useful for duplicating user account information that is the same for a group of users. Because you cannot rename a group, copying a group to a new name also duplicates its membership list and is the next best thing to renaming. Copying user and group accounts results in new accounts being created. As such, each new account has its own new SID assigned to it.

When you copy a user account, the following settings are maintained: the Description, the password options that have been checked off, and if Account Disabled has been selected, it will be unchecked for the copy. Also, group membership and profile information is maintained for the copied account, as are Logon Hours, Logon to Workstations, and Account Expiration and Type, which greatly simplifies the task of creating large numbers of similar users.

Creating and Managing Account Policies, System Rights, and Auditing

Account policy information and user rights are considered part of account management and, as such, are administered through User Manager for Domains. Account policy information includes password-specific information such as password, age, minimum length, and account lockout options.

User rights represent the functional rights a user acquires for a given server when logging on at the console or remotely. You audit file and directory access, print access, and so on by specifying the users or groups whose access you want to audit; you perform auditing at the file, directory, and print levels. You first must enable auditing for those security events for user and group accounts; you perform that through User Manager for Domains as well.

Account Policy

Figure 5.3 shows a typical domain account policy. The options presented in this Account Policy dialog box should be very familiar to network administrators. The policies determined here apply to all domain users.

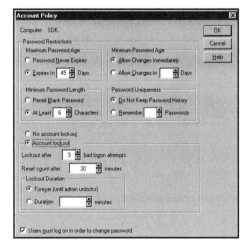

Figure 5.3
In this account policy, the password must be at least six characters and expires every 45 days. Also, if the user forgets the password in three consecutive tries within 30 minutes, the account will be locked out until an administrator releases it.

Table 5.4 describes the various entries you can make for an account policy.

Table 5.4   Account Policy Options

Option	Description
Maximum Password Age	You may set the password to never expire, or you may select a set number of days after which the user is prompted to change the password. The default is 42 days.
Minimum Password Age	The default here is to allow users to change their password at any time. Many organizations now prefer not to allow users to change their passwords whenever they want. Users must wait a specified number of days before they can change their password, which helps to maintain password uniqueness. By forcing users to have a password for several days, organizations make it less likely that users will always change their password back to their child's name.
Minimum Password Length	The default, oddly enough, is to allow blank passwords. As discussed earlier in the section "Password Considerations," you probably will want to define a minimum length for the password. Most network administrators use 8 as the minimum length. The maximum length can be 14.
Password Uniqueness	The default is to not maintain a history of passwords, which allows users to reuse passwords after they expire. Although being able to reuse a password is convenient for users, it is not always the most secure way to deal with passwords. Many organizations require passwords to be unique, which is accomplished by specifying the number of passwords to be remembered by the system for each user (up to 24) and requiring a maximum and minimum password age. By setting the maximum and minimum password age to 30 days and uniqueness to 24, for example, users will not be able to reuse the first password for two years. These settings in effect accomplish uniqueness, simply because users are not likely to be able to remember that far back.
Account Lockout	Lockout prevents an account from being used after several failed logon attempts. The default is to not enable account lockout. In an enterprise where security is essential, this option probably will be enabled, and in fact, it is recommended.
Lockout After	Specifies the number of bad logon attempts (incorrect passwords) the system accepts before locking out that account. The default is 5 and can be set from 1 to 999.

Option	Description
Reset Count After	This number is the number of minutes the system waits between bad logon attempts before resetting the bad logon count to 0. If you mistype your password, for example, the bad logon count is set to 1. If the reset count is 15 minutes, and after 15 minutes you do not log on incorrectly again, the bad logon count is set back to 0. If you do log on incorrectly again within 15 minutes, the logon count is set to 2, and so on. The default is 30 minutes and can be set from 1 to 99,999 minutes (or roughly 70 days, for those of you who couldn't help wondering).
Lockout Duration	You can require an administrator to reset the account after lockout. You also can specify a length of time for the lockout to be in effect before letting the computer hacker try again. The default for this choice is 30 minutes and can be set from 1 to 99,999 minutes.
Users Must Log On in Order to Change Password	Requires that users log on to the system before making password changes. Normally, when a password expires, users are prompted during logon to change the password. With this option selected, users cannot change the expired password, and the administrator must reset it. This option is useful for short-term employee accounts that expire in a specific amount of time to ensure that the employees cannot change their passwords on their own.
Forcibly Disconnect...	By default, logon hour settings merely stop users from logging on during the specified time period. If users already are logged on, the logon hour settings have no further effect on those users. This option causes users to be logged off the system when the logon hours expire. You can use this option to force users off a system before it is backed up or rebooted.

CH
5

User Rights

As mentioned previously, user rights are functional rights and represent functions or tasks that a user or group can perform locally on a given workstation or server, or while remotely connected to a server. User rights include shutting down the computer, formatting a hard drive, backing up files and directories, and so on. Contrast this with permissions, such as read-only, write, and delete, which reflect resource access rights.

In the domain, user rights are granted primarily to local groups, because they usually represent access at the server console itself. You also can grant user rights to global groups, however, especially when remote access and administration are involved.

The user right Log on Locally, for example, defines which users can log on at the server console. Only members of the local Account Operators, Administrators, Backup Operators, Print Operators, and Server Operators groups are granted this access. Note that, unlike Windows NT Workstation, the group Everyone is not listed under User Manager for Domains on Windows NT Server installations by default.

For this discussion, assume that the server in question functions as a print server for a multiple master domain model. You would like print operators from all domains to be able to manage this print server; that includes the capability to log on at the print server itself. Following Microsoft's group-management strategy, you would create a global group in each trusted domain, perhaps called GlobalPrintOps, and then add it to the local Print Operators group on my print server. Those users can log on locally at the print server to manage the printers.

By virtue of the trust relationship, however, you also could have added the GlobalPrintOps global group directly to the Log On Locally user right to let those members log on at the print server. As with all security objects, user rights maintain *access control lists* (ACLs). Groups and users represented by their SIDs are members of the ACL for each user right. Consequently, there is no way to select an account and see what user rights (or file permissions, for that matter) have been assigned to that account, because the rights do not stay with the account.

Table 5.5 highlights the basic user rights on domain controllers and the default groups assigned to each.

Table 5.5   User Rights on Domain Controllers

User Right	Group(s) Assigned
Access This Computer from the Network	Administrators, Everyone
Add Workstations to Domain	No groups explicitly assigned; a default Administrator function
Back Up Files and Directories	Administrators, Backup Operators, Server Operators
Change the System Time	Administrators, Server Operators
Force Shutdown from a Remote System	Administrators, Server Operators
Load and Unload Device Drivers	Administrators
Log On Locally	Account Operators, Administrators, Backup Operators, Print Operators, Server Operators

User Right	Group(s) Assigned
Manage Auditing and Security Log	Administrators
Restore Files and Directories	Administrators, Backup Operators, Server Operators
Shut Down the System	Account Operators, Administrators, Backup Operators, Print Operators, Server Operators
Take Ownership of Files or Objects	Administrators

You can administer accounts assigned to the various user rights by using the User Rights Policy dialog box, which you access by choosing User Rights from the Policy menu (see Fig. 5.4). Select the user right from the Right drop-down list. The default groups assigned this user right appear in the Grant To list box. Click Add to access the Add Users and Groups dialog box (described in the section "Creating a Local or Global Group") and add user and group accounts to the user right's Grant To list. Or click Remove to delete members from the Grant To list.

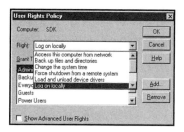

Figure 5.4
The User Rights Policy dialog box shows some of the user rights you can select. Log on Locally has been selected, and in the Grant To box, you can see the groups assigned this user right.

You also can display advanced rights by enabling the Show Advanced User Rights check box at the bottom of the User Rights Policy dialog box. These rights are for use primarily by developers. However, as an administrator on a network, you may need to modify two advanced user rights from time to time:

- **Bypass Traverse Checking:** This advanced user right allows the specified user or group accounts to change between directories and navigate directory trees even if permission has been denied to various directories. This right might be assigned to power users or resource managers.

■ **Log On as a Service:** This advanced user right is intended for user accounts that are used by certain background application tasks or Windows NT system functions, such as Directory Replication. This right allows the service or function to log on as the specified account for the express purpose of carrying out that specific task. No other user needs to be logged on for the task to be performed.

Audit Policy

To audit for events relating to file and directory access, print access, and so on, specify the groups or users whose access you want to audit. You perform this audit at the file, directory, and print levels. You first must enable auditing for those security events for user and group accounts; you do this through User Manager by choosing Policies, Audit. The Audit Policy box appears (see Fig. 5.5).

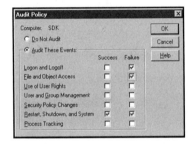

Figure 5.5
This policy audits failed logon and logoff attempts; unsuccessful file and object access; and any events associated with restart, shutdown, or system processes related to this domain controller.

By default, auditing is not enabled because of the additional resources required to monitor the system for related events. You can enable auditing for seven areas:

Audit Area	Monitors
Logon and Logoff	User logon and logoff of the server, the domain, and network connections.
File and Object Access	User access of files, directories, or printers. This access enables the auditing of those objects to take place. The users and groups that are audited are set up at the file, directory, and printer resource levels.
Use of User Rights	When a user right is exercised by a user (such as formatting the hard drive).

Audit Area	Monitors
User and <u>G</u>roup Management	Events related to user and group management, such as the creation of new users, the modification of a group membership, or the change of a password.
<u>S</u>ecurity Policy Changes	Changes made to user rights or account policy information.
<u>R</u>estart, Shutdown, System	Events related to these activities.
<u>P</u>rocess Tracking	Events related to certain process activity, such as starting a program, indirect object access, and so on.

You can log successful and unsuccessful events in the Security Log, which you can view through the Event Viewer, another useful Administrative Tools utility. It is generally not at all useful for you to monitor successful and unsuccessful events for all seven options on a server, because of the resources involved and the volume of data that would be collected in the Security Log. Auditing can be very helpful in troubleshooting events, however, such as unsuccessful logons or unsuccessful file access.

Troubleshooting Account and Policy Management

If you have been reading carefully, you already have the necessary building blocks for understanding and troubleshooting account management. The best tool for learning is to practice.

Most of the problems you will encounter regarding user and group accounts will have to do with permissions to use resources instead of with the account setup itself. Nevertheless, here are some things to keep in mind.

User Cannot Be Logged On By System

When a user cannot log on, fortunately the message(s) that Windows NT displays to the screen are self-explanatory. Usually, the reason why a user cannot log on involves the user incorrectly typing the username or, more likely, the password. Usernames are not case sensitive, but passwords are. Usernames and passwords can both have spaces, but that tends to confuse users more than provide descriptive account names. Be sure to be consistent in your use of usernames. Educate your users on the importance of maintaining the integrity of their passwords, and expect a call every now and then from someone who has forgotten a password or has Caps Lock on when the password should be in lowercase.

If a user forgets a password, the easiest thing for the domain administrator to do is to use User Manager for Domains to give the user a new temporary password and enable the User <u>M</u>ust Change Password at Next Logon check box. If an account lockout policy has been established and the user exceeds the allowed number of incorrect passwords, the Account Lockout check box for that user is enabled. Only an administrator or account operator can remove the lock—again, by using User Manager for Domains.

Unable to Access Domain Controllers or Servers

Another possibility that can slow or inhibit a person's capability to log on successfully is the unavailability of a server. If the user is logging on locally, the user is being validated on the local computer for access to resources on that computer. Unless the computer suddenly turns itself off, the user should be able to log on successfully.

When a Windows NT Workstation or Server is made a member of a domain, the From box on the Logon Security screen displays the local computer as well as the domain name. If one or more trusts are established, the From box displays all available trusted domains. So the first thing to check if a user cannot be authenticated is whether the user chose the correct domain from the list when logging on.

If the user is validating on a network domain controller, the domain controller must be accessible to the user, or the user may not be able to log on. For example, if the PDC is down and no *backup domain controller* (BDC) is identified to the network, the user will be unable to log on. If the user logged on successfully at the computer in a previous session, a message may appear stating that the domain controller is unavailable and that the user will be logged on with cached information from the Registry.

Any changes that may have been made to a profile since the last session probably will not be available.

You troubleshoot this one, of course, by verifying that the domain controller is up and that the computer in question has a valid connection to the network. If you are using *Transmission Control Protocol/Internet Protocol* (TCP/IP) as your protocol, you will want to check that the computer has a valid IP address and subnet mask and, if routing is involved, a valid default router address. If a trust relationship is involved, verify that the trust is valid and working.

Sometimes the location of the BDC can cause a user logon to be slow or to fail due to WAN traffic. Determine whether the location for the BDCs in your domain best meets the needs of your users and the logon traffic they generate. You can track network traffic and performance by using the Network Monitor service and utility that comes with Windows NT Server 4.0.

Sometimes you cannot easily track down network-based errors. Everything may seem to be functioning okay, for example, but you just can't seem to access the network. Sometimes the network card can get confused, and the best thing to do is to shut down the computer and do a cold boot. A warm boot does not always reset the hardware—in this case, the network card.

Other Logon Problems

Other problems may be related to other settings made through User Manager for Domains. Recall that in this utility, the administrator can add logon hour and workstation restrictions for the user, as well as account expiration. Again, the messages Windows NT displays are pretty obvious in this regard and direct you to the appropriate account property to check and modify.

Remote Account Management Tips

You can perform most account management remotely by installing User Manager for Domains on a local Windows NT Workstation. Versions also exist for Windows 95 and Windows for Workgroups.

Two options are available in User Manager for Domains that can facilitate the remote management of accounts across trust relationships and across slow network connections: Select Domain and Low Speed Connection.

The User menu in User Manager for Domains offers a Select Domain option. Choosing this option displays the Select Domain dialog box. Here, you can choose the domain of the account database you want to administer from the Select Domain list (all trusted domains are listed), or type the domain name in the Domain text box. User Manager for Domains displays the account database for that domain, provided you have the appropriate level of access. For example, you must be a member of the trusted domain's Administrators, Server Operators, or Account Operators local groups.

In the Select Domain dialog box, you'll find a check box option for Low Speed Connection. This option, also available from the Options menu, is useful for facilitating administration when the network connection is particularly busy or when administration takes place over a slower-connection medium, such as a 56Kbps line. Selecting this option results in the following modifications to User Manager for Domains:

- The list of user and group accounts does not appear, and the User, Select User option is unavailable, although the administrator can administer accounts by using the other User menu commands.
- The capability to create and manage global group accounts is unavailable, although you can affect global group membership through the group membership of individual user accounts.
- The View menu options are unavailable.

CH

5

Understanding User and Computer Profiles

When speaking of the user profile in Windows NT 4.0, what really is being discussed is managing the user's working environment. In contrast, when speaking of the computer profile, you actually are talking about managing the computer's environment and configuration settings. Both types of profiles involve making modifications to the Windows NT Registry.

In the User Environment Profile dialog box in User Manager for Domains, you can define various elements of the user's environment:

- **User Profile Path:** Identifies the location of the Registry files and profile folders for the user.
- **Logon Script Name:** Identifies the name and optional path of a set of commands that are executed when the user logs on.
- **Home Directory:** Identifies the location of the user's personal data folder.

By using the System Policy Editor, you can modify Registry settings for both the user's environment and the computer's configuration. These settings might include restricting the use of the File, Run command for the user, or configuring a legal notice to display on a Windows NT Workstation when a user attempts to log on.

When the computer boots and the user logs on, the user's computing environment is configured according to predetermined settings.

User Profiles

The user profile represents the user's environment settings, such as screen colors, wallpaper, persistent network and printer connections, mouse settings and cursors, shortcuts, personal groups, and Startup programs. These settings normally are saved as part of the Windows NT Registry on the user's computer and then are loaded when the user logs on to the system.

In Windows NT 3.51 and earlier versions, these settings were kept in the WINNT\ SYSTEM32\CONFIG subdirectory with the other Registry files on the local computer, workstation, or server that the user logged on to. The next time the user logged on, the profile settings were made available and merged into the Registry for that session. If the user moved to another computer, whether the user logged on locally or to the network, a new profile was created on that computer and saved locally. In turn, the settings saved on that computer were merged into the local Windows NT Registry on that computer.

Under Windows NT 4.0, profiles still are saved on the local computer to which the user logs on. However, all information relating to the user's profile now is saved in a subdirectory structure created in the WINNT\PROFILES folder, which contains the Registry data file, as well as directory links to desktop items. Figure 5.6 shows an example of this structure.

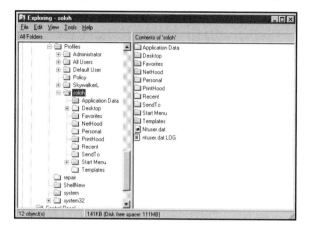

Figure 5.6
In this view of Windows Explorer, the WINNT\PROFILES folder with the profile subdirectory structure for soloh is expanded. Notice the Registry files Ntuser.dat and ntuser.dat.LOG.

Three default profile structures are created during installation:

- **Administrator:** This structure is created because the administrator's account is a default account.
- **Default User:** New user accounts can derive their initial environment settings from this structure.
- **All Users:** This structure is used with the user's profile settings to assign settings that should be common to all users, such as startup items and common groups.

Table 5.6 outlines the directory structure of the user's profile directory.

Table 5.6   Overview of the Profile Folder Directory Structure

Profile Folder	Description
Application	Contains references to application-specific data and usually is modified by the application during installation or when a user modifies a setting for the application
Desktop	Contains references to shortcuts created on the desktop and the Briefcase

...*continues*

Table 5.6 continued	
Profile Folder	Description
Favorites	Contains references to shortcuts made to favorite programs and locations
NetHood	Contains references to shortcuts made to Network Neighborhood items, such as shared folders
Personal	Contains references to shortcuts made to personal group programs
PrintHood	Contains references to shortcuts made to print folder items
Recent	Contains references to items most recently accessed by the user
SendTo	Contains shortcuts to the last items documents were sent to or copied from, such as the A: drive or My Briefcase
Start Menu	Contains references to program items contained on the Start menu, including the Startup group
Templates	Contains references to shortcuts made to template items

When the user first logs on, the settings contained in Default User are used to create that user's own profile folders. In addition, the Registry data file, called Ntuser.dat, is created and stored in the root of the user's profile folder (refer to Fig. 5.6). Windows NT also creates and maintains a corresponding transaction log file, called ntuser.dat.LOG. Changes to the profile actually are recorded in the log file and applied to the Ntuser.dat file when the user logs off. In the event of a problem, the changes are kept in the log file and can be applied the next time the user logs on. So, as the user modifies the environment by changing settings, creating shortcuts, installing applications, and adding programs to the Start menu, Windows NT adds and modifies entries in the appropriate profile folder and updates the Registry log file.

For example, if soloh (the profile folders shown in Fig. 5.6) adds a shortcut to his or her desktop for Word 97, Windows NT adds an entry representing the shortcut to Word 97 in the Desktop folder, under WINNT\Profiles\soloh. If soloh modifies the desktop wallpaper, the change is recorded in soloh's ntuser.dat.LOG file and applied to the Ntuser.dat file when soloh logs off.

The Registry subtree HKEY_CURRENT_USER is actually a cached copy of the Registry data file Ntuser.dat, and as discussed in Chapter 4, "Configuring Windows NT Server 4.0," it contains information related to the user's environment settings, such as color schemes, cursors, wallpaper, and so on.

Key Concept

By default, the `NetHood`, `PrintHood`, `Recent`, and `Templates` folders are hidden from display in Windows Explorer. To view these folders, choose <u>V</u>iew, <u>O</u>ptions, select the View tab, and then choose <u>S</u>how All Files.

Server-Based User Profiles

As you have seen, user profile information is stored in the computer(s) on which the user logs on. If a user routinely logs on to any one of several computers, it might be inconvenient for that user to create or modify preferred settings on each computer before using it. It is far more efficient for the user's work-environment settings to follow the user to whichever computer the user logs on to. This type of user is known as the *roaming user,* and those users' profiles are known as *server-based,* or *roaming profiles.* This type of profile is used more often to provide a level of consistency among an organization's users' desktops than to accommodate roaming users.

Windows NT 4.0 Workstation and Server computers support two types of server-based profiles: roaming user profiles and mandatory user profiles. Both are user profile settings that have been copied to a centrally located server for access by the user when logging on. The location and name of the profile is identified in the user's user environment profile information through User Manager for Domains.

When the user logs on to a computer, a mandatory or a roaming profile is copied to that local computer to provide the best performance (local instead of over-the-network access). Changes made to the roaming profile are updated on both the local computer and the server. The next time the user logs on, the server copy is compared to the local copy. If the server copy is more recent, it is copied to the local computer. If the local copy has the same time and date stamp as the server copy, the local copy is used again to facilitate the logon process. If the local copy is more recent, as might happen if the user uses a laptop that is infrequently connected to the network, the user is notified and asked which copy to use.

The primary difference between mandatory and roaming profiles is that the mandatory profile is created by an administrator for the user and cannot be modified by the user. The roaming profile can be, and is meant to be, modified by the user, and it follows the user as a convenience.

CH
5

Key Concept

The user may change environment settings while in a particular session, but those settings are not saved back to the mandatory profile. Also, a mandatory profile can be configured so that, if the profile is unavailable when the user attempts to log on, the user is prevented from logging on.

Server Profiles over Slow WAN Links

Logging on over a slower WAN connection, such as a dial-up line or a 56Kbps link, can result in slowed response time for the logon process. This can be particularly painful for the user when a server-based profile must be copied across the slow link. If you have told Windows NT to monitor for slow WAN connections (User Manager for Domains), when Windows NT detects a slow link (more than two minutes to respond to a request for the profile), it displays a dialog box that asks the user to select a locally cached profile or the server-based profile. If the user selects the local profile, all changes are saved to the local version.

Users also can make the choice to switch to the local profile during their session. By using the User Profiles tab on the System applet in the Control Panel, users can change their profile from roaming to local, or from local to roaming. Again, if users select local, all changes are saved to the local profile until users switch back to the server profile.

If users require a mandatory profile, they are unable to log on, unless they opt to install the user-based profile over the slow connection.

Creating the Server-Based Profile

Windows NT 4.0 Server no longer provides the User Profile utility that some users are familiar with from using Windows NT Server 3.51. Windows NT Server 4.0 has implemented support for server-based profiles in a couple of interesting ways, however.

A server-based profile always is identified to the user's account by the account administrator, who provides the UNC path and filename of the profile file in the user account's User Environment Profile dialog box (see Fig. 5.7). This path identifies the server on which the profile will be maintained, as well as the shared folder in which it will be stored. If the file specified does not exist, Windows NT creates an empty profile for the user. When the user first logs on and modifies the settings, the server-based profile is updated.

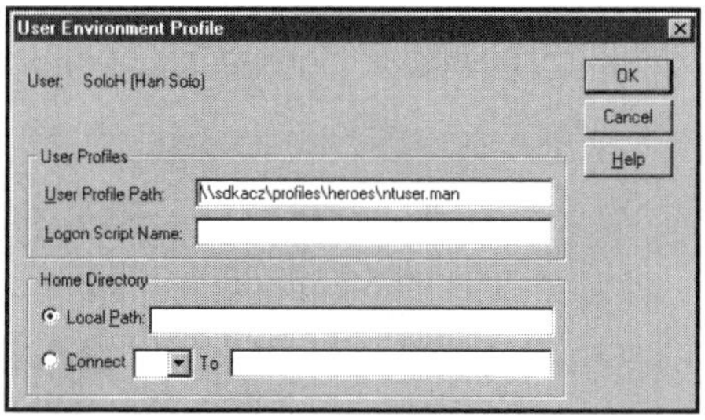

Figure 5.7
The server-based profile file for user SoloH is stored in the heroes subfolder, in the profiles shared folder, on the server sdkacz. The .man extension on the profile file indicates that this is a mandatory profile.

In some cases, the administrator may want or need to predetermine the users' profiles. Windows NT provides management for this type of user profile through the User Profiles tab of the System applet in the Control Panel.

The User Profiles tab of the System Properties dialog box displays the profiles that have been created and stored on that computer. Remember that a profile is created each time a user logs on. If you plan to delete a user, you first should delete the user's profile through this tab. If you first delete the user, you see an Account Deleted entry, as shown in Figure 5.8. This really is not such a big deal if only one or two accounts are involved; if the account is deleted anyway, it is a pretty safe bet that you can delete its profile information. With large numbers of users, deleting the appropriate profiles after the accounts already have been deleted can be confusing. Recall that all settings related to a user account are linked to the user's SID. Deleting the account deletes the SID and renders all previous settings obsolete, including profile information.

The first step necessary to create a roaming or mandatory profile is to identify the users or groups that require this type of profile. The Registry file name NTUSER.DAT cannot be changed, and it is this file that determines whether the profile is mandatory. The next step is to identify the central computer on which you plan to store the users' profiles. This should be a computer that is readily accessible by the users on that network or subnet, particularly if the profiles are mandatory. The directory then should be shared on the network. Within this directory, create subdirectories for the different users or groups that will use the various profiles you create.

CH
5

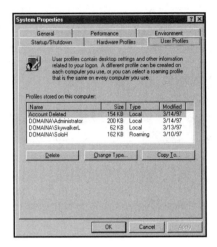

Figure 5.8
Four user profiles are contained on this computer. One of them is for an account that has since been deleted. It should be removed to clean up the Profiles directory on the hard drive.

If you permit several users or a group of users to use the same roaming profile, remember that the profile can be modified by the user. It is possible that multiple users may make multiple changes to the profile. It is better to use mandatory profiles for groups of users. Individual roaming users each should have their own roaming, changeable profile.

You then configure roaming and mandatory profiles by using these steps:

1. Identify a server and shared folder location on which you will save the profile.

2. Identify or create a user account, and make the appropriate changes to that account's environment settings.

3. Select that account's profile on the User Profiles tab, located in the System applet in the Control Panel, and choose Copy To.

4. In the Copy Profile To box, enter the UNC name to the share and directory that will contain the profiles, or click Browse to look for the location.

5. Click Change, and from the Choose User dialog box that appears, select the user or groups you are permitting to use this profile by choosing Show Users.

6. Click OK to save the profile, and then exit the System applet.

Next, you must identify the profile file to the user(s) you are configuring for by using the User Manager utility. Follow these steps:

1. Open User Manager for Domains.

2. From the User Properties for this user's configuration, choose P̲rofile to display the User Environment Profile dialog box.

3. In the U̲ser Profile Path text box, enter the UNC path to the profile file. For example, if the profile NTUSER.DAT is located in the BROWNC directory, in the share PROFILES on the server KITESERVER, enter \\KITESERVER\PROFILES\BROWNC\NTUSER.DAT.

4. Click OK and exit User Manager for Domains.

5. Test the profile by logging on as that user.

Mandatory Profiles

As stated earlier, a mandatory profile is one that does not accept user changes. It always provides the same settings for every user who has been identified as using that profile. For this reason, it is the best choice when maintaining the same configuration settings for large groups of users, or for users who should not be allowed to make configuration changes.

The steps for creating a mandatory profile are the same as those for creating a roaming profile. If you require the profile to become mandatory, you must use Windows Explorer to select the NTUSER.DAT file, and then change the extension to from .DAT to .MAN. This effectively makes the profile mandatory, and any changes that users may make to their desktops will not be saved back to the profile.

Key Concept

If the administrator specifies a mandatory file by name in the user's User Environment Profile settings dialog box, the user is prevented from logging on if the profile is, for any reason, unavailable.

If the administrator does not specify the file by name, the user still is able to log on with default user settings.

Default User Profiles

It is possible for an administrator to create a default profile that all users can receive when they first log on. Perhaps all users should have the same screen colors, for example, or the company logo as their desktop wallpaper. Again, this profile is created as a regular roaming profile. However, this profile must be copied to the NETLOGON share (WINNT\SYSTEM32\REPL\IMPORT\SCRIPTS) for every domain controller in the user's account domain. The user accounts also must be configured, as outlined earlier in the chapter, to use a personal profile.

When the user logs on, Windows NT checks the user account's specified profile path for the existence of a profile file. If that file does not exist, and it is not stored locally on the computer from which the user is logging on, Windows NT checks the NETLOGON share for a folder named Default User and loads the profile stored there. When the user logs off, these settings, and any changes the user makes, are saved to the user's own profile folder.

Key Concept

When copying a profile to a server, you must use the Server applet in the Control Panel. Using Windows Explorer will not make the necessary modifications to the Windows NT Registry to record the location of the profile. Only the Server applet makes the appropriate Registry changes. Profile entries are located in the following Registry subkey: HKEY_LOCAL_MACHINE\Software\Microsoft\Windows NT\CurrentVersion\ProfileList.

Supporting Windows 95 Profiles

Windows 95 administrators also can create and maintain profiles for Windows 95 users. Both Windows 95 and Windows NT 4.0 profiles operate similarly, although Windows 95 profiles are created differently and have some functional differences. Windows 95, for example, does not support the concept of common groups or a centrally stored default profile. For that matter, Windows 95 profiles can be copied only from the user's home folder, as opposed to a specific profile path. In addition, the Registry files created by Windows 95 to support profiles are different than the files of Windows NT 4.0— USER.DAT, USER.DA0, and USER.MAN in Windows 95, as opposed to NTUSER.DAT, NTUSER.DAT.LOG, and NTUSER.MAN in Windows NT 4.0.

Nevertheless, Windows 95 users can obtain their profiles when logging on as a member of a Windows NT domain by creating their profiles as they normally do in Windows 95, which includes storing the profiles in the users' home folders and referencing the locations of the home folders in their account's User Environment Profile dialog box in Windows NT.

Managing Profiles with System Policies

Alternatively (and perhaps more effectively), you can use the System Policy Editor to control user profile settings. It is available only on Windows NT 4.0 Servers. Through the System Policy Editor, you can modify the default settings for all users, or copy the settings and then modify them by individual users or groups. The policy file then is saved as `NTCONFIG.POL` in the `WINNT\SYSTEM32\REPL\IMPORT\SCRIPTS` subdirectory on all validating domain controllers. This concept will seem quite familiar to Windows 95 administrators, because it is similar to the system-policy file they can create for Windows 95 clients (`CONFIG.POL`). However, Windows 95 system policies are not compatible with Windows NT 4.0 system policies because of, in part, differences in their registries.

The System Policy Editor enables administrators to specify both the computer configurations and settings, such as those saved in the `HKEY_LOCAL_ MACHINE` subtree of the Registry, as well as user-environment settings, such as those saved in the `HKEY_USERS` subtree. Settings can affect all computers and users as default or general settings, or you can create settings to affect only specific computers or users.

For example, through the System Policy Editor, you can restrict user activity in the Display applet in the Control Panel; specify desktop settings, such as wallpaper and color schemes; customize desktop folders; create custom folders and Start menu options; restrict the use of Run, Find, and Shutdown; and disable editing of the Registry. Combined with computer-system policies applied to the computer at which a user logs on, the administrator can achieve a finer level of control over the user's work environment.

Working with the System Policy Editor

The System Policy Editor provides two types of policy modes: Registry mode and policy mode. The Registry mode enables an administrator to administer local or remote Registries without using the Registry Editor. The System Policy Editor provides a point-and-click method of implementing Registry changes. Thus, the administrator has a safe and relatively intuitive utility to use to modify a local or remote Registry. Additionally, changes made through the Registry mode of the System Policy Editor take effect immediately, in contrast to those made through the Registry Editor.

You initiate Registry mode by choosing File, Open Registry. The Local Computer icon displays options to implement the changes to the `HKEY_LOCAL_MACHINE` subtree of the local Registry. The Local User icon displays options to implement changes to the `HKEY_Users` subtree. Access the Registry on a remote Windows NT computer by choosing File, Connect from the System Policy Editor, and then enter the name of the Windows NT computer you want to manage.

CH

5

Key Concept

You must have Administrator privileges on the Windows NT computer that contains the Registry you want to manage.

The policy mode provides an administrator with a method of implementing configuration changes for all users or computers, or for selected users and computers. This is done by creating a single policy file that contains references to various computers or users, each with a distinct set of configuration requirements. The policy file then can be saved on a specified server, accessed during user logon, and downloaded to the logon workstation.

Initiate policy mode by choosing File, New Policy from the main menu to create a new policy file. Or choose File, Open Policy to modify an existing policy file. The Default Computer icon displays options that affect all computers connecting to the domain, and the Default User icon displays options that similarly affect all users logging on to the domain. You also can add specific users and computers to the policy file, each with its own set of configuration options selected.

In both modes, when the user logs on, the settings contained in the system policy are merged with the current Registry settings to provide a specific environment for the computer and the user. The options displayed for both modes are the same, so they will not be separated by mode as this section continues.

Policy Templates

The policy options that are displayed when you modify computer or user settings in either mode are determined by a set of template files provided by Windows NT 4.0. These templates provide options for the most common configuration settings that administrators modify. The templates are text files with a specific structure and, as such, can be modified or customized for specific use by the administrator.

Two policies are loaded by default when the System Policy Editor starts. COMMON.ADM offers options that are common to both Windows NT 4.0 and Windows 95, such as Network, Desktop, Control Panel, System, Shell, and System settings. These options primarily make changes to HKEY_Users in the Windows NT 4.0 and Windows 95 Registries. WINNT.ADM offers Windows NT 4.0–specific options, such as Windows NT Network,

Windows NT Printers, Windows NT User Profiles, Windows NT System, Windows NT Remote Access, and Windows NT Shell. These options primarily make changes to HKEY_LOCAL_ MACHINE in the Windows NT Registry.

A third policy also is available, called WINDOWS.ADM, which offers options that are specific to Windows 95 computers, such as the Windows 95 Control Panel, Windows 95 System, Windows 95 Shell, and Windows 95 Network.

Through a combination of these templates, you can create system policies from the same policy file to govern the working environments of all your Windows NT 4.0 and Windows 95 clients.

Setting System Policy Options

When the administrator modifies a system policy by selecting the computer or user icon, a list of option categories is displayed in a manner similar to the Windows Explorer folder screen. The administrator drills down through each option category and makes a selection by checking off the option desired. In many cases, as you check an option, the bottom half of the screen displays additional settings you can make or text you can enter (see Fig. 5.9).

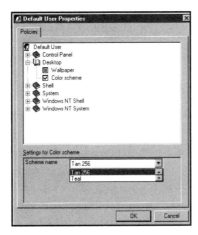

CH
5

Figure 5.9
The Desktop category for the default user is selected. With the selection of Color Scheme, the administrator can choose from a list of available color schemes in the Scheme Name drop-down list box.

Each policy option offers three selection possibilities:

- Checking an option indicates that the option should be merged with the current Registry and override any existing settings.
- Clearing a check box indicates that the option should be merged with the Registry, if there is no current Registry setting for that option. If there is a current setting, the policy setting is ignored.
- Leaving the check box gray, the default, means that the policy setting is not modified at all.

In fact, only the options that are checked or cleared are saved to the policy file; this keeps the file to a manageable size when downloading it across network connections.

Default and Specific User and Computer Settings

Changes made to policy settings under `Default User` or `Default Computer` are applied to all computers and users affected by this policy file. When a user logs on, the policy file is checked first for the default settings that should be applied to all computers and users, and then the Registry is modified accordingly.

However, policy options also can be set for individual computers and users within a domain. Suppose that computer WOOKI5 needs to have a specific network setting configured when a given user logs on. A policy setting can be configured specifically for WOOKI5. When a user logs on at WOOKI5, the policy file is checked for any specific options set for that computer, and then for default settings. It finds WOOKI5 and implements those settings in addition to—or overriding—the default settings. Similarly, specific settings can be provided for individual user accounts. When the user logs on, any specific settings meant for that particular user are implemented in addition to—or overriding—the default settings.

Furthermore, policy settings can be implemented by group membership. Options for specific groups can be set, along with a group priority to determine which settings take precedence when a user belongs to several groups for which policies have been set. If a user has a specific policy, however, any group policy that might otherwise have been set for the user is ignored. Figure 5.10 outlines the specific order for implementing system policy settings.

Follow these steps to create a specific policy for an individual user:

1. Start the System Policy Editor.
2. Choose Edit, Add User.
3. Enter the username of the user you are adding, or click the Browse button to display the domain database.
4. Double-click the new user's icon in the System Profile Editor dialog box and make your choices.

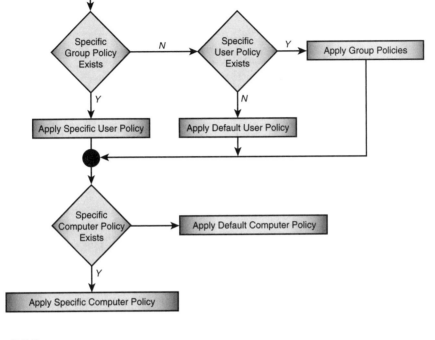

Figure 5.10
A flow chart for applying system policy settings.

Follow these steps to create a specific policy for an individual computer:

1. Start the System Policy Editor.
2. Choose <u>E</u>dit, Add <u>C</u>omputer.
3. Enter the name of the computer you are adding, or click the <u>B</u>rowse button to display the list of computers in the Network Neighborhood.
4. Double-click the new computer's icon in the System Profile Editor dialog box and make your choices.

Follow these steps to create a specific policy for an individual group:

1. Start the System Policy Editor.
2. Choose <u>E</u>dit, Add <u>G</u>roup.

3. Enter the name of the group you are adding, or click the <u>B</u>rowse button to display the domain database.

4. Double-click the new group's icon in the System Profile Editor dialog box and make your choices.

When two or more groups are added to the policy file, you can specify the priority order in which group policy settings are applied to users by following these steps:

1. Highlight a group in the System Policy Editor dialog box.

2. Choose <u>O</u>ptions, <u>G</u>roup Priority.

3. Select a group from the <u>G</u>roup Order list and choose Move <u>U</u>p or Move <u>D</u>own, as appropriate, to create the desired priority order for your groups.

Windows NT 4.0 uses a predefined policy filename to automatically implement system policies across the domain. The file is called NTCONFIG.POL and must be saved in the NETLOGON share (WINNT\SYSTEM32\REPL\IMPORT\SCRIPTS). When the user logs on, Windows NT looks for the existence of this file in the NETLOGON share on all domain controllers for the domain. If the file exists, it is checked for default and specific policy settings (refer to Fig. 5.10).

However, the administrator can choose to create individual policy files for specific users, groups, or computers and save them in an accessible, shared directory on a server. These files can have any filename, but they must have the extension .POL. Also, these policy files must be specified by a UNC path in the user account's Profile Settings dialog box.

Summary

This chapter examined the concepts of users and groups in detail. You looked at using account policies, account management, and troubleshooting.

User Manger for Domains is the tool you use to add and manage users as well as create and administer groups. Groups can be local or global. Local groups can exist on any NT machine (be it server or workstation), whereas global groups exist only on a domain controller and traverse the domain.

User profiles enable users to customize their desktops and environments. By default, the profiles are created locally, and thus are called *local profiles.* Moving the profile to the server creates a *roaming profile,* because users can access it from any workstation they use. If the roaming profile is renamed from NTUSER.DAT to NTUSER.MAN, it becomes a mandatory profile, and users cannot make any changes to it.

The next chapter discusses an issue that is of paramount importance to any type of network: security in the domain. Coupled with what has been addressed so far, this will finish up the discussion of basic Windows NT administration.

QUESTIONS AND ANSWERS

1. The two default user accounts created during an installation of the operating system are _____ and _____.

   A: Guest (which can do nothing and is disabled by default) and Administrator (which can do everything).

2. The three default global accounts created are _____, _____, and _____.

   A: Domain Administrators, Domain Users, and Domain Guests.

3. The syntax `\\servername\sharename\path` is known as _____.

   A: UNC (Universal Naming Convention) path.

4. The tool used for creating new users is _____.

   A: User Manager for Domains. It is similar to User Manager on NT Workstation, but it is enhanced to handle global/domain entities.

5. The feature that maintains a history of passwords and does not allow a user to use the same password twice in a row is known as _____.

   A: Password uniqueness. It is turned off by default, but it may be turned on to enhance security.

CH
5

PRACTICE TEST

1. Which of the following statements is true about the default user accounts created in Windows NT Server 4.0?

   a. The Administrator account is enabled and can be renamed; the Guest account is enabled and cannot be renamed.

   b. The Administrator account is enabled and cannot be renamed; the Guest account is disabled and cannot be renamed.

   c. The Administrator account is enabled and can be renamed; the Guest account is disabled and can be renamed.

   d. The Administrator account is disabled and cannot be renamed; the Guest account is enabled and can be renamed.

Answer a is false, because the Guest account is not enabled and can be renamed. Answer b is false. The Administrator account can be renamed, as can the Guest account. **Answer c is true. The Administrator account is enabled, whereas the Guest account is disabled, and both can be renamed.** Answer d is false. The Administrator account is enabled and can be renamed. Additionally, the guest account is disabled.

2. Everyone should be able to read the files in a certain directory. However, the user who created the file should be able to modify it. What do you need to do?

   a. Do nothing. By default, only the creator of a file has access to it. Windows NT restricts resource access by default.

   b. Give the group Everyone read access and the Creator Owner group change access. By default, Windows NT gives everyone complete access to resources.

   c. Give the group Everyone read access and the Creator Owner group change access. By default, Windows NT restricts resource access.

   d. Give the group Everyone read access and the Users group change access. Windows NT automatically determines who the owner of the file is and restricts the other users.

Answer a is incorrect. You must make changes for this to take place. **Answer b is correct. To meet the criteria, give the group Everyone read access and the Creator Owner group change access.** Answer c is incorrect. By default, NT does not restrict resource access. Answer d is incorrect. The Users group is not the one that will allow for the change needed. You must use the Creator Owner group.

3. On a Windows NT Server in DomainA, you have stored a sales database and a marketing database, and you also have shared a color printer. Five of the users in the domain are salespersons, five are marketers, and the rest are programmers. The users should be able to access their respective databases, but only the team leaders for sales and marketing and the programmers should be able to access the color printer. Which group strategy is the best?

   a. Create local groups for sales, marketing, and team leaders, and assign the appropriate user accounts to the appropriate groups. Then assign permissions for each resource to the appropriate group.

   b. Create global groups for sales, marketing, and team leaders and assign the appropriate user accounts to the appropriate groups. Then assign permissions for each resource to the appropriate global group.

   c. Create global groups for sales, marketing, and team leaders, and assign the appropriate user accounts to the appropriate groups. Then create local groups for each and assign the global group to the local group. Then assign permissions for each resource to the appropriate local group.

   d. Simply assign the appropriate users access to the resources they need to access.

Answer a is incorrect; global groups are needed. Answer b is incorrect. Local groups also must be created, per Microsoft's suggested practice. **Answer c is correct. In order to follow Microsoft's guidelines, create global groups for sales, marketing, and team leaders, and assign the appropriate user accounts to the appropriate groups. Then create local groups for each and assign the global group to the local group. Then assign permissions for each resource to the appropriate local group.** Answer d is incorrect; it avoids the recommended strategy of group management.

4. What are the differences between a local group and a global group? Choose all that apply (true statements).

   a. Local groups can be created on workstations, servers, and domain controllers, whereas global groups can be created and maintained only on a domain controller.

   b. Local groups can contain local users, domain users, and global groups, whereas global groups can contain only users from their domain.

   c. Local groups can contain local users, domain users, global groups, and other local groups, whereas global groups can contain only users from their domain.

   d. Local groups can be used for managing resources only on the local computer, whereas global groups can be used to manage resources on any computer that participates in the domain.

Answer a is true. Local groups can be created on workstations, servers, and domain controllers, whereas global groups can be created and maintained only on a domain controller. Answer b is true. Local groups can contain local users, domain users, and global groups, whereas global groups can contain only users from their domain. Answer c is false, because a local group cannot be nested within any other group (be it local or global). **Answer d is true. Local groups can be used for managing resources only on the local computer, whereas global groups can be used to manage resources on any computer that participates in the domain.**

5. Which of the following sets of usernames and passwords are acceptable for Windows NT?

   Username—Password

   a. `First Ass't Comptroller—FirstComp`

   b. `FirstAsstCompt—1stComp`

   c. `FirstAss*tCompt—COMP1`

   d. `AssComp1—123COMPTROLLER1`

Answer a is invalid because of the number of characters in the username. **Answer b is a valid username and password combination.** Answer c is invalid because of the use of the asterisk (*) in the username. Answer d is invalid because of the number of characters in the password.

**CH
5**

6. Your workstations are members of a domain called `Titan`. You need to create user accounts so that two shifts of temporary employees can log on to the same computer, but only during their shifts. Which of the following are valid solutions?

   a. Use User Manager for Domains on each local Windows NT Workstation to create the temporary accounts and assign each the appropriate logon hours.

   b. Use User Manager on each local Windows NT Workstation to create the temporary accounts and assign each the appropriate logon hours.

   c. Use User Manager for Domains on the domain controller for `Titan` to create domain accounts for the temporary employees and assign each the appropriate logon hours.

   d. Use User Manager on the domain controller for `Titan` to create local group accounts for the temporary employees and assign each the appropriate logon hours.

Answer a is invalid. The tool needs to be run on the domain controller and not locally. **Answer b is correct. Use User Manager on each local Windows NT Workstation to create the temporary accounts and assign each the appropriate logon hours.** Answer c is invalid. User Manager exists only on NT Workstation, whereas User Manager for Domains exists on the domain controller. Answer d is invalid. User Manager exists only on NT Workstation, whereas User Manager for Domains exists on the domain controller.

7. Your boss has advised you that BrownC has left the company and asks that you delete his account. Later, your boss hires BrownC back as a consultant and tells you to put his account back on the network. BrownC calls you the next day and informs you gruffly that he can no longer access any of the network resources that he used to. How do you troubleshoot?

   a. Use the Registry to set BrownC's SID back to what it was before you deleted his account. He then will be able to access all the old resources.

   b. Deleting BrownC's account also deleted his SID. Because security in Windows NT is linked to the user's SID, you need to reestablish all the network resource access that BrownC used to have.

   c. Use the Emergency Repair Disk or your last network backup to copy BrownC's old account back to the Registry.

   d. Install a backup copy of the account database that contains his old account.

Answer a is incorrect. You cannot reuse a SID. **Answer b is the correct assumption. Deleting the account also deleted his SID. When he was added back in, it was with a new SID not associated with old files. You need to reestablish all the network resource access that BrownC used to have.** Answer c is incorrect. Restoring the Registry for one user is not an acceptable practice. Answer d is incorrect. You cannot restore the account database for a single user.

8. Under which of the following situations would you disable the user account instead of deleting it?

a. JaneD has left the company on maternity leave and plans to return in three months.

b. JohnB has taken an emergency medical leave of absence for possibly six or more months, but hopes to return full time.

c. JaniceD has left the company to take a job at Microsoft.

d. FrankP has taken a temporary team leader position in another department and will return when the project is completed.

Answer a is a good reason for disabling the account: A user is off for a time but will return. Answer b is a good reason for disabling the account: A user has left for a time but will return. Answer c is incorrect. This is one of the very few times you would delete a user—when that user leaves for the competition. **Answer d is a good reason for disabling the account: A user has left for a time but will return.**

9. You are creating multiple user accounts for salespersons, marketers, and programmers. Each set of accounts belongs to the same relative groups (sales users in SALES, marketing users in MARKETING, and programmer users in PROGRAMMERS), uses the same logon scripts (SALES.BAT, MARKET.BAT, and PROGRAM.BAT), and saves data in a home directory relative to each group (sales users under USERS\SALES, marketing users under USERS\MARKETERS, and programmer users under USERS\PROGRAMMERS). What is the most efficient way to create these users?

a. Create a separate account for each user. As you create the user, use the %USERNAME% environment variable when specifying the home directory to let Windows NT create it for you.

b. Create a template for each type of user. Make the appropriate choices and entries for groups, logon script, and home directory. Use the %USERNAME% environment variable when specifying the home directory to let Windows NT create the path for you. Then create each user by copying the appropriate template.

c. Create all the users without specifying group membership. After they are all created, select each group of users by Ctrl+clicking them and create the appropriate group.

d. You must create each user individually.

Answer a, although correct, is not the most efficient method. **Answer b is the best answer. Create a template for each type of user. Make the appropriate choices and entries for groups, logon script, and home directory. Use the %USERNAME% environment variable when specifying the home directory to let Windows NT create the entries and path for you. Then create each user by copying the appropriate template.** Answer c is incorrect—this will not work. Answer d is incorrect because the actions can be done.

CH
5

10. To provide a greater level of security, you have decided to create an account policy that requires a minimum password length of eight characters, requires that users change their passwords at least once a month, and does not allow users to use the same password twice in two months. Which Account Policy settings are appropriate?

   a. Max Password Age: 60; Min Password Age: 30; Min Password Length: 8; Password Uniqueness: 2

   b. Max Password Age: 30; Min Password Age: 30; Min Password Length: 8; Password Uniqueness: 6

   c. Max Password Age: 30; Min Password Age: 10; Min Password Length: 8; Password Uniqueness: 6

   d. Max Password Age: 60; Min Password Age: 30; Min Password Length: 8; Password Uniqueness: 1

Answer a is incorrect, because it allows passwords to be used for too long. Answer b is incorrect, because the minimum and maximum ages can never be the same. **Answer c is correct. To meet the criteria given, the parameters are Max Password Age: 30; Min Password Age: 10; Min Password Length: 8; Password Uniqueness: 6.** Answer d is incorrect—the password uniqueness value needs to be higher.

CHAPTER PREREQUISITE

You should be familiar with the concepts of Directory Services and domain models, discussed in Chapter 2, "Understanding Microsoft Windows NT 4.0," as well as the basics of user and group management, discussed in Chapter 5, "Managing Users and Groups."

Security and Permissions

WHILE YOU READ

1. A list of users and groups that can access a resource is maintained by the resource in its _____.

2. When a user logs on, he or she is assigned an _____.

3. The four share-level permissions available are _____, _____, _____, and _____.

4. Of all the administrative shares created by default, the only one not hidden is _____.

5. True or false: Ownership requires NTFS and not FAT.

This chapter discusses more thoroughly the Windows NT 4.0 security model. The security model applies both to Windows NT 4.0 Workstation and Server, as does the method of applying permissions and sharing resources.

Examining the Windows NT 4.0 Security Model

All security provided by Windows NT 4.0 is handled through a kernel mode executive service known as the Security Reference Monitor. When a user logs on, tries to perform a function at the workstation (such as formatting a disk), or tries to access a resource, the Security Reference Monitor determines whether, and to what extent, the user should be granted access. The authentication process provides security through user account location and password protection. User rights are functional and define what actions a user can take at a given workstation, member server, or domain controller, such as shutting down the workstation or formatting a disk. These actions are discussed in Chapter 5, "Managing Users and Groups."

There are also permissions, which define a user's access to network resources. Permissions define what a user can do to or with a resource, such as delete a print job or modify a file. The terms *rights* and *permissions* often are used interchangeably and usually refer to resource access. With Windows NT, the term *rights* invariably refers to the functional user rights you can set through User Manager and User Manager for Domains. The term *permissions* refers to resource access. This book uses the Windows NT definitions of *rights* and *permissions*.

Two types of permissions can be applied in Windows NT:

- **Share-level permissions:** Define how a user can access a resource that has been made available (shared) on the network. This is a resource that resides some place other than the workstation at which the user is sitting and that the user accesses remotely. The owner or administrator of the resource makes it available as a network resource by sharing it. The owner or administrator of the resource also defines a list of users and groups that can access the resource through the share and determines just how much access to give them.

- **Resource-level permissions:** Also define a user's access to a resource, but at the resource itself. The owner or administrator of the resource assigns a list of users and groups that can access the resource and the level of access to grant them. Combined with share-level permissions, resource-level permissions can provide a high degree of security.

The most common resource-level permissions you will encounter are those for files and folders. File and folder permissions are available only on *New Technology File System* (NTFS)–formatted partitions. If you do not have a partition formatted for NTFS, you will be able to use only the *file allocation table* (FAT)–level properties: read-only, archive, system, and hidden. Under NTFS, you get a more robust set of properties, including read, write, delete, execute, and change permissions.

Shared devices, such as printers, also provide a means of assigning permissions to use the device—for example, printing to a print device, managing documents on the print device, and so on.

Key Concept

Any resource for which access can be designated is considered to be a security object. In other network operating systems, such as Novell NetWare, some permissions used to set access to resources are assigned directly to the user or group and stay with the user or group account. This is not true with Windows NT. In all cases, it is important to note that permissions are assigned to, and stay with, the security object and not the user. A user's access to a resource is determined at the time the user tries to access it, not when the user logs on.

When a user logs on to Windows NT, whether at the local workstation or through a domain controller, the user is granted an access token. Permissions ascribed to an object (resource) reside in an *access control list* (ACL) with the object. The Security Reference Monitor compares the user's access-token information with that in the ACL and determines what level of access to grant the user. These concepts are explained further in the following section.

Exploring the Windows NT Logon Process

When a user logs on to Windows NT on a Windows NT–based computer, the username, password, and point of authentication must be provided. This is part of the WIN32 Winlogon service that monitors the logon process. The Winlogon service passes this information to the Security subsystem, which in turn passes it to the Security Reference Monitor (see Fig. 6.1).

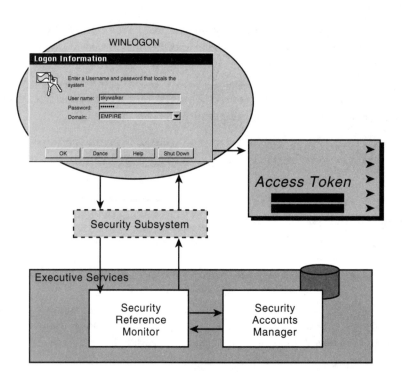

Figure 6.1
A diagram of the Windows NT 4.0 local logon process.

The Security Reference Monitor checks the information entered by comparing it against the *Security Accounts Manager* (SAM) and the account database. If the information is accurate, the Security Reference Monitor authenticates the user and returns a valid access token back to the Security subsystem and the Winlogon process. With Directory Services, users are authenticated by a domain controller in the domain for which they are a member. This domain authentication is governed by another process, called Net Logon. Figure 6.2 shows this process.

Net Logon is very similar to the local logon process. The difference is that the Security subsystem passes the logon information to the Net Logon process on the user's Windows NT computer, which then establishes a secure network *interprocess communication* (IPC) connection with the Net Logon process on an available domain controller.

The Net Logon process of the domain controller then passes the logon information to the SAM and database on the domain controller, where the user is authenticated. The validation confirmation is sent back through the secure connection to the Security subsystem on the user's Windows NT computer, where the access token is generated.

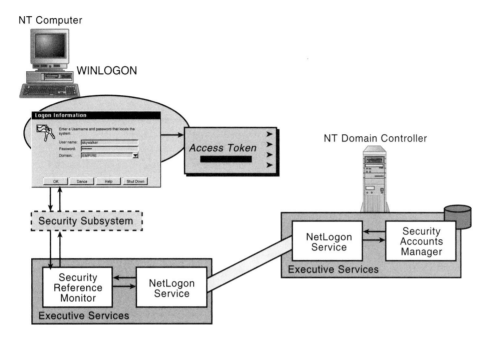

Figure 6.2
Providing network authentication in Windows NT 4.0 by using Net Logon.

The Account Access Token

Many companies that have secure areas provide access to those areas through an electronic key card. A magnetic strip on the back of the card contains the user's information, such as a *security ID* (SID). The card is read by a card reader at the point of entry. Often, the user also has to enter a security number or password on a keypad before the door is unlocked.

The access token is a lot like a key card. It contains important security information about the user. This information includes, most important, the user's SID. Recall from Chapter 5 that the SID is the unique security identifier that Windows NT assigns to the user's account when the account is created. All security-related requests made by the user are linked to, and matched first and foremost against, the user's SID. Other security information includes the username and password, group memberships by name and group SIDs, profile location, home directory information, logon hours, and so on.

CH
6

Key Concept

Windows NT uses the access token to determine whether a user may gain access to a resource, and how much access the user should be provided.

Local Versus Domain Access Tokens

When a user logs on to a local Windows NT Workstation that is participating in a workgroup, the user's account resides in the local Windows NT Workstation's Registry (SAM database). Hence, the user's access token is created on that local Windows NT Workstation and can be used to access only the resources on that workstation.

As Figure 6.2 shows, when a user logs on to a Windows NT computer that is a member of a domain, the user's account resides in the domain Security Accounts Manager's database on the domain controller. Recall that this type of account is called a *domain* or *global account,* because the user can log on just once and gain access to any resource in the network that the account has permission to use. Hence, the user's access token is created on the domain controller for that domain and can be used (because it is a global account) to access any resource throughout the enterprise domain that the account has been given permission to use. This is a hallmark of Windows NT's Directory Services.

Because access to remote resources is determined by comparing the SIDs for each account in the ACL with the SIDs listed in the user's access token, the point of logon validation affects the user's capability to access a resource.

In a domain, the user and group accounts are global and can be used in the ACL of any resource in the domain. When the user logs on to the domain, the access token contains the user's SID (and group SIDs, per group membership), which is global to the network. Both the access tokens and the ACLs obtain their SIDs from the same SAM's database. Thus, the user can access any resource that has granted access permission to any one of the SIDs contained in the user's access token (access to the extent the permission allows).

User access is controlled the same way where trust relationships exist between domains. A trust relationship enables users to log on and authenticate at a Windows NT computer that participates in either the trusting domain or the trusted domain. Also, the trust relationship enables resource managers to assign access to user and group accounts from any trusted domain (including their own).

Among domains where no trust relationships exist, a user's access token is good only in the validating domain. The ACLs for network resources in another domain consist of SIDs from that domain's own account database. If the user has an account in that other domain, the user's SID in that domain is necessarily different (see Chapter 5, "Managing Users and Groups") from the SID the user employs when logging on to his or her own domain. When the user tries to access the other domain's resources, the two SIDs (access token and ACL) do not match, and the user cannot access the resources.

Regardless of whether a trust exists between two domains, Windows NT uses a process called *passthrough authentication* to validate the user on the other domain. When a trust does exist, the NetLogon process determines, as the user logs on, that the user's account does not reside within the trusting domain and therefore passes it through to the Net Logon service on a domain controller in the trusted domain, where it then is authenticated (refer to Fig. 6.2).

When a trust does not exist, the user must log on to the user's own domain. Windows NT then takes the username and password from the user's access token on the user's domain—instead of the user's SID—and "passes it through" to the Net Logon service on a domain controller in the other domain. The user, in effect, then is logged on to the other domain, and a new access token is created with the user's account and group SIDs from the other domain's account database. The user then can access on that domain's computer the resources to which the ACL grants permission.

This all works great as long as the username and password match in both domains. The user can select the resources in the other domain by using Network Neighborhood or browse lists to point and click to those resources. However, the passwords, if not both the username and password, usually do not match. In this case, the user still may be able to access the resource through passthrough authentication, but generally, the user has to connect to the resource by mapping a drive, entering a valid username from the other domain in the Connect As box, and supplying a valid password.

Consider the following example. Suppose that DOMAINA has account BrownC with password ABC. BrownC wants to access a shared printer on Pserver2 in DOMAINB. The first thing the print administrator must do is add BrownC to the ACL for the printer. If DOMAINB trusts DOMAINA, the print administrator just needs to add the account to the printer's ACL because it is available through the trust. However, if no trust exists between the domains, the administrator of DOMAINB can add members of DOMAINB's account database only to the printer's ACL. This means that an account for BrownC must be created in DOMAINB and added to the ACL for the printer.

Suppose that BrownC's account in DOMAINB also expects password ABC. When BrownC uses the Add Printer Wizard to connect to the printer on Pserver2 in DOMAINB, Windows NT uses passthrough authentication and the Net Logon service to pass BrownC and ABC from BrownC's access token in DOMAINA to the Security Reference Monitor on a domain controller in DOMAINB to be authenticated. A new access token is created for BrownC in DOMAINB. This token can be used to access the printer, because now the SID for BrownC in DOMAINB matches the SID for BrownC in the ACL for the printer.

Unlike mapping to shared folders, there is no Connect As text box for shared printers, in which the user can supply a valid username and password for the printer. Thus, if the passwords don't match, BrownC cannot access the printer at all. If BrownC attempts to access a folder under these same circumstances, BrownC can supply his or her username or a valid username from DOMAINB in the Connect As text box that appears when mapping a drive through Network Neighborhood or Windows Explorer. BrownC then is prompted for the appropriate password. If the password is correct, BrownC gains access to the folder with the appropriate level of permissions.

Examining Access Control Lists

When a key card is read by the card reader, the information on the card generally is checked against a central database to see whether this user has the appropriate level of access to be permitted in the secured area. The database may indicate that the cardholder has full access and allow the door to open; or the database may indicate that the cardholder has minimum access and only allow a window in the door to open. If you think of the access token as the key card for access to secured areas, you can think of an ACL as the card reader database.

An ACL is just that—a list of users and groups that have some level of access to the resource. The ACL is created at the object (resource or share) level and stays with the security object. It consists of user and group account entries that reference the accounts' SIDs rather than the accounts' names. These entries are called *access control entries* (ACEs). Each entry has a particular level of permission associated with it, such as read-only, full control, or no access.

When a user tries to access a resource, the request is passed once again to the Security Reference Monitor, which then acts as the card reader. It checks the SID entries in the access token against the SID entries in the ACL (see Fig. 6.3).

The Security Reference Monitor determines all matches, evaluates the permissions assigned to each matching entry, and calculates an overall permission level for the user, which becomes the user's effective access to the resource. It then returns that effective access as a security "handle" to the object—for example, read and write permissions for a file. The security handle becomes part of the access token for as long as the user accesses the object.

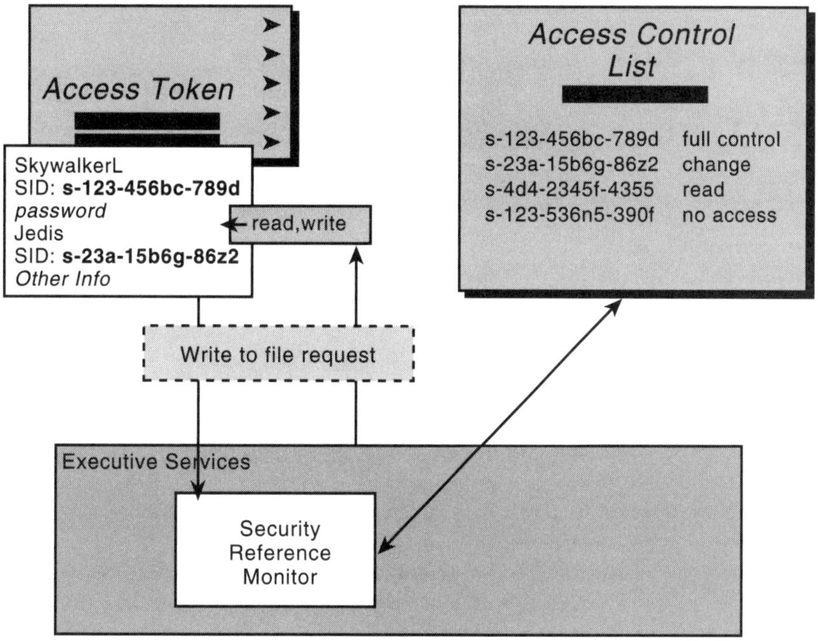

Access Token

SkywalkerL
SID: **s-123-456bc-789d**
password
Jedis
SID: **s-23a-15b6g-86z2**
Other Info

← read,write

Access Control List

s-123-456bc-789d	full control
s-23a-15b6g-86z2	change
s-4d4-2345f-4355	read
s-123-536n5-390f	no access

Write to file request

Executive Services

Security Reference Monitor

Figure 6.3
The security access process.

Key Concept

As long as the user maintains access to the object, the same security handle is in effect, even if the owner or administrator of the resource changes the user's access. The changed permissions do not take effect for the user until the user releases control of the object and tries to access it again.

Sharing Resources and Determining Network Access

A resource, such as a folder or printer, is made available as a network resource by sharing the resource.

CH
6

Key Concept

Only a user who is an administrator, server operator, or print operator (or power user on a member server) can share a resource on a workstation or server.

In addition, the Server Service must be running, and the network card must be operational. If you suspect a problem with the Server Service or the network card, a good place to begin troubleshooting is the Event Viewer. Look for any devices or services that failed to start.

Sharing a folder is a relatively simple process. A folder is shared by selecting the file or folder through Windows Explorer or My Computer, right-clicking it, and choosing Sharing; or through the object's properties sheet. Figure 6.4 shows a folder that has been shared.

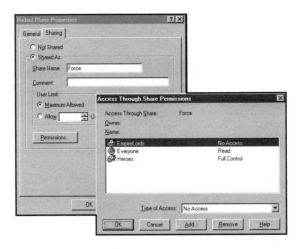

Figure 6.4
Rebel Plans has been shared with the name Force. Notice the list of groups and the permissions assigned to each.

Sharing is enabled by selecting the Shared As option. When you share a folder, the share name defaults to the folder name but can be changed to be more descriptive for its potential users. You also can indicate the number of users that are allowed to access the share at the same time, or accept the default of Maximum Allowed.

Key Concept

The maximum number of remote connections allowed on a Windows NT Workstation is 10. On a Server, the number of connections is effectively unlimited, except as defined by the license option chosen.

If you go no further, Windows NT shares this resource to any and all users. The default permission for every shared resource is Everyone with Full Control.

Key Concept

Windows NT's philosophy of sharing resources is to make information readily and easily available. Therefore, the default is to give every network user access to the resource. Hence, the default permission is always Everyone with Full Control. With printers, the default for Everyone is Print.

If you want to add a layer of security to the shared folder, you must choose <u>P</u>ermissions and <u>A</u>dd the appropriate group and user accounts, modifying the permissions as necessary. By doing this, you are creating and modifying the ACL for the folder.

Key Concept

It is recommended that you either remove the Everyone group and explicitly assign permissions to specific users and groups, or give Everyone the least level of access (read) to provide a greater level of security. Do not give the Everyone group No Access. Because every network user is automatically a member of Everyone, giving it No Access results in locking every user—even the owner and administrator—out of that shared resource.

Table 6.1 explains the four share-level permissions you can assign in your ACL.

Table 6.1 Permissions for Shared Folders	
Permission	*Effect*
Read	Displays the folder and filenames; allows files to be opened and programs to be run; allows similar access to subfolders.
Change	In addition to read permissions, allows changes to be made to files and folders, including creating and deleting files and folders.
Full Control	Allows complete access to the folder and its files and subfolders, including the capability to take ownership of files and change permissions of files and folders.
No Access	Denies access to the folder and its contents.

Key Concept

Share permissions take effect for users accessing the resource remotely over the network. If the user sits down at the computer that has the folder, and no other permissions have been assigned, the user still has complete access to the folder and its files.

If two or more users attempt to access the same file at the same time, the first user is able to modify the file, and the rest see the file in read-only mode.

Permissions assigned to a folder also apply to all files and folders within the shared folder. If you give the group Sales read permissions for the folder DATA, for example, the members of the Sales group also have read permissions for all files and subfolders within DATA.

Effective Permissions

The Security Reference Monitor checks the user's access token against the entries in the ACL, as you have seen already. When it identifies a match or matches, it then must determine the permissions to give the user. The effective share permissions are cumulative. The permissions explicitly assigned to a user, as well as permissions assigned to any groups in which the user is a member, are added together, and the highest level of permission is granted to the user. The only exception to this rule is that the No Access permission always denies access, regardless of any other permissions assigned.

Suppose that BrownC is a member of Managers and Sales. BrownC has been given Change access, Managers has been given Full Control, and Sales has been given Read access to a shared folder. BrownC's effective permissions are Full Control by virtue of BrownC's membership in the Managers group.

The only exception to this rule is No Access. No Access always supersedes any other permission—even Full Control. Using the same example, if BrownC explicitly is given No Access, then BrownC cannot access the shared folder, even though BrownC is a member of the Managers group, which has Full Control.

It is important, therefore, that you take sufficient time to plan your shared folders and their permissions. For example, take a look at the home directory folders. Suppose that users' home directories are created under a share that is called Users. By default, Users are shared to Everyone with Full Control. This means that all files and folders within Users also give Everyone Full Control. Thus, all network users can see all other users' files in their home directories. This probably is not a good idea. This problem is best solved using NTFS file and directory permissions. NTFS permissions are covered later in this chapter in the section "Securing Folders and Files with NTFS Permissions." You can set the permissions on the directory to grant access only to the user who owns the directory. Administrators also are denied access. Although administrators still can grant themselves access to a user's home directory at any time, this action would be recorded in the Security Log.

Administrative and Hidden Shares

When Windows NT is installed, it creates several shares, called *administrative shares,* all of which are hidden, except for Net Logon. *Hidden shares* are shares that exist but cannot be seen by any user in the lists of available shared resources. Hidden shares are meant to be used by either the operating system for specific tasks and services, such as IPC$ and REPL$, or an administrator for security access or troubleshooting, such as the root drive shares.

Table 6.2 summarizes these hidden (and Net Logon) administrative shares.

Table 6.2   Administrative Shares

Share Name	Description
drive$	The root directory of every partition that is recognizable to Windows NT is assigned an administrative share name consisting of the drive letter, followed by $. Administrators, server operators, and backup operators may connect remotely to these shares. CD-ROMs do not count.
Admin$	Used by the operating system during remote administration of the computer. Represents the directory into which the Windows NT system files are installed (such as C:\WINNT40). Administrators, server operators, and backup operators may connect remotely to these shares.
IPC$	Represents the named pipes used for communication between programs and systems. Used by the operating system during remote administration of a computer and when accessing another computer's shared resources.
Netlogon	Created and used on domain controllers only to authenticate users who are logging on to the enterprise domain. This share is not hidden.
Print$	Similar to IPC$; provides remote access support for shared printers.
REPL$	Created and used on a Windows NT Server computer when the Directory Replication Service is configured and enabled. Identifies the location of the directories and files to be exported.

Hidden shares can be identified by the $ after the share name. As an administrator, you can view all the administrative shares on a computer by starting the Server applet from the Control Panel and viewing Shares (or by starting Server Manager on a Windows NT Server, viewing a computer's properties, and then its Shares).

CH
6

Key Concept

You also can create hidden shares personally by adding $ to the end of the share name that you enter. This is a way to keep certain shares more secure. The only users who can connect to these shares are those who know the share name.

Accessing a Shared Folder

Users can access a shared folder in several ways (assuming they have been given permission to do so). Shares can be accessed by connecting directly to the resource through Network Neighborhood or the Find command, or by mapping a drive letter to a shared folder through My Computer or Windows Explorer.

All four utilities offer a point-and-click method of accessing the resource, which means that you do not necessarily have to know exactly where the resource is located. The Computer Browser Service (see Chapter 12, "Windows NT Networking Services") provides the lists of domains, computers, and resources that you see. With Network Neighborhood and Find, you do not waste a drive letter on the resource. With My Computer and Windows Explorer, you use a drive letter for every mapping that you create—and the alphabet is not an unlimited list. Explorer, Network Neighborhood, and Find will not locate hidden shares.

Network Neighborhood

Perhaps the easiest way to connect to a shared folder is to use Network Neighborhood, especially if you need only occasional or short-term access to the folder and its contents (see Fig. 6.5).

To connect to a shared folder by using Network Neighborhood, follow these steps:

1. Double-click Network Neighborhood.
2. All members of your domain are listed under Entire Network. To see members of other domains, double-click Entire Network, then The Microsoft Network, and select the domain from the list.
3. To display a list of the domain's shared folders, double-click the computer that has the shared folder.
4. Double-click the appropriate share name to see the contents of that folder.

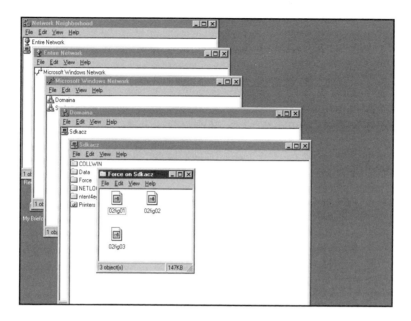

Figure 6.5
Network Neighborhood is used here to display the contents of the Force folder shared
on the computer SDKACZ in DOMAINA.

Find Command

You can use the Find command on the Start menu to search for computers that do not
show up right away in a browse list (such as the list Network Neighborhood displays). Or
you can use Find to search for a specific file or folder in a shared folder when you cannot
recall the name of that folder.

To find a computer, follow these steps:

1. Choose Start, Find, and then Computer from the taskbar.

2. In the Computer Name box, enter the name of the computer that has the shared
   folder.

3. Choose Find Now. Find displays a window that shows the computer it finds.

4. Double-click the computer to display its shared folders.

5. Double-click the appropriate share name to display its contents.

CH
6

To find a file or folder by name, follow these steps:

1. Choose Start, Find, and then Files or Folders from the taskbar.

2. In the Look In box, enter the name of the computer that contains the shared folder. Or, you can choose Browse to browse the Network Neighborhood entry to find the computer.

3. In the Named box, enter the name of the file or folder for which you are looking.

4. Choose Find Now. Find displays a window with its search results. Double-click the appropriate file or folder to work with it.

Key Concept

Several Find options, such as Date Modified and Advanced, are available to help narrow your search. If you are looking for a folder contained only in some particular share on a computer, for example, use Advanced to narrow the search only to folders.

My Computer and Windows Explorer

You can use My Computer to map a network drive to a shared folder on a computer. This is similar to the way logical drives are assigned to Novell NetWare resources (see Fig. 6.6).

Figure 6.6

Making the same connection as in Figure 6.5 to Force on SDKACZ.

Using Windows Explorer probably is most similar to using File Manager in previous versions of Windows NT or Windows for Workgroups. Windows Explorer displays a Map Network Drive dialog box similar to that used with My Computer, and in fact, it operates in much the same way.

To map to a shared folder by using Network Neighborhood, follow these steps:

1. Right-click My Computer and choose Map <u>N</u>etwork Drive. Or, you can start Windows Explorer, choose <u>T</u>ools from the menu, and then <u>M</u>ap Network Drive.

2. The next available drive letter appears in the <u>D</u>rive drop-down list box. Select it or choose another letter.

3. Double-click the appropriate network entry in the <u>S</u>hared Directories list box to display a browse list of workgroups and domains.

4. Double-click the workgroup or domain that contains the sharing computer to display a list of computers with shared resources.

5. Double-click the appropriate computer to display its list of shared resources.

6. Select the appropriate shared folder from the list.

If you do not see the computer or folder in the browse list but know the name of the computer and share, follow these steps:

1. Right-click My Computer and choose Map <u>N</u>etwork Drive. Or, you can start Windows Explorer, choose <u>T</u>ools from the menu, and then <u>M</u>ap Network Drive.

2. The next available drive letter appears in the <u>D</u>rive drop-down list box. Select it or choose another letter.

3. In the <u>P</u>ath drop-down list box, enter the UNC name to the shared folder by using the convention \\server\share, where server is the name of the computer that has the shared folder, and share is the name of the shared folder.

4. Click OK.

Notice that the <u>R</u>econnect at Logon check box in Figure 6.6 may be selected. This is known as a *persistent connection*. When a user maps a drive through Windows NT Workstation 4.0, this option is selected by default. If you select this box, drive J is reconnected to the share every time the user logs on. If this is a resource that the user accesses frequently, this is a convenient tool. If the user does not access this resource frequently, you are just taking up extra system resources to locate the shared folder, make the connection, and monitor for access.

CH
6

Key Concept

When mapped drives are no longer needed, you can disconnect them by right-clicking My Computer and then choosing <u>D</u>isconnect Network Drive. Or you can choose <u>D</u>isconnect Network Drive from the Windows Explorer's <u>T</u>ools menu. Select the drive from the list that you want to disconnect and choose OK.

Likewise, you may need to access a resource on a computer on which you do not have a valid user account. This situation is possible particularly in workgroup configurations, or in the case of administrative access to various workstations or servers. If you know the name and password of a valid user account on that computer (including Guest), you can enter the UNC name in the Path box (as described in Step 3 of the preceding list), and then enter the name of the valid account in the <u>C</u>onnect As box. Windows NT asks you for the password, if it is required or different from your own, before connecting you to the resource.

Securing Folders and Files with NTFS Permissions

Up to this point, you have learned how to make resources available to other network users, how to secure those resources that you share on the network, and how to access those resources. Another level of security can be applied to files and folders stored on an NTFS partition. Among the many benefits of formatting a partition as NTFS (Windows NT's own file system) is the capability to assign permissions directly to the file and folder—that is, at the resource level.

Permissions are set for a file or folder by right-clicking the file or folder, displaying its Properties dialog box, and selecting the Security tab. Choosing Permissions here displays the File or Folders Permissions dialog box, from which you can make your choices.

Effective File and Folder Permissions

When you assign permissions to a folder or file, you are creating an ACL for that folder or file, much like you did for the share. The Security Reference Monitor checks the user's access token against the entries in the ACL, as you learned earlier. When the Security Reference Monitor identifies a match or matches, it then must determine the permissions to give the user. The effective file or folder permissions are cumulative. The permissions explicitly assigned to a user, as well as permissions assigned to any groups in which the user is a member, are added together, and the highest level of permission is granted to the user at the file or folder level.

Suppose that BrownC is a member of Managers and Sales. For a particular file, BrownC has been given Change access, Managers has been given Full Control, and Sales has been given Read access. BrownC's effective permission level for that file is Full Control, by virtue of his membership in the Managers group.

The only exception to this rule is No Access. No Access always supersedes any other permission—even Full Control. Using the same example, if BrownC explicitly is given No Access, he cannot access the file, even though he is a member of the Managers group, which has Full Control.

Unlike share permissions, which are effective for all files and folders within the share, folder and file permissions are effective only for the immediate folder and its contents, or for an individual file, if applied to that file. The permissions for files in a folder, or for subfolders, can trickle down but also can be applied individually. If permissions have been applied to an individual file, the file permission always supersedes the folder permission.

For example, if BrownC has been given Read permission for the folder DATA and Change permission for the file budget.doc, BrownC's effective permission for the file budget.doc is Change because of his folder permission, even though he has only Read access to all the other files in DATA.

As you can see, you have a great deal of discretion, flexibility, and control over the application of permissions to folders, subfolders, and files. It is important, therefore, that you take sufficient time to plan your folder and file permissions. For example, take another look at the home directory folders. Suppose that users' home directories are created under a share called Users. By default, Users is shared to Everyone with Full Control. If the home folders are on an NTFS partition, you can assign each user the NTFS permission Full Control to his or her own home folder only, while assigning the Everyone group List access to the directory. This effectively restricts access to each folder to only the owner of the folder.

Key Concept

If you create the users' home directories on an NTFS partition by using the %USERNAME% variable and NT's User Manager utility (see Chapter 5, "Managing Users and Groups"), Windows NT automatically restricts access to the home directory so that only this specific user account can access the directory.

Assigning File and Folder Permissions

Table 6.3 describes the six individual permissions you can apply to files and folders.

Table 6.3 NTFS File and Folder Permissions		
Permission	Folder Level	File Level
Read (R)	Can display folders, attributes, owner, and permissions	Can display files and file data, attributes, owner, and permissions
Write (W)	Can add files and create subfolders, change folder attributes, and display folder owner and permissions	Can change file contents and attributes, and display file owner and permissions
Execute (E)	Can make changes to subfolders, and display folder owner, attributes, and permissions	Can run executable files and display file owner, attributes, and permissions
Delete (D)	Can delete a folder	Can delete a file
Change Permission (P)	Can change folder permissions	Can change file permissions
Take Ownership (O)	Can take ownership of a folder	Can take ownership of a file

Files and folders can be assigned these permissions individually or, more often, by using standard groupings provided by Windows NT security. There are nine standard folder permissions, which include two choices for setting your own custom choice of folder permissions and file permissions to apply to all files in a folder. There are five standard file permissions, which include an option for setting your own custom choice of file permissions per individual file. Tables 6.4 and 6.5 outline these permissions and what they allow the user to do.

Note that when viewing and setting permissions, Windows NT always displays the individual permissions in parentheses alongside the standard permission. For folder permissions, the first set of parentheses represents the permissions on the folder, and the second set represents the permissions that apply to files globally, including any new file created in the folder.

Table 6.4   Standard Permissions for Folders

Permission	Access
No Access (None)(None)	Supersedes all other file permissions and prevents access to the file.
List (RX)(Not Specified)	Allows the user to view folders and subfolders, and filenames within folders and subfolders. List is not available as a valid permission option for files.
Read (RX)(RX)	In addition to List access, the user can display file contents and sub-folders, and run executable files.
Add (WX)(Not Specified)	The user can add files to the folder, but not list its contents. Add is not available as a valid permission option for files.
Add and Read (RWX)(RX)	In addition to Add, the user can display the contents of files and subfolders, and run executable files.
Change (RWXD)(RWXD)	Allows the user to display and add files and folders, modify the contents of files and folders, and run executable files.
Full Control (All)(All)	In addition to Change, the user is given the capability to modify folder and file permissions, and to take ownership of folders and files.
Special Directory Access	Allows the selection of any combination of individual permissions (R, W, E, D, P, O) for folder access.
Special File Access	Allows the selection of any combination of individual permissions (R, W, E, D, P, O) for file access.

Table 6.5   Standard Permissions for Files

Permission	Access
No Access (None)	No access is allowed to the file.
Read (RX)	Allows the user to display file data and run executable files.
Change (RWXD)	In addition to Read, the user can modify the file contents and delete the file entirely.
Full Control (All)	In addition to Change, the user can modify the file's permissions and take ownership of the file.
Special Access	Allows the selection of any combination of individual permissions (R, W, E, D, P, O) for a file.

CH
6

Key Concept

The folder permission Full Control allows the user to delete files in a folder through the command prompt, even if the user is given No Access permission to a specific file. This is done to preserve Posix application support on UNIX systems, for which Write permission on a folder enables the user to delete files in the folder. This can be superseded by choosing the Special Directory Access standard permission and checking all the individual permissions.

You set permissions for a file or folder by right-clicking the file or folder, displaying its Properties dialog box, and selecting the Security tab. Choosing Permissions here displays the File or Folder Permissions dialog box, from which you can make your choices (see Fig. 6.7).

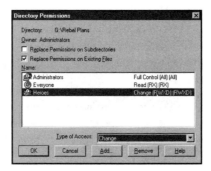

Figure 6.7
The Force folder's ACL shows that Administrators have Full Control access, Everyone has Read access, and Heroes has Change access. The Type of Access drop-down list box displays the standard permission options.

Notice that the Directory Permissions dialog box offers two Replace choices: Replace Permissions on Subdirectories and Replace Permissions on Existing Files (which is enabled by default).

Key Concept

The effect of Replace Permissions on Existing Files is to change any and all permissions that you have set on individual files to the permissions that you have set at the folder level. Because this check box is enabled by default, it is easy to forget when setting permissions at the folder level, and you can accidentally change permissions on files that you do not want to change. Bottom line: Read all screens carefully.

Choosing Replace Permissions on Subdirectories causes Windows NT to apply the permissions set at this folder level to all subfolders. Any new files added to the folder assume the folder's permissions. If Replace Permissions on Existing Files also is left enabled, the permissions are applied not only to the subfolders, but also to their contents.

The Type of Access drop-down list box shows all the standard permissions that are available at the folder level, including the two special options, Special Directory Access and Special File Access, from which you can customize your choice of permissions.

As with share permissions, users and groups can be added or removed from the ACL by clicking the Add or Remove button.

Determining Access When Using Share and NTFS Permissions

A folder (and its contents) is made accessible across the network by sharing it. As discussed, you can create an ACL for the share. The ACL defines which users and group accounts can access the share, and the level of access permitted. You know that the effective permissions are cumulative at the share level.

When you assign NTFS permissions to individual folders and files, you can further refine the level of access by creating an ACL at the file and folder level. You know that the effective permissions at the file and folder level also are cumulative.

When a user accesses a file or folder protected by NTFS permissions across the network through a share, the Security Reference Monitor determines the cumulative permissions at the share and the cumulative permissions at the file or folder. Whichever permission is most restrictive becomes the effective permission for the user.

For example, if BrownC, a member of the Managers group, has been given Read access individually and Change access through the Managers group to a share called Public, then BrownC's effective permission for the share Public is Change. If BrownC has been given Read access to a file budget.doc (contained in the folder that has been shared as Public) and Full Control through the Managers group, BrownC's effective permission at the file level is Full Control. However, BrownC's net effective permission to budget.doc, when accessing it through the network share, is Change, which is the more restrictive of the two permissions.

	Budget.doc Accessed Through the Public Share	Budget.doc File Level
BrownCRead	Read	Read

CH
6

Managers	+ Change	+ Full Control
Effective ChangePermissions	Change	Full Control (more restrictive than Full Control)

Through shrewd use of share- and file/folder-level permissions, you can create a very effective security structure for resources stored on your Windows NT Workstations and Servers.

Understanding the Concept of Ownership

The user who creates a file or folder is considered by Windows NT to be the owner of that file or folder; therefore that user's name is placed in the Creator Owner internal group for that file or folder. Users cannot give someone else ownership of their files or folders. However, users can give someone the permission to take ownership of their files and folders.

The Take Ownership permission is implied through Full Control but also can be assigned to a user or group through the Special Access permission options. A user who has this permission can take ownership of the file or folder. After the user takes ownership, the new owner can modify the file or folder's permissions, delete the file, and so on. Administrators always have the capability to take ownership of a file or folder. All ownership changes are logged in the Security Log.

A user who has the Take Ownership permission can take ownership of a folder or file by following these steps:

1. Right-click the folder or file and choose Properties.
2. In the Properties dialog box, select the Security tab.
3. On the Security tab, choose Ownership. The name of the current owner appears.
4. Choose Take Ownership, and then choose OK.

Key Concept

If any member of the Administrators group takes ownership of a file or folder, or creates a file or folder, the owner becomes the Administrators group.

Taking ownership of files and folders can be useful, especially when users move around from department to department or position to position, or leave the organization permanently. Taking ownership provides a way to assign an appropriate replacement for the files and folders that are no longer being used by a user.

Copying and Moving Files ... and Permissions

When you copy a file from one folder to another, the file assumes the permissions of the target folder. When you move a file from one folder to another, the file maintains its current permissions. This sounds simple enough, except that a move isn't always a move. When you move a file from a folder in one partition to a folder in another partition, you actually are copying the file to the target folder, and then deleting the original file. When permissions are involved, a move is considered a move only when you move a file from a folder in one partition to another folder in the same partition.

Managing Shares and Permissions Remotely

As an administrator, you can create and manage shares and set permissions for folders and files remotely. If you are working on a Windows NT–based computer, simply map a drive to the hidden drive share—for example, D$—and then proceed as described earlier in this chapter, in "Assigning File and Folder Permissions."

If you have installed Server Tools on your computer, you also can use Server Manager to manage shares. Server Manager displays a list of the Windows NT–based domain controllers, member servers, and workstations in your domain. Manage shares by following these steps:

1. Select the computer on which you want to manage the share from the computer list.

2. Choose Computer, Shared Directories to display the Shared Directories dialog box (see Fig. 6.8).

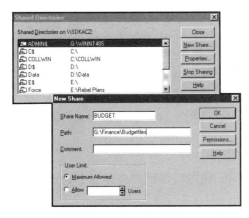

CH
6

Figure 6.8
Server Manager enables an administrator to create and manage shares remotely on Windows NT computers in the domain.

3. Click New Share. In the New Share dialog box, enter a share name and folder path (there is no Browse feature here). Click Permissions to set permissions, and click OK to return to the New Share dialog box. Then click OK to return to the Shared Directories dialog box.

4. Select an existing share from the Shared Directories list, and then click Properties to modify the share's current properties, such as permissions.

5. Select an existing share from the Shared Directories list and then click Stop Sharing to remove the share.

6. Choose Close to save your changes.

If you have administrative access to other domains, through either a valid administrator's account or a trust relationship, you also can remotely administer shares on Windows NT computers in that domain. Follow these steps to switch to that domain:

1. Choose Computer, Select Domain to display the Select Domain dialog box.

2. Select the appropriate domain from the Select Domain list, or enter the domain name in the Domain text box.

3. Click OK. The Server Manager screen refreshes and lists computers in the selected domain.

4. Manage shares as outlined in the steps at the beginning of this section.

File-Level Auditing

File-level auditing allows an administrator to review the Security Log with Event Viewer to determine who may have created, deleted, or modified a specified file or directory. You can use this feature to identify problems in the security model implemented in a domain. To set up file-level auditing, follow these two steps:

1. Enable File and Object Access Auditing in the domain's audit policy. A member of the Administrators local group must enable this auditing feature.

2. Enable the detail of file-level auditing you want to use on specific file and directory objects on an NTFS volume.

Administrators and any users or groups that have been assigned the User Right Manage Auditing and Security Log can set auditing on specific directories and review the Security Log for audit successes and failures.

To set up auditing on a specific directory or file on an NTFS volume, you must bring up the Properties dialog box for that directory or file object. Then select the Security tab of the object and click the Auditing button to set the auditing levels for that object.

You can audit these actions:

Enable This Event	To Determine
Read	Whether an attempt was made to open a file.
Write	When a user attempted to modify the contents of a file.
Execute	When a user attempted to run a program.
Delete	When a user attempted to delete a file object.
Change Permissions	When a user tried to change the permissions on a file or directory.
Take Ownership	When a user attempted to take ownership of a file or directory object.

Troubleshooting Security

The problem you most likely will have with security is a user being unable to access a resource. You must attempt to isolate possible sources of the error. To begin with, have the user log off and then log back on. If this doesn't work, try logging on as that user locally (on the machine providing the resource). If logging on locally works (the user has access), you need to check the share-level permissions. If logging on locally doesn't work, the ACL for that resource is probably in error. You need to carefully check all groups and users in the ACL. Remember, when comparing share permissions to file and folder permissions, Windows NT assigns the most restrictive permission to the user.

When changing permissions on a share, file, or folder, the user will not notice the effect of the change until the next time the resource is accessed. This is because of the way in which Windows NT assigns the permission to the user. Recall that, when the user's access token is compared to the ACL and the effective permission is established, the user's access token receives a permission handle to the resource. This handle remains effective until the user releases the resource.

For example, suppose that BrownC has Change permission to budget.doc. The owner of budget.doc decides to restrict BrownC to Read permission. While BrownC has budget.doc open and in use, the effective permission remains Change. When BrownC closes budget.doc and opens it later, the effective permission changes to Read.

Suppose that BrownC has established a logical drive mapping to the Data share and has Change permission to the share. The owner of the share changes BrownC's permission to Read. BrownC maintains Change permission to the share until disconnecting and reconnecting to the share, or until logging off and logging back on to the share.

In another case, suppose that BrownC is currently a member of the Managers group. BrownC has Read permission to the Data folder but Full Control permission through BrownC's membership in the Managers group. You take BrownC out of the Managers group to ensure

CH
6

that he or she has only Read access to the folder. When BrownC accesses the folder, he or she still has Full Control access to the folder, because BrownC's access token still maintains that he or she has membership in the Managers group. Remember that the access token is created during logon. Thus, the group change is not effective until BrownC logs off and logs back on.

Remote Server Tools

Administrators use Server Tools to administer domain controllers from remote locations. It is quite possible for a domain to be spread out among a number of buildings, towns, cities, or even countries. User and group account changes and additions, password changes, and other administrative duties all are included in the domain administrative functions.

You may recall that to make any change in a directory services database in a domain, an administrator must be located at a domain controller. Even if the administrator is sitting at a *backup domain controller* (BDC), the change is physically made in the database on the *primary domain controller* (PDC). It is possible that not all locations of the domain have a domain controller present. Depending on the location of PDCs and BDCs, it is almost impossible for an administrator to always be at a domain location where a domain controller is located, or to always be in one place and make all database changes from one location.

With Server Tools, an administrator can be physically located at any client computer and still be able to perform a number of domain administrative duties. Server Tools also eliminate the need for a domain controller at each and every remote domain location, thereby lowering the overall cost of required software in the domain.

The reason Server Tools originally were made available for a number of Microsoft clients was to alleviate the problem of the administrator always having to be located at a domain controller in order to administer a domain.

System Requirements

As with any software or utilities, Server Tools require system resources to be installed and to function correctly. The following sections summarize the system requirements for the various client platforms.

Required Resources for Windows NT 4.0 Workstation

The following resources are required to install Server Tools on a Windows NT 4.0 Workstation:

- Microsoft Windows NT 4.0 Workstation software installed
- 486DX/33 or higher CPU
- 12MB of memory
- 2.5MB of free hard drive space
- Workstation and Server Services installed

Required Resources for Windows 95

The following resources are required to install Server Tools on a Windows 95 computer:

- Microsoft Windows 95 installed
- 486/33 or higher CPU
- 8MB of memory
- 3MB of free hard drive space
- Client for Microsoft Networks installed

Required Resources for Windows 3.1 or Windows for Workgroups 3.11

The following resources are required to install Server Tools on Windows 3.1 or Windows for Workgroups 3.11:

- Microsoft Windows 3.1 or Windows for Workgroups 3.11 installed. Both must be running in 386 enhanced mode and have paging (virtual memory—either a permanent or temporary swap file) enabled.
- 8MB of memory
- 5MB of free hard drive space
- The Microsoft Redirector installed

In addition to these requirements, the FILES statement in config.sys must be set to at least 50.

CH
6

Windows NT 4.0 Workstation Server Tools

The following 32-bit Server Tools are available for Windows NT 4.0 Workstation:

- User Manager for Domains
- Server Manager
- System Policy Editor
- Remote Access Administrator
- Services for Macintosh
- DHCP Manager
- WINS Manager
- Remoteboot Manager

After these tools are installed on a Windows NT 4.0 Workstation, they function exactly the same as they do on a Windows NT 4.0 Server installation.

Key Concept

Server Tools installed on a Windows NT 3.5/3.51 Workstation are the same as for a Windows NT 4.0 Workstation, with the exception of System Policy Editor. User Profile Editor is installed on Windows NT 3.5/3.51 instead.

Installing Workstation Server Tools

Installing Server Tools on a Windows NT 4.0 Workstation is relatively easy and can be accomplished in a number of ways. All the required files for any platform for Windows NT 4.0 Workstation are located on the Windows NT 4.0 Server CD-ROM in the CLIENTS\SRVTOOLS\WINNT folder.

Installing from the CD-ROM

Installation can be accomplished simply by accessing the Windows NT 4.0 Server CD-ROM and running the Setup.bat file in the CLIENTS\SRVTOOLS\WINNT folder. The Setup.bat file determines the architecture of the client computer and copies all the Server Tools files and supporting files to the <winntroot>\System32 folder. The Setup file will not create an Administrative Tools program group on the Workstation platform. If you want a specific program group, you must create it manually.

Figure 6.9 shows what events take place when the Setup.bat file executes. Notice that it does display the .exe files that can be included manually in a program group. It does not, however, display the support files loaded with the executables.

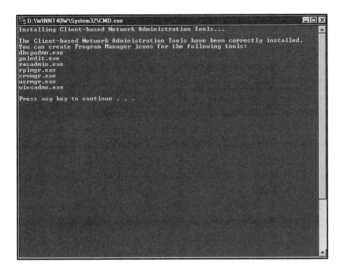

Figure 6.9
The Windows NT 4.0 Workstation Server Tools files.

Creating a Server Tools Share Using Network Client Administrator

The Network Client Administrator application, located on Windows NT 4.0 Server, is a tool used to perform four functions. One of these functions is related to Windows NT 4.0 Server Tools. The Copy Client-Based Network Administration Tools option simply copies the CLIENT\SRVTOOLS folder to a specified location on a network and creates a share for that location. The default location is <diskdrive>\CLIENTS\SRVTOOLS, and the default share name of the SRVTOOLS folder is SetupAdm. From this share, the tools can be installed on any Windows NT 4.0 client workstation computer that can map to or access the share.

You invoke the Network Client Administrator by accessing the Administrative Tools program group on a server and clicking the Network Client Administrator selection. After Network Client Administrator starts, the Network Client Administrator dialog box appears, displaying the four options available. By selecting the third option, Copy Client-Based Network Administration Tools, and then clicking Continue, the Share Client-Based Administration Tools dialog box appears (see Fig. 6.10). Enter the path where the Server Tools files are located, such as a CD-ROM location (<CD-ROM drive>\CLIENTS) or a network location (\\<computername>\<rauth2sharename>\clients). Select the Copy Files to a New Directory, and Then Share option. After you click OK, the files are copied to the specified location.

CH
6

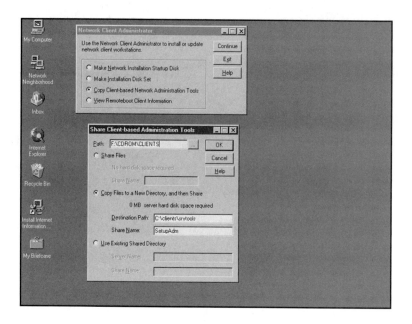

Figure 6.10
The Network Client Administrator and Share Client-Based Administration Tools dialog boxes.

Upon completion of the file copy, a Network Client Administrator information box appears stating how many directories and files were copied; click OK to continue. Next, the srvtools folder is shared, and another Network Client Administrator information box appears, stating that the Network Administration tools now are available in a shared directory; click OK to continue.

Installing Server Tools from a Network Share

When a network share is created with the Network Client Administration application, simply map a client computer to that share. For example, right-click My Computer or Network Neighborhood, select Map Network Drive, and type the path or select the path from the shared directories window (<computername>\SetupAdm).

From the mapped drive, either in Explorer or My Computer, select the WINNT folder and execute the Setup.bat file. Refer to Figure 6.10 for an illustration of the events that take place.

Windows 95 Server Tools

The following 32-bit Server Tools are available for Windows 95:

- User Manager for Domains
- Server Manager
- Event Viewer
- User Manager Extensions for Services for NetWare
- File and Print Services for NetWare (FPNW)

Key Concept

User Manager Extensions for Services for NetWare will be installed only if FPNW or DSNW is installed.

File and Print Services for NetWare will be installed only if FPNW is installed.

In addition, a File Security tab and a Print Security tab are available to establish file, folder, and print permissions.

When these tools are installed on a Windows 95 computer, they function exactly the same as they do on a Windows NT 4.0 Server installation.

Installing Windows 95 Server Tools

Installing the Windows NT Server Tools on a Windows 95 platform requires a few more steps than the Windows NT Workstation version. First of all, the source files must be made available; either the Windows NT 4.0 Server CD-ROM or a network share can be used.

Next, on the Windows 95 computer, access the Control Panel and double-click the Add/Remove Programs icon. After the Add/Remove Programs Properties dialog box appears, select the Windows Setup tab, and then click the Have Disk button. After the Install from Disk dialog box appears, supply the path to the source files, such as <computername>\SetupAdm\Win95 if the files are on the network, or <CdromDriveLetter>\clients\Srvtools\Win95 if the Windows NT 4.0 Server CD-ROM is being used. Click OK.

Next, a Have Disk dialog box appears, asking you to select the check box next to the Windows NT Server Tools item in the Components list box if you want to install the Server Tools (see Fig. 6.11).

CH
6

Figure 6.11
The Have Disk dialog box is part of the Windows 95 Server Tools installation procedure.

After you select the check box, click the Install button and the Windows NT 4.0 Server Tools will be installed. After the tools are installed, a new selection appears in the Start, Programs group.

Figure 6.12 shows the Add/Remove Programs Properties dialog box with the Windows Setup tab selected, after the Server Tools are installed (note the added selection in the Components list box).

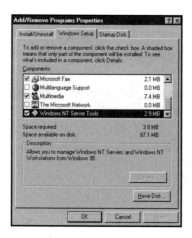

Figure 6.12
The Windows Setup tab in the Add/Remove Programs Properties dialog box.

Windows 3.1 and Windows for Workgroups 3.11 Server Tools

The following 16-bit Server Tools are available for Windows 3.1 and Windows for Workgroups 3.11 installations:

- User Manager for Domains
- Server Manager
- Event Viewer
- Print Manager for Windows NT Server
- File Manager Security menu

Installing Windows 3.1 and Windows for Workgroups 3.11 Server Tools

To install Windows NT Server Tools on a Windows 3.1 or Windows for Workgroups 3.11 platform, the source files must be made available, as mentioned previously in the section "Installation of Windows 95 Server Tools." The Server Tools for these two platforms are located on the Windows NT 3.5/3.51 Server CD-ROM in the Clients\Srvtools directory. The Srvtools directory on this CD-ROM has two subdirectories; one is the Windows directory, and the other is the WINNT directory. The Setup.exe program in the Windows directory is used for the Windows or Windows for Workgroups Server Tools installation. After Setup is run, the Server Tools are available in the Windows NT Server Tools program group.

When Setup.exe is run, a Windows NT Server Tools Setup screen appears, with a Welcome dialog box that gives you the choices to Continue, Exit, or get Help. It also informs you that the Microsoft Win32s and *Remote Procedure Call* (RPC) components and the Windows NT Server Tools will be installed. Clicking Continue displays an Installation Options dialog box, where you decide to do either a Custom Install or Install All Files. You also can change the default installation path of C:\SRVTOOLS from this window. Clicking Continue proceeds with the server tool installation.

The next window that appears is the Time Zone Setup dialog box. Select the correct time zone and click Continue.

Next, the Microsoft Win32s Setup Target Directory dialog box appears, informing you where various components will be installed. Click Continue.

From this point, the files are copied. When the copying is complete, a Windows NT Server Tools Setup dialog box appears, informing you that some system changes will take effect when the system reboots. Clicking OK displays the final dialog box, which informs you that the installation was successful and that you should reboot your system. Click Continue to reboot.

Key Concept

Two files of importance are located in the `<default>\SRVTOOLS` directory: `new-conf.sys` and `new-vars.bat`. You must add the following statements in these two files to the existing `config.sys` and `autoexec.bat`, respectively, and then reboot the system:

```
New-conf.sys includes FILES=50
New-vars.bat includes PATH=<default>\SRVTOOLS and SET TZ=UTC+0DST
```

If you do not make these changes, File Manager will not offer a Security drop-down menu.

Summary

In this chapter, you learned about security and managing network resources. Additional topics covered file-level auditing and troubleshooting security.

Chapter 7, "Managing Disk Resources," focuses on a different aspect of computer and user management—working with the physical system itself.

QUESTIONS AND ANSWERS

1. A list of users and groups that can access a resource is maintained by the resource in its _____.

    A: Access control list (ACL)

2. When a user logs on, he or she is assigned an _____.

    A: Access token. The token then is compared with the resource's ACL to determine whether that user can access that resource.

3. The four share-level permissions available are _____, _____, _____, and _____.

    A: Read, Change, Full Control, and No Access

4. Of all the administrative shares created by default, the only one not hidden is _____.

    A: NetLogon.

5. True or false: Ownership requires NTFS and not FAT.

    A: True. Ownership is an extensible attribute—it requires NTFS and cannot be employed on the FAT file system.

PRACTICE TEST

1. The manager of the Accounting department wants to make next year's budget templates available for the staff accountants to review beginning next month. Staff accountants are all members of the Accountants global group in CORPDOMAIN. The templates will be stored on the department resource server called ACCT1 in a folder called BUDGET97. None of the partitions on ACCT1 are formatted with NTFS. How would you make the folder available only to the Accounting department staff?

   a. Use User Manager for Domains to create a local group on the resource server called Accountants. Make the global Accountants group a member of the local Accountants group. Assign permission to use the folder to the Accountants group through User Manager for Domains.

   b. Use User Manager for Domains to create a local group on the resource server called Accountants. Make the global Accountants group a member of the local Accountants group. Assign the appropriate user rights to the Accountants group to access the BUDGET97 share.

   c. Use User Manager for Domains to create a local group on the resource server called Accountants. Make the global Accountants group a member of the local Accountants group. Use the Security tab on the Properties dialog box for the folder to assign permissions to the Accountants group.

   d. Use User Manager for Domains to create a local group on the resource server called Accountants. Make the global Accountants group a member of the local Accountants group. Use the Sharing tab on the Properties dialog box for the folder to assign permissions to the Accountants group.

Answer a is incorrect. The Sharing tab is needed, and not User Manager for Domains. Answer b is incorrect. User Rights need not be involved. Answer c is incorrect. The Sharing tab (and not the Security tab) is needed. **Answer d is correct. The Sharing tab allows these actions to transpire.**

2. The manager of the Accounting department wants to make next year's budget templates available for the staff accountants to review beginning next month. Staff accountants are all members of the global group Accountants in the domain CORP-DOMAIN. The templates will be stored on the department resource server, called ACCT1, in a folder called BUDGET97. A local group called Budget has been created to manage access to the budget templates. None of the partitions on ACCT1 are formatted with NTFS. How would you make the folder available only to the Accounting department staff? Choose all that apply.

a. Share the BUDGET97 directory.

b. Add the Accountants group to the ACL for the share.

c. Remove the Everyone group from the ACL for the share.

d. Give the Accountants group read and write permissions at the folder level.

Answer a is correct. The directory must be shared. Answer b is correct. The Accountants group must be added to the list of those who can share the directory. Answer c is correct. You must remove the Everyone group, or else the permissions here will apply to all users (including accountants). Answer d is incorrect because it does not meet the requirements.

3. A user's effective access to a resource is determined by

a. Comparing the rights of the user with the permissions assigned through the ACL of the resource.

b. Comparing the permissions in the access token of the user with the permissions assigned through the ACL of the resource.

c. Comparing the user and group SID entries in the user's access token with the permissions assigned through the ACL of the resource.

d. Comparing the user and group SID entries in the user's access token with the user rights listed in the ACL of the resource.

Answer a is incorrect. The access token is reviewed, not the rights. Answer b is incorrect. The access token is the entity examined. **Answer c is correct. A user's effective access to a resource comes from comparing the user and group SID entries in the user's access token with the permissions assigned through the ACL of the resource.** Answer d is incorrect; it is the access token that is scrutinized.

4. The Sales department recently acquired a laser-quality printer with an envelope feed that has been installed on its print server called SalesPrint. The Sales staff is already a member of the local group SALES on SalesPrint. The print operator shared the printer with the default permission. The Sales staff can access the printer, but so can everyone else in the domain. What else must you do to ensure that only the Sales staff can access the printer?

a. Assign the Sales group Print access to the printer.

b. Assign the Sales group Print access to the printer, and remove the Everyone group.

c. Do nothing else.

d. Assign the Sales group Print access to the printer, and give the Everyone group Read access.

Answer a is incorrect. This method still allows access to Everyone. **Answer b is correct. You must assign the Sales group Print access to the printer, and remove the Everyone group to allow access only to the Sales group.** Answer c is incorrect, because this method allows access to Everyone. Answer d is incorrect; Sales is a subset of Everyone.

   5. The permission list defining access to a resource resides
   - **a.** With the resource and is called the Access Control List.
   - **b.** With the user and is called the User Rights Policy.
   - **c.** With the user and is called the Access Control List.
   - **d.** With the resource and is called the User Rights Policy.

Answer a is correct. The permission list resides with the resource and is called the Access Control List (ACL). Answer b is incorrect, because the resource is the ACL. Answer c is incorrect, because the ACL stays with the resource. Answer d is incorrect because the resource is the ACL.

   6. Arlo, a member of the Developers group, currently is editing the file DOOM.DOC in the share TOOLS. The administrator of the share changes permission to the Developers group from Change to Read. Arlo continues to make changes to the document. What else must the administrator do to restrict Arlo's access?
   - **a.** Take Arlo out of the Developers group.
   - **b.** Give Arlo No Access explicitly.
   - **c.** Send Arlo a message to get his authorization.
   - **d.** Nothing. Arlo must disconnect from the share and then reconnect before the new permission takes effect.

Answer a is incorrect, because it does not solve the problem. Answer b is incorrect. It does not update the access token. Answer c is incorrect because it solves nothing. **Answer d is correct. It is only when the user disconnects and reconnects to the share that the new permissions apply.**

   7. The administrator of the TOOLS shared folder wants to limit access to the folder only to the Developers group. To accomplish this, she gives the Everyone group No Access, and the Developers group Change access. The Developers complain that they cannot access any file in TOOLS. What else must the administrator do?
   - **a.** Share the files in the TOOLS folder.
   - **b.** Remove the Everyone group.
   - **c.** Give the Developers group Full Control.
   - **d.** Format the partition as NTFS and assign NTFS permissions in addition to the share permissions.

CH 6

Answer a is incorrect, because those files already are shared. **Answer b is correct. Because Everyone includes all users and groups, it must be removed to avoid assigning No Access to the Developers group.** Answer c is incorrect, because Developers is a subset of Everyone. Answer d is incorrect; this method does not solve the problem.

8. Ned is a member of the Developers group at Springfield Technologies. This group recently was assigned additional responsibilities. As a result of the new assignments, Ned needs to edit the DOOM.DOC file in the TOOLS folder but does not have Write access. What must you do to give Ned—and other developers—access to DOOM.DOC?

    a. Do nothing. The next time Ned logs on, his permissions will change.
    b. Change the Developers group permission to Change.
    c. Add Ned to the Team Leaders group and have him log on again.
    d. Change the Team Leaders group permission to Full Control.

Answer a is incorrect; avoidance will not solve the problem. **Answer b is correct. Changing the Developers group permission to Change will solve this problem.** Answer c is incorrect. No Team Leaders group is mentioned. Answer d is incorrect. No Team Leaders group is mentioned.

9. The TOOLS folder has been shared to the Developers group with Change permission. DOOM is a subdirectory under TOOLS. Team leaders should have access only to DOOM with Read permissions. What can you do to accomplish this?

    a. Add Team Leaders to the TOOLS share with Read permission.
    b. Create a new share called DOOM and give Team Leaders Read permission to it.
    c. Add Team Leaders to the TOOLS share with Change permission.
    d. Add Team Leaders to the TOOLS share with No Access and to the DOOM subdirectory with Read.

Answer a is incorrect; the rights will accumulate. **Answer b is correct. Creating a new share called DOOM and giving Team Leaders Read permission to it will address the needs.** Answer c is incorrect because the rights will accumulate. Answer d is incorrect, because the Team Leaders still need access to TOOLS.

10. The manager of the Accounting department wants to make next year's budget templates available for the staff accountants to review beginning next month. Staff accountants already are members of a global group called Accountants in CORPDOMAIN. The templates will be stored on the department resource server, called ACCT1, in a folder called BUDGET97 on an NTFS partition. The folder has been shared with the default permission, which you do not want to change. How would you further secure the folder's contents so that it is available only to the Accounting department staff?

a. Use User Manager for Domains to create a local group on the resource server called Accountants. Make the global accountants group a member of the local accountants group. Assign the Accountants group permission to use the folder through User Manager for Domains.

b. Use User Manager for Domains to create a local group on the resource server called Accountants. Make the global accountants group a member of the local accountants group. Assign the appropriate user rights to the Accountants group to access the `BUDGET97` share.

c. Use User Manager for Domains to create a local group on the resource server called Accountants. Make the global Accountants group a member of the local Accountants group. Use the Security tab on the Properties dialog box for the folder to assign permissions to the Accountants group and remove the Everyone group.

d. Use User Manager for Domains to create a local group on the resource server called Accountants. Make the global accountants group a member of the local accountants group. Use the Sharing tab on the Properties dialog box for the folder to assign permissions to the Accountants group.

Answer a is incorrect, because it does not meet the requirements. Answer b is incorrect; it is not a valid solution. **Answer c is correct. Creating the appropriate groups/memberships and removing Everyone from the access will solve the problem.** Answer d is incorrect, because it does not solve the problem.

Managing Disk Resources

WHILE YOU READ

1. NTFS supports disks to a theoretical size of _____.

2. You can accomplish file compression from the command line with what utility?

3. The type of backup that includes only files and folders that have changed since the last backup and sets their archive bit off is _____.

4. True or false: You can automate backups with the CRON utility included with NT.

5. True or false: You can use the backup utility included with Windows NT Server 4.0 to back up the local Registry.

This chapter teaches you how to optimize your management of disk resources. It discusses

- Partition support and management
- The Disk Administrator utility
- NT file system support
- The effect of long filenames
- Stripe sets and volume sets
- Microsoft's Backup and Restore utility

Understanding Partitions

Before you can use a computer effectively, you must install an operating system. Before you can install an operating system, you must partition the computer's hard disk(s) into the storage space required by the operating system and the user. You also must format the disk(s) with a file system supported by the operating system, such as a *file allocation table* (FAT).

Many types of partitions are supported by NT 4.0 Workstation and Server. The most common partitions you will encounter are primary and extended. Others include volume sets and stripe sets. NT 4.0 Server adds fault-tolerant partition options, such as stripe sets with parity and disk mirroring.

In MS-DOS, the primary partition contains the boot files needed to start MS-DOS and initialize the system. The primary partition is also called the *active partition,* and it cannot be subdivided any further. Under NT 4.0, a primary partition usually holds the operating system files for NT or an alternative operating system, but it also can simply designate another data or application storage place. Up to four primary partitions are supported per physical disk device under NT 4.0. MS-DOS recognizes only one primary partition per physical disk device. To boot to MS-DOS (or Windows 95), the primary partition must be marked as the active partition.

An extended partition offers a way to get beyond the four-drive-per-physical-disk limit and subdivide a partition into more than four logical drives. Consequently, an extended partition usually consists of the remaining free space on a disk after the primary partition is created. Because MS-DOS recognizes only one primary (active) partition per physical disk, logical drives in an extended partition provide a way to support a larger number of "drives" under MS-DOS. A logical drive is virtually the same as a partition, except that, from the point of view of MS-DOS and NT, a logical drive is a division within a partition. Using logical drives enables the disk administrator to have greater control and flexibility over the storage of applications and data on the physical disk.

There is also the matter of simple arithmetic in the way that NT counts partitions. This becomes more of a concern for NT when the partition scheme changes frequently, or when troubleshooting with a boot disk among a variety of NT computers, because it involves the *advanced RISC computer* (ARC) path to the NT system files.

The ARC path—as you may recall from Chapter 3, "Windows NT Server 4.0 Setup"—specifies the physical location of the partition that contains the NT operating system files (the WINNT40 installation directory). Here is an example of an ARC path used by the BOOT.INI file:

```
multi(0)disk(0)rdisk(0)partition(2)\WINNT40
```

According to this path, the WINNT40 directory is located on the second partition—partition(2)—of the first physical drive—disk(0)rdisk(0)—attached to the first physical controller card—multi(0). Because the ARC path involves the physical path, which includes the controller, disk device, and partition number, if partition schemes change frequently, it is possible that the partition number of the NT system partition also could change.

NT always counts the active primary partition first, or the first primary partition on each additional physical disk, then other primary partitions from the first to the last physical disk, and then the logical drives from the first physical disk to the last (see Fig. 7.1).

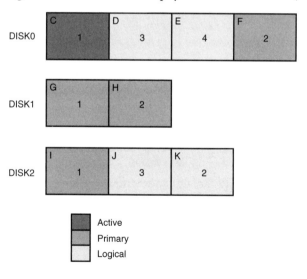

Figure 7.1

In this partition scheme, you see primary, extended, and logical partitions. They are numbered as NT would number them when it boots. Notice that primary partitions are counted before logical drives in an extended partition.

Key Concept

NT refers to the partition from which the computer system boots as the *system partition,* and the partition that holds the system files as the *boot partition.*

Exploring File System Support in NT 4.0

After the partition scheme is decided and applied to the physical disk(s), the disk(s) must be formatted with a file system the operating system can understand. MS-DOS and Windows 95 support the FAT file system. NT supports FAT and its own *New Technology File System* (NTFS). All three support the *CD-ROM File System* (CDFS). NT 4.0 does not support Windows 95 FAT32.

Key Concept

Previous versions of NT provided support for IBM OS/2's *High-Performance File System* (HPFS). This support no longer is available under Windows NT 4.0.

An Overview of FAT

FAT support under NT is somewhat expanded from that offered under MS-DOS. For example, FAT under NT supports long filenames. Here are some characteristics of FAT as supported under NT 4.0:

- FAT is required on at least one partition if you intend to dual boot between NT and MS-DOS or Windows 95.
- FAT supports filenames of up to 255 characters.
- The filename can have multiple sections, separated by periods and, as such, can be considered multiqualified. The last section is treated as the file extension.
- Filenames must begin with an alphanumeric and can contain any characters, including spaces. Filenames cannot contain the following characters:
  " / \ [ ] : ; | = , ^ * ?
- FAT offers only the traditional file attributes: read, archive, system, and hidden. As such, it does not provide the range of security that NTFS permissions provide.
- Folders in a FAT partition can be shared.
- FAT supports a maximum partition (file) size of 4GB.
- FAT is considered most efficient for file access on partitions of less than 400MB.

- Formatting a partition as FAT requires less than 1MB of overhead for the file system.
- The system partition of *reduced instruction set computer* (RISC)–based systems must be at least 2MB, formatted as FAT.

An Overview of NTFS

NTFS provides the most features and benefits for securing your data. However, it is recognized only by NT computers. Also, your old MS-DOS–based disk utilities most likely do not recognize NTFS-formatted partitions—nor do your MS-DOS or Windows 95–based applications. NTFS is used extensively on NT 4.0 Server computers to provide a high level of security and fault tolerance.

The following are some characteristics of NTFS:

- NTFS supports long file and folder names of up to 255 characters, including the extensions.
- Filenames preserve case but are not case sensitive, except when using POSIX-based applications for which case sensitivity is supported.
- File and folder names can contain any characters, including spaces. However, they cannot contain the following characters:
  " / \ < > : ¦ * ?
- NTFS supports a theoretical partition (file) size of up to 16 exabytes. However, on most hardware, this translates to file size limits of 4GB to 64GB, and to a functional partition size of up to 2TB, due to industry-standard limitations of disk sectors.
- NTFS is more efficient on partitions larger than 250MB.
- Formatting a partition as NTFS requires between 4MB and 5MB of system overhead, making it impossible to format a disk with NTFS.
- NTFS provides support for built-in file-level file compression (NT can compress individual files rather than whole partitions). File compression is treated as an attribute of a file and is enabled through the properties of the file or folder.
- NTFS offers automatic *transaction tracking*, which logs all disk activity and provides a means of recovery in the event of a power failure or system crash.
- NTFS offers automatic *sector sparing*, also called *hot fixing*, in which so-called bad clusters are determined and marked, and the data contained therein is moved to a new good cluster.

CH

7

- Through the Services for Macintosh feature on NT 4.0 Server, NTFS provides support for Macintosh files.
- NTFS provides the highest level of security for files and folders through its permission set (see Chapter 6, "Security and Permissions").
- NTFS maintains a separate Recycle Bin for each user.

As you can see, NTFS is quite a robust file system.

Converting a FAT Partition to NTFS

It certainly is not necessary to format a partition as NTFS right away or during installation. One of the nicest things about NTFS is its capability to be applied to an existing FAT partition.

NT provides a conversion tool that you can use to apply NTFS to an existing FAT partition. It is called `CONVERT.EXE` and is located in the `WINNT40\SYSTEM32` subdirectory. No data is lost during the conversion process, because this is not a reformatting operation. At an MS-DOS prompt, the syntax of the command looks like this:

```
CONVERT D: /FS:NTFS
```

where `D:` represents the drive letter of the partition to be converted.

If NT currently is accessing the drive in some way (for example, the pagefile is located on it), or you have the drive window open through My Computer or Windows Explorer, NT displays a message to that effect and offers to schedule the conversion for the next boot. If you choose to accept the offer, when NT boots, it detects that the partition is marked for conversion. It reboots and performs the conversion, and then it reboots again to start the operating system and lets the user log on.

Considering Long Filenames

Both FAT and NTFS under Windows NT 4.0 support long filenames for files and folders. Not all Microsoft Network clients support or recognize long filenames, however. MS-DOS and Windows 3.x–based computers and their applications, for example, do not recognize long filenames. NT has allowed for this variety in operating systems. When you create a file or folder and use a long filename to identify it, NT assigns an 8.3 format version of the name. This method allows DOS and Windows-based systems to be able to "see" the files and folders. You should keep several considerations in mind as you work with long filenames.

How 8.3 Names Are Created

The internal algorithm NT uses to generate an 8.3 name from a long filename is really quite simple within the first four iterations. NT takes the first six characters of the name, minus spaces, and adds a tilde (~) followed by a number increment. Notice the convention followed in this example:

Long Filename	NT 8.3 Filename
1995 Budget Summary Spreadsheet.XLS	1995Bu~1.xls
1995 Budget Detail Spreadsheet.XLS	1995Bu~2.xls
Budget Overages.DOC	Budget~1.doc

As you can see, the short filename does not give anywhere near the level of description that the long filename does. If several long filenames start with the same first six characters, the 8.3 versions are identifiable only by the number increment. After the fifth iteration, NT's algorithm performs a name hash, retaining the first two characters of the long filename and generating the remaining characters randomly, as shown in this example:

Long Filename	NT 8.3 Filename
KiteFlyers Corp Budget—January.XLS	KiteFl~1.XLS
KiteFlyers Corp Budget—February.XLS	KiteFl~2.XLS
KiteFlyers Corp Budget—March.XLS	KiteFl~3.XLS
KiteFlyers Corp Budget—April.XLS	KiteFl~4.XLS
KiteFlyers Corp Budget—May.XLS	Kia45s~1.XLS
KiteFlyers Corp Budget—June.XLS	Ki823x~1.XLS

On a network with a variety of clients that include NT, MS-DOS, and Windows 95, the short names can become a source of confusion for people who are using clients and applications that only support and display the short name. Consequently, in a mixed environment, try to keep the long filenames unique within the first six characters.

Additional Thoughts on Long Names

Here are some additional considerations:

- When referring to long names at a DOS prompt, most DOS commands require that you place the name in quotation marks. If copying the file MY BUDGET SPREAD-SHEET.XLS from C:\Apps to the D:\Data directory, for example, you need to use this syntax:

```
COPY "C:\Apps\MY BUDGET SPREADSHEET.XLS" D:\Data
```

CH

7

- Some DOS and Windows 16-bit applications save files by creating a temporary file, deleting the original file, and renaming the temporary file to the original name. This deletes not only the long filename, but also any NTFS permissions associated with the file.

- Third-party DOS-based disk utilities that manipulate the FAT also can destroy long filenames contained in the FAT because they do not recognize those entries as valid DOS files. Most of these utilities do not run under NT in any case.

- You can display the 8.3 version of the long filename at a DOS prompt by typing DIR /X at the prompt.

- Every long filename uses one FAT directory entry for the 8.3 name (called the *alias)* and a hidden secondary entry for up to every 13 characters of the long filename. MY BUDGET SPREADSHEET.XLS, for example, uses one FAT directory entry for the 8.3 name—MYBUDG~1.XLS—plus two secondary entries for the long filename (25 characters divided by 13), for a total of three FAT directory entries. The FAT root directory has a hard-coded limit of 512 directory entries. It therefore is possible to run out of directory entries if using very long filenames consistently.

As you can see, if you are supporting a variety of clients in an NT network enterprise, you must carefully consider the use of long filenames. If these filenames will be used widely, you must explain their use thoroughly to the end users who will encounter them.

Chapter 4, "Configuring Windows NT Server 4.0," makes a concerted effort to dissuade you from ever modifying the Registry if a utility is available to you. That having been said, there are occasions when you can accomplish a change only by modifying the Registry. Preventing the support of long filenames is an example of this for your NT 4.0 Server.

You can prevent the support of long filenames on FAT partitions altogether by modifying a Registry entry. Use the Registry Editor to expand the HKEYLOCALMACHINE subtree to the following subkey:

HKEYLOCALMACHINE\SYSTEM\CurrentControlSet\Control\FileSystem\

Change the parameter setting for Win31FileSystem from 0 to 1. This is particularly useful when several clients are accessing files stored on a central server and there is any chance of confusion. Clients are able to name files and folders only by following the 8.3 convention on the FAT partitions.

Exploring File Compression Under NTFS

When a partition is formatted as NTFS, among the features provided is the capability to compress files and folders. Compression is treated as another attribute of the file and folder and is, in fact, enabled through the General Properties dialog box for the file or folder. This compression is handled on-the-fly, and like all compression algorithms, although it results in greater disk capacity, it can result in a performance decrease—especially across heavy-traffic networks.

NTFS compression follows roughly a 2:1 ratio, with slightly more compression for data files and slightly less compression for executables. In general, compression can be most effective for files that are not accessed on a regular basis but that cannot be archived because ready access is required. Good file candidates also are those that are fairly large and located on disk partitions where storage space is at a premium.

How to Enable Compression

As stated earlier, compression is considered an attribute of the file or folder on an NTFS partition. To enable compression for a file or folder, right-click the file or folder and display its Properties dialog box. On the General tab, select Compress.

If a folder's Compress attribute is set, any new files placed in the folder also have their Compress attribute set. Also, for folders, you can choose to apply the Compress attribute down through that folder's subfolders. Disable compression for folders and files by deselecting the Compress attribute.

You can configure Windows Explorer to display compressed files and folders in blue. Choose View, Options, and select Display Compressed Files and Folders with Alternate Color.

You can compress the WINNT40 installation folder and all its files and subfolders if disk space is an issue. However, because NT accesses these folders and files rather frequently, compressing them almost certainly will result in a noticeable decrease in performance on that computer. This is especially unwise on an NT 4.0 Server computer or domain controller. NTLDR and the current pagefile can never be compressed.

 Managing Compression from the Command Prompt

NT provides a command prompt utility called COMPACT.EXE, described in Table 7.1, that you can use to enable and disable file and folder compression on NTFS partitions. The basic syntax is one of the following:

```
COMPACT /C d:\path\filename

COMPACT /C d:\foldername

COMPACT /?
```

CH

7

Table 7.1   COMPACT.EXE Switches

Switch	Description
/C	Enables compression of specified files and folders.
/U	Disables compression of specified files and folders.
/S	Applies the command to files in the specified folder and to all subfolders.
/A	Displays hidden and system files (omitted by default).
/I	Continues the operation, even if errors are encountered. By default, Compact stops when it encounters an error.
/F	Forces compression on all specified files, even if they already are marked as compressed. If a file is being compressed when power is lost, the file may be marked as compressed without actually being compressed.
/Q	Displays summary information about the operation.

Key Concept

When you *copy* a file from one folder to another, it assumes the compression attribute of the target folder. When you *move* a file from one folder to another, it retains its compression attribute.

Managing Disks with Disk Administrator

Now that you have explored partitions and file systems, you'll take a look at another utility in the Administrative Tools group called Disk Administrator.

Disk Administrator is essentially a GUI FDISK. You should remember the MS-DOS FDISK utility that you used to create the primary and extended partition and logical drives. Disk Administrator does the same for your NT Workstation and Server, plus a whole lot more. This section discusses Disk Administrator's capabilities.

Creating and Managing Partitions

You'll begin with the simplest task: creating a new partition. Recall that you can create up to four primary partitions per physical disk and one extended partition that can contain many logical drives. Refer to Figure 7.2 as this discussion continues.

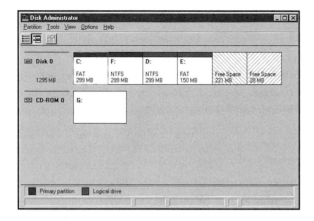

Figure 7.2
A Disk Administrator screen.

To create a partition, follow these steps:

1. Start Disk Administrator by choosing Start, Programs, Administrative Tools.

2. Click an area of free space on a physical disk.

3. Choose Partition, Create to create a new primary partition. Or, choose Partition, Create Extended to create an extended partition.

4. The Create Primary or Create Extended Partition dialog box appears, showing you the smallest-size (2MB) and the largest-size partition you can create. In the Create Partition of Size text box, enter the size partition you want to create.

5. Click OK. The new primary partition appears in Disk Administrator as Unformatted. The new extended partition is set apart from any additional free space with an opposing crosshatch.

After you create an extended partition, you need to create logical drives within it to store data and other files. You can create a logical drive by following the same basic steps you used to create a partition:

1. Start Disk Administrator by choosing Start, Programs, Administrative Tools.

2. Click an area of free space in the extended partition.

3. Choose Partition, Create to create a new logical drive.

4. The Create Logical Drive dialog box appears, showing you the smallest-size (2MB) and the largest-size drive you can create. In the Create Logical Drive of Size spin box, enter the size drive you want to create.

5. Click OK. The new logical drive appears in Disk Administrator as Unformatted.

CH

7

The Format Process

The next step, of course, is to format the new primary partition or logical drive. Before you can do that, you must confirm your partition changes to NT. Choose Partition, Commit Changes Now. Disk Administrator asks that you confirm your changes and then reminds you to update the Emergency Repair Disk with this new configuration information by using the RDISK.EXE command-line utility.

To format the new primary partition or logical drive, follow these steps:

1. Select the partition or drive.
2. Choose Tools, Format. The Format Drive dialog box appears. If you are formatting a drive or partition that already has been formatted, the Capacity text box displays its size. Otherwise, it simply says Unknown Capacity.
3. In the File System list box, select FAT or NTFS.
4. Specify an Allocation Unit Size. Unless you know something different, stick with Default.
5. Enter a Volume Label if you want. The label appears in Disk Administrator and Windows Explorer and helps describe the drive and/or its contents.
6. Select Quick Format if the disk has been formatted and you know it is not damaged. Quick Format removes all files and does not perform a scan for base sectors before formatting. It is faster but potentially more risky.
7. Select Enable Compression if you are formatting as NTFS and want to turn on the Compression attribute for the entire drive or partition.
8. Click Start. The dialog box charts the progress of the format operation. Click OK when the formatting is complete, and then click Close.

Deleting Partitions and Drives

Deleting a partition is as simple as choosing Partition, Delete. Disk Administrator warns you that deleting the partition or drive irrevocably loses any data stored on the partition. Always check the contents of a drive or partition before you delete it to ensure that you will not inadvertently lose something valuable—something that you don't have backed up!

Disk Management Extras—Drive Letters, Properties, and Display Options

Besides the Format option, the Tools menu gives you the capability to assign a specific drive letter to a logical drive or primary partition. By default, NT assigns the next available drive letter to your primary partition or logical drive. Some programs require that a particular drive letter be used for the partition that holds the application files. Or you can choose to assign drive letters for consistency. Sometimes a persistent connection to a mapped drive takes up a drive letter that you would prefer to assign to a logical drive or primary partition after you have disconnected.

To assign a drive letter, follow these steps:

1. Select the drive or partition in Disk Administrator.
2. Choose Tools, Assign Drive Letter.
3. In the Assign Drive Letter text box, select the desired drive letter. Only the available drive letters are shown. If a drive letter you want to use is currently in use by a persistent connection, disconnect that mapping first to release the drive letter.

You have the option of not assigning a drive letter at all. Because there are a limited number of letters in the alphabet, and some are reserved up front, this option enables you to create additional drives and partitions now and assign drive letters to them as you need to access them.

You can quickly display the Properties dialog box for any partition or logical drive by selecting that drive and choosing Tools, Properties. In the dialog box, you can see usage statistics, change the volume label, run volume scan and defragmentation tools, and view sharing information for the drive.

As you create primary partitions, logical drives, volume sets, and so on by using Disk Administrator, it uses various color codes and crosshatching to facilitate your interpretation of the disks' partition and formatting schemes. The Options menu includes options for changing Colors and Patterns used in the legend, whether to show partition and drive sizes to scale through Disk Display, and whether and how to show a specific physical disk only through Region Display. By using Customize Toolbar, you can even create and customize your own icon toolbar to facilitate your most frequent activities.

System, Boot, and Active Partitions

As mentioned earlier, NT refers to the partition that contains the NT boot files (NTLDR, NTDETECT.COM, NTBOOTDD.SYS, BOOT.INI, BOOTSECT.DOS) as the *system partition,* and the partition that contains the WINNT40 installation directory as the *boot partition.* Only one partition can be marked as active. On MS-DOS computers, this usually refers to the C: drive. In NT, on dual-boot computers (booting between NT 4.0 and MS-DOS or Windows 95), this probably is still the C: drive. However, it must be the partition that contains the NT boot files. Your computer may have multiple operating systems, such as NT 4.0 and UNIX or NT 4.0 and OS/2. Each expects its boot files to be on the partition marked as active. You are most likely to find this type of configuration on test servers.

CH

7

You use the Boot Manager utility that comes with the other operating system to mark the NT system partition as the active partition when you want to restart your workstation and boot into NT. When you are in NT and ready to restart your system and boot into another operating system, you use Disk Administrator as your boot manager.

To change the active partition marker, follow these steps:

1. Start Disk Administrator.
2. Select the partition to be marked as active (primary partitions only).
3. Choose Partition, Mark Active. Disk Administrator displays a confirmation message stating that the partition has been marked as active and will boot with whatever operating system is on the partition the next time you restart your system.

You can spot the active partition if you look very closely in the color bar above the drive letter. The active partition is marked with a star. You can see this better if you choose Options, Colors and Patterns and change the color bar to something other than dark blue.

Creating and Managing Volume Sets

You can think of a *volume* as any partition or logical drive on any physical disk that can be accessed as a single unit. In NT, a volume can be a single contiguous area of disk space or a collection of noncontiguous areas of disk space. The latter is called a *volume set*.

A volume set can consist of from two to 32 areas of free disk space on one or more physical disk drives. These areas are combined and treated by NT as though they are one large volume and can be formatted as FAT or NTFS. After these areas are combined, they cannot be split apart. Consequently, deleting any part of a volume set deletes the entire volume set.

You can use volume sets to clean up areas of free space that, by themselves, may not be large enough to be useful, or to create storage areas larger than any one physical disk can provide.

Here are some more fun facts about volume sets:

- Volume sets can contain areas of free space from different drive types, such as *small computer system interface* (SCSI), *Enhanced System Device Interface* (ESDI), and *Integrated Device Electronics* (IDE).
- NT system and boot partitions may not participate in a volume set.

- Like NTFS, on workstations that dual boot between NT and MS-DOS or Windows 95, volume sets are not accessible by MS-DOS or Windows 95.
- If any member of a volume set fails, or the disk on which a member resides fails, the entire volume set is corrupted.

Key Concept

When you choose areas of free space of very disparate sizes, Disk Administrator sizes each member of the volume set proportionate to the amount of free disk space selected. For example, if you choose to create a 50MB volume set out of a 10MB and 200MB area of free space, you might expect Disk Administrator to use all of the 10MB space for the first member of the volume set, and then 40MB from the remaining 200MB free space for the second member of the volume set. However, Disk Administrator determines that proportionate to the size of the free areas selected, the first member is 4MB and the remaining is 47MB (see Fig. 7.3). This same note applies to extended volume sets.

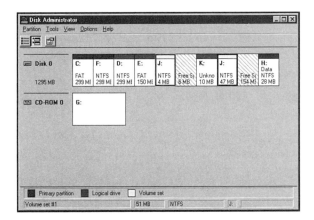

Figure 7.3
Volume set J: consists of two noncontiguous areas of disk space and has been formatted as NTFS.

Creating and Formatting a Volume Set

To create a volume set, follow these steps:

1. Start Disk Administrator.

2. Select from 2 to 32 areas of free disk space by clicking on the first free-space area, and then Ctrl+clicking the other areas.

3. Choose Partition, Create Volume Set. The Create Volume Set dialog box appears, showing the smallest-size (2MB) and largest-size volume set you can create from your selections.

4. In the Create Volume Set of Total Size text box, enter the total size you want for the volume set.

5. Click OK. Disk Administrator displays the new volume set, similar to the example shown in Figure 7.3.

6. Format the new volume set as FAT or NTFS.

Extending a Volume Set

If you have formatted a partition, logical drive, or volume set as NTFS, and you are running out of space on it, never fear: NTFS-formatted space can be extended into free space without any loss of data and without having to reformat the space. This process is called *extending the volume set.*

This feature can be particularly helpful in adding extra print spool space to a partition or allowing for the growth of a database.

To extend a volume set, follow these steps:

1. From Disk Administrator, select the NTFS partition, drive, or volume set.

2. Ctrl+click an area of free space that will be added to the existing partition.

3. Choose Partition, Extend Volume Set to display the Extend Volume Set dialog box. The minimum and maximum total size for the extended volume is shown.

4. In the Create Volume Set of Total Size text box, enter the total size you want the volume set to be.

5. Click OK. Disk Administrator creates what appears to be a volume set and applies NTFS to the new volume set member (see Fig. 7.4).

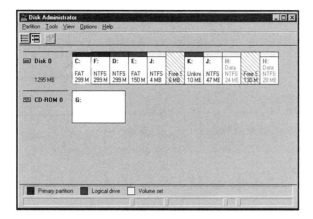

Figure 7.4
Note how the H: drive has been extended from 28MB to a total of 52MB. Because it was formatted as NTFS, NTFS is applied automatically to the extended volume.

Creating and Managing Stripe Sets

A stripe set in NT is quite similar to a volume set; both involve combining areas of free disk space into a single large volume. The similarities end there, however.

There are two common confusions regarding stripe sets, also known as *redundant array of inexpensive/independent disks* (RAID) 0:

- Data is written to each member of a volume set in turn. In other words, when one member is filled, the next member is written to, and so on. Therefore, a volume set really does not improve disk I/O performance.

- A stripe set consists of free space from at least two, and up to 32, different physical drives. The area of free space chosen on each disk must be the same size on each disk. For example, if you have three disks with 100MB, 200MB, and 300MB of free space each, and you want to combine all three to create a stripe set, the largest any member can be is the smallest of the areas of free space, or 100MB, providing a total stripe set across all three disks of 300MB (100MB * 3 disks). Or, you can combine two 200MB areas from the second and third disks to create a total stripe set size of 400MB. It's all just a matter of arithmetic.

Unlike volume sets, in which the first member gets filled up before the second member is written, in stripe sets, data is written uniformly in 64KB blocks across all members of the stripe set (see Fig. 7.5). Because data can be written concurrently across the physical disks, a stripe set normally results in an overall disk I/O performance increase.

CH
7

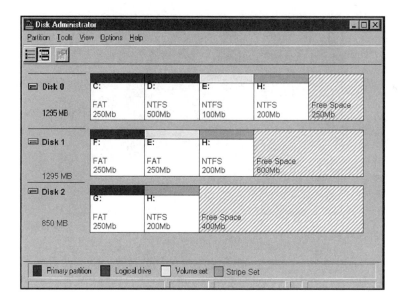

Figure 7.5
Here, the H: drive represents a 600MB stripe set distributed across three physical disk drives.

Here are some more fun facts about stripe sets:

- NT system and boot partitions cannot participate in a stripe set.
- Like NTFS, on workstations that dual boot between NT and MS-DOS or Windows 95, stripe sets are not accessible by MS-DOS or Windows 95.
- If any member of a stripe set fails, or the disk on which a member resides fails, the entire stripe set is corrupted.

To create a stripe set, follow these steps:

1. From Disk Administrator, select from 2 to 32 areas of free disk space on different physical disks. Click the first area and Ctrl+click the remaining areas. The areas should be approximately the same size. If not, Disk Administrator sizes the stripe set based on the smallest area of disk space selected.

2. Choose Partition, Create Stripe Set to display the Create Stripe Set dialog box. The minimum and maximum total sizes for the stripe set are shown.

3. In the Create Stripe Set of Size text box, enter the total size stripe set you want.

4. Click OK. Disk Administrator displays the equal-sized members of the stripe set distributed across the physical disks selected.

5. Format the stripe set.

6. Quit Disk Administrator or choose Partition, Commit Changes Now to save your changes in the Registry.

The System Partition and RISC

The system partition on a RISC-based computer must be formatted as FAT, because these computers can only boot from FAT. There is no way to protect the system partition in this environment with local security. However, Disk Administrator provides an additional menu choice called Secure System Partition. When this option is selected, only administrators on that computer are able to access the system partition.

Fault Tolerance

In addition to the partition, volume set, and stripe set options that you have seen, Disk Administrator on an NT 4.0 Server provides disk-fault tolerant options. From the menu option Fault Tolerance, you can create stripe sets with parity, also called RAID 5, and disk mirroring, as well as regenerate data lost because of failed stripe sets with parity or mirrored disks.

This is software-based fault tolerance that is built into the NT operating system. When enabled, it places additional stress on the processor for resource management and disk I/O. Also, when a member of a stripe set fails, or a disk mirror fails, NT must be shut down, the drive replaced, and the data regenerated. Hardware-based fault-tolerant systems generally allow for hot swapping failed disks without shutting down NT. However, NT's software-based fault tolerance is less expensive than its hardware counterparts. If you are just getting started and need to secure your servers with fault tolerance, this is a good way to go.

Backing Up and Restoring Data

By now, if you have spent any length of time working with microcomputers, especially within a network environment, you have heard the words "backup and restore" at least once. Perhaps you have heard yourself utter them, as in, "Why didn't I...?"

Backing up data and having the capability to recover it is perhaps the most important part of disk management, especially within an enterprise network environment. As companies move faster and closer toward electronic media for conveying information (and in spite of rhetoric to the contrary, believe that it is happening), the backup process has taken on a much more prominent and integral role in securing data.

CH
7

You can follow several strategies when implementing a backup procedure, and you have just about as many hardware and software options to choose from. This section is not intended to drive home the importance of developing and implementing a sound backup/restore policy. If you haven't yet been convinced, you will be the first (and last) time you lose $20 million worth of financial records because the incremental daily backup failed to occur and no one monitored it.

The purpose of this section is to introduce you to the backup/restore utility included with your installation of NT 4.0 Server, to explain some terms Microsoft uses (and that you are apt to encounter on the server exam), and to present a few backup and restore strategies.

Requirements, Terms, and Strategy

The Windows NT Backup utility is designed for use with an NT-compatible tape backup device. To determine whether your tape backup device is compatible, as with any new piece of hardware, consult the NT 4.0 *hardware compatibility list* (HCL).

The Windows NT Backup utility is meant primarily as a file and folder backup product and does not back up data at the sector level. Consequently, NT's Backup utility cannot be used to perform volume recovery—restoring an entire partition. If you need this kind of functionality or want built-in scheduled backups, you should review the many third-party backup programs available now for NT. Nevertheless, the Windows NT Backup utility is a fine product and does allow the backup of the Registry.

The following persons can perform the backup and restore function:

- Administrators
- Members of the local Backup Operators group
- Members of the local Server Operators group
- Users granted the user right Backup (Restore) Files and Directories
- Users can back up files and folders to which they have Read permission

As for strategy, Microsoft promotes the following three areas of consideration when planning your backup procedure:

- What do you need to back up? What is the significance of the data?
- Where are you backing up from—centrally stored data or locally distributed?
- How often do you need to back up? What is the frequency with which the data should be backed up to provide recovery?

The significance of the data is always subjective. For the purposes of your strategy, you need to determine how much data is significant in order to plan for the appropriate number of backup devices, the right-sized media, the location of devices, and so on.

Data stored centrally tends to be easier to maintain than data stored at local computers. For one thing, although you can back up users' data remotely with NT's Backup utility or various third-party products, you rely more heavily on the users to back up their own data or make their computer available for the remote backup, share folders, close files, and exit applications. The backup of centrally stored data is usually the responsibility of one or two persons who can monitor network use and ensure that important files are closed and can be backed up regularly.

The obvious recommendation, then, is to store critical files in a central location and always back them up. Files that you cannot live without—including the Registry, especially on the domain controller (SAM and Security databases)—should be backed up regularly, perhaps daily. Files that change infrequently or are of less importance also might be backed up on a regular basis, perhaps weekly. Temporary files and files that are used once and forgotten probably never need to be backed up.

Table 7.2 lists some backup terms that NT uses and with which you already may be familiar.

Table 7.2   Tape Backup Categories

Term	Backs Up
Normal	All selected files and folders and sets their Archive attribute.
Copy	All selected files and folders but does not set the Archive attribute. This option generally is used for creating tape copies outside the regular backup routine.
Incremental	Only selected files and folders that have changed since the last backup, and sets their Archive attribute.
Differential	Only selected files and folders that have changed since the last time they were backed up, but does not set their Archive attribute.
Daily	Only files and folders that changed that day without setting their Archive attribute.

The use of the Archive attribute is significant for any backup strategy. The Archive attribute indicates whether the file has been previously backed up. The difference between a differential and incremental backup is examined next as an example.

According to Table 7.2, differential and incremental backups do precisely the same thing, except for setting the Archive attribute: The incremental sets it, and the differential does not.

CH

7

Suppose that you have a data folder in which users make frequent contributions and modifications. If you employ an incremental backup each day of the week, starting with a normal backup on Monday, the backup would proceed like this:

Monday	Back up all files, and set their Archive attribute.
Tuesday	Back up all files that are new or have changed since Monday, and set their Archive attribute.
Wednesday	Back up all files that are new or have changed since Tuesday, and set their Archive attribute.
Thursday	Back up all files that are new or have changed since Wednesday, and set their Archive attribute.
Friday	Back up all files that are new or have changed since Thursday, and set their Archive attribute.

By the end of the week, you have created five backup tapes, each containing data that changed since the previous day. If data is lost in the folder on Friday, you can use all tapes to recover the data that is lost, because you would not necessarily know which day's data was lost. The backup process is faster, but the restore can take longer.

Now back up the same folder by using a normal backup on Monday and a differential backup the rest of the week:

Monday	Back up all files, and set their Archive attribute.
Tuesday	Back up all files that are new or have changed since Monday, but do not set their Archive attribute.
Wednesday	Back up all files that are new or have changed since Monday, but do not set their Archive attribute.
Thursday	Back up all files that are new or have changed since Monday, but do not set their Archive attribute.
Friday	Back up all files that are new or have changed since Monday, but do not set their Archive attribute.

Notice that each day's tape contains files that are new or have changed since the beginning of the week. This backup process takes a little longer, but if data is lost from the folder on Friday, only the Monday and Thursday tapes need to be restored, because Monday contains all the original data, and Thursday contains everything that has changed since Monday.

Another twist on these strategies is to perform a complete normal or copy backup once every week or every month, and archive that tape off site. By designating a series of tapes in rotation, you can cycle your off-site archive tapes into the regular routine and always maintain a valid and timely recovery system that includes off-site data storage.

Table 7.3 lists some additional terms that Microsoft uses regarding the backup process.

Table 7.3 Backup Terms

Term	Description
Backup set	The group of files and folders backed up during a backup session. A tape may contain one or more backup sets.
Family set	The group of tapes that contains files and folders backed up during a single backup session.
Backup Log	The backup text file the Backup utility creates that records details relating to the session, such as the date, type of backup, which files and folders were backed up, and so on.
Catalog	A listing of the files stored on the backup tape that are loaded during the restore process. Displays the backup sets on a tape and the files and folders contained in a backup set.

Initiating Backup

The first step in initiating a backup is to determine what you will be backing up (see Fig. 7.6). It helps to know ahead of time what files and folders you want to back up and where they are located. For example, if you are planning on backing up files located on a remote server or a user's workstation, the folder containing the files first must be shared, and then you must connect to that share from the computer that is doing the backup. Unfortunately, you cannot back up the Registry from a remote computer. All files, of course, must be closed, because backup cannot operate on open files. After you make these preparations, you can start the Backup utility.

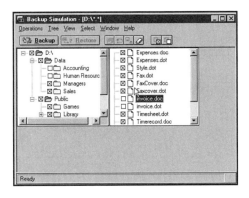

Figure 7.6
Files and folders on the D: drive are selected by a simple point-and-click method.

To back up files and folders, follow these steps:

1. Start the Windows NT Backup utility by choosing Start, <u>P</u>rograms, Administrative Tools, Backup.

2. In the Backup dialog box, select the drives, folders, and/or files to be backed up by pointing to and clicking in the appropriate check boxes. Your selections are hierarchical; if you select a drive or folder, you automatically select its contents and subfolders (refer to Fig. 7.6).

3. Choose <u>O</u>perations, <u>B</u>ackup, or just click the <u>B</u>ackup button to display the Backup Information dialog box (see Fig. 7.7).

Figure 7.7
This tape for the files selected on Kite Server includes an incremental backup of the Registry and is restricted to the user who performed the backup.

4. In the <u>T</u>ape Name text box, enter a name for the tape, which can be up to 32 characters. If you are appending to an existing tape, the <u>T</u>ape Name box is not available.

5. Choose the appropriate tape options (see Table 7.4).

6. Enter a <u>D</u>escription for the backup set you are creating.

7. Choose a <u>B</u>ackup Type.

8. In the <u>L</u>og File text box, enter the name and path for the text file you want to use to record details about the backup operation, and select whether you want to capture all backup information (<u>F</u>ull Detail), only major operations such as starting, stopping, and failing to open files (<u>S</u>ummary Only), or D<u>o</u>n't Log at all.

9. Click OK. Backup displays the status of the operation as it takes place and a summary when it is complete (see Figure 7.8).

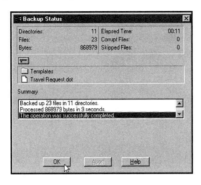

Figure 7.8
The statistics compiled for a successful backup of the files and folders selected in Figure 7.6.

10. Click OK to complete the operation. Store your tape in a safe place.

Table 7.4 Tape Options	
Option	Description
Append	Adds a new backup set to an existing tape.
Replace	Overwrites the data on an existing tape.
Verify After	Compares files selected with files backed up, and Backup confirms that they are backed up accurately.
Backup	In addition to the files selected, copies the Registry to the Registry backup set. (At least one file in the volume containing the Registry must have been selected in order for the Registry to be backed up successfully.)
Restrict	Only administrators, backup operators, or the user that Access performed the backup for is allowed access to the backup set for purposes of recovery.
Hardware	If the tape drive supports data compression, select this Compression option to enable it.

CH
7

Initiating a Restore

The restore process is much the same as the backup process, but in reverse. The same rules apply regarding who can perform the operation, and your restore strategy pretty much depends on what type of backup strategy you implemented. Refer back to the two backup examples outlined earlier in the section "Requirements, Terms, and Strategy."

Also, as with backup, the first step in initiating a restore is to determine what you will be restoring. You will make good use of the backup logs created during the backup process to determine which files and folders you want to restore, on what backup set they are located, and to where you need to restore them. If you are planning to restore files to a remote server or a user's workstation, for example, you must connect to the appropriate drive on that computer.

Key Concept

The Registry cannot be backed up from or restored to a remote computer.

To restore files and folders, follow these steps:

1. Start the Windows NT Backup utility.
2. The Tapes window displays the name of the tape in the device and information regarding the first backup set on the tape.
3. To see additional backup sets, load the tape catalog by choosing <u>O</u>perations, <u>C</u>atalog. The Catalog Status dialog box appears.
4. Click OK when the process is complete. A new window with the tape's name appears.
5. In this window, select the appropriate backup set to load its catalog.
6. Select the drives, folders, and/or files to be restored by pointing to and clicking in the appropriate check boxes. Your selections are hierarchical—if you select a drive or folder, you automatically select its contents and subfolders.
7. Choose <u>O</u>perations, <u>R</u>estore, or just click the <u>R</u>estore button to display the Restore Information dialog box (see Fig. 7.9).
8. In the Restore to <u>D</u>rive text box, the original drive and path are displayed. You can accept this default or select an <u>A</u>lternate Path.
9. Select the appropriate restore option (see Table 7.5).

Figure 7.9
This operation restores the selected files and folders to the original D: drive, as well as the Registry, and maintains the original permission settings.

   10. Enter the name and path for the text file you want to use to record details about the restore operation in the Log File text box, and select whether you want to capture all restore information (Full Detail), only major operations, such as starting, stopping, and failing to restore files (Summary Only), or Don't Log at all.

   11. Click OK. Restore displays the status of the operation as it takes place and a summary when it is complete, as shown in Figure 7.10.

Figure 7.10
The summary statistics for the restore operation you began in Figure 7.9.

   12. Click OK to complete the operation.

CH
7

Table 7.5 Tape Restore Options	
Option	Description
Restore Registry	Restores the local Registry to the target computer.
Restore Permissions	Restores the NTFS permissions to the files as they are recovered. If this option is not selected, files assume the permissions of the target folder. If you restore to a different computer, be sure that you have valid user and group accounts, or your permissions may be inaccurate.
Verify After Restore	Compares files selected with files restored and confirms that they are restored accurately.

Troubleshooting Backup and Restore

You are not likely to encounter any problems with the Backup utility, as long as you are using a supported tape device and have the appropriate level of permission to perform the operation—by virtue of membership in the Administrators, Backup Operators, or Server Operators group; by assignment of the Backup (Restore) Files and Directories user right; or through Read permission to the files and folders.

If you have chosen to log the backup and restore operations, any exceptions to the process, such as open files that couldn't be backed up, are duly recorded in the log. You can use that file to troubleshoot what did and did not get backed up, where it was backed up from, in which backup set it is located, and so on.

Also, you should review the catalog for the selected backup set before restoring files. Corrupted files and folders are highlighted with a red X. Obviously, you probably should not restore these files and folders.

Scheduling a Tape Backup

NT provides a command-line backup utility that you can use in combination with NT's AT command to schedule a tape backup operation. To accomplish this scheduling, you need to create a batch file that contains the backup command syntax, and then use the AT command to schedule the batch file to run. The schedule service must be running in order for the AT command to work.

Here is the basic backup command syntax:

```
NTBACKUP BACKUP path\filenames options
```

where path\filenames indicates the location of any selected files, and options is any of the items listed in Table 7.6.

Table 7.6 NTBACKUP Options

Option	Description
/A	Adds (appends) the backup set to the existing tape.
/b	Backs up the local Registry.
/d "text"	Adds a description for the backup set.
/e	Creates a Summary Log rather than a Detail Log.
/hc:on/off	Turns on or off hardware compression for tape devices that support the option.
/l filename	Assigns a filename (other than the default) to the Backup Log.
/r	Restricts access to only administrators, backup operators, server operators, or users who perform the backup.
/t type	Indicates the type of backup (Copy, Incremental, Differential, Daily) other than the default, Normal.
/v	Verifies that files were backed up accurately.

If you need to connect to a remote share to back up files, begin the batch file with a connection to that remote share by using the following syntax:

```
CMD /C net use d: \\server\share
```

where d: is the logical drive mapping, and \\server\share is the *Universal Naming Convention* (UNC) path to the remote share. At the end of the batch file, include the same line with a /d at the end to disconnect from the share.

The following is an example of a batch file called DATABACK.BAT; it connects to a share called DATA on server ACCT1, does an incremental backup of the files (including the Registry) in that share, restricts access, and verifies the backup:

```
CMD /C NET USE M: \\ACCT1\DATA
NTBACKUP M: /a /t Incremental /b /r /v
CMD /C NET USE M: /D
```

To use the AT command to schedule this batch file, the Scheduler Service must be running. Use the Services applet in the Control Panel to enable and configure this service.

The AT command uses the following syntax:

```
AT \\computer time options batchfilename
```

where computer is a remote computer (otherwise, the local computer is assumed), time indicates the 24-hour time hour:minute (00:00) notation for the operation to take place, and batchfilename indicates the command or batch file you want to execute. For an explanation of options, see Table 7.7.

CH

7

For example, if you want to schedule your ACCT1 backup to occur at 11 p.m. every week-day, the AT command would look like this:

```
AT 23:00 /every:M,T,W,Th,F DATABACK.BAT
```

Table 7.7 AT Command Options

Option	Description
/delete	Cancels a scheduled command by the ID number assigned to it.
/interactive	Lets the job interact with the currently logged-on user.
/every:date	Runs the command on the specified day(s) of the week (M,T,W,Th,F,S,Su) or on one or more days of the month by using numbers (1–31). The default is the current day.
/next:date	Runs the command on the next occurrence of the day(s) specified or one or more days of the month.

Troubleshooting Disk Management

As with all the troubleshooting sections so far in this book, if you have read the material and understand it, and have taken the opportunity to experiment with the utilities discussed, you already have the basic tools you need to troubleshoot most problems. Here are a few more considerations.

Saving Disk Configurations

When you have made changes to the partition and format scheme on your computer, it is important to update that information. Of course, the current Registry settings are updated. However, if you are using the *Emergency Repair Disk* (ERD) as a recovery tool, you must remember to update it. You can do so by running the RDISK command at the command line. This command updates the Emergency Repair information with any Registry changes, including the disk configuration.

You also can choose Partition, Configuration, Save from the Disk Administrator menu to save assigned drive letters, volume sets, stripe sets, stripe sets with parity, and mirror sets to a blank disk or the ERD. This information can be particularly useful when planning migrations, software upgrades, and so on.

Other Considerations

If NT fails to recognize a drive, it is most likely an incompatibility problem or driver problem. Always check the HCL before upgrading any hardware on your NT 4.0 computer. Detected hardware errors are listed in the Registry in this key:
HKEY_LOCAL_MACHINE\Hardware.

Generally, you should delete corrupted files and folders and restore good versions from your most recent backup. The worst cases require that you reformat the disk and then restore from backup.

When dual booting to MS-DOS, running some third-party MS-DOS–based utilities that modify the FAT entries can result in corruption or loss of data in NT, especially if long filenames are used. To avoid file corruption or loss, don't use these utilities and don't disable long filename support for FAT partitions.

Disk drives that are 1GB IDE drives and follow the *Enhanced Integrated Device Electronics* (EIDE) standard have a *basic input/output system* (BIOS) limit of 1,024 cylinders, which restricts NT's capability to access all of the available storage space on these disks. The BIOS needs to be able to get around the limit through sector translation or relative cluster addressing, or NT needs to be able to communicate with the disk's controller. NT currently supports Western Digital 1003–compatible controllers.

Summary

This chapter examined the basics of disk management and discussed the differences in file systems. You also learned about the Disk Administrator utility, volume sets, and stripe sets. The topic of fault tolerance was introduced and will be covered in greater detail in a later chapter.

Next up on your agenda is a trip through the wonderful world of monitoring and printing—still an adventure after all these years. Before you journey on, be sure to go through the review questions and lab for this chapter.

QUESTIONS AND ANSWERS

1. NTFS supports disks to a theoretical size of _____.

   A: 16EB

2. You can accomplish file compression from the command line with what utility?

   A: Compact

3. The type of backup that includes only files and folders that have changed since the last backup and sets their Archive bit off is _____.

   A: Incremental. Other backup types include Copy, Full (Normal), Differential, and Daily.

CH
7

...*continues*

...continued

---

4. True or false: You can automate backups with the CRON utility included with NT.

   A: False. The CRON service/daemon is not included with Windows NT. You can automate backups with the AT utility included with NT.

5. True or false: You can use the Backup utility included with Windows NT Server 4.0 to back up the local Registry.

   A: True. Although it cannot back up remote Registries, the Backup utility included with Windows NT Server 4.0 can back up the local Registry.

PRACTICE TEST

1. Lucy has been appointed the backup coordinator for the network. What must you do to enable her to accomplish this task and still maintain security on the data? Choose all that apply.

   a. Make Lucy a member of the local Backup Operators group on each computer that needs to be backed up.

   b. Make Lucy a member of the Server Operators group on each server computer that needs to be backed up.

   c. Assign Lucy the Backup Files and Directories user right.

   d. Give Lucy Full Control over all files and folders.

Answer a is correct. You must make Lucy a member of the local Backup Operators group on each computer that needs to be backed up. Answer b is correct. You must make Lucy a member of the Server Operators group on each server computer that needs to be backed up. Answer c is correct. You must assign Lucy the Backup Files and Directories user right. Answer d is incorrect. Giving Lucy Full Control is much more power than she needs and defeats security.

2. You need to extend a FAT partition to allow more space for a growing database. Which option best explains your strategy?

   a. Use Disk Administrator to select the FAT partition and an area of free space and choose Partition, Create Volume Set.

   b. Use Disk Administrator to select the FAT partition and an area of free space and choose Partition, Extend Volume Set.

   c. Use Disk Administrator to select the FAT partition and an area of formatted space and choose Tools, Combine Volume Sets.

   d. Convert the drive to NTFS and create a volume set.

Answer a is incorrect. A FAT volume set is not a good idea—after you create it, you cannot change its size. Answer b is incorrect. A FAT volume set cannot be extended. Answer c is incorrect. Volume sets cannot be combined. **Answer d is correct. Converting the drive to NTFS and creating a volume set addresses the problem.**

3. You are ready to implement your backup strategy and want to back up files from all Windows NT computers remotely to an archive directory on your local computer. All remote shares have been implemented. What is the best solution?

   a. Connect to the shares, start Backup, and select the files and folders to be backed up. Choose Backup, and enter the UNC path to the target archive directory in the Backup Path text box.

   b. Connect to the shares, start Backup, and choose Operations, Select Target from the menu. Enter the path to the archive directory in the Backup Path text box.

   c. Connect to the shares, start Backup, and redirect the backup path by using Tools, Options.

   d. You cannot back up to disk.

Answer a is incorrect. Backups must be done to removable media. Answer b is incorrect; backups must be done to removable media. Answer c is incorrect—backups must be done to removable media. **Answer d is correct. You cannot back up to disk.**

4. The Anderson office is running an internal Web server and suddenly has become very sensitive to security and access rights across the domain. You need to convert a partition on the server from FAT to NTFS and do not want to lose any data in the process. How can you best accomplish this task?

   a. Use Disk Administrator to select the partition and choose Tools, Format. Then select NTFS.

   b. Use the command-line utility CONVERT.EXE to convert the partition.

   c. Use the Windows NT Backup utility to back up the partition data to disk. Then format the partition for NTFS and restore the data.

   d. You cannot convert a FAT partition to NTFS without loss of data.

Answer a is incorrect. Format operations erase data. **Answer b is correct. Use the command-line utility CONVERT.EXE to convert the partition.** Answer c is incorrect. Format operations erase data. Answer d is incorrect, because the CONVERT utility enables you to do this.

CH
7

5. Which of the following statements are true regarding volume sets and stripe sets? Choose all that apply.

   a. Stripe sets can contain the system partition, and volume sets cannot.

   b. Stripe sets must combine areas of equal size, whereas volume sets can combine areas of any size.

   c. Stripe sets cannot contain the system partition, and volume sets can.

   d. Stripe sets write to all members of the set concurrently, whereas volume sets fill each member of the set in turn.

Answer a is false. Stripe sets cannot contain the system partition. **Answer b is true. Stripe sets must combine areas of equal size, whereas volume sets can combine areas of any size.** Answer c is false. Volume sets cannot contain the system partition. **Answer d is true. Stripe sets write to all members of the set concurrently, whereas volume sets fill each member of the set in turn.**

6. Windows NT calls the active primary partition its:

   a. Boot partition

   b. System partition

   c. Startup partition

   d. Extended partition

Answer a is incorrect. The active partition is known as the system partition. **Answer b is correct. In Windows NT, the active partition is known as the system partition.** Answer c is incorrect; the active partition is known as the system partition. Answer d is incorrect—the active partition is known as the system partition.

7. You need to recover a lost folder for a user. Before you do so, what can you do to minimize errors?

   a. Review the Backup Set Catalog for any corrupted files before proceeding with the backup.

   b. Review the Backup Log file to see whether any files were missed during the backup process.

   c. Select the Verify Files Restore option.

   d. Do nothing. Windows NT verifies files while restoring to disk.

Answer a is correct. Never restore files from a corrupted backup. Answer b is correct. Make certain the files you need were included on the backup. Answer c is correct. Do not restore the entire backup, but select the needed files before starting. Answer d is incorrect, because it does not address the problem.

8. Which of the following statements are true regarding FAT and NTFS? Choose all that apply.

    a. FAT supports long filenames, and so does NTFS.

    b. NTFS supports long filenames, but FAT does not.

    c. FAT supports a maximum partition size of 4GB, and NTFS supports a maximum partition size of 16EB.

    d. Formatting a partition as FAT requires less than 1MB of overhead, whereas NTFS formatting requires at least 4MB.

Answer a is correct: **FAT and NTFS support long filenames.** Answer b is incorrect. Both FAT and NTFS support long filenames. **Answer c is correct. FAT supports a maximum partition size of 4GB, and NTFS supports a maximum partition size of 16EB. Answer d is correct. Formatting a partition as FAT requires less than 1MB of overhead, whereas NTFS formatting requires at least 4MB.**

9. Which of the following statements accurately describe NTFS? Choose all that apply.

    a. NTFS provides built-in transaction tracking.

    b. NTFS supports file compression as a file property.

    c. NTFS requires less than 4MB of overhead for formatting.

    d. NTFS offers file- and folder-level security.

Answer a is correct. **NTFS provides built-in transaction tracking. Answer b is correct. NTFS supports file compression and does so as a property (or attribute) of the file.** Answer c is incorrect. NTFS requires between 4MB and 5MB. **Answer d is correct: NTFS offers file- and folder-level security.**

10. You are deciding whether to support long filenames on FAT partitions for your server. You have a variety of client platforms that connect to the server, including MS-DOS and Windows 95. Some of the platforms support older 16-bit applications. Which of the following considerations would influence your decision?

    a. There are no significant concerns. All applications support long filenames on all platforms in a Microsoft network.

    b. Most Microsoft applications support long filenames, but some older applications save changes by deleting the old file and renaming a temporary file to the original filename. This method could eliminate the long filename.

    c. Long filenames saved in the root of the drive require one directory entry for the alias, and one for up to every 13 characters of the name. Because the root is hard coded for 512 directory entries for FAT partitions, you could run out of entries.

    d. If long-filename support is disabled for the FAT partition, it is disabled for all partitions on that computer, including NTFS.

CH

7

Answer a is incorrect. Not all older applications support long filenames. **Answer b is correct. Most Microsoft applications support long filenames, but some older applications save changes by deleting the old file and renaming a temporary file to the original filename. This method could eliminate the long filename. Answer c is correct. Long filenames saved in the root of the drive require one directory entry for the alias, and one for up to every 13 characters of the name. Because the root is hard coded for 512 directory entries for FAT partitions, you could run out of entries.** Answer d is incorrect. Although a uniform policy should be in place, what is set for one partition does not affect another.

CHAPTER

8

CHAPTER PREREQUISITE

This chapter discusses a monitoring utility that charts Windows NT's system and network performance, so you should have a working knowledge of networking and computer systems. An understanding of the basic concepts of Windows NT Server 4.0, outlined in Chapters 1 through 7, also is beneficial.

Performance Monitor

WHILE YOU READ

1. After selecting a computer name in Performance Monitor, the next level of incrementation to choose is _____.

2. All Performance Monitor activity should be compared against a _____.

3. The two types of counters are _____ and _____.

4. True or false: The default view in Performance Monitor is Log.

5. TCP/IP counters require the installation of _____.

6. When there are multiples of an object (such as multiple processors), Performance Monitor allows you to select a(n) _____.

7. True or false: You cannot save charts in Performance Monitor for viewing later.

This chapter explores Windows NT 4.0's Performance Monitor utility. This utility provides an administrator with the capability to chart a Windows NT–based computer's performance in a given situation.

Monitoring System Performance with Performance Monitor

Windows NT Server 4.0 offers a performance-tracking tool called Performance Monitor, which collects data about system resources and presents that data in a graphical chart format. You can use Performance Monitor to

- Create a baseline of normal system performance.
- Monitor use of system resources for given periods of time.
- Identify periods of abnormal system activity.
- Predict system resource use given specific parameters.
- Justify upgrades to hardware and resources.

The Performance Monitor treats system resources as objects with characteristics or counters that can be tracked (see Fig. 8.1). Multiple occurrences of an object and counter, or variations on them, are called *instances*. The processor is an object that can be monitored, for example. It has counters that can be charted, such as the total percentage of processor use, the percentage of the processor used by the kernel mode, and so on. Recall that Windows NT Server 4.0–based computers can support up to 32 processors. If a given system has multiple processors, each processor is considered an instance. You then can track each processor's total percentage of use, total percentage of kernel mode use, and so on for each instance of the processor.

Most counter instances include a Total selection that provides the activity generated by all of the instances. For example, each of four processors installed in a computer would have a Processor>%Processor Time instance. You can monitor data for each processor. However, if you want a total value for processor use by all four processors, you can select the Total instance.

With Performance Monitor, you also can create and view log files, view summary statistics, and create system alerts based on monitored values. You use Performance Monitor primarily for two purposes: to create baselines of performance and to monitor aberrations from the baselines—in other words, to troubleshoot.

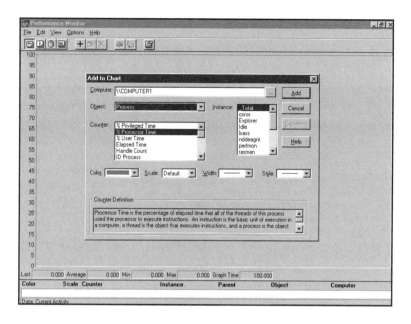

Figure 8.1
The Add to Chart dialog box displays some of the objects and instances the Performance Monitor can track.

 Key Concept

It does you no good as an analyst to turn on Performance Monitor to monitor system activity after you have detected a problem if you have no normal baseline of activity against which to measure the problem. A baseline represents the normal level of activity for a system. The certification tests assume that having a baseline for each system is desirable.

Eleven core objects can always be selected in Performance Monitor (see Table 8.1). However, numerous other objects appear, depending on whether certain services and devices are installed. Each object has numerous counters, also available by default. Every additional protocol, service, driver, and in some cases, application you install on your Windows NT Workstation or Server will likely add additional objects and counters to the list. The number of instances varies greatly with each object.

In this chapter, Performance Monitor counters are referred to by using the following notation: objectname>countername, where objectname represents the object to select, and countername is the corresponding counter for that object.

Two types of counters are described in the following list:

- **Averaging:** Averaging counters measure a counter's value over a period of time and show the averaged value of the last two measurements.
- **Difference:** These counters sometimes are included with other applications that are installed on your system. Difference counters subtract a measurement from the previous measurement and display the difference if the value is positive. Otherwise, a zero is displayed.

The Add to Chart dialog box contains an <u>E</u>xplain button. This button expands the dialog box to display a full explanation of the counter and the resource it monitors (refer to Fig. 8.1). This explanation is very useful, especially for those counters you might use infrequently.

Table 8.1   Core Objects in Performance Monitor

Object	Monitors
Cache	Effectiveness of physical memory used for caching disk operations
Logical Disk	Disk activity by logical partitions and drives
Memory	Use of physical and logical/virtual memory
Objects	Synchronization objects
Paging File	Pagefile activity
Physical Disk	Disk activity for each physical disk installed in the system
Process	Activity of programs currently running on the system
Processor	Activity of the CPU(s) installed on the system
Redirector	Activity of network requests generated by this system
Server	Activity of network requests to which this system responds
Thread	Activity of process threads

Key Concept

Logical Disk breaks the disk into partitions, whereas Physical Disk looks at the whole entity. Both can be useful—and answers to test questions—based on the scenario.

Key Concept

Five specific objects are of particular concern when troubleshooting your system and are the focus in this chapter: Processor, Memory, Disk, Process, and Network.

This is not to say that other objects aren't important to monitor. These five objects are simply the objects most often looked at first to determine aberrations from the baseline and bottlenecks in the system. After all, if the system is running with poor performance, the most likely problem spots are the processor (too many programs and processes running), memory (not enough RAM for the number of processes running), disk (too many disk requests), or the process itself (an application that overuses resources).

Configuring Performance Monitor

You can find Performance Monitor with the other Administrative Tools. You can configure four types of views with Performance Monitor: Chart, Report, Log, and Alert.

Creating a Performance Monitor Chart

The most frequently used view is the Chart view. The Chart view plots a real-time graph of the system activity being generated by the objects and counters selected (see Fig. 8.2).

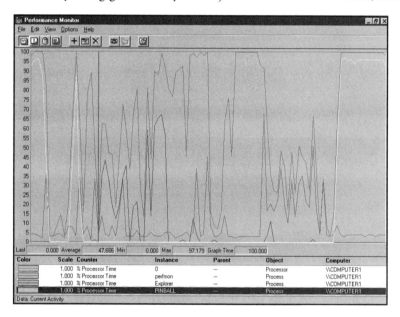

Figure 8.2
This chart tracks Processor>% Processor Time for the total system, as well as for three individual processes.

Here are the basic steps to follow when configuring a Performance Monitor chart:

1. From the taskbar, choose Start, Programs, Administrative Tools, Performance Monitor.

2. Choose Edit, Add to Chart to display the Add to Chart dialog box.

3. In the Computer text box, enter or browse for the computer you want to monitor.

4. Select the Object you want to monitor.

5. As you select an object, the Counter list displays counters associated with that object that you can chart. Select the counter you want to track. Select multiple counters by clicking the first counter, and then Ctrl+clicking the others.

6. If you are unsure about what a counter measures, click Explain to display descriptive text about the counter.

7. If appropriate, choose an Instance for each object counter. Again, select multiple instances for each counter by selecting the first instance and then Ctrl+clicking the rest.

8. Modify the legend characteristics as you want (Color, Scale, Width, and line Style).

9. Click Add to add the counter(s) to the chart window.

10. Repeat Steps 3 to 9 for any additional objects you want to monitor.

11. Click Done when you are finished.

Key Concept

Monitoring other Windows NT computers remotely requires an Administrator account.

Remote monitoring is recommended by Microsoft, because you can skew performance results locally due to Performance Monitor itself using resources.

Performance Monitor, by default, displays a line chart that charts activity for every second in time. You can modify these defaults by choosing Options, Chart to display the Chart Options dialog box.

Most of the options in the Chart Options dialog box are self-explanatory. However, note the Update Time section. The Periodic Interval is set to 1 second, the default. If you want to capture information in smaller or larger time intervals, modify the value accordingly. The value you enter will affect the Graph Time value on the Statistics bar at the bottom of the graph. At a setting of 1 second, it will take 100 seconds to complete one chart pass in the window. A setting of 2 seconds will take 200 seconds to make a complete pass. A setting of .6 seconds will take 60 seconds, or one minute, to complete a pass, and so on.

Key Concept

Chart view plots a real-time graph of the system activity being generated by the objects and counters selected. You can modify the defaults by choosing Options, Chart.

To save chart settings for future use, such as creating a chart to compare against baseline activity, choose File, Save Chart Settings. You then can load the chart settings later to monitor system activity as designed.

Creating a Performance Monitor Log

As was mentioned before, charting values really is ineffective unless you have some baseline values against which you can compare activity. Log files are designed to collect this kind of information for viewing later. Object and counter values, as well as values from multiple computers, can be collected and saved in a log file (see Fig. 8.3).

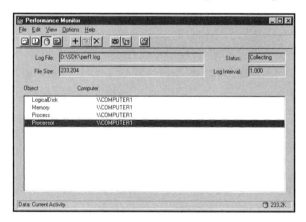

Figure 8.3
The log file as it is recording data for specific objects.

While the log file is collecting data, you cannot view its contents. If you want to monitor what kinds of data the Log view is recording, you must start another copy of Performance Monitor and configure the Options, Data From option so that it will display chart data from the running log.

To create a log file, use these steps:

1. Start Performance Monitor.
2. Choose View, Log to display the log window.
3. Choose Edit, Add to Log. Select all the objects for which you want to capture data and choose Add. The log now will record activity for every counter associated with each object. Choose Done when you are finished.
4. Choose Options, Log.
5. Enter a name for the log file and a directory to save it in, and set the Periodic Update interval if you want.
6. Choose Start Log to begin recording system activity.
7. Monitor the file size counter (shown in bytes) until the file grows as large as you like, or simply use your watch to collect data over a specific period of time.
8. When you have collected the desired amount of data, choose Options, Log, Stop Log.
9. Choose Options, Log, Save to save the log file.

To view the contents of a log file, use these steps:

1. Start Performance Monitor.
2. Choose View, Chart to display the Chart window.
3. Choose Options, Data From to display the Data From dialog box.
4. Choose Log File and enter the pathname and filename of the log file, or browse for it. Choose OK.
5. Choose Edit, Add to Chart. The only objects listed are those you captured in the log file. Select the object and each appropriate counter for which you want to view chart values. Choose Add to add them to the chart. A static Chart view is created.
6. Adjust the time view of the chart by choosing Edit, Time Window, and then make your adjustment.

Key Concept

Chart view is the default that Performance Monitor opens to. Performance Monitor does not enable you to print charts.

Although Performance Monitor does not enable you to print charts, you do have an alternative. Press Print Screen to copy a Chart window to the Clipboard. Then paste the window into a word processing document and print it that way. You also could export the data to an Excel spreadsheet and use its utilities to create graphs and analyze the data.

Creating a Performance Monitor Report

The Report view enables you to see a summary window of the object and counter values recorded in a given log file, or collected dynamically for specified values from a current chart (see Fig. 8.4). Each object and its counters and instances are summarized in this view.

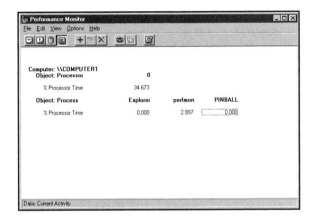

Figure 8.4
This report is based on and summarizes the values charted in Figure 8.2.

To create a report, use these steps:

1. Choose View, Report from the menu.
2. Choose Edit, Add to Report. The Add to Report dialog box appears, which is similar to the Add to Chart dialog box.
3. Add the desired objects, counters, and instances as you did when creating a chart (see "Creating a Performance Monitor Chart," earlier in this chapter).

Creating a Performance Monitor Alert

The Alert view enables the administrator to monitor a system, and record and receive alerts when a specified threshold is reached for given counters and instances. You configure alert settings in the Add to Alert dialog box (see Fig. 8.5). This feature enables an administrator to continue to work—perhaps remotely—until notified of an alert.

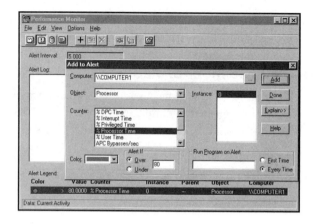

Figure 8.5
An alert is generated when the Processor>% Processor Time counter exceeds 80 percent for a period of five seconds.

Many counters can be measured concurrently in Alert view, and up to 1,000 alerts can be recorded before the oldest are overwritten with new information. As with charts, logs, and reports, alerts can be saved for future reference. For example, you might use alerts as documentation of increases in resource use when specific applications are run or when services are started. You then can use the saved files for troubleshooting or as growth-prediction tools.

To create an alert, use these steps:

1. Choose View, Alert.

2. Choose Edit, Add to Alert to display the Add to Alert dialog box (surprisingly similar to the Add to Chart and Add to Report dialog boxes).

3. Add the desired objects, counters, and instances as you did when creating a chart (see "Creating a Performance Monitor Chart," earlier in this chapter).

4. Enter an alert threshold appropriate to the counter selected in the Alert If section. For example, select Over and 90 for the Processor>% Processor Time counter if you want to generate an alert when the counter exceeds 80 percent over a default period of time. (The default is five seconds.)

5. Optionally, enter the name of a program or command prompt command to execute when the threshold is reached in the Run Program on Alert text box. You can configure the program or command to execute the first time the alert is generated, or every time the alert is generated. For example, you might enter the command

   ```
   NET SEND COMPUTER1 Processor Limit Exceeded
   ```

to send a system message to COMPUTER1, where the administrator is currently working, to notify the administrator of the alert.

Key Concept

Alerts inform you only *after* a situation has occurred—for example, when processor use has reached 100 percent.

Considering Specific Objects to Monitor

There are five useful objects to monitor, especially when creating a baseline of normal system activity: processor, process, disk, memory, and network. This section outlines specific counters that can be useful to monitor for each object.

Monitoring the Processor

The Processor object monitors processor use by the system. There are four counters that you may want to chart.

Processor>%Processor Time (refer to Fig. 8.2) tracks the total processor use and gives a picture of just how busy the processor is. This counter alone is not enough to tell you what is driving the processor to a particular level of use, but it does help to indicate whether the problem or bottleneck is related in any way to the processor.

Processor>%User Time and Processor>%Privileged Time define processor use by displaying what percentage of the total processor use pertains to the user mode (application) or the kernel mode (Executive Services) components of the Windows NT 4.0 operating system activities. Again, these counters do not indicate what specific activities are driving the percentages. Microsoft recommends that these three counters (%Processor Time, %User Time, and %Privileged Time) should, in general, remain below 75 to 80 percent, depending on computer use. For example, you would expect these values to be lower on a desktop computer, but consistently higher on a server running a client/server or system management application—for example, Microsoft Systems Management Server.

Processor>Interrupts/Sec tracks the number of device interrupt requests made from hardware devices, such as network cards or disk controllers, which are serviced by the processor. The optimum number of requests will vary from processor to processor. For example, you would expect a Pentium-based processor to handle perhaps three times as many requests as a 486 processor. In general, the higher the number (greater than 1,000 suggested for 486), the more likely the problem is related to the hardware rather than the processor.

If you suspect a hardware-related problem, you might next monitor queue lengths for the suspected hardware devices, such as the disk controller or network card. Optimally, only one request should be waiting in the queue for each device. Queue lengths greater than 2 indicate which device (which may need to be replaced or upgraded) is the likely culprit causing the bottleneck. Processor object counters, as with all object counters, should never be monitored alone. As pointed out previously, the mere indication of activity beyond the norm does not in itself point to the processor as the focus of the problem. Use these and the other object counters recommended to draw attention to a problem. Then add other object counters to help pinpoint and troubleshoot the problem.

You can use two additional counters other than Processor object counters to identify the processor as a potential bottleneck. The first is the System>Processor Queue Length. This counter tracks the number of requests currently waiting for processing. At least one process thread also must be monitored for any data to be collected for this counter. Microsoft suggests that the queue length value should not be greater than 2. Even if it is greater than 2, it may not necessarily mean that the processor is the bottleneck. A particular application or process may be generating excessive requests. Your next step would be to monitor %Processor usage for individual suspected processes to obtain further results.

The other counter is the Server Work Queues>Queue Length counter. Similar to the System>Processor Queue Length counter, this one indicates the number of requests for network resources currently in the queue. Again, this value should not exceed 2 on average.

Monitoring Processes

For every service that is loaded and every application that is run, a process is created by Windows NT—a process that can be monitored by Performance Monitor. Each process is considered an instance in this case, and each Process object instance has several counters that can be charted.

Notice that the %Processor Time can be tracked for each process instance (see Fig. 8.6). This is how you can determine which specific process is driving the processor to higher-than-normal use.

Another useful process counter is the Process>Working Set. This counter actually tracks the amount of RAM required by the process and can be used to help determine when additional RAM is necessary. For example, if paging appears to be excessive, you might monitor the working sets of the processes suspected of causing the increased paging. The Memory>Pages/Sec example in the next section gives a complete scenario for combining counters to determine a need for additional RAM.

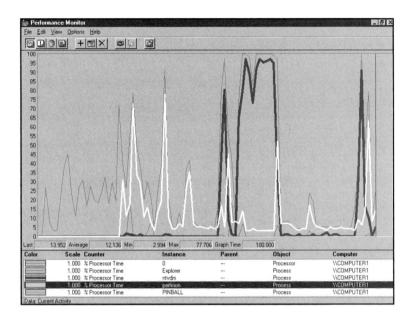

Figure 8.6
The Performance Monitor is driving the total percentage of processor use.

Monitoring Memory

Perhaps the most common problem encountered on heavily used computers is inadequate RAM for the processes to perform at their optimum rates. Several Memory object counters can be of particular service to you (see Fig. 8.7). In this chart, the Memory>Pages/Sec counter (thick dark line) is somewhat high, with the Memory>Committed Bytes counter (highlighted in white) at about 22MB larger than available RAM (16MB on this computer). This indicates that the computer may need to add more RAM to improve performance and reduce paging.

Memory>Committed Bytes indicates the amount of virtual memory currently stored in physical RAM or the pagefile. If this value is consistently larger than the total RAM installed on the computer, you may need to install additional RAM to accommodate the system's memory requirements and reduce paging.

Memory>Commit Limit indicates the number of bytes that can be written (committed) to the pagefile without extending or growing the pagefile. As this number falls, the pagefile is more likely to grow. Whenever the page file needs to expand or grow, it must allocate additional disk storage space. This allocation requires extra disk I/O. Any time additional disk I/O is generated, your system will experience a performance hit. Use this counter to help you determine whether you need to adjust the size of your pagefile.

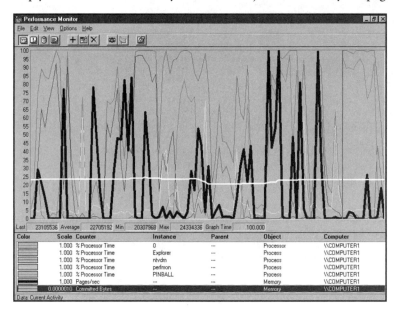

Figure 8.7
Some useful memory object counters.

For example, if you are running several large applications simultaneously (which is quite probable on a Windows NT Server), it is likely that the initial size of your pagefile is inadequate. If, as you load and run each application, the Memory>Commit Limit quickly expands and the pagefile expands, you can assume that the initial size is inadequate. You first need to determine the expanded size of the pagefile, which you can do by using Windows Explorer. Then modify the pagefile size so that the initial size matches the expanded size, which enables you to start with the right-size pagefile and eliminate the disk I/O involved with growing the pagefile. Although you can use Windows Explorer to monitor the size of the pagefile, the size shown for the pagefile stored on an NTFS volume probably will be inaccurate. This is because in NTFS, file size is not updated while the file is open; it is updated only when it is closed. Of course, the pagefile always opens to its initial size when Windows NT boots.

Key Concept

The pagefile always opens to its initial size when the system boots. For that reason, it is important to tune the pagefile so that it is large enough to accommodate your operations.

There is a way around this phenomenon. Try to delete the pagefile through Windows Explorer. You will get a message that the file is in use by another process (of course, Windows NT). Now refresh Windows Explorer, or type DIR at a command prompt to display the correct pagefile size.

Memory>Pages/Sec (refer to Fig. 8.7) indicates the number of pages requested by a process that were not in RAM and had to be read from disk, or had to be written to disk to make room available in RAM for another process. In itself, this value should remain rather low—Microsoft suggests between 0 and 20 pages per second.

Multiply the Memory>Pages/Sec counter's average value by that of the Logical Disk object's Avg. Disk Sec/Transfer counter. This counter indicates the average number of seconds for each disk I/O. The resulting value shows the percentage of disk I/O used by paging. Microsoft suggests that if this value consistently exceeds 10 percent, paging is excessive and you probably need more RAM. The actual threshold is based on the function of the particular computer. You might expect more paging to occur on a SQL server than on a desktop, for example. When combined with the Process>Working Set counter (described in the preceding section, "Monitoring Processes"), you can determine approximately how much additional RAM you may need to install in the computer.

Suppose that you have determined that paging is excessive by multiplying the Memory object's Pages/Sec counter by the Logical Disk>Avg. Disk Sec/Transfer counter and receiving a value of 20 percent. You presume that you need additional RAM. But how much?

You also have been tracking the Processor>%Processor Time for the processor as a whole, and for several suspect processes. You note three processes that really push the processor.

For each process, also monitor that process' Process>Working Set counter. Recall that this is the amount of RAM required by the process. Make note of the amount of RAM used by each process. Now terminate one of the processes. Check the percent of disk I/O used by paging. Has it dropped below the acceptable threshold (10 percent, as recommended by Microsoft)? If so, then the amount of RAM required by that application is the minimum amount of additional RAM to add to your computer. If not, terminate another application and check the results again. Keep doing this until the pagefile I/O drops to an acceptable level, and add up the working set values for the terminated processes. The total represents the minimum amount of RAM to add to your computer. Administrators often round this value up to the nearest multiple of 4.

Monitoring Disk Activity

Two objects actually are related to disk activity: the physical disk object and the logical disk object. The physical disk object counters track activity related to the disk drive as a whole and can be used to determine whether one disk drive is being used more than another for load-balancing purposes (see Fig. 8.8). For example, if the activity of a disk is particularly high because of operating system requests and pagefile I/O, you might want to move the pagefile to a disk that is being underused, especially if the disk controller can write to each disk concurrently. The number of instances will be the number of physical drives installed on the computer.

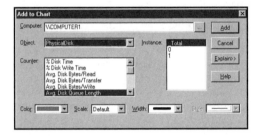

Figure 8.8
Some of the counters available for tracking activity on the physical disk. Note that there is an instance for each of two disk drives, as well as a Total option that measures both drives together.

The Logical Disk object counters track activity related to specific partitions on each disk and can be used to locate the source of activity on the disk—for example, on what partition the pagefile is located. The number of instances will be the number of partitions created by drive letter.

Both objects pretty much have the same group of counters for tracking activity. The following five counters, in particular, can be useful:

■ **Avg. Disk Sec/Transfer:** You saw this counter when reviewing Memory object counters in the preceding section, "Monitoring Memory." This counter shows the average amount of time for disk I/O to complete and can be used with the Memory object's Pages/Sec counter to determine whether paging is excessive.

■ **Current Disk Queue Length:** This counter represents the number of requests for disk I/O waiting to be serviced. This number generally should be less than 2. Consistently high numbers indicate that the disk is being overused or should be upgraded to a faster access disk.

- **Disk Bytes/Sec:** This counter indicates the rate at which data is transferred during disk I/O. The higher the value, the more efficient the performance.

- **Avg. Disk Bytes/Transfer:** This counter is the average number of bytes of data transferred during disk I/O. As with Disk Bytes/Sec, the larger the value, the more efficient the disk transfer.

- **%Disk Time:** This counter represents the amount of time spent servicing disk I/O requests. A consistently high number indicates that the disk is being heavily used. You may choose to determine which processes are driving this use and partition or move the applications to a less heavily used disk to load balance disk activity.

These counter values, when used with the others already discussed, can help you determine bottlenecks and possible courses of action to alleviate disk-related problems. In Figure 8.9's sample chart, the %Disk Time, Avg. Disk Sec/Transfer, and Current Disk Queue Length values are consistently high, indicating that the disk is being heavily used. Additional analysis can determine what is being accessed (files, applications, and so on) and whether anything can be done to improve disk performance.

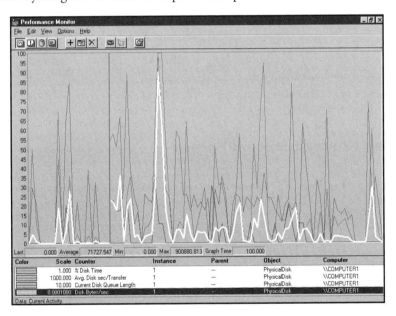

Figure 8.9
Counters that can help determine bottlenecks in a system.

Key Concept

Although Disk object counters are visible in the Add to Chart dialog box, they are not enabled by default. This is because the resource required to monitor disk activity is rather demanding. You must enable Disk object monitoring before any charting can take place; otherwise, your chart will always display a flat-line graph.

Enable disk monitoring by typing the following command at a DOS command prompt:

```
DISKPERF -Y \\computername
```

where `\\computername` optionally references a remote computer for which you want to monitor disk activity.

When you are finished capturing your data, type

```
DISKPERF -N \\computername
```

to disable disk monitoring.

Disk bottlenecks generally are resolved by upgrading the disk or its controller, increasing the amount of controller caching that can take place (if possible), implementing striping on a server and load balancing applications across physical disks, or even moving heavily used applications to their own servers.

Monitoring Network-Related Objects

Perhaps one of the more difficult components of system activity to monitor and analyze is network activity. Windows NT Server 4.0 provides a rather thorough network-analysis tool called Network Monitor. This is a frame analysis tool that helps isolate and identify network traffic related to different types of network activity generated between two or more computers.

You also can use some network-related objects and counters to determine the performance of network-related processes on the computer. These include Server, Redirector, and entries for the protocols installed on the computer, such as *Transmission Control Protocol/Internet Protocol* (TCP/IP), NWLINK (the Microsoft IPX/SPX-compatible transport protocol), and *Network BIOS Extended User Interface* (NetBEUI). As additional network services are installed—*Remote Access Service* (RAS), *Dynamic Host Configuration Protocol* (DHCP), *Windows Internet Name Service* (WINS)—objects and counters relating to those services are added to Performance Monitor. If you have multiple network adapter cards installed on your computer, each of them will be considered an instance, making it possible to chart network objects and counters for each network adapter.

Protocol counters include Bytes Total/Sec, Datagrams/Sec, and Frames/Sec. In general, a high value is desirable, because this indicates a high rate of throughput for network activity. High values also can indicate excessive generation of traffic, however, such as excessive frames caused by browser broadcasts.

Key Concept

TCP/IP counters are enabled only if the *Simple Network Management Protocol* (SNMP) service agent is installed on the computer. When the SNMP service is installed, it also adds some TCP/IP-related counters to the Performance Monitor.

The Workstation Service on a computer can be monitored by charting Redirector object counters. One counter of interest is Redirector>Network Errors/Sec. This counter indicates the number of errors detected by the Workstation Service as it attempted to direct frames onto the network. The higher this number is, the more serious the problem may be. Use Network Monitor to observe and detect network traffic as a whole, especially to and from this computer.

Two more Redirector counters are Redirector>Reads Denied/Sec and Redirector>Writes Denied/Sec. If either of these numbers rises significantly, it may indicate that the server with which this computer is communicating may be having difficulty handling the number of network requests for resources it is receiving. You would want to monitor activity on that server to pinpoint the problem and devise a solution, perhaps by using one or more of the following Server object counters:

- **Server>Bytes Total/Sec:** Indicates the number of bytes sent and received by the computer responding to network resource requests. This counter gives you an idea of how busy the Server Service is on the computer.

- **Server>Logon/Sec:** Indicates how many logon attempts took place during the last second on the computer—locally, over the network, or by a service account.

- **Server>Logon Total:** Indicates the total number of logon attempts that took place during the current computer session. This counter, together with Server>Logon/Sec and the protocol counters, is particularly beneficial when used with Network Monitor to get a complete view of network activity relating to a domain controller.

■ **Server>Pool Nonpaged Failures:** Indicates how frequently the server tried to allocate memory for server-based request handling but was unable to because of a lack of physical RAM. Similarly, Server>Pool Paged Failures indicates how frequently the server tried to allocate paged memory but was unable to because physical RAM was inadequate or the paging file was full. In either case, it may be appropriate to reconfigure memory use by the server. You can do this by accessing the Server Service properties through the Network Properties dialog box. You can select four memory options:

- **Minimize Memory Used:** Allocates the smallest amount of memory to handle server-based requests for network resources. This value is adequate for workgroups in which the number of users accessing the server is small—no more than 10—or the server functions primarily as a workstation.

- **Balanced:** Allocates enough memory to handle up to 64 network connections to the server. This might be a member server in a moderately used network environment.

- **Maximize Throughput for File Sharing:** An optimal choice for file and print servers, because it allocates enough memory for heavier user access.

- **Maximize Throughput for Network Applications:** Allocates the greatest amount of memory for network connections to the server while minimizing the memory cache. This setting is most appropriate for servers running client/server applications, because it also takes into account that the applications will need to perform some functions in RAM on that computer. It also is recommended for domain controllers with large numbers of users configured in a master or multiple master domain model.

Key Concept

For the exam, know the four memory options available and when to use them:

■ **Minimize Memory Used:** 10 or fewer users

■ **Balance:** 64 or fewer users

■ **Maximize Throughput for File Sharing:** Ideal for Access server, file server, and so on

■ **Maximize Throughput for Network Applications:** Any BackOffice service server

Summarizing Performance Monitoring and Optimization

Here are some suggestions for collecting meaningful performance data, analyzing it, and using it effectively for problem solving and planning.

First, establish a performance baseline for the computer. If you do not understand what normal performance is like, you will not be able to accurately identify, resolve, or predict abnormal performance. Microsoft recommends that processor use should not consistently exceed 80 percent, for example. However, some BackOffice applications normally exceed 80 percent processor use when performing their regular functions and service cycles. Your baseline should include counters from each of the objects discussed in this chapter.

You will notice that as you select an object, one counter already is highlighted by default. This is the counter that Microsoft considers to be most commonly included in a measurement baseline.

Next, analyze performance for specific functions and during specific periods. If you are analyzing a file and print server, for example, you might monitor the Server>Pool Nonpaged Failures and Pool Paged Failures counters to determine whether the server memory is configured appropriately. You also might want to keep track of the number of users connected to the server concurrently, as well as the number of files open, by monitoring Server>Server Sessions and Server>Files Open, respectively. Because a high level of disk activity on a file and print server is expected (for example, file reads and writes, and print spooling), it is beneficial to track Physical Disk>Avg. Disk Bytes/Transfer, %Disk Time, %Disk Read Time, and %Disk Write Time. These counters can help you determine, among other things, whether one disk is enough, whether additional disks should be added and the files load balanced, or even whether disk striping might be considered as a viable optimizing solution.

On a domain controller, you might monitor the number of simultaneous logons the server is receiving and the number that it can handle at peak logon periods throughout the day by using Server>Logon/Sec and Server>Logon Total. Other useful counters include Memory>Available Bytes and Committed Bytes to identify how RAM and the pagefile are being used.

On servers functioning as WINS, DHCP, and *Domain Name Service* (DNS) servers, it is advantageous to monitor the object counters associated with those services to see how they affect performance on a given computer, in conjunction with the Network Monitor utility as it tracks network traffic associated with that service. For example, WINS servers perform NetBIOS name registration and resolution. The WINS Server>Total Number of Registrations/Sec and Queries/Sec counters can provide data relating to those functions as they take place on this computer and affect resources. Network Monitor can identify how many frames are generated for each function, how large the frames are, how long it took to send them, and where the requests for registration and name resolution originated.

Key Concept

As you add other services to the server (such as WINS, DNS, and so on), additional counters and objects corresponding to them are added to Performance Monitor.

Remember that you can monitor performance on computers remotely. This method is suggested particularly to avoid skewing the data collected due to the activities of Performance Monitor itself. Remotely monitoring a computer can be especially useful when trying to pinpoint network bottlenecks. If you suspect that a particular server may be the source of a network bottleneck, for example, you might consider remotely monitoring the Server object counters described in the preceding section, "Monitoring Network-Related Objects." A consistently high Server>Pool Paged Failures counter indicates that the server is trying to allocate paged memory but cannot—perhaps because it doesn't have enough RAM or the page file is full or inadequately sized. This causes server performance to denigrate, resulting in a potential bottleneck of network requests.

Document your performance measurements and convey the information appropriately. If the system as it currently is configured—hardware purchased, software installed, network traffic generated—can perform only at a particular level, document that fact. If a higher level of performance is required, use your data to justify to management upgrading in hardware, load balancing heavily used applications by purchasing additional servers and moving applications to them, upgrading *wide-area network* (WAN) links, and so on.

Extrapolating data collected for the current system can give a rough estimate of future performance. This process is more commonly referred to as *trend analysis*. Performance Monitor can help facilitate the identification of potential resource requirements, hardware and software upgrades, and budget needs.

Summary

This chapter explored the Performance Monitor tool and all the functionality it includes. Performance Monitor breaks the system into *objects,* and objects are divided further into *counters*. If multiples of objects exist, the counters or objects can be divided further into *instances*.

When you start Performance Monitor, it defaults to Chart view, but three other options are available: Report, Log, and Alert. Before you can draw any assumptions or conclusions about anything Performance Monitor shows regarding the current status, you must establish a *baseline*. A baseline gives you a historical perspective from which to gauge all future deviations.

Counters that appear in Performance Monitor are based on services and operations installed. For example, IPX-SPX–related counters appear as choices only if you are using the NWLink protocol. TCP/IP counters require the addition of the SNMP, and physical disk counters must be turned on with the DISKPERF command.

The next chapter continues the discussion of managing resources by examining fault tolerance (introduced in Chapter 7) in greater detail. RAID levels 0, 1, and 5, as well as the requirements and troubleshooting of each, are examined.

QUESTIONS AND ANSWERS

1. After selecting a computer name in Performance Monitor, the next level of incrementation to choose is _____.

    A: Object. Objects further break into counters.

2. All Performance Monitor activity should be compared against a _____.

    A: Baseline. In the absence of such, you do not know whether what you are viewing is an abnormality or normalcy.

3. The two types of counters are _____ and _____.

    A: Averaging and Difference

4. True or false: The default view in Performance Monitor is Log.

    A: False. The default view in Performance Monitor is Chart.

5. TCP/IP counters require the installation of _____.

    A: *Simple Network Management Protocol* (SNMP)

6. When there are multiples of an object (such as multiple processors), Performance Monitor allows you to select a(n):

    A: Instance. You can choose an instance of any object where there are multiples.

7. True or false: You cannot save charts in Performance Monitor for viewing later.

    A: False. To save chart settings for future use, such as creating a chart to compare against baseline activity, choose File, Save Chart Settings.

PRACTICE TEST

1. Frederick recently loaded two more C++ applications to modify on his Windows NT 4.0 Workstation. He has noticed that when he boots and loads all his applications, Windows NT takes longer to respond to application requests. You use Performance Monitor and notice that pagefile use has increased and that the commit limit for the pagefile increases rapidly when the applications are loaded. What is the *best* solution you can offer Frederick based on this data?

   a. Purchase more RAM for Frederick's computer.

   b. Move the pagefile to another disk partition.

   c. Increase the initial size of the pagefile so that it doesn't have to grow right away as the applications load.

   d. Move the C++ applications to another disk partition.

Answer a is a good choice but is not the best answer. Answer b is valid but is not the best answer. **Answer c is correct; increasing the initial size of the pagefile is the best solution.** Answer d is incorrect. It does not solve the problem, because the applications still must load, regardless of the partition on which they reside.

2. Desiree, a Visual Basic developer, has noticed that her system's performance has decreased since she began work on a large VB application. You use Performance Monitor to determine that the pagefile use has increased. You also notice that the pagefile, Windows NT system files, and the VB application are all stored on the same partition. In addition, the working set for the VB application shows that it consistently requires 16MB for itself. What solutions can you recommend? Choose all that apply.

   a. Add more RAM in the computer.

   b. Move the pagefile to a disk partition other than the system or application partition.

   c. Increase the maximum size for the pagefile.

   d. Create multiple pagefiles.

Answer a is correct. Adding more RAM allows the operating system and the application to stop sharing such a small amount, thus decreasing use of the pagefile. Answer b is correct. Moving the pagefile to another partition allows the pagefile to not have to read and write to the same partition from which the operating system is being accessed. Answer c is incorrect. It does not solve the problem and is invalid in this scenario. **Answer d is correct. Multiple pagefiles can be read and written to only as needed—offloading the pressure on a single file that must be accessed constantly.**

3. Which Processor object counter is useful to determine how much processor time is being used by application requests?

   a. %Processor Time

   b. %User Time

   c. %Application Time

   d. %Privileged Time

Answer a is incorrect. %Processor Time does not show the amount of time being used by application requests. **Answer b is correct. %User Time shows how much processor time is being used by application requests.** Answer c is incorrect. %Application Time does not exist. Answer d is incorrect. %Privileged Time does not show the amount of time being used by application requests.

4. Which Process object counter is useful in determining the amount of memory required by an application?

   a. %Application Memory

   b. Commit Limit

   c. Working Set

   d. Avg. Disk Sec/Transfer

Answer a is incorrect. %Application Memory does not exist. Answer b is incorrect. Commit Limit does not show the amount of memory required by an application. **Answer c is correct. Working Set shows the amount of memory required by an application.** Answer d is incorrect. Avg. Disk Sec/Transfer does not show the amount of memory required by an application.

5. Which Memory object counter helps to identify when to right-size a pagefile?

   a. %Pagefile

   b. Commit Limit

   c. Working Set

   d. %Disk Time

Answer a is incorrect. %Pagefile will not help with the identification of right-sizing the pagefile. **Answer b is correct. Commit Limit is the memory object counter to use to monitor the pagefile.** Answer c is incorrect. Working Set will not help with the identification of right-sizing the pagefile. Answer d is incorrect. %Disk Time will not help with the identification of right-sizing the pagefile.

6. On your Windows NT 4.0 development workstation, you have concluded that performance as a whole has decreased. You are not sure which process is driving this, but you have noticed that your disk drive has had a lot more activity lately. What objects should you monitor through Performance Monitor to troubleshoot this situation?

CH 8

a. Check the Processor>%Processor Time counter, determine the percent of disk I/O used for paging through the Memory>Pages/Sec counter and the Logical Disk>Avg. Disk Sec/Transfer counter, and check the Process>Working Set for every process running.

b. Check the Processor>%Processor Time counter, and determine the percent of disk I/O used for paging through the Memory>Pages/Sec counter and the Logical Disk>Avg. Disk Sec/Transfer counter. Track the Process>%Processor Time counter for every process running to determine which processes are pushing the processor excessively. Monitor the Process>Working Set counter for these processes in particular.

c. Check the Processor>%Processor Time counter, determine the percent of disk I/O used for paging through the Logical Disk>Disk Queue Length counter, and check the Process>Working Set for every process running.

d. Check the Processor>%User Time counter, determine the percent of disk I/O used for paging through the Logical Disk>%Disk Time counter, and check the Memory>Commit Limit counter for the pagefile.

Answer a is incorrect and does not point to the Working Set counter. **Answer b is correct and points to the Working Set counter.** Answer c is incorrect. It does not look at the memory pages. Answer d is incorrect. It does not look at the processor.

7. Which counter provides you with the total percent of time spent servicing disk requests for a given partition on a disk?

a. Logical Disk>%Disk Time

b. Logical Disk>Disk Queue Length

c. Physical Disk>%Disk Time

d. Physical Disk>Disk Queue Length

Answer a is correct. The Logical Disk represents a single partition, and %Disk Time shows the total percentage of time spent servicing disk requests. Answer b is incorrect because it is not a percentage. Answer c is incorrect. It does not look at a partition, but rather the whole disk. Answer d is incorrect, because it is not a percentage.

8. Which of the following counters provides you with the total number of bytes transferred during disk I/O for all the disks in your computer?

a. Logical Disk>Disk Bytes/Sec, Total instance

b. Logical Disk>Disk Bytes/Sec, for each partition instance

c. Physical Disk>Disk Bytes/Sec, Total instance

d. Physical Disk>Disk Bytes/Sec, for each disk instance

Answer a is incorrect. It does not look at the whole disk. Answer b is incorrect. It does not look at the whole disk. **Answer c is correct. It examines the whole disk and views them in terms of total value.** Answer d is incorrect. It does not look at all I/O.

9. Which objects are most beneficial to include in a log file when creating a baseline measurement of your system's performance? Choose the best three.

   a. Memory

   b. TCP/IP

   c. Processor

   d. Physical and Logical Disk

Answer a is correct. Memory use is something to monitor over time. Answer b is incorrect. It is relevant to the network and not the system. **Answer c is correct. Processor use is something to monitor over time. Answer d is correct. The use of the physical and logical disks is something to monitor over time.**

10. You plan to use Performance Monitor to help predict and troubleshoot server activity under various conditions. Which of the following is the best way to begin?

   a. Create and monitor a real-time chart during peak activity, and note the percent of processor use during these periods.

   b. Create a series of baseline logs of specific objects (processor, memory, disk, and network), each representing a different condition. Use these logs to predict activity under those conditions and to troubleshoot abnormal system activity.

   c. Create a baseline log that measures system activity during periods of average activity. Compare this to real-time charts created during peak activity on the system.

   d. Network Monitor is a better tool to predict system activity.

Answer a is incorrect. It does not reference a baseline—a necessary item for any measurement. **Answer b is correct. The use of baseline logs enables you to view normal operations and see changes over time, as well as suddenly.** Answer c is incorrect. It does not include multiple baselines. Answer d is incorrect, because it is invalid.

Disk Management and Fault Tolerance

WHILE YOU READ

1. RAID is implemented in Windows NT Workstation through which utility?

2. Disk duplexing constitutes what RAID level?

3. True or false: Disk striping with parity requires a minimum of three disks.

4. True or false: Backups are a form of RAID.

5. RAID is an acronym for _____.

This chapter discusses the Windows NT 4.0 Server fault-tolerance disk options available and some decisions you must make prior to the actual implementation. The concepts you learn will help you maintain data integrity and maximize the performance of your server's disk subsystem.

What Is Fault Tolerance?

Fault tolerance is the capability for your Windows NT Server to continue to do its designated tasks, even though the machine has lost one of its disk drives. Another part of fault tolerance is the capability to quickly return to operational status with all the data intact after a power failure. The goal of the enterprise administrator is to have as much "up" time as possible. This translates to no hardware failures and no software restores or rebuilds. The last problem the administrator wants is to have a server disk or any other type of hardware failure to cause the server to be down for any length of time. The network must be producing 100 percent of the time.

Windows NT provides some inroads to these networking needs. Hardware vendors also are helping to meet these fault-tolerance goals with redundant motherboards, power supplies, and other components. Microsoft's clustering services are making even further inroads into the zero-downtime objective.

Windows NT uses a fault-tolerant driver, FTDISK.SYS, and a software-implemented system called *RAID*. The acronym originally stood for *redundant array of inexpensive disks,* but now has come to also stand for *redundant array of independent disks.* Windows NT 4.0 also supports hardware-based RAID subsystems. You should create a RAID subsystem whenever you need to retain data integrity, increase logical disk space, or improve performance. In the event of a drive failure, your RAID subsystem will ensure data integrity and prevent downtime.

Windows NT–Controlled Software RAID

Windows NT software fault tolerance supports RAID 1 and 5 only. RAID 1 is called *disk mirroring.* RAID 5 is called *striping with parity.* The fault-tolerant disk driver also is used for a process known as *cluster sparing.* Cluster sparing marks a bad sector, reads or regenerates the information from the remaining fault-tolerant disk partition(s), and writes the data to the new cluster.

Key Concept

RAID 1 and 5 are supported by Windows NT. The subsystem solution RAID 0 is known as *disk striping.* Striping is not fault tolerant but is used to speed disk operations.

Hardware-Controlled RAID

Windows NT supports hardware-implemented fault tolerance. Support for most current RAID configurations is widely available through various third-party vendors. Be sure to check the *hardware compatibility list* (HCL) or check with the vendor before you purchase the hardware. Hardware RAID solutions use disk array controller cards, which handle the processing necessary to protect your data on the drives.

When Windows NT is managing a drive in a fault-tolerant manner, it sends separate I/O requests to each drive. It collects all the data from the drives and assembles it for use. When hardware RAID is involved, Windows NT treats the entire array of disks as one large drive and sends a single request to the RAID controller, which in turn sends requests to each of the individual drives.

CH
9

Key Concept

You can use both software- and hardware-based RAID systems in the same Windows NT box. However, you should use hardware-based RAID whenever the CPU has the potential of becoming the bottleneck, such as in an application server.

Disk Striping

Disk striping can be implemented through software or hardware configurations. Once again, disk striping is not part of fault tolerance. The data integrity—or in this case, the capability to keep any data—is as good as your last backup. Two reasons to implement striping are for high-speed transactions that involve both reading and writing; and to address the need for a large, logical drive. Disk striping normally is configured to be a logical drive larger than the largest physical disk storage devices.

You can create stripe sets using the Disk Administrator tool. The drives can be composed of the same-size segments, but with different types and manufacturers. For example, you can configure a combination of disks—including a mix of ESDI (Enhanced System Device Interface), *Integrated Development Environment* (IDE), and *small computer system interface* (SCSI) drives—and their free space into one logical drive. You can use multiple controllers in your subsystem. You must have a minimum of two physical drives, up to a maximum of 32 drives. Because the drives still function the same whether they are striped or independent, by putting them together as a stripe, you have concurrent I/O activity. Data is written and read simultaneously from all drives in this logical unit.

Key Concept

A stripe set isn't the same as a volume set. In a *stripe set,* Windows NT considers consecutive sectors to occur on each drive in turn. Because Windows NT reads and writes to all drives simultaneously, performance is enhanced. *Volume sets,* however, aren't written to each disk in turn. Instead, the information is written to drive 1 until it fills up, then to disk 2, then disk 3, and so on.

Stripe sets require partitions of the same size and increase performance. Volume sets do not require partitions of the same size and do not enhance performance.

Follow these steps to create a stripe set:

1. Select one area of free space on one of the drives to be used in the stripe set.
2. Select additional areas of free space on all other drives you want to use for the stripe set. You can select only one area of free space on each drive. You can select multiple free-space areas by pressing Ctrl while clicking the additional free-space areas.
3. Choose Partition, Create Stripe Set.
4. Select the size of the stripe set. Windows NT allows you to create a stripe set only as large as the number of free-space segments selected multiplied by the smallest free-space area. When the stripe set is created, it is made of an equal-sized partition on each of the drives where free space was selected.

Suppose that you have five disk drives. Four of them are 1GB drives, and one drive is a 500MB drive. When you combine the free space of all five drives, the smallest is the 500MB; therefore, Windows NT allocates 500MB on each of the five drives to be considered the maximum stripe size of 2.5GB. This is also the case when implementing RAID 5.

RAID 5 is discussed in the following section, "Disk Striping with Parity."

At this point, you need to select the desired actual logical disk size. You have 2.5GB available, and you only need 1GB. Using the spin box, reduce the 2.5GB to 1GB. Disk administrator makes the adjustments to the drives automatically. You now have occupied 200MB of physical space on each drive. Choose Partition and then Commit Changes Now.

Key Concept

Remember that whenever you make changes to the partitions on your system, you must commit the changes before formatting the partition.

Disk Striping with Parity **307**

Now you may format your logical drive as a *file allocation table* (FAT) or *New Technology File System* (NTFS). It is ready to use. You can use the remaining free space as a logical drive, another stripe set, a volume set, or a stripe set with parity.

Key Concept

Always format stripe sets, stripe sets with parity, and volume sets with NTFS. The advantage of DOS and Windows 95 being able to read a FAT is not valid with stripe sets, because DOS and Windows 95 don't understand stripe sets and can't use them even if they are formatted as a FAT.

Windows NT accesses the logical drive using 64KB units on each drive. Reading and writing are simultaneous across all physical drives and controllers used in making the stripe set.

Disk Striping with Parity

Disk striping with parity (known as a RAID 5 configuration) is the first fault-tolerant disk configuration you'll look at in this chapter. Windows NT takes care of the configuration process and the control. Windows NT 4.0 supports two software RAID configurations: RAID 1 and RAID 5. RAID 1 is disk mirroring (discussed in the next section, "Disk Mirroring or RAID 1"). Microsoft Windows NT 4.0, 3.5, and 3.51 support one striping with parity configuration: RAID 5. Using RAID 5 is the best choice for databases or other crucial data you don't want to lose.

If a drive fails, the server continues to function and no data is lost. The failed drive can be replaced, and the striping with parity configuration can be rebuilt. Table 9.1 lists the most common configurations.

Table 9.1	Raid Configurations
Type	Description
RAID 1	Disk mirroring
RAID 2	Disk striping using error correction code (not supported in NT)
RAID 3	Disk striping with ECC stored as parity (not supported in NT)
RAID 4	Disk striping parity stored on one drive (not supported in NT)
RAID 5	Disk striping parity stored on all drives evenly

As previously mentioned, you can create stripe sets by using the Disk Administrator tool. The steps are the same; however, for disk striping with parity, you must have a minimum of three physical drives, up to a maximum of 32 drives.

Follow these steps to create a stripe set with parity:

1. Select one area of free space on one of the drives to be used in the stripe set.

2. Select additional areas of free space on all other drives you want to use for the stripe set. You can select only one area of free space on each drive. You can select multiple free-space areas by pressing Ctrl while clicking the additional free-space areas.

3. Choose Fault Tolerance, Striping with Parity.

4. Select the size of the stripe set. Windows NT allows you to create a stripe set only as large as the number of free-space segments selected, minus 1, multiplied by the smallest free space area. When the stripe set is created, it is made of an equal-sized partition on each of the drives where free space was selected. The extra segment is necessary overhead to provide fault tolerance.

Let's use the striping example once more. You have five disk drives. Four of them are 1GB drives, and one drive is a 500MB drive. When you combine the free space of all five drives, the smallest is the 500MB. Therefore, Windows NT allocates 500MB on each of the five drives to be considered the maximum physical stripe size of 2.5GB.

Because you are creating a fault-tolerant disk subsystem, and this is RAID 5, you know there will be space used for the parity block. Every time you write to the disk, there is a parity stripe block for each row. Every new row written by the parity block moves to the next physical disk. Remember that RAID 5 parity moves from drive to drive. It is not random; it moves to the next physical drive. Because you do have a parity block, it also takes up space. Your 2.5GB physical space being used yields only 2GB. You lose 1/n storage space, where n is the number of physical drives.

Disk Mirroring or RAID 1

Mirroring is also a fault-tolerant disk configuration. The Windows NT 4.0 fault tolerance disk driver (FTDISK.SYS) writes the same data to only two physical drives. System and boot partitions, as well as data drives, are eligible for mirroring. You can mirror a FAT or NTFS. In the event of a hardware failure, the data on the mirrored drive survives and is up to date.

Follow these steps to create a mirror set:

1. Select a previously formatted partition.

2. Select an area of free space on the other drive you want to use for the mirror set. You can select the free-space area by pressing Ctrl while clicking the free-space area. The free space must be at least as large as the existing partition.

3. Choose Fault Tolerance, Establish Mirror.

4. Select the size of the mirror set.

Key Concept

RAID 5 (stripe sets with parity) performs better when the data is mixed with both read and write operations, because information is written 1+1/n times (where n is the number of drives in the stripe set) and the reads can be accomplished by reading all the drives simultaneously.

RAID 1 (mirroring) performs better when the data is largely read-only, because Windows NT can read either drive to get the information. However, writing incurs a slight performance penalty because the information must be written twice.

With mirroring, you're prepared for a drive failure; however, you're still susceptible to a controller failure. Disk duplexing is a level above mirroring in terms of fault tolerance and just requires another disk controller. If you want the added protection of disk duplexing, set up a mirror set with one drive on one controller and the second drive on the second controller.

Recovering from Hard Drive Failure

If there is a failure of a hard drive in either fault-tolerant disk configuration (RAID 1 or RAID 5), the fault-tolerant driver directs all I/O requests to the remaining drives in the chosen configuration.

The RAID 5 system uses the remaining drives and continues to implement the parity. Mirroring continues to read and write to the remaining partition. If the system partition being mirrored experiences the failure, you need to restart using a Windows NT fault tolerance boot disk.

Breaking and Building a Mirror Set

To logically break the mirror set, use these steps:

1. Using Disk Administrator, choose Mirrored Partition.

2. Choose Fault Tolerance from the menu bar.

3. Choose Break Mirror.

4. Assign the original drive letter to a good drive.

5. Delete the failed partition.

6. Select the drive and free space to make a new mirror.

7. Exit and restart.

Regenerating a Stripe Set with Parity

To rebuild a failed RAID 5 set, use these steps:

1. Shut down the Windows NT Server.

2. Replace the failed disk drive.

3. Run Disk Administrator.

4. Use the left mouse button and select the failed drive set.

5. Choose Fault Tolerance, Regenerate.

6. Shut down and restart the server.

Regeneration occurs at bootup time using the parity.

Performance Enhancement

To enhance the performance of any Windows NT disk subsystem, you should consider a few basic items:

- Disk controllers
- Caching
- Type and performance of the drive
- Type of work

Disk Controllers

Disk controllers can have a huge impact on server performance as well as disk performance. The cost difference between a good, fast, disk controller and a poorly performing disk controller is relatively minor. It makes sense to put good disk controllers in place. The server will perform faster disk requests and general tasks, because the disk controller won't be demanding as much CPU attention.

Multiple disk controllers and busses improve performance even more. The more disk controllers and busses, the more commands that can take place simultaneously.

Key Concept

Microsoft recommends that you use a Fast SCSI-2 controller as the minimum controller. However, a SCSI-3 Ultra Wide controller connected to a PCI bus would be a good choice as well.

Note the following approximate throughput that various controller types can provide.

Controller Type	Throughput
IDE controllers	2.5Mbps, depending on bus
ISA Bus standard SCSI controllers	3Mbps
SCSI-2 controllers	5Mbps
Fast SCSI-2 controllers	10Mbps
PCI bus controllers with SCSI	Nearly 40Mbps

You may have not noticed, but the farther you scan down the list, the faster the cards become. Keep in mind that you need the appropriate drive type to connect with the controller chosen.

Caching

Caching is the process of keeping a copy of some information close at hand. This ensures that it doesn't take quite so long to find important information when you really need it.

Key Concept

Caching is easy to understand if you think of the process in terms of an address book. Most of the numbers and addresses we keep in our address books are ones we could look up in the local phone book. However, it would take longer to search a thick phone book than it would to simply flip through our address book; so in a way, our address books are a kind of cache for telephone numbers.

Windows NT uses any available memory for cache when running. There are also disk controllers that have cache built in. When information is needed from the disk, the cache is checked first to see whether the information is available there.

Whenever possible, memory should be added to Windows NT instead of cache on a disk controller. When system memory is used as cache by Windows NT, it can retrieve the information without even going to the bus. The result is faster operations than even a disk controller cache can provide.

In addition, if Windows NT needs the memory, it can use it rather than use virtual memory, which greatly enhances performance.

Drive Types

As stated earlier, you must match the drive type to the controller. If you have standard SCSI controllers, you need SCSI drives. Additional considerations for disk subsystems include disk-access times. Typically, the shorter the disk-access time, the faster the transfer rate. Also look for transfer-rate numbers that the vendor sometimes supplies.

In addition to disk-access time, the speed of the drive—specifically, how fast the medium is spinning—can have a significant impact on the sustained throughput. Drives originally spun at 3,600 RPM, but speeds as high as 10,000 RPM are available today. Consider drives that spin at a fast rate for server applications.

Type of Work

Knowing the nature of the data greatly helps your decision-making process. If you know that the data is mission critical and you cannot afford any downtime or loss, consider RAID 5. Remember that you can lose a drive, and the data is still intact while the drive continues to function. The read performance is approximately a 20 percent improvement over a single drive. The write performance is marginal at best because of the CPU time needed to generate the parity block. If your data is mixed between reads and writes but is not critical, consider striping with no parity (RAID 0). RAID 0 provides the fastest read and write operations, but it is not fault tolerant.

Summary

In this chapter, you looked at the various types of fault tolerance—all of which employ RAID technology. RAID 0 is best exemplified by disk striping. Disk striping provides no fault tolerance, but it can speed disk reads and writes by accessing multiple disks instead of just one.

Beyond RAID 0, all other RAID levels enable you to recover from the failure of a single piece of hardware. RAID 1 can be disk mirroring or disk duplexing and involves making two hard disks exactly the same—thus enabling you to recover from the failure of either.

RAID 5 is known as disk striping with parity, and it requires between three and 32 disks. Data is written in blocks across the drives, with parity computed and written as well. In the event of a failure of any one drive, parity can be computed to reconstruct the value of the data that had to be there.

QUESTIONS AND ANSWERS

1. RAID is implemented in Windows NT Workstation through which utility?

    A: RAID cannot be implemented in Windows NT Workstation. In Windows NT Server, RAID is implemented through the Disk Administrator utility.

2. Disk duplexing constitutes what RAID level?

    A: Disk duplexing, a hardware enhancement over disk mirroring, constitutes RAID 1.

3. True or false: Disk striping with parity requires a minimum of three disks.

    A: True. Disk striping with parity requires a minimum of three disks and a maximum of 32. Disk striping without parity (not fault tolerant) requires a minimum of two disks and a maximum of 32.

4. True or false: Backups are a form of RAID.

    A: False. Backups are something that should never be overlooked, but they employ removable media and not an array of disks—thus, they are not a form of RAID.

5. RAID is an acronym for _____.

    A: Redundant array of inexpensive/independent disks.

PRACTICE TEST

1. What Windows NT software RAID configurations are supported?

    a. 1
    b. 2
    c. 5
    d. 10

Answers a and c are correct. Windows NT Server 4.0 supports RAID levels 0, 1, and 5. Answers b and d are incorrect. Windows only supports RAID levels 0, 1 and 5.

2. What hardware RAID configurations can be implemented in Windows NT Server?

    a. 0
    b. 1
    c. 5
    d. 12

Answers a, b, and c are correct. All RAID implies hardware (an array of disks). Windows NT Server 4.0 supports RAID levels 0, 1, and 5. Answer d is incorrect. Windows only supports RAID levels 0, 1, and 5.

3. A Windows NT Server has been configured with striping across six disk drives, and one of the drives has failed to spin up. How can you recover your data?

  a. Add the new drive and choose Regenerate.

  b. Add the new drive and do nothing. Windows NT does it automatically.

  c. Create a new stripe set and restore data from the backup.

  d. Delete the stripe set and add it back.

Answer c is correct. Disk striping does not include any fault-tolerance capabilities, and you must restore from another source. Answers a, b, and d are incorrect. These answers discuss fault-tolerance features native to mirroring and disk striping with parity that are not available in a standard stripe set.

4. A Windows NT file and print server have been configured with striping with parity across four disk drives. Users have complained of poor response time. Checking the event view, you discover disk errors. What steps should you take?

  a. Reformat the logical drive.

  b. Replace the failed drive.

  c. Using Disk Administrator, choose Regenerate and restart the server.

  d. Restore data from backup.

Answers b and c are correct. When a drive fails, you must replace it and then use the Regenerate command to compute parity and restore the data to the new drive. Answers a and d involve operations that need not be taken.

5. What is the minimum number of drives needed for striping with no parity?

  a. 32

  b. 3

  c. 2

  d. 1

Answer c is correct. Only two drives are needed for a stripe set without parity, and 32 is the maximum number that can be used. Answers a, b, and d are incorrect. A stripe set needs a minimum of two drives.

6. Your assistant called and wants to know why he cannot set up his mirrored disk on his workstation. Your answer is:

  a. He does not have the correct password.

  b. Only RAID 5 is available for workstations.

c. Striping with no parity is not available for workstations.

d. RAID 1 is not available to workstations.

Answer d is correct. Only Windows NT Server 4.0 supports fault tolerance. Answers a, b, and c are incorrect. Windows NT Workstation does not support fault tolerance.

7. You have SCSI and IDE controllers, and three disks for each controller to install on the BDC you are building. What configurations can you use?

a. Logical drive.

b. Striping with no parity.

c. Striping with parity.

d. Mirroring.

Answers a, b, c, and d are all correct. Logical drives, striping with no parity, and mirroring only require two drives, and mirroring needs only three.

8. You have a file and print server configured for striping with no parity using one *Industry Standard Architecture* (ISA) controller and four disk drives. You want to increase the read and write performance. What is the best option to use?

a. Add a second ISA controller to your configuration.

b. Add a fifth drive to your configuration.

c. Format the stripe set as an NTFS partition.

d. Replace the one ISA controller with two bus master ISA controllers.

Answer d is correct. Two controllers will allow operations to be split out and processed faster. Answer a uses two controllers but is not the quickest option available. Answer b adds another drive to an already full controller and is not a good answer. Answer c is incorrect because it is not the best option available.

9. Your Windows NT file server is configured with mirroring on one of the data drive partitions. Users have complained about the `disk full` errors and poor response time. You have 500MB available on each drive. What steps do you take to remedy this situation?

a. Back up data, extend the mirrored partition, and restore data.

b. Back up data, break the mirror, create a larger mirror set, and restore data.

c. Implement disk duplexing.

d. Implement RAID 5 on the free space and assign permissions to the users.

Answer b is correct. A mirror set first must be broken before it can be extended. Answer a is incorrect. You cannot extend a mirror set—you must break it and re-create it. Answer c is incorrect because it involves adding a second controller but not changing the size at all. Answer d does not address the question at hand and requires additional disks.

10. Which disk controller has the highest throughput?

  a. IDE standard

  b. SCSI-2 bus mastering

  c. Fast SCSI-2

  d. PCI with SCSI

Answer d is correct. PCI combined with SCSI offers the fastest throughput of any combination listed here. Answers a, b, and c are incorrect because they do not offer the highest throughput of all the choices listed here.

CHAPTER PREREQUISITE

You should understand the concept of Directory Services presented in Chapters 2 to 5. You also should have a general concept of Windows NT share-level security.

Managing Printers in the Domain

WHILE YOU READ

1. When does the print process start in NT?

2. In the printing process, the local _____ service makes a *Remote Procedure Call* (RPC) connection to the print server and copies the print job to the print server spooler directory.

3. True or false: By default, NT sends a separator page between print jobs.

4. True or false: The most common print job type is RAW.

5. The highest print priority is _____.

This chapter provides a short discussion of the Windows NT 4.0 print process, followed by discussions on adding and configuring network printing devices and working with printer pools and printer priorities. You'll also look at troubleshooting network printing. The concepts and procedures examined in this chapter apply to both workstation and server installations.

Examining the Windows NT 4.0 Print Process

In the past, configuring a printer was somewhat of a problem—not only from a local desktop, but also across the network. Microsoft has expended great effort in the Windows NT 4.0 operating system to streamline and simplify management of the printing process, particularly on the network.

Microsoft has been aware of the problems associated with local and network printing and has, throughout its history, successfully enhanced the process. For example, each MS-DOS application generally requires its own print driver to be loaded to successfully print to a given printing device. With Windows, Microsoft introduced a single set of print drivers that can be used with all applications. In other words, Windows requires the installation of one printer driver, which all its applications use, instead of a driver for each application.

Windows NT follows this same concept by using a generic set of drivers along with a specific printer minidriver that is used by all applications running under Windows NT. Windows NT 4.0 also takes this concept a step further by requiring a set of drivers to be installed only on the printer server and not on every installation using the printing device.

Before we begin, take a look at some of the terminology used in the Windows NT 4.0 print process. A *printer* in Windows NT 4.0 is the software interface between the application and the physical printing device, which consists of the *print driver* and the *print queue*. The physical hardware that does the printing is referred to as the *print device*. A print request or print job can be sent to a local print device (connected directly to the user's local computer) or a remote print device (attached to and managed by another computer or print server on the network). Requests also can be sent to a network interface print device, which is controlled and managed by a print server on the network but is connected directly to the network and not to a print server.

The printer, or software interface, interacts with the print device to ensure that the print device receives a print job that has been formatted appropriately for that device. The printer also provides the print management interface from which print jobs can be viewed and manipulated.

After a print device is made available to users on the network, any valid Microsoft network client (Windows NT, DOS, Windows 95, Windows for Workgroups, Windows 3.1, LAN Manager 2.x, NetWare, or Macintosh) and even OS/2 and UNIX clients are able to direct print jobs to that device.

When a print device is made available on the network as a remote printer, you are not actually sharing the print device itself. The actual printer, or the management interface, is being shared. A given print device might have several printers associated with it, each with a different set of characteristics, priorities, or permissions. This concept is discussed further in the section "Sharing a Printer," later in this chapter.

Windows NT 4.0 Print Process

The print process starts when an application makes a print request. As mentioned previously, print drivers do not have to be installed on each Windows NT installation. Let's explore this further. One of the innovative accomplishments Microsoft has brought about with the Windows NT 4.0 print process is to automatically download the required print drivers to Windows NT clients (all versions), as well as Windows 95 clients. Although these clients do need a print driver to process print requests, they do not require that a print driver be manually installed locally. When any Windows NT or Windows 95 client connects to a network printer server through the Print Wizard application, the Windows NT print server automatically downloads the required print driver to the client. For that reason, it is important that an administrator load all print drivers for all the different clients that will be accessing that printer (Windows 95, Windows 98, NT Workstation and NT Server) on the system.

From that point on, if the client is a Windows NT client, any time the client prints to the network printer, a version check is done to make sure the latest print driver exists on the client. If the latest version does not exist on the client, the print server downloads a copy of the newer print driver to the client computer.

Key Concept

Currently, no version checking is done between Windows NT 4.0 print servers and Windows 95 clients. If a new print driver is installed on the Windows NT 4.0 print server, each Windows 95 client will require the newer print driver to be installed manually.

The automatic downloading of print drivers to Windows NT and Windows 95 clients enables network administrators to easily provide a greater number and variety of print devices to their clients. Print drivers do not have to be manually installed on every client computer. Figure 10.1 gives a graphic representation of the print process.

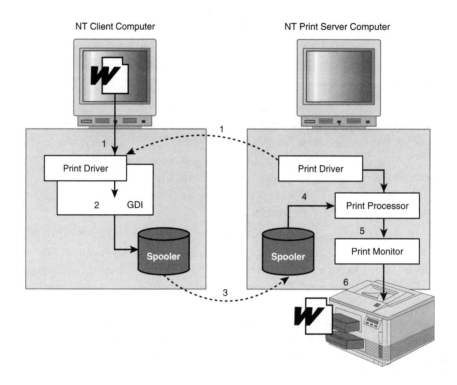

Figure 10.1
The Windows NT 4.0 print process for Windows NT and Windows 95 clients.

The print process involves six specific steps:

1. When a Windows NT client makes a request for printing on a print device attached to a print server, the client computer checks to see whether it has a local print driver installed. If it does not, or if the local copy is older than the copy on the print server, the print server downloads a copy of the print driver to the client. (If a Windows 95 client's print driver is older than the print server, the newer print driver must be loaded manually on the Windows 95 client.)

2. By default, the *graphics device interface* (GDI) component of a Windows NT 4.0 client operating system creates a print job in enhanced metafile format. This some-times is called a *journal file* and represents the print job formatted to print on most any print device type, such as HPPCL or PostScript. It then is sent to the local spooler.

3. The local spooler service makes an RPC connection to the corresponding service on the print server and copies the print job to the print server spooler directory. The bulk of the print process now continues on the print server.

4. The print job is routed to the appropriate print processor, where the print job is further rendered into a format compatible for the specific print device. This usually is referred to as a RAW file (refer to the section "Print Processor," later in the chapter). If a separator page has been requested, it is attached to the beginning of the print job.

5. The print job is passed to the appropriate print monitor, which controls access to print devices, directs jobs to the correct port, and monitors the status of the job.

6. The print device receives the print job from the print monitor and generates the final print product.

Printing from other clients is essentially the same, except that the appropriate print driver must be installed on that local client computer. The fully formatted RAW print job file is generated locally and routed to the print server spooler. Because no further rendering is needed, a separator page is added if required, and the print monitor sends the print job to the print device.

Windows NT 4.0 supports MS-DOS–based applications and Windows-based applications. In general, these applications take advantage of the Windows NT print driver and print successfully. Some MS-DOS applications that produce graphic print output, however, probably require that the print driver native to that application be installed for that application. It is safe to say that if the print output from MS-DOS or Windows-based applications is not correct, you need to install an application-specific driver.

Print Process Components

The print process consists of four basic components: print driver, print spooler, print processor, and print monitor. Each component is discussed in the following paragraphs.

Print Driver

As stated earlier, the print driver interacts with the print device to allow applications to generate printed output. It also provides the graphic interface through which the print device and queue can be managed. The print driver consists of three pieces—two dynamic links libraries (DLLs) and a characterization data file:

- The printer graphics driver DLL converts the print job output from an application to a print device–ready format.
- The printer interface driver DLL provides the interactive management screen through which the print jobs and the print device can be manipulated.
- The characterization data file provides information concerning device-specific characteristics of the print device, such as the amount of memory, internal cartridges, additional form trays, and so on.

CH
10

Here is an example of the three print driver files for an HP LaserJet 4 printing device:

- `Rasdd.dll`   Printer graphics driver DLL
- `Rasddui.dll`   Printer interface driver DLL
- `Pcl5ems.dll`   Characterization data file

Print Spooler

The print spooler actually refers to the spooler service running in Windows NT 4.0. The spooler is responsible for making a connection to the spooler on a remote print server. It also tracks print jobs, sends print jobs to the appropriate ports, and assigns jobs an appropriate print priority.

You can think of the spooler as the print queue for the Windows NT print process. Because the spooler is a Windows NT service, you can control it through the Services applet in the Control Panel. If a print job gets stuck or hangs, simply select the spooler service from the list, choose, Stop and then choose Start. This effectively cancels the stuck print job waiting in the spooler. If a print job hangs, or the spooler does not seem to be responding, you also can purge the spooler. If the spooler is purged, all jobs in the spooler also are purged.

Key Concept

It always is preferable to use the printer interface to try to pause or delete a problem job instead of stopping and starting the spooler service, which may cause you to lose any other jobs in the queue. If the spooler is not responding and jobs cannot be deleted, however, you must stop the spooler service and then start it again.

By default, print job files are spooled to the `<winnt root>\SYSTEM32\SPOOL\PRINTERS` directory. Depending on the size of the partition, as well as the number and size of the print jobs spooled, it is possible to run out of disk space.

Key Concept

You can use the folder Compression attribute, available through the Properties dialog box for files and folders on an NTFS partition, to compress the spool files and conserve disk space. However, keep in mind that compression does add overhead to your system and could, with large print files, result in a performance decrease.

If the spool folder is located on an NTFS partition, you can use the Disk Administrator to extend the partition into a volume set to increase the space available for the spooler folder. Windows NT also provides a Registry entry through which you can modify the location of the spooler folder globally for all printers, as well as for individual printers.

Use the Registry Editor to select the HKEY_LOCAL_MACHINE subtree and expand through to find the following key:

```
SYSTEM\CurrentControlSet\Control\Print\Printers
```

Look for a parameter entry called DefaultSpoolDirectory and modify its value to correspond to the new spool location. This change affects all printers installed on the computer.

On the next level below the Printer key, you will find an entry for each printer you created on the computer. Each of these also has a SpoolDirectory entry that, if modified, changes the spool location just for that printer. Figure 10.2 shows these two Registry locations.

CH
IO

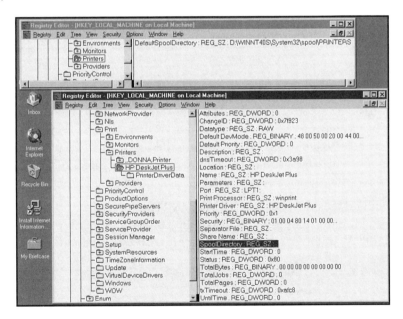

Figure 10.2
Two print spooler locations in the Registry.

When planning an installation of Windows NT 4.0, especially if the installation will be a print server, allow for enough print spooler disk space.

Print Processor

The print processor is responsible for carrying out any further formatting or rendering of the print job required for the specific printer to understand it. The default print processor for Windows NT 4.0 is WINPRINT.DLL. It recognizes and renders the print job types listed in Table 10.1.

Table 10.1 WINPRINT.DLL Print Job Types

Type	Description
Raw Data	The most common print job type. It represents a print job that has been fully rendered and ready for the specific print device, such as PostScript.
Enhanced Metafile (EMF)	A portable format that can be used with any print device.
Text	Represents a print job rendered with raw, unformatted ASCII text and minimal control codes (linefeeds and carriage returns).
PSCRIPT1	Used on Windows NT Servers running Services for Macintosh, it represents PostScript code from a Macintosh client destined for a non-PostScript print device on a Windows NT print server.

Print Monitor

As mentioned previously, the spooler tracks the location of the job and ensures that the print job reaches the appropriate destination. The Windows NT 4.0 print monitor is responsible for tracking the status of the print job. It controls the stream of jobs to the printer ports, sends the job to its destination print device, releases the port when finished, returns print device messages such as out of paper and out of toner, and notifies the spooler when the print device has completed the generation of print output.

Table 10.2 outlines the print monitors supplied by Windows NT 4.0. The print monitor installed depends on the print driver you are using, the print device type (such as PostScript, HPPCL, or DEC), and the network protocol used to direct print traffic.

Table 10.2 Windows NT 4.0 Print Monitors

Print Monitor	Description
LOCALMON.DLL	Monitors print jobs targeted for print devices connected to local ports.
HPMON.DLL	Monitors print jobs targeted for Hewlett-Packard network print devices. You must install the *Data Link Control* (DLC) protocol on the print server and identify the printer port by supplying the print device's hardware address.

Print Monitor	Description
SFMMON.DLL	Monitors Macintosh print jobs routed using the AppleTalk protocol to network print devices.
LPRMON.DLL	Monitors print jobs targeted for print devices communicating through the *Transmission Control Protocol/Internet Protocol* (TCP/IP), such as UNIX print devices and print spooler services.
DECPSMON.DLL	Monitors print jobs targeted for DEC's Digital PrintServer and other DEC print devices. You may use either the DECnet protocol or TCP/IP to communicate with these print devices. You can obtain the DECnet protocol from Digital Equipment Corporation.
LEXMON.DLL	Monitors print jobs targeted for Lexmark Mark Vision print devices using DLC, TCP/IP, or *Internetworking Packet Exchange* (IPX) to communicate.
PJLMON.DLL	Monitors print jobs targeted for any bidirectional print device that uses the *Printer Job Language* (PJL) standard, such as the HP LaserJet 5Si.

Additional LPD Device Information

The Line Printer Port print monitor (LPRMON.DLL) is loaded when the TCP/IP Printing Support Service is installed on the print server. This print monitor facilitates the routing and tracking of print jobs destined for network-ready print devices that communicate using TCP/IP, or print devices that are connected to certain UNIX-based computers.

Windows NT provides two command-line utilities for directing and monitoring print jobs targeted for UNIX host printers: LPR.EXE and LPQ.EXE. If you are familiar with the UNIX environment, you probably have used these commands.

To direct a print job to a UNIX host print device, open a command prompt window and enter this command:

```
LPR -S <IP address of UNIX host> -P <printer name> <filename>
```

where IP address of UNIX host is the TCP/IP address of the printer or host computer to which the printer is attached, printer name is the shared name of the printer, and filename is the name of the print job that you are directing.

To receive queue information on the print server, enter this command:

```
LPQ -S <IP address of UNIX host> -P <printer name> -l
```

Key Concept

Note that the LPR and LPQ command switches (such as -S and -P) are case sensitive.

Adding and Configuring Network Printing

This section examines how to create and share printers, set their characteristics and properties, assign security, and manage print jobs.

Adding a Printer

Recall the definition of a *printer*. When you speak of a printer in Windows NT 4.0, you are referring to the print driver and the interface through which you interact with the print device and from which you can monitor and manipulate print jobs.

The first step in creating a printer is to ensure that the print device is compatible with Windows NT 4.0. You can verify this information from the *hardware compatibility list* (HCL).

Only certain users can create printers and share them on the network. Administrators, of course, have this capability by default. However, members of the Print Operators and Server Operators groups on domain controllers, and Power Users group members on any other Windows NT Workstation or Server also can perform this task.

You add and connect to printers by using the Add Printer Wizard, which is accessible through the Printers folder in My Computer or by choosing Start, Settings, Printers. The following paragraphs and figures step through the process of adding a new printer that is physically connected to a local computer. The local computer (either workstation or server platform) acts as a print server for users on a network (a workgroup or a domain).

To create a new printer, follow these steps:

1. From the Printers folder in My Computer, start the Add Printer Wizard by double-clicking Add Printer (see Fig. 10.3).
2. If the printer is connected directly to this computer, keep the default setting of My Computer. Network Printer Server is used to connect to a remote printer. Click Next.
3. Select the port that the printer is physically attached to, such as LPT1: or COM1: (see Fig. 10.4). Click Configure Port to modify transmission retry of an LPT port or baud rate settings of the designated COM port. Click Next.

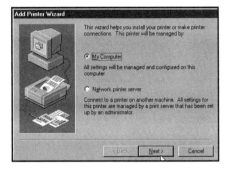

Figure 10.3
The Add Printer Wizard dialog box.

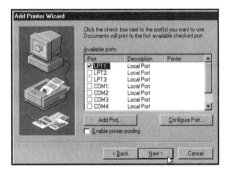

Figure 10.4
The Available Ports list box in the Add Printer Wizard dialog box indicates that the print device is physically attached to LPT1.

If the print device is a network printer or is identified through a hardware or IP address, click Add Port to provide new port information, or select or add the appropriate print monitor. (This information is covered later in this chapter.) You also have the option of enabling a printer pool. Printer pools and their benefits are discussed later in this chapter in the section "Print Pools."

4. The list of supported print driver options has grown tremendously (see Fig. 10.5). The driver selection menu now is divided into a Manufacturers list and a Printers list. If the device you are installing does not appear in the list, and you have an *original equipment manufacturer* (OEM) disk with a Windows NT–compatible driver on it, click Have Disk to install it. Click Next.

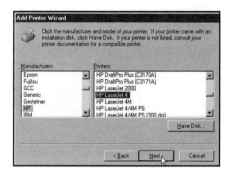

Figure 10.5
In the Add Printer Wizard dialog box, you can see the selection of a print driver for the
HP LaserJet 4.

5. Enter a Printer Name that is descriptive of the print device (see Fig. 10.6). This is
the name print administrators will use to identify the printer. Also, if the printer is
being installed for local use, you can identify it as the default printer for use by
applications. The first installed printer always is designated as the default. Click
Next.

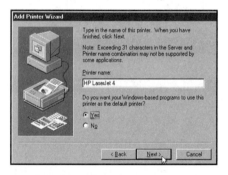

Figure 10.6
Here, the Printer Name remains the default name of the print device and will be the
default print device for applications run on this computer.

6. If the printer is to be shared, you can do so by selecting the Shared radio button
and supplying a Share Name; otherwise, by default, the Not Shared radio button
is selected. You can always share the printer later. When sharing a printer, enter a
share name that is descriptive for the users who will connect to this printer (see
Fig. 10.7). Click Next.

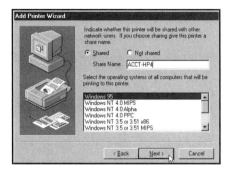

Figure 10.7
This printer has been shared using the user-friendly name of ACCT-HP4.

7. The Printer Wizard then asks whether you want to print a test page to the print device. This is usually a good idea, especially if you are identifying a network print device through a hardware or IP address. Click Finish.

8. As Windows NT installs the print driver, note the various driver files, DLLs, monitor files, and so on being loaded. If asked, supply the path to the location of the Windows NT 4.0 source files.

9. As the installation completes, the Printer Wizard adds an icon to represent the printer in the Printer folder and asks whether the test page printed successfully (see Fig. 10.8). If it did, the installation is complete. If it did not, you have the opportunity to go back and modify your settings. The new printer icon is your access to the print manager for that printer, its jobs, and its print device(s).

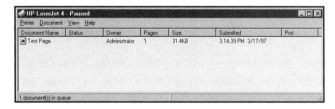

Figure 10.8
Notice the new HP LaserJet 4 icon created in the Printers box. You can double-click the HP LaserJet 4 icon to display the print manager window for that printer.

Sharing a Printer

If a printer was not shared during installation, you can share it later and configure permissions. The default permission for shared printers allows Everyone to print permissions.

To share a printer, use these steps:

1. Display the printer's Properties dialog box by right-clicking the printer's icon in the Printers box and choosing Properties. Or, double-click the printer's icon in the Printers box and choose Properties from the Printer menu.
2. In the Properties dialog box, select the Sharing tab.
3. Enter a user-friendly share name. This is the name users will see when they are determining which printer to connect to. Make the share name descriptive and informative.

Key Concept

Printer share names, as is true with all share names, must remain within the eight-character range in order for non–Windows NT/Windows 95 clients to be able to see the share name. If the share name is longer than eight characters, MS-DOS and Windows 3.1/3.11 network clients may not be able to connect to the printer.

4. Optionally, choose to install an alternative platform printer driver if needed.
5. Click OK. The printer now will be shared.

Setting Permissions for the Shared Printer

There are no permissions that you can set directly on a printer share. Instead, you set permissions on the printer itself. You can use four permissions to secure a printer in Windows NT 4.0:

- **No Access:** Regardless of whatever permission you have been assigned through group membership, if you get No Access explicitly or through a group, you will not be able to access the printer to print or view the print jobs.
- **Print:** The default permission for the Everyone group. It allows users to connect to the printer, send print jobs to the printer, and manage their own print jobs. Users can delete, pause, resume, or restart print jobs owned by the user.

- **Manage Documents:** Allows all the permissions of Print and extends job management to all print jobs.

- **Full Control:** In addition to the permissions allowed for Manage Documents, lets the user modify printer settings, enable or disable sharing, delete printers, and modify permissions.

Like file and folder permissions, the permission list is actually the *access control list* (ACL) for the printer. By default, Administrators and Power Users are given Full Control on Windows NT Workstations and Member Servers. Administrators, Print Operators, and Server Operators have Full Control on Windows NT domain controllers. On all Windows NT computers, the Everyone group has Print permission, and Creator Owner has Manage Documents permission. The Creator Owner group is a special internal group that Windows NT uses to identify the owner of a file, folder, or in this case, a print job. By assigning the Manage Documents permission, you are basically saying that only the owner of any given print job can pause, resume, delete, resend, or cancel it.

To secure a printer, use these steps:

1. Display the printer's Properties dialog box by right-clicking the printer's icon in the Printers box and choosing Properties. Or, double-click the printer's icon in the Printers box and choose Properties from the Printer menu.

2. In the Properties dialog box, select the Security tab.

3. Choose Permissions to display the Printer Permissions dialog box. The current ACL for the printer appears in the Name list box (see Fig. 10.9).

Figure 10.9
In the Printer Permissions dialog box for the HP LaserJet 4, the Everyone group has been removed and the Developers group has been added with Print permission.

4. Modify the access of the current ACL entries by selecting the entry and choosing a Type of Access. Click Remove to remove entries from the list (such as Everyone, Print), or click Add to add user and group accounts from the local or domain *Security Accounts Manager* (SAM) database.

5. Click OK to save the permissions.

Auditing the Printer

As with files and folders, access to a printer can be audited, provided that auditing has been enabled in User Manager (see Fig. 10.10). The audit events are saved as part of the Security Log, which you can view through the Event Viewer utility after auditing is enabled through User Manager or User Manager for Domains from the Policies menu. File and Object Access must be selected after auditing is enabled.

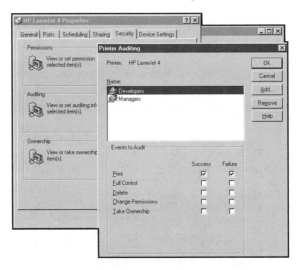

Figure 10.10
Here, users who are members of the Developers and Managers groups who print to this printer are recorded in the Security Log of the Event Viewer.

You can configure auditing for the printer by selecting Auditing on the Security tab on the printer's Property dialog box. Recall that you audit the activities of specific users and groups regarding the printer instead of general access to the printer.

In the Printer Auditing dialog box, click Add to display the account database. Select the users and groups for whom you want to record printer activity, and click OK. In the Printer Auditing dialog box, select the activities you want to audit.

Key Concept

Auditing causes additional overhead on resources and the processor. It is designed as a troubleshooting technique rather than as a reporting tool.

Taking Ownership of a Printer

The user who creates the printer becomes the owner of the printer (usually an administrator). If for some reason that user is no longer able to manage a printer, another user can be given permission to take ownership of a given printer.

Members of the Administrators, Print Operators, Server Operators, and Power Users groups can take ownership of a printer. Also, any other user or group that has been given Full Control permission for the printer can take ownership of that printer.

To take ownership of the printer, navigate to the printer's Properties dialog box, select the Security tab, and choose Ownership. Then choose Take Ownership.

Working with Printer Properties

Up to this point, this chapter has reviewed only two tabs of the printer's Properties dialog box: the Sharing tab and the Securities tab. This section explores the remaining tab on the printer's Properties dialog box.

General Tab

The General tab gives you the option of entering a descriptive comment about the printer, such as who can use it, what options it provides, and so on (see Fig. 10.11). You also can enter a descriptive location of the printer. This is useful when users are browsing for printers, viewing print manager screens, or receiving device-specific messages.

Using the General tab, you also can identify a Separator Page, select an alternative Print Processor, or choose the Print Test Page option.

Separator pages, sometimes called *banner pages,* identify and separate print output by printing a page before the document that indicates who submitted the document, as well as the date and time it was printed. Separator pages also have the function of switching a printer between modes. Windows NT provides three separator pages located in <winnt-root>\SYSTEM32 (see Table 10.3). You can select separator pages by clicking the Separator Page button.

Figure 10.11

In this printer's Properties dialog box, a comment and descriptive location have been added. When users view the printers or receive device-specific messages, they will see the location as well.

Table 10.3   Windows NT 4.0 Separator Pages

Separator File	Description
SYSPRINT.SEP	Causes a page to print before each document and is compatible with PostScript print devices
PCL.SEP	Causes the device to switch to PCL mode for HP devices and prints a page before each document
PSCRIPT.SEP	Causes the device to switch to PostScript mode for HP devices and does not print a page before each document

Separator pages are text files and can be created and saved with a .SEP extension in the <winnt root>\SYSTEM32 directory using any text editor. You can use the following control characters to customize a separator page:

\N	Returns the name of the user who sent the document
\D	Returns the date the document was printed
\T	Returns the time the document was printed
\Hnn	Sets a printer-specific control sequence based on a specified hexadecimal ASCII code

You can find more information about creating custom separator pages in the online help and in the Books folder on the Windows NT Server CD-ROM. Simply choose Find and search for "separator."

The P<u>r</u>int Processor button lets you specify an alternative print processor for the print device and port, and modify the job types it creates to accommodate your applications. For example, WINPRINT.DLL offers five default print job types: RAW (the default), RAW (FF appended), RAW (FF auto), NT EMF 1.003, and TEXT.

If an application is not adding a formfeed to the end of the document when the application sends a print job to a particular printer, the last page may remain stuck in the printer. You might choose RAW (FF appended) to force a formfeed on the end of any document sent to the printer, or RAW (FF auto) to let the print processor decide.

Key Concept

You can click the Print <u>T</u>est Page button at any time to test a change in printer configuration.

Ports Tab

You use the Ports tab for many different activities. First, you can use it to view which port the printer and print device are associated with and what kind of print device it is.

On this tab, you also can change the port associated with a given printer. For example, if the LPT1 port has failed and you move the print device to the LPT2 port, you just need to change the port designation here instead of having to create a new printer.

You also can use the port associations listed here to redirect print output from one printer to another. For example, if the printer stalls for some reason (perhaps because of a failed port, broken printer, or problem print job), you can redirect the output of the printer from the current printer to another printer, such as a remote printer (see Fig. 10.12).

Key Concept

It is a good idea to test this type of redirection before implementing it. If the spooling has been done in *Extended Metafile Format* (EMF), the print job will print correctly. If not, the remote print device needs to be identical to the printer from which you are redirecting.

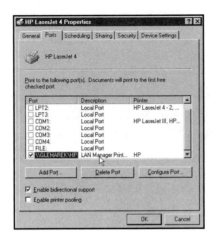

Figure 10.12
Here, the HP LaserJet 4 has been redirected from LPT1 to a remote printer HP on a server named Glemarek.

Click the Add Port button to add additional ports, such as a network port IP address for an LPD-enabled print device. If you need to redirect print jobs from an existing printer to a network printer, for example, use Add Port to add the remote printer to the list of ports, and then select the port from the list on the Ports tab. Click the Delete Port button to delete ports you no longer need. Click Configure Port to modify the LPT transmission retry value, COM port settings, and so on.

Bidirectional Support

When the print device associated with the printer you installed supports the sending of setting and status information back to the printer, it is said to provide *bidirectional support*. Any extra information about the print process that you can get will be helpful in troubleshooting. If the print device supports this feature, select Enable Bidirectional Support from the Printer Properties dialogue box.

Print Pools

One of the most useful configuration activities you can perform from the Ports tab is the creation of a printer pool. A *printer pool* represents one printer (queue or software interface) associated with two or more print devices. In other words, the same printer driver and management window are used to interact with two or more print devices that are compatible with that printer driver. This type of arrangement is particularly efficient on a network with a high volume of printing. Print jobs sent to the pool will print on the next available print device, thus reducing the time jobs stay in the queue. In addition, you only need to manage one printer instead of several.

As Figure 10.13 shows, three print devices are available for use on a print server computer. An HP LaserJet 4 is connected to LPT1, another HP LaserJet 4 is connected to LPT2, and an HP LaserJet III is connected to COM1. Three separate printers (one for each print device) can be created; however, this does not stop users from favoring one printer over another. Users may not choose, for example, the HPIII printer because of its slower performance. Consequently, print jobs may get stacked up in the queue on the other two printers.

Figure 10.13
Three printers are configured as a printer pool in this example.

By associating one printer with all three devices, users have only one shared printer choice to make, and their print jobs are serviced by any of the configured print devices. However, the user will not know which printing device the job will be printed to. For this reason, physically position all printing devices in the printer pool in the same location.

To set up a print pool, use these steps:

1. Choose Enable Printer Pooling on the Ports tab.
2. Check the ports connected to the print devices you want as part of the pool.
3. Click OK.

Key Concept

Make sure that the print device you associate with the printer in the printer pool supports that print driver. If it does not, print output may be unintelligible.

You can combine printer pools with other printers to produce a variety of output control options for the print manager. For example, three shared printers are created: one for developers, one for accountants, and one for managers. Permissions are configured so that members of each group can print only to their specified printer; however, it is imperative that any of the managers' print jobs are printed as quickly as possible.

The managers' printer is configured into a print pool by associating it with the other two print devices. Now the Developers and Accountants groups each have one print device that services their print jobs, but all of the Managers group's print jobs can be printed on any of three printers.

Scheduling Tab

In addition to defining the time when the printer can service jobs, you can use the Scheduling tab to set a priority for the printer and define additional spool settings (see Fig. 10.14). All three of these option settings help a print administrator further refine how and when print jobs are serviced.

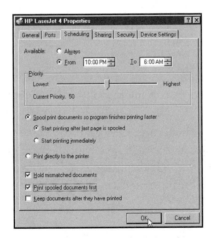

Figure 10.14
This printer begins sending print jobs to the print device after 10 p.m. It also waits until the entire job is spooled before it sends it, and it prints jobs that have finished spooling ahead of jobs that still are spooling.

Available Time

Defining the time during which the printer can service jobs is fairly straightforward. Select the Available: From radio button and select the time range you want. Print jobs sent to this printer still will be spooled but will not print until the designated time.

Suppose that you have a color LaserJet print device to which several groups of users send print jobs. One group, Graphics, tends to send very large graphic files that cause the other group's print jobs to wait in the spooler. You could create a separate printer for that print device and assign only the Graphics group print access. Then you could set the printing time to print at off-peak hours. The Graphics group's print jobs then will wait in the queue until the print time for its printer.

Priority

When you configure a priority for a printer, you really are setting the priority for all print jobs received by that printer. You can set the printer priority from 1 (lowest) to 99 (highest).

Setting a priority on a printer really only makes sense when you want documents sent to the same print device to have different priorities to that device.

Key Concept

The key to making a priority effective is to associate two or more printers with the same print device. This is the exact opposite of creating a printer pool, in which only one printer is associated with two or more print devices.

After you create and associate a number of printers with one print device, you can configure the priority for each printer on the Scheduling tab by using the Priority slider.

The following example will help illustrate the priority theory. Three groups—Managers, Developers, and Accountants—will all be using the same HP LaserJet 5Si network print device. Accountants send large spreadsheets to the printer, and Developers send small to medium source files. Managers, on the other hand, always want their documents to print as soon as possible.

To solve this printing scenario, create three printers and associate each with the same HP LaserJet 5Si print device. Set permissions so that each group can print only to its respective printer, and then set the priority for each printer:

99 (highest) for the printer used by Managers

50 (medium) for the printer used by Accountants

1 (lowest) for the printer used by Developers

Because the managers' printer has been given the highest priority, their print jobs will print ahead of the accountants' and developers' print jobs. Likewise, because the accountants' printer has been given a medium priority, their print jobs will print ahead of developers' print jobs. Because the developers' printer has the lowest priority, their print jobs will always wait until print jobs from the Managers and Accountants groups finish printing.

Key Concept

Priorities do not affect a job that has begun printing. If a developer's print job has begun printing, the manager's print job will wait until it is finished. However, any subsequent developers' print jobs will wait until managers' and accountants' print jobs have completed.

Other Spool Options

You can use several other options to determine how jobs are spooled. These options, in combination with print pools and priorities, give the print administrator many choices for affecting how, when, and where print jobs are printed.

The first option is Spool Print Documents so Program Finishes Printing Faster. This option is set by default and simply means that print requests are spooled in the Printers folder instead of being sent directly to the printer, which results in a faster return to the application for the user.

If you choose Spool Print Documents so Program Finishes Printing Faster, two secondary options are available. Start Printing Immediately—set by default—indicates that the print job will be sent to the print device for printing as soon as enough information is spooled. Printing, of course, will be faster overall. The other option, Start Printing After Last Page Is Spooled, indicates that the print job will not be sent to the print device for printing until the entire job is spooled. When used with printers of different priorities, this option can effectively prevent large documents from hogging the print device. Smaller documents are printed first, because they are spooled first.

You also can select Print Directly to the Printer. In this case, the print job is not spooled. It decreases printing time, because the rendered print job is sent directly to the print device. However, the user must wait until the print job is complete before control is returned to the application.

Did you ever experience the problem of sending a legal-size print job to a print device that only had a letter-size tray? The print job hangs the print device. The Hold

Mismatched Documents option is designed to prevent that from happening by comparing the format of the print job with the configuration of the printer. If the formats do not match, the print job is held in the queue and is not allowed to print while other print jobs in the queue proceed.

The Print Spooled Documents First option allows print jobs that have completed spooling to print ahead of those that still are spooling, even if their priority is lower. When used with the Start Printing After Last Page Is Spooled option, this option virtually assures that smaller print jobs print ahead of larger print jobs. If no print jobs have finished spooling, larger jobs print ahead of smaller jobs.

When a print job finishes printing, the spooler deletes the print job from the queue (the Printers folder), which deletes it from the printer management window. If you would like to keep the document in the queue to see its complete status, to keep open the option of resubmitting the job, or to redirect the job to another printer if it prints incorrectly, select the Keep Documents After They Have Printed option. After the print job completes, it is held in the spooler instead of deleted, and its status is displayed. For example, if you have an end-of-month report that is difficult to reproduce and you would like to resubmit it, use this option to keep the job in the spooler. On the other hand, because the jobs do remain in the spooler folder taking up space, it becomes the responsibility of the print administrator to remove these jobs when they are no longer needed.

Device Settings Tab

You use the Device Settings tab to assign forms to paper trays, indicate the amount of memory installed in the print device, specify font cartridges, and configure other device-specific settings—such as soft font or halftone settings.

Configuring these options is as easy as selecting the option you want to configure and choosing a setting from the list box displayed in the lower portion of the dialog box. The available options and their settings depend on the print device (or the printer) you installed. For example, whereas an HP LaserJet 4 only has one paper tray, an HP LaserJet 5Si may have several, including an envelope feed. The Device Settings tab reflects these device features. Some printers offer page protection as a feature, and this option is displayed on the Device Settings tab. Page protection ensures that the print device prints each page in memory before creating the output page. If you regularly send print jobs with pages containing complex text and graphics, enabling this option helps ensure that the print device prints the page successfully instead of possibly breaking the page up as it prints it.

CH
IO

Managing the Printer and Its Documents

Double-clicking a printer icon in the Printers box displays its print management window. You can choose from four menus: Printer, Document, View, and Help. View and Help are fairly self-explanatory. Most of your time will be spent using the Printer and Document options.

Printer Menu

From the Printer drop-down menu, you can pause the printer, change the default printer for the computer, manage sharing and permissions, purge all documents from the spooler, and manage printer properties. In addition, you can set document defaults that apply to all print jobs sent to the printer. Among the options that can be set are the paper size, paper tray, number of copies, orientation, and resolution settings.

Document Menu

From the Document drop-down menu, you can pause, resume, restart, and cancel print jobs. Each print job also has individual properties that can have their properties set just like printers. However, the most important options, such as scheduling a time and priority for the job, are available (see Fig. 10.15). Only users who have Full Control or Manage Documents permissions, or the owner of the document, can modify the print job's properties.

Figure 10.15
The Budget document is scheduled to print between 12 a.m. and 1:30 a.m. with the highest priority.

You display a print job's properties by highlighting the document in the printer management window and choosing Document, Properties or by double-clicking the print job.

The General tab displays statistics about the print job, such as its size, number of pages, data type, print processor, owner, and when it was submitted. In addition, you can specify a user account to send a message to when the print job is complete.

You can set an individual priority for the job here just as you did for the printer; however, the priority selected here overrides the printer priority. If there is one particularly large print job that has been sent to a low-priority printer that needs to be printed as soon as possible, you can set its priority higher from this tab. The priority change only affects the specific print job; other jobs use the priority setting of the printer (print queue).

Finally, you can set time restrictions for the individual print jobs. Using Figure 10.15 as an example, suppose that the Budget document is a large job that has been sent to the low-priority Developers printer. Other jobs have undoubtedly been sent to the Managers and Accountants printers that have higher priorities. Budget's individual property settings are being set from this document's properties sheet to ensure that it prints with the highest priority between 12 a.m. and 1:30 a.m.

The Page Setup and Advanced tabs let you set additional options for the particular document, such as the paper size, paper tray, number of copies, orientation, and resolution settings.

CH
IO

Exploring DLC, TCP/IP, and Macintosh Installation Options

This section describes the installation options for installing and configuring network print devices using the DLC, TCP/IP, and AppleTalk protocols.

DLC Printing

When configuring a print server to communicate with a network interface print device using DLC, you first must install the DLC protocol on the print server. This must be done in order to select any of the available network interface print devices. After the DLC protocol is installed, the Hewlett-Packard Network Port choice becomes available in the Printer Ports dialog box (see Fig. 10.16).

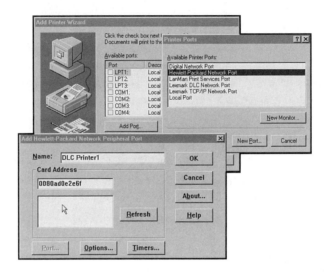

Figure 10.16
Adding a Hewlett-Packard Network DLC printer port.

After you select the Hewlett-Packard Network Port and click the New Port button, the Add Hewlett-Packard Network Peripheral Port dialog box appears. In the dialog box where the pointer is positioned (refer to Fig. 10.16), all available network interface print device *Media Access Control* (MAC) addresses are displayed. Simply select the desired print device for this port by its MAC address, give the device a name, and click OK. After you create a port for each available network interface print device, you can configure each port as shared on the print server. You also can configure printer pools using any number of the DLC ports.

You can access additional DLC configuration options by clicking the Options and Timers buttons from the Add Hewlett-Packard Network Peripheral Port dialog box. The Advanced Options for All HP Network Ports dialog box, shown in Figure 10.17, is accessed by clicking Options. The HP Network Peripheral Port Timers dialog box, shown in Figure 10.18, is accessed by clicking Timers.

The DLC Timers options control the network timing parameters and include the Response Timer (T1), the Acknowledgment Timer (T2), and the Inactivity Timer (Ti). The only time these parameters should be changed is if timeouts consistently occur on extremely busy networks.

The Logging Level options control how much information is placed in the Event Log. By default, all errors, warnings, and information events are entered in the Event Log.

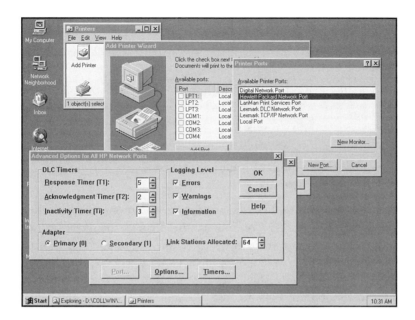

Figure 10.17
Setting advanced options for all HP Network ports.

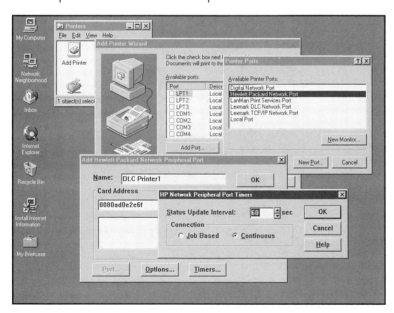

Figure 10.18
Selecting configuration options from the HP Network Peripheral Port Timers dialog box.

CH
IO

The Adapter Primary (0) or Secondary (1) option allows the HPMON software to use one of two possible adapter cards installed in the computer. Figure 10.17 shows the default—Primary (0).

The Link Stations Allocated option specifies how many network peripherals can be configured on this print server. The default is 64, with a range of 1 to 255. One link station is required for each print device configured.

In the HP Network Peripheral Port Timers dialog box, the Status Update Interval is simply the interval at which the status of print devices is updated. The default is 60 seconds, with a range of 1 to 32,767 seconds.

The Connection options control how the print server communicates with the network interface print device. If you select Continuous (the default), the server maintains a connection with the print device until either the server or the peripheral is turned off. This option allows a single server to monopolize the network interface print device. If you select Job Based, the workstation establishes a connection with the print device during each print job. No connection is maintained between jobs. This option allows other print servers to use the network interface print device when this specific print server is not using it.

Figure 10.19 shows the Add Printer Wizard dialog box with a DLC Printer1 port configured.

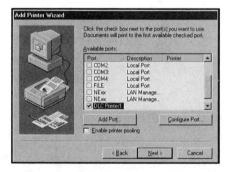

Figure 10.19
Select a DLC configured print device using the Add Printer Wizard dialog box.

TCP/IP Printing

Printing to TCP/IP network interface print devices also requires a specific installation configuration. This section outlines these requirements.

In addition to the TCP/IP, the Microsoft TCP/IP Printing service must be installed on the print server. Recall that both the TCP/IP and the Microsoft TCP/IP Printing service are installed from the Network icon in the Control Panel. Figure 10.20 shows the Microsoft TCP/IP Printing service installation.

CH
10

Figure 10.20
Installing the Microsoft TCP/IP Printing Service.

After the Microsoft TCP/IP Printing service is installed, the LPR Port option is available for adding and configuring LPR ports in the Printer Ports dialog box (see Fig. 10.21).

In the Printer Ports dialog box, click the New Port button to access the Add LPR Compatible Printer dialog box. You must configure two options in this dialog box: Name or Address of Server Providing LPD and Name of Printer or Print Queue on That Server. These configuration options can be extremely misleading. The first option, Name or Address of Server Providing LPD, requires the name or address of the MAC installed in the network interface print device, or the address of the MAC installed in a special electronic controller attached to the print device. This could be a UNIX computer that controls a print device, or a Fiery PC controlling a Savin color laser print device.

 Key Concept

The address required in the Name or Address of Server Providing LPD text box is not the IP address of the print server.

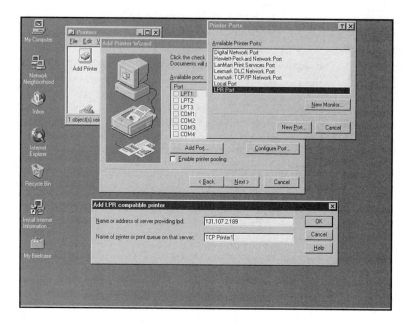

Figure 10.21
Adding and configuring an LPR printer port.

After the port is added, it is accessible in the <u>A</u>vailable Ports list box to be selected and configured with the specific type of print device (see Fig. 10.22).

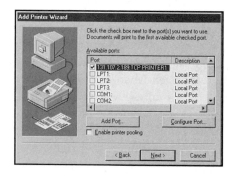

Figure 10.22
Select a TCP/IP configured print device using the Add Print Wizard dialog box.

Macintosh Printing

After the AppleTalk protocol is installed on the Windows NT Workstation platform or the Services for Macintosh service is installed on a Windows NT Server platform, either platform can function as a print server for AppleTalk print devices. Simply highlight the AppleTalk Printing Devices option in the Printer Ports dialog box and click the Add Port button. The Available AppleTalk Printing Devices dialog box appears, listing the AppleTalk print devices available (see Fig. 10.23).

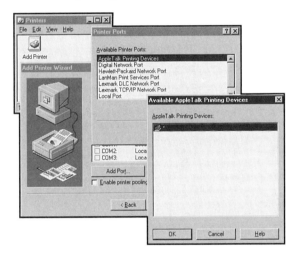

CH
IO

Figure 10.23
Select one of the print devices for each port, and configure each port in the print server.

Key Concept

Print devices attached to and configured on the Windows NT print server will be available for selection on the Macintosh computers in Chooser.

Troubleshooting Printing

This troubleshooting discussion contains some extremely basic steps to follow when the printing process fails. The following bullets outline this troubleshooting checklist:

- Check to see whether the print device is turned on and is online.
- Check to see whether the physical print device connection is good. Swap out cables, and check the network card and IP address. Also verify the configured MAC address.

- Verify that the printer driver installed is compatible with the print device. Verify that the correct version of print driver is installed (3.1, 3.5/3.51, 4.0, or 95). Also verify that the print driver for the correct platform is installed (I386, Alpha, MIPS, or PowerPC).

- Confirm that the printer is available and has been selected. Verify that sharing has been enabled and that the permissions allow printing to take place for the users affected.

- Verify that the appropriate print port has been selected and configured by printing a test page.

- Monitor network traffic in the case of remote printing to verify that print jobs are being routed correctly and are not being dropped.

- Check the amount of disk space available for spooling. Recall that the default spool directory is `<winnt root>\SYSTEM32\Spool\Printers`. The installation partition often contains only the Windows NT files and is kept purposely small. If there is not enough space for the spooled files, printing will fail. Either add more disk space (extend the partition if it is NTFS), or move the spool folder to a disk with adequate space by editing the Registry. Disk compression also could be enabled for the spool directory; however, this could have a negative effect on printing performance for large print jobs. Recall that the Registry location to change the default spool folder is `HKEY_LOCAL_MACHINE\System\CurrentControlSet\Control\Print\Printers`.

- Determine whether the printing problem is caused by a specific application error or occurs within all applications. Some MS-DOS and Windows 16-bit applications may require that their own print drivers are installed to successfully print their documents.

- Determine whether the printing problem is because a nonupdated print driver is installed on a Windows 95 client. Recall that no version checking is done between a Windows NT print server and a Windows 95 client; the update must be done manually on the Windows 95 client.

- Resubmit the print job to print to a file, and then copy the file to a printer port. If the job prints successfully, the problem may be related to the spooler or transmission process. If the job does not print successfully, the problem probably is related to the application or printer driver.

Another source of help for troubleshooting printing problems is the built-in Windows NT Help program. It also provides a set of troubleshooting steps and tips to help resolve printing-related problems. Access help for printing problems by following these steps:

1. Choose <u>H</u>elp, <u>H</u>elp Topics from the menu of any window opened through My Computer or Network Neighborhood; or choose Start, <u>H</u>elp.

2. Select the Contents tab in the Help dialog box.

3. Double-click the Troubleshooting contents entry.

4. Select the topic If You Have Trouble Printing.

5. Find the problem you are having and click it.

6. Help guides you through a series of questions and suggestions to help resolve the problem.

7. Exit Help when you are finished by closing the Help window.

Additional Considerations

As noted earlier, most printing problems stem from an improper print driver, inadequate disk space, incorrect port or address settings, or restrictive permissions. Also, recall that most older MS-DOS–based applications and some Windows-based applications require that their own printer driver be installed. Be sure to consider these possibilities as well when troubleshooting.

Windows-based applications print just like they did under Windows. Settings saved in WIN.INI or CONFIG.SYS are copied into the Windows NT Registry and are used for these applications printing under Windows NT. Applications that produce PostScript-specific graphics probably will print incorrectly or not at all. If no default printer has been selected, these applications produce an out-of-memory error message when loading or do not allow the selection of fonts.

If print jobs stall in a printer, or no one is able to print to it any longer, the spooler probably has stalled. You can purge the spooler of its documents by starting the Print Manager for that printer and choosing Purge Print Documents from the <u>P</u>rint menu. You also can stop and restart the spooler service through the Services applet in the Control Panel to purge the specific job that has stalled.

If your print server and clients happen to be of different or mixed platforms, and you want the print server to download the appropriate driver to all the Windows NT Workstations, you need to install the appropriate platform drivers on the print server. A given print server may have multiple platform drivers installed for just this purpose.

Suppose that your print server is a *reduced instruction set computer* (RISC)–based DEC Alpha computer. The Windows NT clients connecting to shared printers on the print server are Intel-based computers. You must install the Windows NT 4.0 Alpha printer driver in order for the print server to interact successfully with the print device. In addition, the Windows NT 4.0 Intel print driver must be installed on the print server for it to automatically download the Intel print driver to Intel clients. When an Intel client accesses the shared printer, the Intel driver is downloaded to them. The Alpha print server, in turn, uses the Alpha driver to manage the print job on the print device.

Table 10.4 lists the folders in which the drivers will be located for Windows 95 and the different Windows NT versions. The printer driver location starts with `<Winnt root>\System32\Spool\Drivers\`.

Table 10.4 Windows NT Printer Driver Locations

Location	Description
Win40	Windows 95 drivers
w32?86\0	Windows NT 3.1 Intel drivers
w32?86\1	Windows NT 3.5/3.51 Intel drivers
w32?86\2	Windows NT 4.0 Intel drivers
Alpha\0	Windows NT 3.1 Alpha drivers
Alpha\1	Windows NT 3.5/3.51 Alpha drivers
Alpha\2	Windows NT 4.0 Alpha drivers
MIPS\0	Windows NT 3.1 MIPS drivers
MIPS\1	Windows NT 3.1/3.51 MIPS drivers
MIPS\2	Windows NT 4.0 MIPS drivers
PPC\0	Windows NT 3.1 PPC drivers
PPC\1	Windows NT 3.5/3.51 PPC drivers
PPC\2	Windows NT 4.0 PPC drivers

Summary

This chapter dissected the printing process. You learned how the operations take place, how to use the wizard, and how to manage the process.

Printers are added through the Add Printer Wizard and can work in pools and with different priorities. Priorities do not affect a job that already has begun printing.

Printing to and from other platforms (such as UNIX) is possible if the correct services are installed. Installing TCP/IP Printing Service enables printing between UNIX hosts via the LPR command and the LPD service.

If the spooler is not responding, and you are unable to delete jobs, you must stop the spooler service and then start it again. It always is preferable to use the printer interface to try to pause or delete a problem job instead of stopping and starting the spooler service—this method helps you avoid losing any other jobs in the queue.

In the next chapter, "Windows NT Architecture and Boot Sequence," you will look at the underlying design behind Windows NT and what transpires when the system boots.

QUESTIONS AND ANSWERS

CH
10

1. When does the print process start in NT?

    A: The print process starts in NT when an application makes a print request.

2. In the printing process, the local _____ service makes a *Remote Procedure Call* (RPC) connection to the print server and copies the print job to the print server spooler directory.

    A: Spooler. This is the third step in the printing process.

3. True or false: By default, NT sends a separator page between print jobs.

    A: False

4. True or false: The most common print job type is RAW.

    A: True

5. The highest print priority is _____.

    A: 99 (and the lowest is 1)

PRACTICE TEST

1. Which of the following sets of Windows NT network clients do not require print drivers to be installed manually on the local computer?

    a. All Microsoft Network clients
    b. Windows NT and Windows 95
    c. Windows NT, Windows 95, Windows for Workgroups 3.11
    d. Windows NT, Windows 95, LAN Manager 2.x for DOS

Answer a is incorrect. All clients other than Windows NT and Windows 95 require the drivers to be installed manually on the local computer. **Answer b is correct. All clients other than Windows NT and Windows 95 require the drivers to be installed manually on the local computer.** Answer c is incorrect. Windows for Workgroups 3.11 clients require the drivers to be installed manually on the local computer. Answer d is incorrect. LAN Manager 2.x for DOS clients require the drivers to be installed manually on the local computer.

2. Which of the following steps apply to the Windows NT 4.0 print process on Windows NT computers? Select all that apply.

   a. The GDI component of the client computer generates an enhanced metafile print job.

   b. The bulk of the print process completes in the spooler on the client computer before forwarding the print job to the print server.

   c. The print monitor controls access to the print devices and device ports and monitors the status of the print job.

   d. The local printer spooler makes a remote connection to the print server spooler and copies the print job there.

Answer a is correct. The GDI component of the client computer generates an enhanced metafile print job. Answer b is incorrect. The bulk of the print process does not complete in the client computer spooler. **Answer c is correct. The print monitor controls access to the print devices and device ports and monitors the status of the print job. Answer d is correct. The local printer spooler makes a remote connection to the print server spooler and copies the print job there.**

3. Nicole calls to say that her print jobs seem to have stopped running. You check the printer that she sent the jobs to and see that the jobs are stuck in the queue. What steps should you take to clear the stuck jobs? Select all that apply.

   a. Select the stuck jobs and choose Document, Cancel.

   b. Choose Printer, Purge Printer.

   c. Use the Control Panel Services applet to stop and restart the spooler service.

   d. Select each stuck job and change its priority.

Answers a, b, and c are correct. They are legitimate steps that could solve the problem. Answer d is incorrect. It is not a legitimate step that could solve the problem. The priority is important before the job is submitted and cannot be changed after.

4. Several users have called you within the past half-hour to complain that their print jobs are not printing. In fact, they get system messages that tell them that the spooler is not responding. You have verified that the spooler directory partition does not have adequate free space to hold all the print jobs sent to it. What steps should you take to resolve this situation?

  a. Use the Control Panel Services applet to more frequently stop and restart the spooler service to keep the print jobs from becoming fragmented.

  b. Change the location of the spool directory to a partition with enough disk space by modifying the `HKEY_LOCAL_MACHINE\System\CurrentControlSet\Control\Print\Printers` `DefaultSpoolDirectory` parameter.

  c. Change the location of the spool directory to a partition with enough disk space by modifying the `HKEY_Current_User\Control\Print\Printers\Spool` `SpoolDirectory` parameter.

  d. If the partition is formatted with NTFS, compress the spool directory.

Answer a is incorrect. Stopping and restarting the spooler service frequently is not recommended. **Answer b is correct. Changing the location via the Registry solves the problem.** Answer c is incorrect. It points to the wrong Registry key. Answer d is incorrect. You should not compress the spool directory.

5. If the final print output is corrupted, what print process component should you check?

  a. Spooler service on the client computer

  b. Spooler service on the print server

  c. Print processor on the print server

  d. Print monitor on the client computer

Answer a is incorrect. The print processor is responsible for rendering the final job. Answer b is incorrect. The print processor is responsible for rendering the final job. **Answer c is correct. The print processor is responsible for rendering the final job.** Answer d is incorrect. The print processor is responsible for rendering the final job.

6. Which print monitor is loaded with TCP/IP and tracks print jobs targeted for TCP/IP print hosts?

  a. `IPMON.DLL`

  b. `LPDMON.DLL`

  c. `LPRMON.DLL`

  d. `LOCALMON.DLL`

Answer a is incorrect—it is an invalid option. Answer b is incorrect. It is an invalid option. **Answer c is correct. It is the LPR (Line PRinter) MONitor.** Answer d is incorrect; it is an invalid option.

7. What is the purpose of the print monitor SFMMON.DLL?

   a. SFMMON.DLL monitors Macintosh print jobs routed using the AppleTalk protocol to network print devices.

   b. SFMMON.DLL is the System File Manager print monitor, which tracks print jobs sent directly to or printed directly from a file.

   c. SFMMON.DLL is the software print job compression DLL, which compresses the print job before it is sent from the local print spooler to the print server.

   d. SFMMON.DLL is not a valid print monitor.

Answer a is correct. SFMMON.DLL monitors Macintosh print jobs routed using the AppleTalk protocol to network print devices. Answer b is incorrect. SFMMON.DLL monitors Macintosh print jobs routed using the AppleTalk protocol to network print devices. Answer c is incorrect. SFMMON.DLL monitors Macintosh print jobs routed using the AppleTalk protocol to network print devices. Answer d is incorrect; it *is* a valid print monitor.

8. You can direct a print job directly to a UNIX host print device and check its status using which two command-line utilities?

   a. LPD and LPR

   b. LPD and LPQ

   c. LPR and IPCONFIG

   d. LPR and LPQ

Answer a is incorrect. LPD is a service and not a utility. Answer b is incorrect. LPD is a service and not a utility. Answer c is incorrect. IPCONFIG shows IP configuration but does not relate to printing. **Answer d is correct. LPR submits print jobs to the Line PRinter, and LPQ is the Line Printer Query utility.**

9. Michelle has been selected to assist you as a print administrator in the Dry Gulch office, because you are unable to travel there frequently, although you'd really like to. What is the minimum level of access you need to give Michelle so that she can perform basic print management tasks, such as creating and sharing printers and managing print jobs?

    a. Make Michelle a member of the Printer Operators local group on her print server.

    b. Make Michelle a member of the Server Operators local group on her print server.

    c. Make Michelle a member of the Administrators local group on her print server.

    d. Give Michelle Full Control permission for each printer on her print server.

Answer a is correct. Making Michelle a member of the Printer Operators local group on her print server gives her the necessary capabilities and does not jeopardize any other security. Answer b is incorrect. This does not give her the minimum level of access that making her a member of the Printer Operators group does. Answer c is incorrect. This does not give Michelle the minimum level of access that making her a member of the Printer Operators group does. Answer d is incorrect. This does not give her the minimum level of access that making her a member of the Printer Operators group does.

10. You have created four printers. Each printer will be used by a specific group of users. Select all the steps that are required to successfully make each printer available to the appropriate users.

    a. Share each printer.

    b. Set the share permissions for each printer so that only the appropriate group has access.

    c. Set the printer permissions for each printer so that only the appropriate group has access.

    d. Create a printer pool so that each group can access all the print devices.

Answer a is correct. You must share the printer before you can make it available. Answer b is incorrect, because it is not a necessary step. **Answer c is correct. After you share the printer, you must set the printer permissions for each printer so that only the appropriate group has access.** Answer d is incorrect, because it is not a necessary step.

CHAPTER PREREQUISITE

Chapter 2, "Understanding Microsoft Windows NT 4.0" (cursory knowledge of device drivers, threads, interrupts, and swap files), Chapter 3, "Windows NT Server 4.0 Setup," and Chapter 4, "Configuring Windows NT Server 4.0." Also, it is very useful to have actually installed Windows NT Server 4.0.

Windows NT 4.0 Architecture and Boot Sequence

WHILE YOU READ

1. Kernel mode services are also known as _____.

2. Hardware platform support is provided to Windows NT Server via the _____.

3. The menu of operating system choices available at boot are derived from what file?

4. The NT boot switch to display driver names is _____.

5. True or false: Boot files are contained in the system partition.

6. User mode constitutes what ring in Intel architecture?

7. Kernel mode constitutes what ring in Intel architecture?

8. What is the name of the NT page file?

An integral part of understanding Windows NT for the exam is a discussion of the internal architecture of the NT operating system. Recovering from serious errors often entails changing the way Windows NT boots. Understanding the sequence of events and knowing from where input information is being gathered are critical pieces of knowledge.

Understanding Modes

The Windows NT 4.0 architecture consists of two primary processing areas: user or application mode and kernel or privileged processor mode. User mode, as it implies, provides operating system support primarily for user applications and the environment. Figure 11.1 shows this basic architecture.

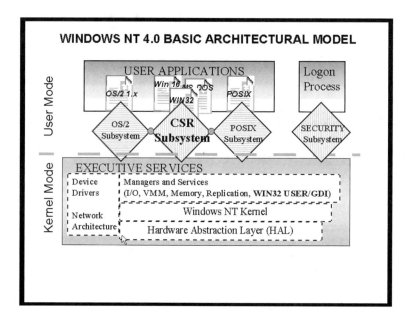

Figure 11.1
The user mode basic architectural model is for user applications.

The kernel mode provides operating system support services for just about everything else, including kernel processing, memory management, hardware access, and so on. These kernel mode services are referred to as *Executive Services*.

Understanding User (Application) Mode

The user mode of the operating system provides application processing support. Applications in Windows NT run in one of three subsystems—the WIN32, OS/2, and POSIX subsystems—provided by the operating system. The primary subsystem, which is loaded at boot time, is WIN32. WIN32 supports both 32-bit Windows and Win95 applications, as well as 16-bit DOS and Windows applications.

The OS/2 subsystem provides support for 1.x character-based OS/2 applications. *Portable Operating System Interface for UNIX* (POSIX) provides support for POSIX-based applications. Any application program calls from these two subsystems that read/write to the display are forwarded to the WIN32 subsystem. Any other calls to drivers or other Executive Services are communicated directly to the kernel mode.

In NT 3.51, the user and *graphics device interface* (GDI) portions of the operating system were included in the WIN32 subsystem—thus, in user mode. The user is the Window Manager and responds to user input onscreen. The GDI processes graphics primitives such as pixels, lines, fills, and so on. The GDI also performs graphics rendering for print files.

If an application needed the user or GDI for processing, it would have to create an *interprocess communication* (IPC) to it. This process would involve a context switch from user mode to kernel mode (Ring 0 to Ring 3 of the processor) as well as 64KB buffering. Then, another context switch would take place back to user mode. This obviously involves some time and decreases overall performance.

NT 4.0 moves the user and GDI into kernel mode. This move significantly improves application performance by eliminating the 64KB buffer and leaving only a kernel transition. You can see the benefit particularly in applications that involve direct draw to the screen, such as Pinball, as well as in multimedia applications, such as QuickTime.

Key Concept

Windows NT is broken into user and kernel mode. User mode provides support for applications.

Understanding Kernel (Privileged Processor) Mode

Kernel mode provides support for all major operating system functions. The kernel controls access to memory and the execution of privileged instructions. All kernel mode processes run in the protected mode of the processor—Ring 0. As such, the applications running in user mode are effectively buffered from direct access to hardware. Thus, 16-bit applications that are designed to access hardware directly will not run successfully under Windows NT. You must rewrite these to "talk" to the NT kernel mode services before you can run them under Windows NT.

The kernel mode consists of three parts:

- Executive Services
- Windows NT kernel
- Hardware Abstraction Layer (HAL)

Executive Services

Executive Services make up most of the kernel mode functionality. Executive Services provides support for processes, threads, memory management, I/O, IPC, and security. It is here that most NT services and process managers execute. This layer provides device driver support, including NT's network architecture support drivers and protocols. This layer is written in C code to help make NT portable across platforms. It is this C code that is recompiled for each of platforms that NT supports, such as Dec Alpha, PowerPC, and MIPS.

Windows NT Kernel

The NT kernel provides support for thread management and context switching, synchronization among services and processes in the Executive Services layer, multiprocessor load balancing, and exception and interrupt handling.

Hardware Abstraction Layer (HAL)

The HAL provides hardware platform support. It isolates specific platform details from the Executive and the NT kernel. It is largely because of the HAL that 16-bit applications that like to talk directly to hardware are unable to run. Users' applications therefore are effectively isolated from base hardware interaction under Windows NT.

 Key Concept

Windows NT is broken into user and kernel mode. Kernel mode manages the processor and isolates the hardware from the user.

Understanding Windows NT Virtual Memory Management

One Executive Services manager is the Virtual Memory Manager (see Fig. 11.2). The memory architecture of Windows NT is a 32-bit, demand-based flat model. This model allows the Virtual Memory Manager to access up to 4GB of RAM—far more than the amount of physical RAM installed in most computers.

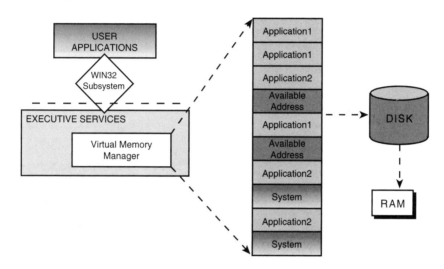

Figure 11.2
Virtual Memory Manager manages up to 4GB of memory.

If you remember Windows' swap file model, you know that there are two types of swap files: permanent and temporary. Both swap files manage available RAM in 4KB pieces by using an internal Windows algorithm called the *least recently used* (LRU). Essentially, the LRU assumes that the piece of code in memory that was least recently accessed by a process is the best choice of memory to be swapped to disk when more RAM is needed. On computers with the minimum required RAM for Windows, a considerable amount of swapping takes place when several applications are open.

The main difference between permanent and temporary swap files is that a permanent swap file has a preallocated amount of space reserved on the disk. Temporary swap files begin at 2MB and then grow as needed to a predetermined amount. Thus, although a permanent swap file actually provides better swap performance because the space is always there and available, it also reduces the amount of available disk storage. Similarly, although temporary swap files do not reduce the amount of disk storage available up front, more resources are expended in finding additional storage space when the swap file needs to grow.

Windows NT combines the best of these swap files. The NT pagefile (PAGEFILE.SYS) is created when NT is installed and generally defaults to an initial preallocated size (à la permanent swap files) of physical RAM (plus 12MB for Workstation) and a maximum size of three times physical RAM (depending on the amount of disk space available). So, on a server with 16MB of physical RAM, the default initial pagefile size would be 16MB, while on Workstation it would be 28MB (12MB + 16MB), and the maximum size on both would be about 48MB (3 * 16MB). NT boots with the initial-size pagefile available. The pagefile subsequently grows as applications are loaded and demands for physical RAM increase.

Key Concept

For the exam, know that the initial size of the pagefile in NT Workstation is RAM + 12MB; for Windows NT Server, it is just RAM.

It is important to realize that although NT allows the addressing of up to 4GB of physical RAM, the *Virtual Memory Manager* (VMM) can allocate up to 2GB of virtual storage for each application. Another 2GB is allocated for all system (kernel mode) processing.

The VMM addresses application memory like this:

1. When an application is loaded, the VMM assigns it virtual memory addresses in physical RAM.
2. The data then is moved in pages out of physical RAM and into the pagefile.
3. As the application needs the data, it calls for the virtual memory addresses.
4. The VMM moves those pages on demand into available locations in physical RAM.

This process of assigning virtual addresses to the application effectively hides the organization of physical RAM from the application. The various pages of the application may wind up in noncontiguous space in physical RAM (that is, in sectors that may be distributed at different locations on the disk instead of next to each other). But because the VMM is providing the application with its addresses, it really doesn't care. This allows NT to use available physical RAM most efficiently and to provide an overall performance increase for application processing.

Understanding the NT Boot Process

The Windows NT 4.0 boot process, although a bit more complicated during the operating system load phase, is still pretty much like any other operating system. Most operating system boot processes follow five basic steps:

1. The *power-on self-test* (POST) occurs. This process takes place with every computer when you first power it on. This is the BIOS check of installed hardware, interrupts, I/O, memory, and so on.

2. The *master boot record* (MBR) is read to determine which *operating system* (OS) governs the boot process.

3. The OS system file recorded in the MBR is loaded, the OS is initialized, hardware is initialized, and drivers and configuration files are loaded.

4. The OS kernel is loaded.

5. Environment settings are initialized.

Windows NT 4.0 follows these same basic steps, with some variation in Steps 3, 4, and 5.

The Windows NT boot process has two primary phases: boot and load.

The boot phase consists of the preboot sequence, during which the operating system is initialized, hardware is detected, and Executive Services is loaded. When Windows NT is installed, it replaces the MS-DOS entries in the MBR with its own system file, NTLDR. Along with NTLDR, the following boot files are read during the boot phase: BOOT.INI, NTDETECT.COM, NTOSKRNL.EXE, NTBOOTDD.SYS (all files with any of the hidden, read-only, or system file attributes are stored in the root directory of the boot partition), NTOSKRNL.EXE and HAL.DLL (stored in the NT system directory), and the HKEY_LOCAL_MACHINE\SYSTEM hive.

Here is the entire boot sequence for Windows NT:

1. NTLDR loads a mini-OS and changes memory to a flat 32-bit model.

2. NTLDR next reads the BOOT.INI file to display the operating system menu.

3. If the user chooses NT, or that is the default, NTLDR loads NTDETECT.COM, which determines what hardware is installed on the computer and then uses this information to build the HKEY_LOCAL_MACHINE\HARDWARE hive.

   If the system boots NT from a SCSI drive for which the SCSI adapter BIOS is disabled, NTLDR loads NTBOOTDD.SYS to initialize and access that device.

   If the user chooses MS-DOS or Microsoft Windows (for Windows 95), NTLDR loads BOOTSECT.DOS, which records the boot sector location of the alternative OS system files and loads them. OS initialization then continues as normal for that OS.

4. NTLDR next loads NTOSKRNL.EXE, which initializes the Executive Services of the

CH

II

operating system. Think of this as NT's `COMMAND.COM`.

5. `NTLDR` then loads the `HAL.DLL` and the `SYSTEM` hive and any drivers that need to initialize at boot time to continue building the Executive Services.

6. At this point, the screen displays progress dots across the top indicating the loading and initialization of drivers as defined in `HKEY_LOCAL_MACHINE\SYSTEM\CURRENTCONTROLSET\CONTROL\GROUPORDERLIST`. The user is prompted to press the space-bar to invoke the Last Known Good boot configuration. Control is passed to `NTOSKRNL.EXE`, and the load phase begins.

During the load phase, the rest of the kernel and user modes of the operating system are set up. The kernel is initialized, control set information is initialized, NT services are loaded, and the WIN32 subsystem starts.

7. The blue screen is displayed, indicating that the kernel is initializing, drivers are initialized, and the `CurrentControlSet` is created and copied to the `CLONE` control set.

8. The Services load phase begins with the starting of `SMSS.EXE`, the Session Manager. The Session Manager runs the programs listed in `HKEY_LOCAL_MACHINE\SYSTEM\CURRENTCONTROLSET\CONTROL\SESSION MANAGER\BootExecute`, usually containing at least `AUTOCHK.EXE` (which performs a `CHKDSK` of each partition). If a drive has been flagged to be converted to NTFS, the drive is added to `BootExecute` and conversion takes place at this time. Next, the pagefile is configured, as defined in `HKEY_LOCAL_MACHINE\SYSTEM\CURRENTCONTROLSET\CONTROL\SESSION MANAGER\MEMORY MANAGEMENT` parameters.

Finally, the required subsystem, defined in `HKEY_LOCAL_MACHINE\SYSTEM\CURRENTCONTROLSET\CONTROL\SESSION MANAGER\SUBSYSTEMS\Required`, is loaded. The only required subsystem at this time is WIN32.

9. With the loading of the WIN32 subsystem, `WINLOGON.EXE` (the service that governs the logon process) is loaded and started. `WINLOGON`, in turn, starts the Local Security Authority (`LSASS.EXE`), which displays the Ctrl+Alt+Del screen, and the Service Controller (`SCREG.EXE`), which starts services that are configured to start automatically, such as the computer browser, workstation, and server.

10. Finally, the user enters the username and password and logs on to the computer or domain. If the logon is successful, the `CLONE` control set is copied to the Last Known Good boot configuration. If the boot is not successful, the user can power off or shut down and choose Last Known Good to load the last values that resulted in a successful logon.

Key Concept

For the exam, understand the boot process thoroughly. Above all else, remember that boot files are located in the system partition, and system files are located in the boot partition.

BOOT.INI

The BOOT.INI file is a read-only system, ASCII text file that is created by NT during installation. BOOT.INI is stored in the root directory of the primary boot partition of the computer. It contains the information that NT uses to display the boot menu when the computer is booted (refer to Step 2). It is divided into two sections: Boot Loader and Operating System. The Boot Loader section contains the default operating system and timeout values, and the Operating System section displays operating system choices and the location of the system files. You can modify the BOOT.INI file using any ASCII text editor, after first turning off the system and read-only properties.

Key Concept

You can locate the BOOT.INI file by using Windows Explorer, Windows Find, or My Computer. To change its properties, right-click the file and choose P̲roperties. Deselect Read-Only and System. Be sure to reselect these attributes when you finish modifying the file.

In the following example, the default timeout value is 30 seconds. If the user does not make a selection during that time, the default operating system is loaded. Notice that the unusual-looking path to the WINNT40 directory matches a line under the Operating Systems section:

```
[Boot Loader]
Timeout=30
Default=multi(0)disk(0)rdisk(0)partition(4)\WINNT40
[Operating Systems]
multi(0)disk(0)rdisk(0)partition(4)\WINNT40="Windows NT
➥ Workstation Version 4.00"
multi(0)disk(0)rdisk(0)partition(4)\WINNT40="Windows NT
➥ Workstation Version 4.00 [VGA mode]"
    /basevideo /sos
C:\="Microsoft Windows"
```

CH

II

That unusual-looking path is called an *advanced RISC computer* (ARC) path. The best way to describe an ARC path is as a hardware path. By now, everyone has used a DOS path. It indicates the drive and directory location of a specific file. An ARC path indicates the physical disk location of the NT system files—the specific partition on a specific physical disk connected to a specific physical controller.

Referring to the preceding example, the ARC path

```
multi(0)disk(0)rdisk(0)partition(4)\WINNT40
```

can be interpreted as described next.

The first value can be either `multi` or `scsi`. This really has no direct relation as to whether the controller is a SCSI controller. NT chooses `scsi` if the controller does not have its card BIOS enabled. Otherwise, the choice is `multi`. The number that appears in parentheses is the ordinal number of the controller.

The next two values are `disk` and `rdisk`. If the first value choice is `scsi`, the disk number represents the SCSI bus number and is incremented accordingly (the physical disk attached to the card), and the `rdisk` value is ignored. If the first value is `multi`, the disk value is ignored and the `rdisk` value representing the physical disk on the adapter is incremented accordingly.

Next, the partition value indicates on which disk partition the directory `\WINNT40` is located. Recall that this is the NT system directory that you selected during installation.

Key Concept

To tie it all together for this example, during boot, if the user lets the timeout value expire or specifically selects NT from the menu, NT can find the Windows NT system files (specifically, the location of the `NTOSKRNL.EXE` file) in the `WINNT40` directory, on the fourth partition of the first disk, attached to the first controller in this computer. If the user chooses Microsoft Windows from the menu, `NTLDR` loads `BOOTSECT.DOS` and proceeds to boot (in this case) Windows 95.

The Boot Menu

The operating system's section values build the boot menu you see during startup. Each ARC path has a text-menu selection associated with it that is enclosed in quotes. By default, there are always two entries for NT and one for the other operating system— usually MS-DOS (`C:\="MS-DOS"`)or Windows 95 (`C:\="Microsoft Windows"`). The second entry for NT represents a fallback entry that loads NT with a generic *video graphics adapter* (VGA) driver. If you make changes to the display settings that make it difficult or impossible to read the screen, selecting this choice during startup ignores those settings and loads a generic VGA driver so that you can see the screen and rectify the problem. This is accomplished through the /basevideo switch.

Key Concept

NT provides a variety of switches you can add to these or additional NT boot entries to modify the way NT boots. For example, you might want to create another entry in your boot menu that displays all the driver files that are loaded during boot. You can copy the first line in the Operating Systems section to a new line, modify the text to read Windows NT Workstation 4.0 Driver Load, and add the /SOS switch to the end of the line. Thus, if you are having trouble booting or aren't sure whether a particular driver is being located, you can select this choice to display these items during the load phase (refer to Step 6 in the "Understanding the NT Boot Process" section earlier in this chapter).

Table 11.1 describes the more practical boot switches you can use in the BOOT.INI file. You'll find an exhaustive list in the Windows NT Resource Kit.

Table 11.1	NT Boot Switches for BOOT.INI
Switch	*Description*
/Basevideo	Boots NT with the standard VGA display driver in 640×480 resolution.
/SOS	Displays driver filenames instead of progress dots during the load phase.
/Crashdebug	Used for troubleshooting, enables automatic recovery and restart mode for the NT boot process and displays a system memory dump during the blue-screen portion of the load phase.
/Maxmem:n	Specifies the maximum amount of RAM, in megabytes, that NT will recognize and work with. This is helpful when you suspect a bad SIMM or memory chip and are trying to pinpoint its location.

Understanding Control Sets and the Last Known Good Option

The HKEY_LOCAL_MACHINE\System hive contains several control set subkeys. NT uses these subkeys to boot the system, keep track of configuration changes, and provide an audit trail of failed boot attempts. In general, there are four control sets: Clone, ControlSet001, ControlSet002, and CurrentControlSet. There is also a subkey called Select, with parameter values that point out which control set is being used for the current settings, default settings, failed settings, and Last Known Good settings. If the value for `Current` is `0x1`, for example, 1 indicates that `CurrentControlSet` is being derived from or mapped to `ControlSet001`.

`Clone` is used by NT during the boot process (refer to Step 7 in the "Understanding the NT Boot Process" section earlier in this chapter) as a temporary storage area for the boot configuration. Settings from `CurrentControlSet` are copied into `Clone` during the load phase. When a user logon results in a successful boot, the configuration settings in `Clone` are copied to another control set, such as `ControlSet002`, and are referred to as the *Last Known Good settings.* If the boot attempt is unsuccessful, these values are copied to a different control set number.

`ControlSet001` generally is the default control set and produces the `CurrentControlSet`. As such, by default, it also contains the NT boot configuration.

`ControlSet00x` represents other control sets. The control set with the highest number increment usually is pointed to in the `Select` subkey as the Last Known Good configuration. Other control set numbers invariably refer to failed boot configurations.

`CurrentControlSet` is mapped back to `ControlSet001`. These settings are copied to `Clone` during the load phase of the boot process. Whenever an administrator makes a change to the configuration of the computer, such as modifying the virtual memory parameters, adding a new driver, or creating a hardware profile, those changes are saved to `CurrentControlSet` (and thus to `ControlSet001`, if that control set is specified as the default in the `Select` subkey).

Key Concept

During the load phase, the settings in `CurrentControlSet` (derived from `ControlSet001`) are copied to `Clone` and are used to determine service order, the driver files to load, startup configurations, hardware profiles, and so on. If the boot is successful (in other words, it logs on to NT successfully), `Clone` is copied to the control set designated as the Last Known Good control set—for example, `ControlSet002`. If changes made by the administrator result in a failed boot attempt, the failed configuration in `Clone` is copied to `ControlSet002`, what used to be the Last Known Good control set becomes `ControlSet003`, and the user has the option of selecting to boot with the Last Known Good control set.

The Last Known Good control set contains the last boot configuration that resulted in a successful logon to the computer. The user is given the option to use Last Known Good when the load phase begins and the progress dots are displayed. The user has five seconds to press the spacebar to invoke the Last Known Good control set.

If the system detects a severe or critical device initialization or load error, it displays a message recommending that the user choose Last Known Good as the boot option. Users can choose to bypass this message, but they do so at their own risk.

Key Concept

Last Known Good enables the server to boot after a failed boot. But remember that a failed boot is one in which a user cannot successfully log on to NT. The user may be able to log on successfully but still may have a system that fails to run correctly because of a configuration error. Last Known Good is not helpful in this situation, because it is created as soon as the boot is successful—in other words, as soon as you log on successfully.

Troubleshooting the Boot Process

The most common errors you are likely to encounter during the boot process are caused by corrupt or missing boot files. NT needs these boot files:

NTLDR

BOOT.INI

BOOTSECT.DOS

NTDETECT.COM

NTOSKRNL.EXE

If the NTLDR file is missing or corrupt, the following message is displayed after the POST:

```
BOOT: Couldn't find NTLDR
Please insert another disk.
```

Although there are various reasons for this file to become missing or corrupt, the most common reasons are a virus attacking the *master boot record* (MBR) and a user inadvertently reinstalling MS-DOS on the computer. If the problem involves a virus, use a virus-protection program to restore the MBR. If this is unsuccessful, you can use the Emergency Repair Disk to reestablish NTLDR in the MBR. The worst-case scenario is that you will have to reinstall NT from scratch, which you should try to avoid.

If the problem involves a user reinstalling MS-DOS, you need to use the Emergency Repair Disk to reestablish the NTLDR. Again, in the worst-case scenario, you will have to reinstall NT.

If BOOT.INI is missing or corrupt, NT looks for the system partition. If NT cannot locate it, the following message is displayed after the prompt for Last Known Good:

```
Windows NT could not start because the following file is missing or corrupt:
\winnt root\system32\ntoskrnl.exe
Please reinstall a copy of the above file.
```

If the ARC path to the NT system file directory is incorrect in the BOOT.INI file, NTLDR may display this message:

```
Windows NT could not start because of a computer disk hardware configuration
problem. Could not read from the selected boot disk. Check boot path and disk
hardware. Please check Windows NT ? documentation about hardware disk
configuration and your hardware reference manuals for additional information.
```

Incorrect paths are relatively easy to fix. Because BOOT.INI is a text file, turn off its system and read-only attributes and edit the ARC path by using your favorite text editor.

Key Concept

The ARC path indicated in the default parameter in the Boot Loader section of the BOOT.INI must match an ARC path for a parameter under the Operating Systems section. If it does not match, the menu displays a phantom selection option called NT (default), which may result in the same error message that was discussed for a missing BOOT.INI file.

If BOOTSECT.DOS is missing, NTLDR displays the following error message when the user tries to select the other operating system from the boot menu:

```
I/O Error accessing boot sector file
multi(0)disk(0)rdisk(0)partition(1):\bootsect.dos
```

Because this file is unique to each computer, the best ways to recover it are to restore the file from the backup you create regularly (!) or to use the Emergency Repair Disk.

If NTDETECT.COM is missing or corrupt, expect the following message after the user selects NT from the boot menu or the menu times out to NT:

```
NTDETECT v1.0 Checking Hardware...
NTDETECT v1.0 Checking Hardware...
```

Again, recover by using the Emergency Repair Disk or a backup.

If NTOSKRNL.EXE is missing or corrupt, NTLDR displays this message after the prompt for Last Known Good:

```
Windows NT could not start because the following file is missing or corrupt:
\winnt root\system32\ntoskrnl.exe
Please reinstall a copy of the above file.
```

As before, you can recover this file by using the Emergency Repair Disk or a file backup.

The Emergency Repair Disk

The *Emergency Repair Disk* (ERD) usually is created during the NT installation process (see Chapter 3, "Windows NT Server 4.0 Setup"). However, you can create (and update) the ERD at any time by running the NT command RDISK.EXE at an NT DOS prompt.

To use the ERD, you first must boot the computer by using a Windows NT Startup disk.

Key Concept

If you do not have a Windows NT Startup disk set, but you have access to the original installation files, you can create a Startup disk by typing the command **WINNT /OX**. Be sure to have three disks available.

From the Startup menu, choose <u>R</u>epair. The repair process offers four options:

- **Inspect Registry Files:** Prompts the user for the replacement of each Registry file, including system and SAM.

Key Concept

The files on the ERD overwrite the files in the Registry. For this reason, the ERD is not the best way to recover damaged security or account information. A backup is much more useful for maintaining the integrity of existing account entries.

- **Inspect Startup Environment:** Checks the BOOT.INI file for an entry for Windows NT. If it doesn't find an entry, it adds one for the next boot attempt.
- **Verify Windows NT System Files:** Verifies whether the NT system files match those of the original installation files. For this option, you need to have access to the original installation files. This option also looks for and verifies the integrity of the boot files.

Key Concept

If you updated Windows NT with a service pack, you need to reinstall the service pack after initiating a repair.

> ■ **Inspect Boot Sector:** Checks the MBR for NTLDR. If the MBR is missing or corrupt, it restores the boot sector.

If you know specifically which file is missing or corrupt, you can replace the file directly from the source files by using the NT EXPAND utility. At an NT prompt, type **EXPAND -R**, followed by the compressed filename. If NT is inoperable on your system, use another NT system to expand the file and then copy it to your computer.

NT Boot Disk

Another useful tool to have in your toolkit is an NT boot disk. This is not a disk formatted with NTFS. Instead, it is a disk that was formatted under NT that contains copies of the boot files.

Key Concept

You can format a disk from My Computer. Right-click the A: drive icon and choose <u>F</u>ormat. Make the appropriate selections and choose OK.

When you format a disk under NT, NT creates a boot sector on that disk that references NTLDR. Simply copy the five boot files to this disk, and you have an NT boot disk. This disk can be used in a variety of NT computers, because it is not unique to each installation. The only file you may need to modify for each computer is the BOOT.INI file. This makes it much easier to replace missing or corrupt boot files.

Summary

This chapter examined the architectural design and implementation of Windows NT Server, as well as the boot process. The boot process often can be one of the most aggravating to troubleshoot, and a good understanding of the steps involved is important to problem solving.

The BOOT.INI file provides the boot menu that offers the operating system choices you can choose from. NTLDR begins the initial load of the system, while NTDETECT.COM detects the hardware. You can place these three files, along with two other startup files, on a startup disk to use in case of emergency.

You can use WINNT /OX at any time to create/re-create the initial three-disk set needed to boot NT. You can create the Emergency Repair Disk (not bootable) with the RDISK command.

The next few chapters discuss basic networking architectures and Microsoft's implementation of these architectures and protocols. The two most popular networks, TCP/IP and Novell NetWare, are discussed in detail.

⌐ QUESTIONS AND ANSWERS ─────

1. Kernel mode services also are known as _____.

   A: Executive Services

2. Hardware platform support is provided to Windows NT Server via the _____.

   A: *Hardware Abstraction Layer* (HAL)

3. The menu of operating system choices available at boot are derived from what file?

   A: The BOOT.INI file

4. The NT boot switch to display driver names is _____.

   A: /SOS

5. True or false: Boot files are contained in the system partition.

   A: True. Boot files are contained in the system partition; the boot partition contains system files.

6. User mode constitutes what ring in Intel architecture?

   A: User mode is Ring 0.

7. Kernel mode constitutes what ring in Intel architecture?

   A: Kernel mode is Ring 3.

8. What is the name of the NT page file?

   A: The NT page file is PAGEFILE.SYS.

PRACTICE TEST

1. Which two subsystems are loaded when Windows NT boots?
   a. WIN32 and security subsystems
   b. CSR and OS/2 subsystems
   c. Environment and security subsystems
   d. OS/2 and POSIX subsystems

Answer a is correct. WIN32 and security subsystems are both loaded when Windows NT boots. Answer b is incorrect—the OS/2 subsystem is not loaded when NT boots.

Answer c is incorrect—the environment subsystem is not loaded when NT boots. Answer d is incorrect. Neither the OS/2 nor the POSIX subsystem is loaded when NT boots.

2. Following the power-on self-test, NT loads the

   a. Environment settings

   b. Master boot record

   c. OS kernel

   d. OS system file

Answer a is incorrect. NT loads the MBR following the POST. **Answer b is correct because NT loads the MBR following the POST.** Answer c is incorrect because NT loads the MBR following the POST. Answer d is incorrect because NT loads the MBR following the POST.

3. The two primary phases of the NT boot sequence are

   a. Boot and load

   b. Boot and initialize

   c. Load and initialize

   d. Startup and shutdown

Answer a is correct. The two primary phases of the boot sequence are boot and load. Answer b is incorrect because initialize is not a primary phase of the boot sequence. Answer c is incorrect because initialize is not a primary phase of the boot sequence. Answer d is incorrect. Neither startup nor shutdown is a primary phase of the boot sequence.

4. The operating system choices displayed during bootup are stored in

   a. the Registry

   b. the master boot record

   c. BOOT.INI

   d. CONFIG.SYS

Answer a is incorrect, because the BOOT.INI file holds the startup choices. Answer b is incorrect—the BOOT.INI file holds the startup choices. **Answer c is correct. BOOT.INI holds the startup menu choices.** Answer d is incorrect—the BOOT.INI file holds the startup choices.

5. Which files are read before NT displays the blue screen? Circle all that apply.

   a. BOOT.INI

   b. CONFIG.SYS

   c. NTLDR

   d. COMMAND.COM

Answer a is correct. The BOOT.INI file is read during boot. Answer b is incorrect. The CONFIG.SYS file is not a necessary file and is not read prior to the blue screen. **Answer c is correct. NTLDR is read during boot.** Answer d is an invalid file used in DOS systems.

6. The switch you can use in BOOT.INI to show all drivers as they are loaded is

   a. /BASE
   b. /DRIVERS
   c. /SOS
   d. /ORDINAL

Answer a is incorrect; it is an invalid option. /SOS shows all the drivers. Answer b is incorrect because it is an invalid option. /SOS shows all the drivers. **Answer c is correct: /SOS shows all the drivers.** Answer d is incorrect—it is an invalid option. /SOS shows all the drivers.

7. The HAL.DLL file is located in the

   a. NT system directory
   b. root directory
   c. NT boot directory
   d. BOOT.INI

Answer a is correct. HAL.DLL is located in the NT system directory. Answer b is incorrect. HAL.DLL is located in the NT system directory. Answer c is incorrect. HAL.DLL is located in the NT system directory. Answer d is incorrect. HAL.DLL is located in the NT system directory.

8. If you need to replace a corrupted system file, you can do so from the compressed files on the CD-ROM. To do so, however, you need to uncompress the file with

   a. UNPACK
   b. UNZIP
   c. EXTRACT
   d. EXPAND

Answer a is incorrect. The Expand utility is used to uncompress system files. Answer b is incorrect. The Expand utility uncompresses system files. Answer c is incorrect. The Expand utility is used to uncompress system files. **Answer d is correct. The Expand utility is used to uncompress system files.**

CH
II

CHAPTER PREREQUISITE

You should have an understanding of the networking concepts. Ideally, you have studied for and passed the Networking Essentials exam.

Windows NT Networking Services

WHILE YOU READ

1. A two-way IPC connection channel that guarantees that data is sent, received, and acknowledged is called _____.

2. A one-way IPC connection channel is called _____.

3. What is the default networking protocol in NT 3.5, which offers fast, efficient communications but no routing capability?

4. Which protocol does the Internet use?

5. Which protocol do NetWare servers use?

This chapter reviews the Windows NT 4.0 network architecture, including the protocols supported by NT 4.0, and the newest advantages of this release. This chapter is meant as a primer for the TCP/IP and Novell chapters that follow.

Exploring the NT 4.0 Networking Model

Networking capabilities are fully integrated into Windows NT 4.0 Workstation and Server. Network support is supplied for Microsoft network clients, such as Windows 95 and Windows for Workgroups, and also for Apple Macintosh clients (through Services for Macintosh on the NT Server), NetWare clients and servers (through a variety of NetWare connectivity products for both NT 4.0 Workstation and Server, but primarily for Server), and *Transmission Control Protocol/Internet Protocol* (TCP/IP) systems, such as Internet connectivity and UNIX hosts. In addition, dial-in capabilities are supported and fully integrated.

The NT 4.0 network architecture is positioned as part of the Executive Services running in kernel mode. In fact, the NT 4.0 network architecture is itself a three-tiered model that is an integrated part of the NT Executive Service called the *I/O Manager* (see Fig. 12.1). The I/O Manager is primarily responsible for determining whether a request for resource access is locally or remotely directed. If it is remotely directed, the request enters the layers of the network model.

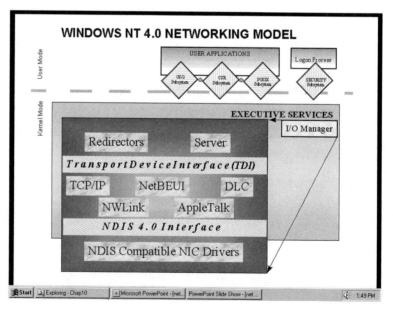

Figure 12.1
Windows NT 4.0 networking model.

The three layers are the File System or Redirector layer, the Protocol layer, and the *network interface card* (NIC) or Adapter layer. Each layer communicates by using a boundary or transmission interface.

After the request is made, a path to the location of the resource is established by finding the most appropriate path through the layers of the client computer, through the network connection, and then up through the layers of the server computer—the computer that has the resource. These paths through the layers are known as the *bindings* for that computer. The established connection between a client and server computer is called the *interprocess communication* or IPC mechanism, which enables data to flow between the computers. This type of interaction often is referred to as *distributed processing*. A computer may have several bindings to various protocols to enable the establishment of various IPC mechanisms for different networking platforms, such as NetWare IPX or UNIX TCP/IP. Table 12.1 outlines some of these mechanisms.

Table 12.1 IPC Connections

Type of Connection	Description
Named pipes	A two-way connection channel that guarantees data is sent, received, and acknowledged by both computers.
Mailslots	A one-way connection channel in which data is sent with no acknowledgment of receipt. NetBIOS broadcasts are examples of a mailslot IPC connection.
Windows Sockets	A Windows application-based programming interface (API) that enables two-way acknowledged data transfer between the computers.
NetBIOS	Another application-based programming interface (API) that enables two-way acknowledged data transfer between the computers.
Distributed Component Object Model	A new IPC model in Windows NT 4.0 that enables the distribution of processes across multiple servers in the NT network for the purpose of optimizing access and performance of network-based programs.

Now take a look at the various components of the NT 4.0 network architecture.

File System Layer

The File System layer also is known as the *Redirector layer,* because the NT I/O Manager determines where to redirect the request for the resource in this layer. If the request is for a local resource, a file on an NTFS partition, the request is kept local and directed to the appropriate file system—in this case, to NTFS on the partition.

CH

12

If the request is for a resource on another computer in the network, the request must be redirected to that remote location. As you learned, the remote location might be on another NT Workstation or Server. Therefore, the I/O Manager redirects the request to NT's own built-in network redirector, RDR.SYS, also known as the *Workstation Service*. Every NT computer, whether Workstation or Server, has a Workstation Service configured to load and run automatically upon booting NT. Every NT computer has the capability of making, and does make, requests for resources on other computers.

However, the request may be for a resource on a NetWare server or a UNIX host; therefore, the request must be redirected accordingly. In the case of NetWare, this process involves loading another redirector that can interpret requests meant for a NetWare server and finding the appropriate binding and IPC connection to which to send the message. On an NT Server, this additional redirector is the *Gateway Services for NetWare* (GSNW) service that comes with NT 4.0 Server as an installable service. You may need to obtain other network redirectors from the network manufacturer.

Protocol Layer

Protocols are responsible for creating the packets of information sent from one computer to another across the network connection. Various networks support or require specific protocols when communicating with a computer in that network. UNIX hosts generally require TCP/IP, for example, whereas NetWare networks prefer *Internetworking Packet Exchange/Sequenced Packet Exchange* (IPX/SPX).

Windows NT 4.0 supports five protocols:

TCP/IP	A routable protocol supporting enterprise networking and NetBIOS connections, and is used to connect to the Internet and UNIX hosts.
NWLink IPX/SPX	Microsoft's 32-bit implementation of IPX/SPX. It also is routable and supports enterprise networking among NT network clients, as well as connection to Novell servers.
NetBEUI	A fast, efficient, but non-routable protocol used within smaller networks and thus is not well-suited for enterprise networking.
Data Link Control (DLC) protocol	Provides connection support to *Systems Network Architecture* (SNA) mainframe computers and network-connected printers.
AppleTalk protocol	Used primarily on NT 4.0 server computers that provide remote access support for Apple Macintosh computers through Services for Macintosh.

TCP/IP, NWLink, and NetBEUI are examined in more detail in the next section. Windows NT 4.0 supports the installation of any number of protocols in each NT computer.

Network Adapter (NIC) Layer

The Network Adapter layer is the hardware layer that consists of the NDIS 4.0-compatible *network interface card* (NIC) drivers that initialize and manage communications through the hardware device connected to the network. NT 4.0 supports the installation of one or more NICs in each NT computer, provided that the card is compatible with NT and has an NDIS 4.0–compatible driver available to support it. All cards that are supported by Microsoft for use with NT will be on the *hardware compatibility list* (HCL) available from Microsoft.

Key Concept

The File System layer serves as the redirector. When it encounters something that must be redirected, it turns to the Protocol layer to find the language and specifics to use. The Protocol layer, in turn, talks with the Network Adapter layer to perform the actual redirection.

Transport Device Interface

The *Transport Device Interface* (TDI) is a boundary interface between the Redirector layer and protocols. The TDI provides a common programming interface that any redirector can use to build a path (bind) to any and all appropriate installed protocols. This capability enables the redirectors to remain independent of the protocols installed and makes it extremely easy (and attractive) for network manufacturers to write redirectors for NT. The TDI provides the translation necessary to enable the redirector to "talk" successfully with the protocol. This is called *binding the redirector to a protocol.*

NDIS 4.0 Interface

The NDIS 4.0 boundary interface does for network cards what the TDI does for redirectors. It provides a common programming interface between the protocols and the NICs. Protocols are written to communicate with the NDIS 4.0 interface. NIC drivers also are written to communicate with the NDIS 4.0 interface. Consequently, only one set of drivers needs to be written for a protocol or an NIC. In other models, each protocol requires drivers to communicate with every NIC installed in a computer. This requirement is no longer necessary in NT 4.0. As with the TDI, the NDIS 4.0 interface makes it attractive and easy to write protocol and card drivers to work with NT.

Benefits of TDI and NDIS 4.0

The ultimate benefit of this model is that the TDI and NDIS 4.0 interfaces do all the work of finding the appropriate path for a resource request out on the network. These interfaces provide the bindings between the layers. As a result, you can install any number of compatible protocols, redirectors, and NICs in a given NT computer. TDI and NDIS 4.0 will neatly manage communications among them.

Furthermore, each network card can have multiple protocols bound to it. Thus, your NT Workstation can "talk" with any computer on the network that is running any of your installed protocols. It is possible for your computer to have two NICs installed on your NT 4.0 Workstation, for example. One NIC can use the NetBEUI protocol to communicate with computers on one subnet, while the other NIC can use TCP/IP to communicate with computers on another subnet. You can access resources on computers in either subnet with this arrangement.

As the administrator, you have the capability to fine-tune these bindings and even turn them off if they're not being used. You also can install any number of network cards in the same machine and configure each independently; changing *interrupt requests* (IRQs), I/O base, or memory addresses for one card does not affect the others. To change any of these items, double-click on an adapter in the Adapters tab and change the settings in the Setup dialog box.

Examining NetBEUI

Of the five communication protocols supported by NT 4.0, three are most likely to be used for computer-to-computer communications: NetBEUI, NWLink, and TCP/IP. The last section briefly reviewed each. This section covers *Network BIOS Extended User Interface* (NetBEUI), a protocol typically found only in small Microsoft-only networks. The next two chapters cover TCP/IP and NWLink in detail.

NetBEUI is a fast, efficient networking protocol used mostly for small, single-subnet LANs rather than large, multiple-subnet *wide-area networks* (WANs) because NetBEUI is not a routable protocol.

This protocol heavily relies on network broadcast messages to provide communications between computers. Consequently, NetBEUI LANs have a relatively high level of broadcast traffic. Think of a broadcast as a computer sending a message to every computer on the network, even if the message is intended for a specific computer.

Key Concept

NetBEUI is an excellent protocol for use on small workgroups and networks because of its size and efficiency. This is why it was the default protocol used by the first versions of Windows NT, as well as Windows for Workgroups, LAN Manager, and others.

NetBEUI cannot be routed, however, and that makes it an impractical choice for any large network.

NetBEUI has no configuration parameters that can be changed through the user interface in NT 4.0.

Configuring and Installing Network Options

Network-based options are installed, configured, and maintained through the Network applet in the Control Panel, also accessible through the Network Neighborhood properties (see Fig. 12.2). Five tabs are included with the network applet, three of which are of particular interest to the current discussion. Those three tabs are Protocols, Adapters, and Bindings. The other two tabs are Identification and Services tabs.

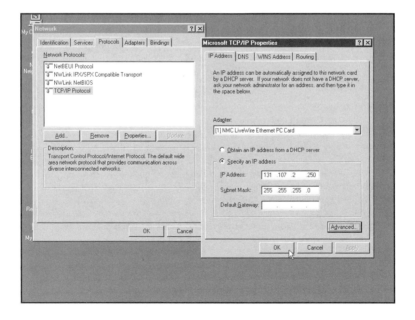

Figure 12.2
The Network applet showing the Protocols tab, and the Properties dialog box for the TCP/IP protocol.

The Protocols tab displays a list of the currently installed network protocols. Choosing Add displays a list of all the protocols that are available for installation through NT, or through an *original equipment manufacturer* (OEM) disk. You can Remove protocols from the computer and Update a protocol driver. You can configure a protocol during installation of the protocol or by selecting the protocol from the list and then choosing Properties. For example, notice the TCP/IP configuration parameters displayed in Figure 12.2.

The Adapters tab displays the installed network adapter cards (see Fig. 12.3). Again, if you choose Add, NT displays a list of all supported adapter cards for which NT supplies a *Network Device Interface Specification* (NDIS)–compatible driver. You also can install a card by using a manufacturer-supplied driver, provided it is NDIS-compatible. You can Remove and Update drivers as well. You configure network adapter card drivers during installation of the card or by selecting the card from the list and choosing Properties. Settings associated with the card are displayed in a dialog box similar to the one in Figure 12.3. Settings such as IRQ level, *direct memory access* (DMA) base, I/O base, and transceiver type can be viewed and modified here.

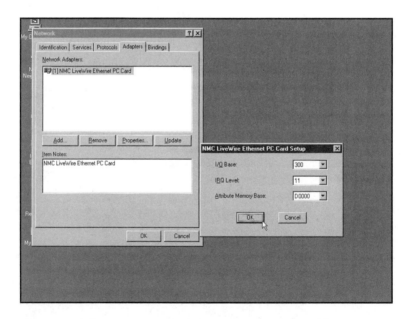

Figure 12.3
You can use the Adapters tab to view and configure adapter card settings.

The Bindings tab displays, in a graphic format, the paths network-bound communications may take to complete their tasks. These paths are arranged like Windows Explorer, so you easily can expand through a protocol or service to see what that protocol or service is bound to. For example, Figure 12.4 shows that an application using NetBIOS communicates with the network through NWLink NetBIOS bound to NWLink IPX/SPX, or through NetBEUI to other computers running NWLink and/or NetBEUI.

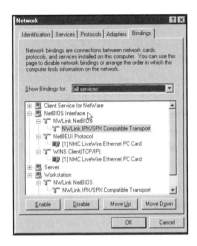

Figure 12.4
Some of the bindings for NetBIOS and Workstation.

As you can see by looking at the available buttons on the Bindings tab, you can enable or disable bindings and change their order. If you think of network bindings as being a path that a communications request can take, all enabled bindings are possibilities, and NT checks each one to find the best path to take. Furthermore, NT searches the paths in the order in which it encounters them. Therefore, you can improve network performance somewhat by moving up in the list the paths most likely to be taken so that they are encountered and chosen ahead of the other paths, or by disabling paths that are used infrequently.

Suppose that you can communicate with several computers throughout your network by using TCP/IP and NWLink. Some of the computers have only NWLink, but most use TCP/IP or both. You most frequently communicate with the computers by using TCP/IP. If NWLink appears ahead of TCP/IP in the bindings list, NT has to check the NWLink binding first before choosing TCP/IP (which it usually winds up choosing anyway, because you most frequently talk with the TCP/IP computers). If you move the bindings for TCP/IP ahead of NWLink for those computers that you most frequently talk with by using TCP/IP, NT has to check only the first binding for TCP/IP and never go any farther.

CH
12

Key Concept

The workstation goes through the protocols available to it in the binding order, trying to find a common language with the server. Placing the most-used protocols at the top of the binding order reduces the number of attempts that must be made to find a common language (protocol) on which the workstation and server can communicate.

As another example, suppose that you maintain an archive computer on your subnet that you use to back up data once a month by using NetBEUI. There is no particular reason to leave the binding for NetBEUI active, because you use it only once a month. That binding is taking up resources and very likely is sending out many broad-cast messages that can affect network traffic. In this case, you can disable the binding for NetBEUI and enable it only when you need to use the protocol to communicate with the archive computer.

The Identification tab displays the current computer (NetBIOS) name and workgroup or domain in which the computer participates. You can change either setting by using the <u>C</u>hange button.

The Services tab displays NT services that are currently installed on the computer. Recall that *services* are programs and processes that perform specific tasks, which are added to the Executive Services portion of the NT operating system. For example, if you want your Windows NT 4.0 Workstation to be able to log in to a NetWare server, you need to install Client Services for NetWare on your computer. You can add that service through the Services tab by clicking <u>A</u>dd and then by selecting the service from the list of available services.

Three of these services—Workstation, Server, and Computer Browser—are discussed in particular in the next section.

Reviewing Workstation and Server Services

The Workstation and Server services are both integral to your ability to share and access resources on the network. Recall the earlier reference to the redirector that determines for which network and binding a resource request is intended. The NT 4.0 redirector file is RDR.SYS, which is more commonly called the *Workstation Service.* In addition to accessing network resources, the Workstation Service provides the capability to log on to a domain, connect to shared folders and printers, and access distributed applications. It is your outgoing pipe to the NT network.

The incoming pipe is the *Server Service.* The Server Service enables the creation and sharing of network resources, such as printers and folders. The Server Service also accepts incoming requests for resource access, directs the requests to the appropriate resources (or file systems, such as NTFS), and forwards resources back to the source computer.

Now try to put the whole process together. A request for an NT network resource is made and sent to the I/O Manager on a computer. The I/O Manager determines that the request is not for a local resource and sends it to the appropriate network redirector—in this case, the Workstation Service. Through the redirector and the bindings, the appropriate protocol is chosen and a packet is created and sent through the NIC out onto the network.

The target computer (determined by the NetBIOS name, IP address, NWLink hardware address or frame type, and so on) receives the request. The request then is serviced by the Server Service on the target computer, which determines which resource is required and where it is located (local printer, NTFS folder, and so on); the service then directs the request there. After the *access control list* (ACL) for the resource determines the effective access to the resource, the appropriate resource response (printer driver, file, and so on) is forwarded back through the now-established IPC connection to the client computer.

Two additional components play a part in determining the name and redirector resolution for network requests. The *Multiple Universal Naming Provider* (MUP) enables the client computer to browse for and request network resources by their *Universal Naming Convention* (UNC) names. This is the syntax in which a resource path is established by naming the server and share name for the resource. For example, a folder shared as DATA on server ACCT1 can be accessed by mapping a network drive in Windows Explorer to \\ACCT1\DATA, its UNC name. Along with the MUP, the *Multiple Provider Router* (MPR) ensures that, on computers with multiple redirectors to multiple networks, requests for network resources are routed to the appropriate network redirector. After a connection has been established to a network, it is cached for that session and the MPR again provides the route for additional requests for that network.

Becoming a Member of a Domain

Chapter 2, "Understanding Microsoft Windows NT 4.0," covers the various models of network computing available with NT and compared workgroup computing with domain computing. When you participate in a workgroup, you are part of a logical grouping of computers that may or may not share resources with one another, and for which there is no single point of logon or authentication. Recall that every computer in the workgroup (workstation or server) maintains its own account database. When a user

CH
12

logs on at a computer, that user is authenticated on that local workstation and receives an access token for resources used on that local workstation.

As your network grows and as workgroups merge together, it may become appropriate to migrate to a domain model. A domain centralizes account information in one or more domain controllers. Thus, users have a single point of logon. They can log on to the domain from any computer that participates in the domain, be authenticated by a domain controller for the domain, and receive an access token that can be used to access any resources available in the domain.

You can switch your computer's participation from workgroup computing to a domain by using the Identification tab in the Network applet, which you can access through the Control Panel (or through the properties of Network Neighborhood). In order for your NT computer to join a domain, it must have a computer account created for it on the domain controller. This can be done ahead of time by a domain administrator, or it can be done during the change process by providing the name and password of a valid administrator's account. A standalone server can become a member of a domain, but a member server cannot be promoted to a backup domain controller or a primary domain controller.

Key Concept

Only NT Workstation and member server computers require a computer account in an NT domain; other network clients do not. However, Windows 95 workstations will appear in the list of computers in the domain if their workgroup setting matches the name of the domain.

Key Concept

For the exam, and the real world, be sure that the computer name you are using is unique in the domain you are joining. If it is not unique, you can run into some serious connection problems in the domain.

If you need to change your computer name to make it unique, modify the entry in the Computer Name text box in the Changes dialog box.

As Figure 12.5 shows, clicking the Change button on the Identification tab displays a Changes dialog box. Select the Domain option and enter the name of the domain your computer is joining. If the computer account for your computer already has been created, click OK and wait for NT to confirm that you have successfully joined the domain.

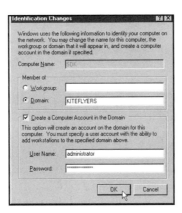

Figure 12.5
This computer is about to join the KITEFLYERS domain by using the administrator's account from that domain to create a computer account for it there.

If you do not have a computer account already created, but you know the name and password of a valid administrator account for the domain, enable the Create a Computer Account in the Domain check box. Enter the administrator account name in the User Name text box and the valid password in the Password text box. Then click OK.

After the computer account is created for your computer, you can move back and forth between a workgroup and a domain. However, you cannot be a member of both simultaneously.

Troubleshooting Networking

If you encounter network-related difficulties, they are more likely caused by traffic problems, protocol incompatibilities, or hardware failures than anything else. Troubleshoot your NT network as you would troubleshoot any other network. A good network-traffic analysis tool is beneficial for the network administrator, such as the NT Network Monitor utility that comes with NT 4.0 Server.

If you experience a network problem after the first installation of NT, or after installing an adapter card, double-check the adapter settings. Recall from Chapter 3, "Windows NT 4.0 Server Setup," that NT uses the default factory settings for most NICs. As a result, if you did not change the settings, your card might not be properly configured for the network.

Performance Monitor also provides objects and counters relating to the protocols installed, as well as to the Workstation and Server Services. For each protocol installed on an NT 4.0 Server, for example, you can chart total bytes/sec, session timeouts and retries, frame bytes sent and received, packets sent and received, and adapter failures. TCP/IP object counters become available when the *Simple Network Management Protocol* (SNMP) service is installed.

Other tips include double-checking all protocol configuration options. Be sure that the TCP/IP address and subnet mask are correct, for example, and that the IP address is unique (described further in the next chapter). If you are using *Windows Internet Name Service* (WINS), be sure that the correct address to these servers has been configured for the workstation. Recall that NWLink autodetects the network frame type. If NWLink detects multiple frame types, it simply defaults to 802.2, which may restrict access to certain resource servers. If necessary, determine what frame types are in use on the network and manually configure NWLink to recognize them.

Check the Services applet in the Control Panel and the Event Viewer to see whether any network-related services failed to start, and why. If the Workstation Service is not running, you cannot connect to network resources. Similarly, if the Server Service is not running, you cannot share resources or service network requests.

Table 12.2 describes which network protocols and TCP/IP services each of the client systems supports.

Table 12.2   Network Protocol and TCP/IP Service Support for Windows NT Client Systems

Network	TCP/IP	IPX-	IPX/	Net-	TCP/IP	DLC	DHCP
NetworkClient for MS-DOS	X	X		X	X	X	
LAN MAN2.2c for MS-DOS	X			X	X	X	
LAN MAN2.2c for OS/2	X			X			
Windows95	X	X	X		X	X	X
WindowsNT Workstation	X	X	X	X	X	X	X

Summary

This chapter introduced the networking concepts of Windows NT Server. It talked about the networking model, Workstation and Server Services, and troubleshooting networking.

Windows NT Server can work with a number of protocols, and five are included with it. NetBEUI was the default protocol in many earlier versions of NT, as well as other Windows-based products. The small size and efficiency of NetBEUI make it ideal for small networks, but the inability to route makes it unusable for large networks.

Network adapter card binding order can enable workstations and servers to find a common protocol quickly and reduce negotiation time. The Workstation Service is necessary for a server to access remote resources, while the Server Service is needed to share resources across the network.

Sharing a printer is a simple operation, but such things as allowing it to be accessed by TCP/IP hosts can require the addition of other services.

The next two chapters discuss the TCP/IP and NWLink protocols in detail.

QUESTIONS AND ANSWERS

1. A two-way IPC connection channel that guarantees that data is sent, received, and acknowledged is called _____.

   A: Named pipes. Named pipes represent a two-way IPC connection channel that guarantees that data is sent, received, and acknowledged.

2. A one-way IPC connection channel is called _____.

   A: A mailslot. Unlike named pipes, mailslots are a one-way IPC connection channel.

3. What is the default networking protocol in NT 3.5, which offers fast, efficient communications but no routing capability?

   A: NetBEUI. The default networking protocol in NT 3.5, NetBEUI, offers fast, efficient communications but no routing capability.

4. Which protocol is used by the Internet?

   A: TCP/IP.

5. Which protocol is used by NetWare servers?

   A: IPX/SPX (NWLink is NT's compatible answer to IPX/SPX).

CH
12

PRACTICE TEST

1. You install protocols by accessing the Network applet in the Control Panel and

    a. Selecting the Protocol tab and clicking the Add button.

    b. Selecting the Protocol tab and selecting the protocol.

    c. Selecting the Protocol tab and selecting all protocols.

    d. Selecting the Protocol tab; nothing else has to be selected.

Answer a is correct. You click the Add button from the Protocol tab. Answer b is incorrect. You must click the Add button. Answer c is incorrect. You must click the Add button. Answer d is incorrect. You must click the Add button.

2. The three layers of the networking model are

    a. The File System layer

    b. The Protocol layer

    c. The NIC layer

    d. The IP layer

Answers a, b, and c are correct. The three layers are the File System or Redirector layer, the Protocol layer, and the NIC or Adapter layer. Answer d is incorrect. The three layers are the File System or Redirector layer, the Protocol layer, and the NIC or Adapter layer.

3. Which of the following protocols is not considered routable?

    a. TCP/IP

    b. NetBEUI

    c. NWLink

    d. AppleTalk

Answers a, d, and c are all incorrect, because TCP/IP, NWLink, and AppleTalk are all routable. **Answer b is correct, because NetBEUI depends on broadcasts and cannot be used across routers.**

4. A Windows API that enables two-way acknowledged data transfer between computers is

    a. Named pipes

    b. Mailslots

    c. Windows Sockets

    d. NetBEUI

Answer a is incorrect. Named pipes are not implemented as an API. Answer b is incorrect. Mailslots are a one-way connection channel. **Answer c is correct. Windows Sockets are APIs that perform this function.** Answer d is incorrect. NetBEUI is a networking protocol and not an API or connection type.

5. Which service must be running in order to access resources residing on another machine?

   a. Server
   b. Replicator
   c. Browser
   d. Workstation

Answer a is incorrect. The Server Service makes resources on this machine available remotely. Answer b is incorrect. The Replicator Service performs replication. Answer c is incorrect. The Browser Service maintains a browse list of available resources across the network. **Answer d is correct. The Workstation Service enables you to access remote resources on this machine.**

6. All NICs supported by Windows NT can be found in

   a. NTHQ
   b. HCL
   c. POP
   d. Readme

Answer a is incorrect. NTHQ is a text for querying what is on your system, not what is compatible. **Answer b is correct. The *Hardware Compatibility List* (HCL) lists all known compatible hardware.** Answer c is incorrect. POP is a protocol used to look for the presence of email and is not a valid choice. Answer d is incorrect; it is invalid.

7. Associating a protocol with a NIC is known as

   a. Tying
   b. Linking
   c. Binding
   d. Browsing

Answer a is incorrect. This process is known as *binding*. Answer b is incorrect. Linking commonly involves shortcuts on the desktop and similar operations. **Answer c is correct. Binding is the process of associating protocols with the network cards.** Answer d is incorrect. Browsing involves seeing what resources are available to the network user.

CH
12

TCP/IP and Windows NT

WHILE YOU READ

1. What is the IP address used for testing the internal stack down to the card?

2. What is the default subnet mask for a class B address?

3. IP addresses can be issued automatically to workstations via the use of what type of server?

4. True or false: To see all IP configuration data, use the PING /ALL utility.

5. What is the maximum number of hops you can configure on the Relay tab?

6. What class does the IP address 192.16.12.14 fall into?

7. An IP address consists of how many bits?

Transmission Control Protocol/Internet Protocol (TCP/IP) is the default protocol selected at installation time for Windows NT 4.0 for both the Workstation and Server platforms. Currently, TCP/IP is the protocol of choice because of its capability to connect to many types of computing equipment and to the Internet.

TCP/IP Addressing

To install TCP/IP, access the Network property sheet, select the Protocol tab, and click the Add button. During the installation process, you must configure an IP address and subnet mask for at least one *network interface card* (NIC) in the machine (a unique IP address is required for every network adapter card using TCP/IP). You can obtain this IP address and subnet mask from a *Dynamic Host Configuration Protocol* (DHCP) server, or you can enter the address manually if no DHCP server exists on the network. Installing DHCP is covered later in this section.

An IP address consists of 32 bits of address information and is denoted in a dotted decimal notation, such as 131.107.2.200. Each octet of the address is made up of 8 bits of information, with each bit assigned a binary weight. Each byte (8 bits) can contain any value from 0 to 255.

Table 13.1 shows the corresponding bits (bolded) in each octet of an IP address of 131.107.2.200.

Table 13.1   A Sample IP Address

First Octet		Second Octet		Third Octet		Fourth Octet	
131	107		2		200		
128	8	128	**8**	128	8	**128**	**8**
64	4	**64**	4	64	4	**64**	4
32	**2**	**32**	2	32	**2**	32	2
16	**1**	16	**1**	16	1	16	1

An IP address consists of two parts: the network address and the workstation address. IP addresses are divided into classes: class A through class C. Each class, by default, denotes the number of networks and workstations available. The class of an address is resolved by the value in the first octet of the address. Table 13.2 shows the three classes of addresses, as well as the number of networks and workstations available by default in each class.

Table 13.2 IP Address Class Definitions

Class	Value in First Octet	Available Networks	Available Workstations
A	1–126	254	16,777,214
B	128–191	65,534	65,534
C	192–255	16,777,214	254

Key Concept

Address 127 is reserved for loopback testing. You can use the IP address 127.0.0.1 on any machine to test the TCP/IP stack down to the card.

If the address is a class A address, the first octet (far left octet) of the address is the network address, and octets 2, 3, and 4 are the workstation address. If the address is a class B address, the first and second octets are the network address, and octets 3 and 4 are the workstation address. If the address is a class C address, the first, second, and third octets are the network address, and octet 4 is the workstation address.

A subnet mask is used to divide the address octets. If all bits are on (value 255) in the subnet mask for a specific octet, the bits are considered masked out when determining the address of a specific machine on a subnet. If no bits are on in the subnet mask for a specific octet, they are not masked out. By default, a class C address of 192.123.234.xxx has a subnet mask of 255.255.255.0, for example. The values in octets 1, 2, and 3 (192.123.234) are the network number. All workstations on this subnet will be on network 192.123.234 and will have a unique value from 1 to 254. In an IP address, the network number remains constant, and the workstation addresses change.

Here are the default subnet mask parameters for each class of address:

Class A	255.0.0.0
Class B	255.255.0.0
Class C	255.255.255.0

CH
13

Key Concept

The subnet mask enables you to divide all possible hosts into multiple locations. The chances of having a class B address and 65,000 hosts in one building are small. By using a subnet mask, you can divide the 65,000 hosts into a number of subnetworks.

Note that the previous subnet mask parameter values are default values. Each class of addresses has a corresponding minimum value for the subnet mask. For example, a class B address can have a class C subnet mask (131.107.2.200 and 255.255.255.0), but it cannot have a subnet mask below 255.0.0.0.

A subnet mask can be any value from 0 to 255. A subnet mask of 255.255.240.0 allows 1,048,575 network addresses and 4,096 workstations on each network. A subnet mask cannot have any 0s to the left of any 1s (binary).

Another parameter you may need to configure is a default gateway or router parameter. Gateways and routers enable the computer to communicate with another computer on another TCP/IP network in or outside the enterprise. If you are going to use your computer to communicate with another computer on another TCP/IP network in or outside the enterprise, you need to configure a default gateway or router parameter.

Figure 13.1 shows the IP address, subnet mask, and default gateway parameters.

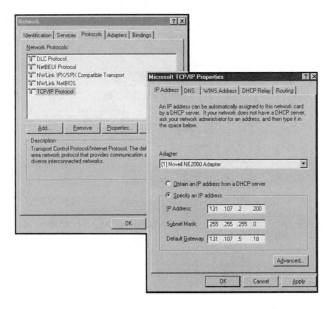

Figure 13.1
The Microsoft TCP/IP Properties dialog box.

You can click the Advanced button on the Microsoft TCP/IP Properties dialog box to add up to five additional IP addresses and up to five additional default gateway (router) addresses. Machines that have more than one TCP/IP address are typically computers that are connected to more than one network.

Figure 13.2 shows an additional default gateway address being added to the already configured default gateway address of 131.107.5.18.

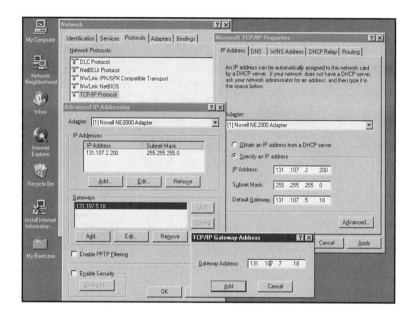

Figure 13.2
You can add more default gateway parameters.

PPTP Filtering and Enable Security Options

In addition to the parameters previously mentioned, you can configure other protocols and security options—including PPTP; Filtering; and Enable Security for TCP Ports, UDP Ports, and IP Protocols—by using the Advanced button. Figure 13.3 shows *Point-to-Point Tunneling Protocol* (PPTP) filtering enabled and the TCP/IP Security dialog box with TCP Port 23 (Telnet), UDP Port 137 (nbname), and all IP Protocols (or ports) enabled.

Key Concept

Enabling PPTP filtering effectively prevents all other TCP/IP packets from passing through the selected network adapter card. Only PPTP packets are allowed through.

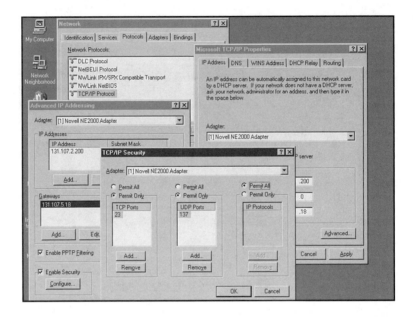

Figure 13.3
Clicking the Advanced button displays PPTP Filtering and TCP/IP Security options.

Dynamic Host Configuration Protocol (DHCP)

As mentioned previously, each network card installed in a computer requires an IP address to communicate in a TCP/IP network. You can configure IP addresses manually or obtain them dynamically from a *Dynamic Host Configuration Protocol* (DHCP) server. Windows NT 4.0 Server can be configured as a DHCP server. A DHCP server dynamically allocates IP addresses to DHCP-enabled clients in lieu of manual IP address configuration.

To configure a Windows NT 4.0 Server to become a DHCP server, you must manually give the specific computer a static IP address and subnet mask; then you can add the DHCP service. In fact, the following message appears when you load the DHCP service:

```
If any adapters are using DHCP to obtain an IP address, they are now required
to use a static IP address. Press Close on the Network Control Panel and the
TCP/IP Property Sheet will be displayed, allowing you to enter an address.
```

After the service is added, you can configure the DHCP server by using the DHCP Manager tool in the Administrative Tools program group.

Key Concept

A DHCP server dynamically allocates IP addresses to DHCP-enabled clients in lieu of manual IP address configuration. DHCP Manager is used to add and remove DHCP servers; create, configure, and manage scopes and reservations; and configure and manage DHCP options.

Figure 13.4 shows the DHCP Manager and Scope Properties dialog boxes, with a scope configured and a range of excluded IP addresses. The figure also shows a default lease duration of three days.

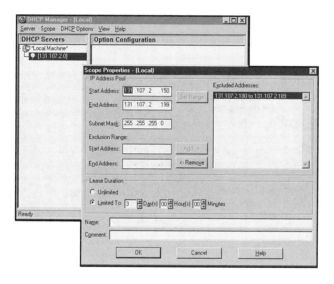

Figure 13.4
Configuring a DHCP scope.

Key Concept

If more than one DHCP server is configured on a network or an enterprise, it is extremely important to note that each DHCP server must be configured with a unique scope of IP addresses. Failure to observe this warning results in duplicate IP addresses on the network.

You configure DHCP options that a DHCP server assigns to clients by using the DHCP Options drop-down menu on the DHCP Manager dialog box. You can set options for a single scope (scope selection) or all scopes (global selection). If you select the default choice, you can change the default values for the default options, and you can delete default options or add options. Active global options apply unless overridden by scope or client options. Refer to Windows NT 4.0 online help for a description of all default options.

If you want to assign a specific IP address to a network card, you can configure a reservation by using DHCP Manager. You can make a reservation by associating an IP address with a unique 12-digit Mac address of a network card on the network. You find the 12-digit Mac address by activating a command prompt and typing **ipconfig /all**. The resulting display includes a line that indicates the physical address of the network card(s) in the computer. Figure 13.5 shows an example of the ipconfig command.

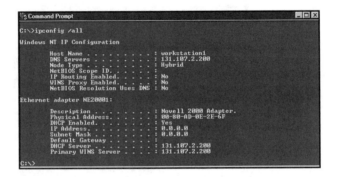

Figure 13.5
The command prompt ipconfig /all command.

Key Concept

The TCP/IP must be running for the ipconfig command to function.

Figure 13.6 shows the Add Reserved Clients dialog box, which you use to specify an IP reservation. A reserved IP address of 131.107.2.180 is being assigned to a client computer named workstation1.

If the routers that connect the IP subnets in an enterprise can function as a DHCP/BOOTP-relay agent (specified in RFC 1542), a DHCP server can lease IP addresses to clients in multiple subnets on the network. If the routers are not RFC 1542–compliant, a DHCP server must be configured on each subnet. The DHCP relay option is configured on one or two computers on each network that act as proxies for all DHCP traffic.

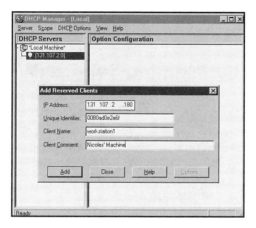

Figure 13.6
The DHCP Manager and Add Reserved Clients dialog boxes.

The DHCP Relay tab is located on the TCP/IP Properties dialog box, as Figure 13.7 shows.

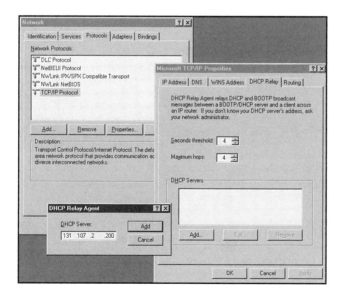

Figure 13.7
Configuring a DHCP relay agent.

Key Concept

You can configure a maximum of 16 hops on the DHCP Relay tab of the TCP/IP Properties dialog box.

Windows Internet Naming Service (WINS)

The TCP/IP communicates with other network devices by using an IP address. In order for an application to communicate with another computer through the *Network Basic Input/Output System* (NetBIOS) session-level interface by using a computer name, the computer name must be mapped or resolved to an IP address. Table 13.3 lists the methods used to map or resolve NetBIOS computer names to IP addresses.

Table 13.3 NetBIOS-Name-to-IP-Address Resolution Methods

Mapping Method	Configured
IP broadcasts	NetBIOS name queries
Host files	Manually configured
LMHost files	Manually configured
DNS configuration	Manually configured
WINS configuration	Dynamically configured

Windows NT 4.0 Server can be configured as a *Windows Internet Naming Service* (WINS) server, and multiple WINS servers can be configured in one network or enterprise. Multiple WINS servers help divide the load of handling computer-name registrations and queries, as well as database backup and redundancy.

Key Concept

Unlike DHCP servers, WINS servers can be configured to communicate with one another, and to replicate their databases with one another to ensure a current database structure.

WINS is designed to lessen the use of IP broadcast messages on the network to establish IP addresses of specific network devices. Because WINS maintains a dynamic database that maps NetBIOS names to IP addresses, the administrative task of maintaining a Host or LMHost file is eliminated.

WINS is installed and configured as a service in the same way that the DHCP service is installed and configured.

After WINS is installed, you can manage it from WINS Manager in the Administrative Tools program group. Figure 13.8 shows the WINS Manager dialog box.

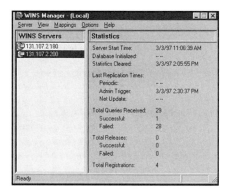

Figure 13.8
Managing WINS from the WINS Manager dialog box.

The WINS Manager dialog box displays the configured WINS servers and a Statistics window. The five menus are S̲erver, V̲iew, M̲appings, O̲ptions, and H̲elp.

WINS Manager Server Menu

The Server menu provides options to add or delete WINS servers, display detailed information about a WINS server, display a WINS server configuration dialog box, display a replication partner configuration dialog box, and exit. Figure 13.9 shows the default settings for the WINS Server Configuration dialog box. Here, the Advanced button has been clicked, and information appears in the Advanced WINS Server Configuration section at the bottom of the screen.

You use the WINS Server Configuration dialog box to configure parameters that are used to manage the WINS database and replication partner relationships. Figure 13.10 shows the Replication Partners dialog box.

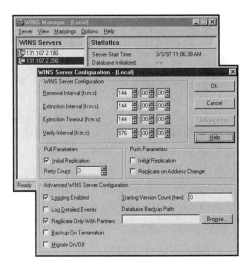

Figure 13.9
The WINS Server Configuration dialog box.

Figure 13.10
The WINS Replication Partners dialog box.

You use the Replication Partners dialog box to add or delete WINS replication partners and to display the status of each WINS server on the network. The display shows whether a WINS server is a push partner, a pull partner, or both. You use the Replication Options area of the dialog box to configure the update count parameter for push partners specifies how many changes or additions you can make in the WINS database before a replication is triggered. (The minimum value is 20.) If you click the Configure button adjacent to Pull Partner, a time interval parameter for pull partners specifies when replication of the WINS database should begin and how often replication should occur.

Other options you can select from this dialog box include Send Replication Trigger Now for both push and pull partners to replicate the WINS database immediately, without waiting for the time interval to time out for the pull partners or the update count to be exceeded for the push partners. Another available choice is the Replicate Now button to initiate replication immediately in both directions.

WINS Manager View Menu

You use the WINS Manager View menu simply to select/deselect two options. One option is to clear the Statistics window on the right pane of the WINS Manager dialog box; the other option is to refresh the Statistics window.

WINS Manager Mappings Menu

You use the WINS Manager Mappings menu to display the WINS database, initiate scavenging, add static mappings, and back up and restore the WINS database. Figure 13.11 shows an example of a WINS database.

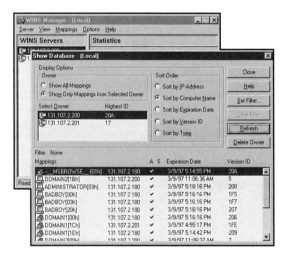

Figure 13.11
A WINS database mapping NetBIOS names to IP addresses.

CH
13

The Show Database dialog box displays the WINS servers and the actual database mappings—either all mappings or individual WINS server mappings.

You can initiate scavenging from the Mappings menu; however, by default, it is performed automatically. *Scavenging* is the process of cleaning out the database by removing old released mappings and old mappings from other WINS servers that did not get deleted. Scavenging is done automatically, based on the renewal interval time and extinction interval time defined in the WINS Server Configuration dialog box.

Static mapping and importing mapping files, such as LMHost files, also can be accomplished from the Mappings drop-down menu. Figure 13.12 shows an example of adding a static mapping for a computer named Michelle, configured with an IP address of 131.107.2.182.

Figure 13.12
Adding static mappings.

WINS Manager Options Menu

The one important option in the Mappings drop-down menu is the Preferences option, which enables you to configure a default setting for two parameters that were discussed earlier (clear the Statistics pane on the right side of the WINS Manager dialog box and refresh the Statistics window). As Figure 13.13 shows, most of the options are self-explanatory. However, by clicking the Partners button, two additional parameters become available: the New Pull Partner Default Configuration and the New Push Partner Default Configuration options. Values entered here are configured automatically for the pull and push partners if you select the Set Default Value option in the Pull Partners Properties and the Push Partner Properties dialog boxes. Recall that you access these two property sheets from the Server menu in the Replication Partners dialog box. Figure 13.13 shows the Preferences dialog box with the Partners button clicked.

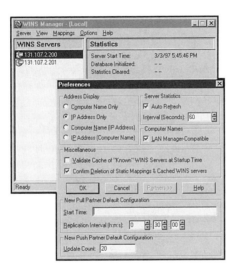

Figure 13.13
The Preferences dialog box.

WINS Client Installation and Configuration

When the TCP/IP is installed on a WINS-compliant client (such as a Windows NT domain controller or member server, a Windows NT Workstation, or a Windows 95 computer), WINS can be installed and configured. You configure WINS from the WINS Address tab in the TCP/IP Properties dialog box (see Fig. 13.14). The only thing that has to be configured is the IP address of a primary or secondary WINS server. From that point, any time the WINS client is started, it registers its name, IP address, and user with a designated WINS server. When WINS client computers are shut down properly, the clients send a WINS server a name-release request, and then the computer name/IP mapping is released from the WINS database.

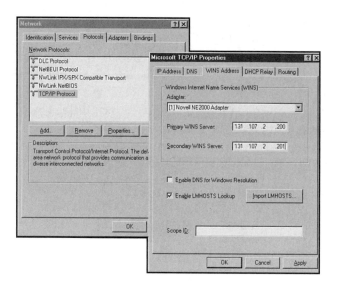

Figure 13.14
A WINS client configuration.

The TCP/IP Properties dialog box also has options called Enable DNS for Windows Resolution and Enable LMHOSTS Lookup (which is selected by default). You can import an LMHost file from this screen and configure a scope ID.

Domain Name System Server

Windows NT 4.0 Server also can be configured as a *Domain Name System* (DNS) server. You install DNS by selecting Microsoft DNS Server in the Select Network Service dialog box.

In a DNS or Internet/intranet environment, clients (resolvers) query DNS servers and their databases for computer name resolution. DNS servers map DNS domain names to IP addresses.

DNS Server Configuration

After the DNS service is installed, open the TCP/IP Properties dialog box from the Network dialog box and select the DNS tab. The first thing you must define is a domain name, as well as the IP addresses of the DNS servers in the DNS Service Search Order box (see Fig. 13.15).

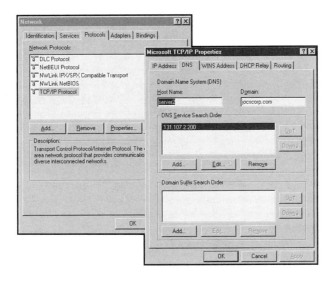

Figure 13.15
A DNS domain and server configuration.

The next step in the process of configuring a DNS server is to start DNS Manager from the Administrative Tools program group. Then, in the DNS Servers pane, define a new server or group of servers that will be managed from this computer's DNS Manager.

The menus in DNS Manager include DNS, View, Options, and Help. Except for configuring preferences from the Options menu, all other DNS configuration is performed from the DNS menu. Choosing Preferences from the Options menu gives you choices such as Auto Refresh Statistics, Show Automatically Created Zones, and Expose TTL (TimeToLive). Right-click the Server List icon and choose New Server. Or, choose New Server from the DNS menu to access the Add DNS Server dialog box (see Figure 13.16). Figure 13.17 shows what you see after you enter a server name or IP address and click OK.

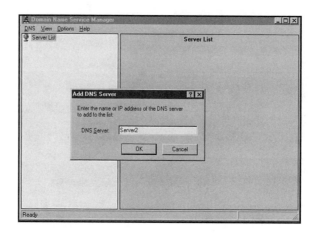

Figure 13.16
The Add DNS Server dialog box.

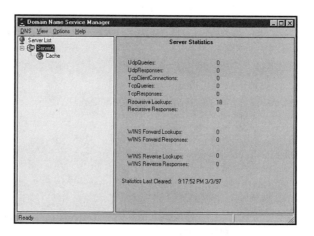

Figure 13.17
The results of adding a DNS server.

After you successfully create a DNS server and, if required, define forwarded information in the Servers Properties dialog box, you can create a zone by right-clicking the server and selecting a new zone. In the Creating New Zone for Server dialog box, enter the zone name in the Zone Name text box and press the Tab key to move to the Zone File text box. A zone filename appears automatically (see Fig. 13.18). Click Next to see an information screen stating that all the information for the new zone has been entered. To create the new zone, click Finish.

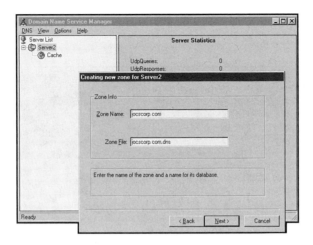

Figure 13.18
Creating a new DNS zone.

When a new zone is created, the DNS Manager appears, as Figure 13.19 shows. In this figure, two additional records already have been added. The first is the A record (address record) for server2; the second is the CNAME record (canonical or alias record).

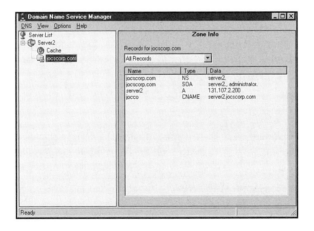

Figure 13.19
The newly created DNS zone and DNS record associations.

Figure 13.20 shows the Ping utility being used to ping both server2's address of 131.107.2.200 and the alias or CNAME of server2. Pinging the alias was successful because of the CNAME record (refer to Fig. 13.19). The alias computer name to IP address is resolved by the DNS database.

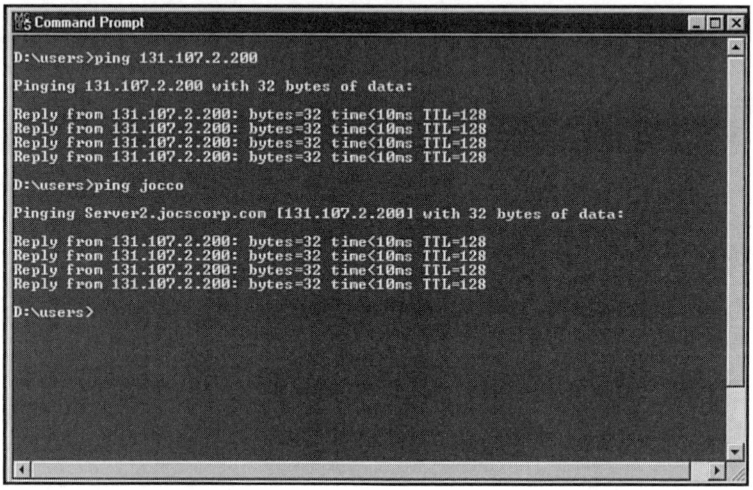

```
Command Prompt                                                    _ □ X

D:\users>ping 131.107.2.200

Pinging 131.107.2.200 with 32 bytes of data:

Reply from 131.107.2.200: bytes=32 time<10ms TTL=128
Reply from 131.107.2.200: bytes=32 time<10ms TTL=128
Reply from 131.107.2.200: bytes=32 time<10ms TTL=128
Reply from 131.107.2.200: bytes=32 time<10ms TTL=128

D:\users>ping jocco

Pinging Server2.jocscorp.com [131.107.2.200] with 32 bytes of data:

Reply from 131.107.2.200: bytes=32 time<10ms TTL=128
Reply from 131.107.2.200: bytes=32 time<10ms TTL=128
Reply from 131.107.2.200: bytes=32 time<10ms TTL=128
Reply from 131.107.2.200: bytes=32 time<10ms TTL=128

D:\users>
```

Figure 13.20
Pinging an IP address and alias name.

IP Routing

The *Routing Information Protocol* (RIP) for *Internet Protocol* (IP) is another service available in Windows NT 4.0. After you install the service, a Windows NT 4.0 system can act as an IP router in a TCP/IP network. You install the service from the Services tab in the network application.

When RIP for IP is installed, the Routing tab in the TCP/IP Properties dialog box displays an Enable IP Forwarding check box, which is enabled by default (see Fig. 13.21). The Routing tab also states that IP Forwarding (IP Routing) allows packets to be forwarded on a multi-homed system. A *multihomed* system is a system with more than one network card installed—each connected to a unique subnet. Windows NT 4.0 can forward TCP/IP packets between subnets.

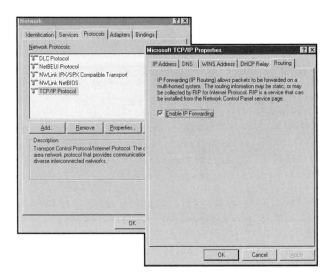

Figure 13.21
Using the Routing tab to configure NT as a network router.

TCP/IP and the Registry

Registry keys and values for the TCP/IP and all its additional services are located in many places in the Registry. To display all locations would be virtually impossible as well as impractical. The following figures, however, show a number of default keys and values. Figure 13.22 shows the default TCP parameters.

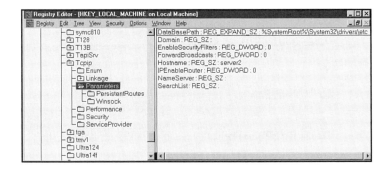

CH
13

Figure 13.22
The default TCP Registry parameter values.

Figure 13.23 shows the default NE20001 network adapter card parameters for TCP/IP. Values can change depending on the network adapter card used.

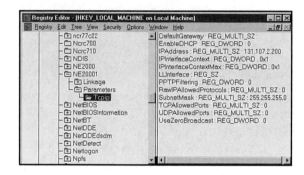

Figure 13.23
The default TCP NE20001–compatible network adapter card parameters.

Default NetBIOS over TCP/IP parameters are established in the Registry when TCP/IP is installed. Figure 13.24 shows the NetBT over TCP/IP default Registry values.

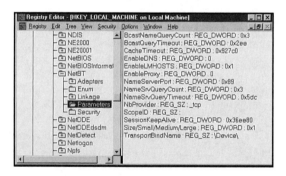

Figure 13.24
The default NetBT over TCP/IP Registry parameters.

Figures 13.25 and 13.26 show the default Windows Sockets Registry entries.

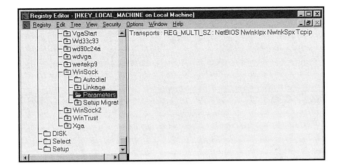

Figure 13.25
The default WinSock Registry parameters.

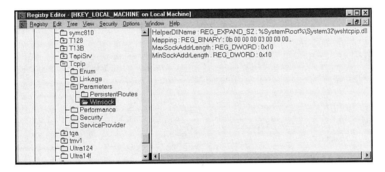

Figure 13.26
The default TCP/IP Winsock Registry parameters.

Figure 13.27 shows the default DHCP Server Registry parameters.

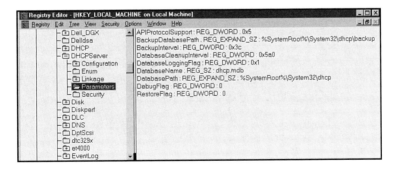

Figure 13.27
The default DHCP Server Registry parameters.

CH
13

Figure 13.28 shows parameter information relating to the DHCP client portion of DHCP. Many parameter options are available at this location; however, only one option, 15, is shown in the figure. Table 13.4 lists all the default options and their relationship to DHCP.

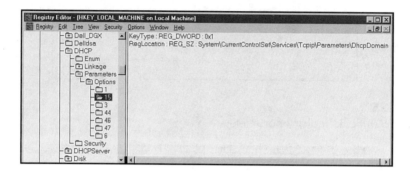

Figure 13.28
The default DHCP Client Registry parameters.

Table 13.4   DHCP Client Registry Options

Option	Relationship
1	DhcpSubnetMaskOption
15	DhcpDomain (see Fig. 13.29)
3	DhcpDefaultGateway
44	DhcpNameServer
46	DhcpNodeType
47	DhcpScopeID
6	DhcpNameServer

Figure 13.29 shows default Registry parameters for WINS. No default parameters are listed in this location; however, in this example, the pull and push partners are shown. Figure 13.30 shows default DNS Registry parameters.

For additional information on the TCP/IP, options, and Registry parameters, refer to the online help files in Windows NT 4.0 and the Windows NT 4.0 Resource Kit.

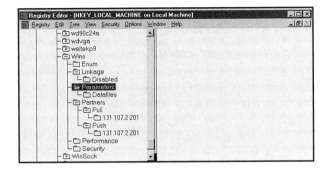

Figure 13.29
The default WINS Registry parameters.

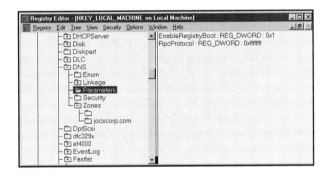

Figure 13.30
The default DNS Registry parameters.

Summary

In this chapter, you examined TCP/IP from all angles. You learned about the necessary components to configure the protocol to work with Windows NT Server, as well as enhancements to the protocol that simplify management, such as DNS, DHCP, and WINS.

DNS lets you use hostnames—alphanumeric entries such as Kristin1 to be converted to IP addresses. The *Windows Internet Name Service* (WINS) is similar to DNS, only it allows NetBIOS computer names—found only in Windows operating systems—to be converted to IP addresses. DHCP, on the other hand, simplifies IP configuration for an administrator by leasing addresses and other configuration data to clients.

The next chapter explores IPX/SPX and Novell NetWare networks.

CH
13

QUESTIONS AND ANSWERS

1. What is the IP address used for testing the internal stack down to the card?

A: 127.0.0.1.

2. What is the default subnet mask for a class B address?

A: 255.255.0.0.

3. IP addresses can be issued automatically to workstations via the use of what type of server?

A: A *Dynamic Host Configuration Protocol* (DHCP) server.

4. True or false: To see all IP configuration data, use the PING /ALL utility.

A: False. Ping is used to test connectivity to another host. To see all IP configuration data, use the IPCONFIG /ALL utility.

5. What is the maximum number of hops you can configure on the DHCP Relay tab?

A: 16

6. What class does the IP address 192.16.12.14 fall into?

A: Class C. Class A has the first octet between 1 and 126. Class B is between 128 and 191, and Class C is 192–223.

7. An IP address consists of how many bits?

A: 32

PRACTICE TEST

1. An IP address of 191.191.191.191 will have a default subnet mask of

   a. 255.255.255.0
   b. 255.255.0.0
   c. 255.0.0.0
   d. 0.0.0.0

Answer a is incorrect. It is the default subnet mask for a class C address, whereas the address given is within the class B realm. **Answer b is correct for a class B address.** Answer c is incorrect. It is the default subnet mask for a class a address, whereas the address given is within the class B realm. Answer d is incorrect; it is an invalid address.

2. An IP address consists of what two parts in the order from left to right?

    a. A network address and a workstation address

    b. A workstation address and a network address

    c. A subnet mask address and a default gateway address

    d. A default gateway address and a subnet mask address

Answer a is the correct answer. An IP address consists of a network address and a workstation address. Answer b is incorrect. It contains the correct components, but in the wrong order. Answer c is incorrect. It has two wrong entities. Answer d is incorrect. It has two wrong entities.

3. The Advanced button on the Microsoft TCP/IP Properties dialog box enables you to add

    a. Five additional WINS server IP addresses

    b. Ten additional default gateways

    c. Five additional DHCP server IP addresses

    d. Five additional default gateways

Answer a is incorrect. You use the WINS tab to configure WINS functionality, not the Advanced button. Answer b is incorrect, because only five additional default gateways can be configured. Answer c is incorrect. You configure DHCP from the DHCP Manager after you have installed the service. **Answer d is correct; the maximum number of additional default gateways is five.**

4. A DHCP server eliminates the need to manually configure

    a. A DHCP scope

    b. A WINS database

    c. An IP address and subnet mask for DHCP clients

    d. An IP address and subnet mask for non-DHCP clients

Answer a is incorrect. You must give DHCP the scope (the pool of addresses) it can issue. Answer b is incorrect. DHCP works independently of WINS. **Answer c is correct: DHCP can issue configuration values to DHCP clients only.** Answer d is incorrect. DHCP does not work with non-DHCP clients.

5. A DHCP reservation is assigned to a

    a. Computer

    b. Network adapter card

    c. Domain

    d. Workgroup

CH 13

Answer a is incorrect. The addresses are assigned to the NIC. **Answer b is correct: The configuration information is issued to the NIC.** Answer c is incorrect, because the addresses are assigned to the NIC. Answer d is incorrect—the addresses are assigned to the NIC.

6. A WINS database is used to dynamically map
    a. IP addresses to network adapter card names
    b. IP addresses to subnet masks
    c. IP addresses to NetBIOS names
    d. IP addresses to a username

Answer a is incorrect. WINS maps IP addresses to NetBIOS names. Answer b is incorrect, because WINS maps IP addresses to NetBIOS names. **Answer c is correct. WINS dynamically maps IP addresses to NetBIOS names.** Answer d is incorrect, because WINS maps IP addresses to NetBIOS names.

7. The DLC protocol is used on Windows NT 4.0 computers to communicate with
    a. HP JetDirect printing devices
    b. AppleTalk PostScript printing devices
    c. Novell file servers and client computers
    d. IBM mainframes and front-end processors

Answer a is correct. DLC is used to talk to HP printers. Answer b is incorrect, because DLC does not communicate with AppleTalk. Answer c is incorrect, because DLC does not communicate with Novell (IPX/SPX/NWLink). **Answer d is correct. DLC is used to communicate with mainframes.**

CHAPTER PREREQUISITE

Before reading this chapter, you should be familiar with fundamental protocols and networking concepts.

Novell NetWare Connectivity Tools

WHILE YOU READ

1. The frame type used by NetWare 2.2 servers is _____.

2. The frame type used by NetWare 3.12 servers is _____.

3. The frame type used by NetWare 4.1 servers is _____.

4. The service that allows you to manage your NetWare servers from an NT Server is _____.

5. True or false: Gateway Service for NetWare converts Novell's *NetWare Core Protocol* (NCP) to Microsoft's *Server Message Block* (SMB) packets.

Corporations and businesses today are faced with the challenge of a complex computing environment. Most of the issues associated with the management of this environment are related to the integration of components within that architecture. In recognition of that, Windows NT has intensified its efforts for connectivity tools. The efforts have included the development of NWLink (the Microsoft IPX/SPX–compatible transport protocol), *File and Print Services for NetWare* (FPNW), *Directory Service Manager for NetWare* (DSMN), *Gateway Service for NetWare* (GSNW), *Client Services for NetWare* (CSNW), and the Migration Tool for NetWare.

NWLink IPX/SPX–Compatible Transport

One of the key components for integrating NetWare is the NWLink protocol. This protocol is an IPX/SPX–compatible protocol and also is compatible with SPX II. IPX/SPX stands for *Internetwork Packet Exchange/Sequenced Packet Exchange* and is the group of transport protocols used in the Novell NetWare environment. Because NWLink is a Microsoft product, NWLink follows the *Network Driver Interface Specification* (NDIS) and is fully compliant with NDIS.

Key Concept

For any communication to take place between Windows NT and NetWare, those operating systems must share a common protocol. NetWare uses the proprietary IPX/SPX, and Windows NT's answer to this is NWLink—an IPX/SPX–compatible protocol.

NWLink provides support for both Windows Sockets APIs, *Remote Procedure Calls* (RPCs), the Novell *Network Basic Input/Output System* (NetBIOS), and the NWLink NetBIOS. NWLink ships with both Windows NT Server and Windows NT Workstation.

Application programming interfaces (APIs) are a set of program segments used to perform common operating system functions. These functions can be as simple as supplying the look and feel of the Windows interface and as complicated as providing an *interprocess communication* (IPC) method such as Windows Sockets. The availability of all the APIs is one of the reasons Windows has become so popular. It allows the use of standard methods to access system resources and services. Additionally, the availability of the prewritten program segments has reduced the amount of time necessary to develop Windows applications.

NWLink is the transport protocol necessary to implement any of the integration tools and can be loaded with any other transport protocol you might need. You add the protocol as you add other protocols—from the Network icon in the Control Panel or from the Properties selection from the Network Neighborhood context menu. Figure 14.1 shows the access screen.

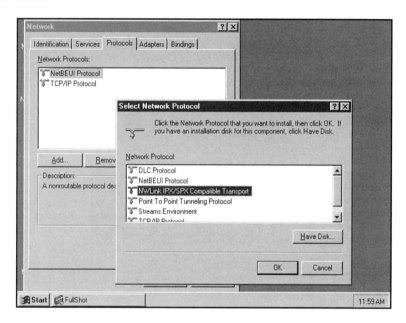

Figure 14.1
From the Select Network Protocol dialog box, highlight the desired protocol and click OK.

The configuration parameters for NWLink are straightforward. Some of these parameters can be provided by the NetWare *local area network* (LAN) administrator. NetWare routers use the NetWare Internal Network Number to determine whether the packet belongs on that LAN or the network. You can find additional information on these parameters in the Novell manuals. If NWLink does not detect that number, it defaults to zeros.

Another configuration parameter relates to selecting Ethernet frame types (see Fig. 14.2). On the General tab of the NWLink IPX/SPX Properties dialog box, you are offered two choices: Auto Frame Type Detection and Manual Frame Type Detection. The first option is to set the frame type for the Ethernet card to Auto Frame Type Detection. When automatic detection is selected, Windows NT goes through the list of frame types, as they are listed in the Frame Type selection box, and tests each until Windows NT gets a response.

When using Auto Frame Type Detection, Windows NT selects the default protocol if there is no response.

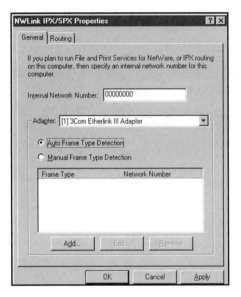

Figure 14.2
The frame type for the Ethernet card can be selected automatically on the NWLink IPX/SPX Properties screen.

The other possibility is to set the frame type manually using the Manual Frame Type Detection option (see Fig. 14.3). If you choose this option, the Manual Frame Detection dialog box opens. Select a frame type from the Frame Type drop-down list and click Add.

Key Concept

Usually a NetWare 2.x or 3.x server uses 802.3 frames types. The exception to this is NetWare 3.12, which uses 802.2. A NetWare 4.x server typically uses 802.2 frame types.

Key Concept

When using NWLink, a fast way to determine the frame type is to use the IPXROUTE CONFIG command. The results of this command include the frame type.

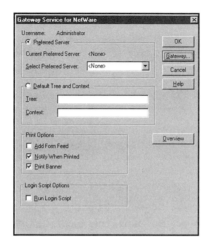

Figure 14.3
Manually select a frame type by choosing the Manual Frame Type Detection option and searching the Frame Type drop-down list.

When using token ring, the configuration parameters concern the token ring source routing table, which is kept on each computer in a token-ring environment. The source routing table is used in determining the route the packet will take. If a packet is received without a corresponding *Media Access Control* (MAC) address in the source routing table, there is a slight problem. When this happens, the packet is passed on as a single route broadcast. The IPXROUTE is useful in this situation also, because it indicates whether a single route broadcast packet is being sent.

File and Print Services for NetWare

File and Print Services for NetWare (FPNW) is an emulator that presents itself to NetWare clients in the same manner as a NetWare 3.x server, not a NetWare 4.x server. It is written to run on all Windows NT platforms, MIPS, Intel, Alpha, and PowerPC machines. It is actually a service that runs on the Windows NT Server. Included in the FPNW package are the Administration Tools and the FPNW product. Generally, the complete package is installed on the *primary domain controller* (PDC), and the Administrative Tools are installed on each *backup domain controller* (BDC). When FPNW is running, the Windows NT Server can be a server for any NetWare client—without modifying the client workstation. The file and print services are supported by using Netx (the NetWare shell) or VLM (the DOS requester).

CH
14

Key Concept

File and Print Services for NetWare (FPNW) is an add-on product not supplied with Windows NT Server. After it is purchased and installed, FPNW allows the Windows NT Server to service NetWare clients.

You add FPNW as you add other Windows NT services—from the Network Properties Protocol tab. Because FPNW is an add-on, you use the Have Disk button to install the service.

The installation process requests a Windows NT directory, which actually will become the SYS volume. Microsoft recommends that the directory named to be the SYS volume be on an NTFS partition. This setup allows the maximum amount of security and may duplicate the security provided on the NetWare volume. After the installation process, the directory structure has the required NetWare directories—MAIL, LOGIN, PUBLIC, and SYSTEM. FPNW provides NetWare-compatible commands in the PUBLIC directory, such as SLIST, USERLIST, MAP, CAPTURE, and so on.

Also requested is a server name, which is the Windows NT computer account the NetWare clients are using to access the SYS volume. Windows NT uses a default of the server's computer name followed by FPNW.

The installation process creates a Supervisor account (this account is the equivalent of the Administrator account in NT), which is added to the Administrators group. A system restart is done at this point, and the process is continued when adding new users. The new users are added from the FPNW icon in the Control Panel. When accessing the New User dialog box from User Manager for Domains, notice the additional selection at the bottom—the Maintain NetWare Compatible Logon check box. Checking this box enables the user logon for FPNW.

Directory Service Manager for NetWare

Directory Service Manager for NetWare (DSMN) is like FPNW—it has to be purchased separately. Understanding the advantages of DSMN requires an understanding of working in an environment that has multiple NetWare 3.x file servers. In the NetWare environment, if a user needs access to files on various servers, that user needs to be defined in the appropriate servers accounts database (bindery). For example, if a user needs access to three NetWare 3.x servers, an account has to be created on each server for that user. Although at first glance this may not seem to be a problem, it is. The requirement for multiple definitions of users has been an extra administrative task with associated problems, such as password synchronization and directory mappings.

Key Concept

Directory Service Manager for NetWare (DSMN) is an add-on product not supplied with Windows NT Server. After you purchase and install DSMN, you can manage your NetWare servers through the Windows NT interface/tools.

DSMN is a time-saver because it brings the administrative tasks into one location—the Windows NT Server. You only have to create a user in one location—the Windows NT Server. DSMN updates the NetWare 3.x servers. DSMN is installed on the PDC, and the account information is replicated in the ordinary manner. Essentially, DSMN does not require any changes on the client's workstation. What happens is that core files are replaced in the SYS:PUBLIC directory.

DSMN needs to have *Gateway Service for NetWare* (GSNW) installed. GSNW is covered in the next section, "Gateway Service for NetWare." You install DSMN as you install other services—from the Network icon.

Key Concept

If you install FPNW before DSMN, the users defined for FPNW are not automatically synchronized to the NetWare server.

Gateway Service for NetWare

Gateway Service for NetWare (GSNW) is included with Windows NT. There are a number of ways to understand GSNW. From the bit/byte perspective, GSNW converts the *server message block* (SMB) packet to Novell's *NetWare Core Protocol* (NCP). From the user perspective, GSNW allows Microsoft clients to access NetWare resources through the gateway running on the Windows NT Server.

The Microsoft clients do not have to have NetWare client software or Microsoft's *Client Services for NetWare* (CSNW) on their workstations. The Windows NT Server shares the NetWare resources and presents these resources to the Microsoft clients for use. The clients attach to the Windows NT Server share, which is actually a NetWare resource. GSNW works for NetWare 3.x and for NetWare 4.x servers, which use bindery emulation mode.

From the NetWare view, there is one attachment to the NetWare server, and access rights are assigned to that account. The Windows NT Server can allow multiple attachments to the share, so many people may actually be using the NetWare resource. This process could be slow due to speed considerations for the translation between SMB and NCP.

CH
14

Also, because access rights are assigned to that account, all users from the Windows NT side who are accessing the resource have the same rights.

Key Concept

Whereas FPSN allows NetWare clients to access the Windows NT Server, *Gateway Service for NetWare* (GSNW) allows Windows clients to access NetWare servers through the Windows NT Server. GSNW is not an add-on and is included with the basic NT product.

One of the ideal uses for GSNW is to allow access to NetWare print queues. To accomplish this, the Windows NT Server machine needs to add a logical printer and direct it to a NetWare print queue (a printing device, from Windows NT's perspective). After this, the driver is added from the Windows NT installation disk, and the printer appears in the printer folder as if it were a local printer. The Windows NT administrator just needs to share the printer, and it will be available for all to use. GSNW allows the creation of a gateway for resources on the *NetWare Directory Services* (NDS) tree in addition to the resources available on any NetWare server with bindery security.

The installation process for GSNW follows the same process as installing other services. However, there are a few preinstallation tasks:

■ From the NetWare server, create a group called NTGATEWAY. From this group, assign the access rights to the resource.

■ From the NetWare server, create a user and put the user into the group NTGATEWAY.

■ Log on as a member of the Administrators group.

You double-click the Network applet icon in Control Panel to access the network configuration options. Or you can access these options by right-clicking the Network Neighborhood icon and choosing Properties from the context menu. After the configuration screen appears, select the Services tab. Highlight the service and click Add to install the Gateway (and Client) Services for NetWare, as shown in Figure 14.4.

Key Concept

If NWLink has not been installed previously, it is installed automatically when Gateway Service for NetWare is installed.

Figure 14.4
Installing the Gateway (and Client) Services for NetWare from the Select Network Service screen.

After you select the service, the Gateway Service for NetWare dialog box appears, as shown in Figure 14.5.

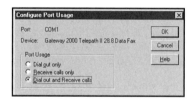

Figure 14.5
You use the Gateway Service for NetWare dialog box to enter configuration information.

In the Preferred Server section, enter the name of the NetWare server to which the Windows NT Server is attaching. If the NetWare server is using NDS, enter the name of the tree where the resource is located in the Tree box. The Context box refers to the position of the object in the tree. You use the Print Options section to specify further print instructions. You use the Login Script Options section to control whether the login script should execute at login time.

Clicking the Gateway button displays the Configure Gateway dialog box (see Fig. 14.6).

CH
14

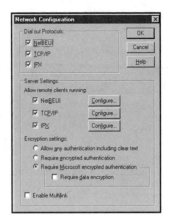

Figure 14.6
You use the Configure Gateway dialog box to input configuration information.

Enter the gateway username in the Gateway Account text box; here it is Gateway_User. You can use any name, but it is wise to use names that remind the administrator of the original intentions in creating the account. The NetWare configuration, therefore, should have a group named NTGATEWAY, with a user in it named Gateway_User. Remember, of course, that the group and user were created in the preinstallation steps.

Click the Add button to add new shares that are going to be accessed (see Fig. 14.7).

Figure 14.7
You use the New Share dialog box to enter specific information related to new shares.

Enter the name of the share in the Share Name text box. The share name should be named as any other Windows NT share is named. The share name appears in the browse list. In the Network Path text box, enter the volume that is being shared—this is the NetWare volume and pathname. In the Use Drive drop-down list box, enter the drive letter to be used to establish the gateway share. You use the User Limit area to control the number of users accessing the share.

After you configure the share as shown in Figure 14.7 and click OK, you return to the Configure Gateway dialog box with the share information entered. From this screen, you can set the permissions. As with other Windows NT shares, the default is Full Control for the group Everyone. The trustee rights that are set in NetWare override the Windows NT share-level permissions.

After you make the gateway configurations and set permissions, the process is finished. The GSNW icon appears in the Control Panel for future use (see Fig. 14.8).

Figure 14.8
Here the GSNW icon is in the second row of the Control Panel.

Client Services for NetWare

Client Services for NetWare (CSNW) is packaged with Windows NT. This software is also a service, but it runs on the client Windows NT Workstation. This service allows users to access NetWare resources. CSNW supports NetWare 2.x, 3.x, and 4.x running in bindery emulation mode or NDS.

You install CSNW on Windows NT Workstation the same way you install a service on Windows NT Server. It is significant to note that when CSNW is installed, it is installed on the Windows NT Workstation machine. When that occurs, the Control Panel of the Windows NT Workstation machine includes a CSNW icon that brings up a screen similar to the screen shown in Figure 14.3. The Windows NT Workstation screen is titled Client Services for NetWare and asks for the same information. Of course, the CSNW screen does not have a button for Gateway configuration, which applies only to Gateway Service.

Key Concept

Client Services for NetWare (CSNW) allows a Windows NT Server or Windows NT Workstation to be a client on a NetWare network. It is not an add-on and is included with the basic NT product.

Migration Tool for NetWare

Windows NT ships with Migration Tool for NetWare. The purpose of this tool is to seamlessly move the users from NetWare to Windows NT. It works with FPNW for the migration of the logon scripts; if FPNW is not running, the logon scripts aren't migrated. Essentially, the Migration Tool reads the NetWare bindery and creates the users and groups on the Windows NT Server. File and directory permissions also can be migrated if the receiving Windows NT volume is NTFS.

The Migration Tool has the added capability of migrating more than one NetWare server to the Windows NT PDC (or BDC). The receiving Windows NT Server must have NWLink and GSNW already installed before using this utility. Working with this utility requires both Supervisor (for NetWare) and Administrator (for Windows NT) rights.

The Migration Tool for NetWare dialog box enables you to specify servers for migration (see Fig. 14.9). After you click the <u>A</u>dd button, another screen appears to indicate the selection for the target and destination server. Clicking the ellipsis (...) button allows the administrator to select the server from a screen similar to Network Neighborhood (see Fig. 14.10).

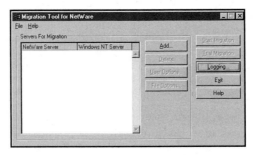

Figure 14.9
The first Migration Tool screen. This screen keeps the list of the involved servers and enables you to set user and file options, as well as the actual migration options.

Figure 14.10
The Select Windows NT Server dialog box is helpful for the selection of the Windows NT Server participating in the migration.

The <u>U</u>ser Options dialog box enables you to control user accounts and groups. The default of this transfer is that all the users and groups get migrated to the Windows NT domain, unless there is a name conflict. If the administrator chooses, he or she can create a mapping file with a listing for each user and specific information for their accounts.

Key Concept

The Migration Tool for NetWare is included with Widows NT Server and is used to move from NetWare to a Windows NT–based network.

Novell NetWare uses an encryption scheme for password storage, so the passwords from a NetWare server cannot be migrated. To assign some type of password, an administrator can use a mapping file to include the password information. If the administrator chooses to use a mapping file, the password information also can be included with the group and user options. Possible options for password information include assigning all accounts a null password, setting the new password to the user's name, indicating a single password for all migrated accounts, and specifying that the password must be changed at the next login.

Key Concept

No matter what you do, you cannot keep the NetWare passwords and import them into Windows NT when using the Migration Tool for NetWare. Passwords are the one value that will always be lost.

The File Options button gives the administrator greater control over the transfer of folders and files. The preferred option is to have these migrated to an NTFS partition to retain the effective rights.

The most helpful option is to run a trial migration. When the trial migration is run, it creates various log files (see Table 14.1).

Table 14.1   Trial Migration Log Files

Log Filename	Content
Logfile.log	User and group information
Error.log	Failures and error messages
Summary.log	Summary of trial migration, names of server, users, groups, and files

The Migration Tool for NetWare dialog box also has a convenient feature that gives the administrator the option to save the configuration. You can save all the configuration information entered for users and files by choosing File, Save Configuration (see Fig. 14.11).

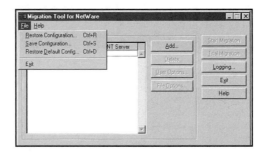

Figure 14.11
The Migration Tool for NetWare dialog box offers four options on the File menu.

Summary

In this chapter, you reviewed material on migrating NetWare users to Windows NT. You also reviewed additional services for NetWare, such as the Client Service and File and Print Services.

For any communication to take place between Windows NT and NetWare, those operating systems must share a common protocol. NetWare uses the proprietary IPX/SPX, and Windows NT's answer to this is NWLink—an IPX/SPX–compatible protocol.

File and Print Services for NetWare (FPNW) and *Directory Services for NetWare* (DSNW) are add-on products not supplied with Windows NT Server. When purchased and installed, they allow the Windows NT Server to service NetWare clients, and Windows NT Servers to manage NetWare servers, respectively.

The *Client Services for NetWare* (CSNW) and *Gateway Service for NetWare* (GSNW) are included with NetWare and allow Windows clients to access NetWare servers and Windows NT to be a client on a NetWare network, respectively.

The Migration Tool for NetWare migrates your network from NetWare to Windows NT but cannot maintain passwords during this process.

In Chapter 15, "Network Client Configuration and Support," you'll learn about the Network Client Administrator utility, how to use client-based server tools, and methods of working with Macintosh clients.

QUESTIONS AND ANSWERS

1. The frame type used by NetWare 2.2 servers is _____.

   A: 802.3

2. The frame type used by NetWare 3.12 servers is _____.

   A: 802.2; all earlier versions of the 3.x network operating system used 802.3—confusing, to say the least

3. The frame type used by NetWare 4.1 servers is _____.

   A: 802.2

4. The service that allows you to manage your NetWare servers from an NT Server is _____.

   A: Directory Service Manager for NetWare or DSMN. You must purchase the add-on service product separately.

5. True or false: Gateway Service for NetWare converts Novell's *NetWare Core Protocol* (NCP) to Microsoft's *Server Message Block* (SMB) packets.

   A: True—and does the opposite as well for traffic going in the other direction.

CH
14

PRACTICE TEST

1. Gateway (and Client) Services for NetWare is _____. (Pick one.)

    a. Both are sold as a part of Services for NetWare.

    b. Both are included with Windows NT Workstation.

    c. Both are included with Windows NT Workstation and Server.

    d. Both are included with Windows NT Server.

Answer a is incorrect. CSNW is included with Windows NT Workstation and Server, and GSNW is included with Windows NT Server only. Answer b is incorrect. CSNW is included with Windows NT Workstation and Server, and GSNW is included with Windows NT Server only. Answer c is incorrect. CSNW is included with Windows NT Workstation and Server, and GSNW is included with Windows NT Server only. **Answer d is correct. CSNW is included with Windows NT Workstation and Server, and GSNW is included with Windows NT Server only.**

2. You need for your existing Novell NetWare clients to access a new Windows NT Server without changing the client software. What approach would you take?

    a. Install File and Print Services for NetWare on the Windows NT Server.

    b. Install File and Print Services for NetWare on the Novell NetWare Server.

    c. Install Gateway (and Client) Services for NetWare on the Windows NT Server.

    d. Install Gateway (and Client) Services for NetWare on the Novell NetWare Server.

Answer a is correct. Installing File and Print Services for NetWare (FPNW) on the server allows NetWare clients to access it. Answer b is incorrect. The service must be installed on the Windows NT Server. Answer c is incorrect. The service needed is File and Print Services for NetWare. Answer d is incorrect. The service needed is File and Print Services for NetWare, and it must be installed on the Windows NT Server.

3. You have clients who only have the Microsoft client installed but need access to a Novell NetWare server. How can you allow these clients to have access to the NetWare server? (Choose all that apply.)

    a. Install Gateway (and Client) Services for NetWare on the Novell Server.

    b. Install Gateway (and Client) Services for NetWare on the Windows NT Server.

    c. Install the Novell NetWare requestor on the client.

    d. Install File and Print Services for NetWare on the Windows NT Server.

Answer a is incorrect. The Gateway Service must be installed on the Windows NT Server and not the NetWare server. **Answer b is correct. Installing the Gateway Service on the Windows NT Server allows clients to access the NetWare server through the Windows NT Server. Answer c is correct. Placing the client requestor on every client is an option, although using the Gateway Service is preferred.** Answer d is incorrect because it involves the wrong service. The Gateway Service must be used in place of File and Print Services for NetWare.

4. When migrating NetWare servers to Windows NT, what are the options for passwords? (Choose all that apply.)

    a. Set them to blank.
    b. Set them to the username.
    c. Set them to a password set in a map file.
    d. Set them to a random password from a dictionary.

Answer a is correct. During migration, you can choose to set passwords to blank. Answer b is correct. During migration, you can choose to set passwords to the username. Answer c is correct. During migration, you can choose to set passwords to a value in a map file. Answer d is incorrect. During migration, you cannot choose to use random passwords.

5. What do Gateway (and Client) Services for NetWare require in order to function?

    a. A user with membership in an NTGATEWAY group on the Windows NT Server
    b. A user with membership in an NTGATEWAY group on the Novell NetWare Server
    c. Supervisor access to the Novell NetWare Server
    d. A translation file that translates Windows NT usernames to Novell NetWare usernames

Answer a is incorrect. The membership must be on the NetWare server. **Answer b is correct. The user must be a member of the group on the NetWare server.** Answer c is incorrect. The user must be a member of the NTGATEWAY account group. Answer d is incorrect. Translation tables are not used anywhere in the gateway process.

CH
14

CHAPTER PREREQUISITE

You should be familiar with the concepts presented in Chapter 12, "Windows NT Networking Services," as well as basic networking concepts.

CHAPTER

15

Network Client Configuration and Support

WHILE YOU READ

1. What is the utility used to create client installation startup disks?

2. What enables Microsoft and Apple clients to share files and printer resources with each other?

3. True or false: The minimum requirement to install Windows NT Server Tools is 8MB of RAM on Windows 95 or 12MB of RAM on NT Workstation.

4. What client tools are available when Windows NT Server Tools for Windows NT Workstation is installed that are not available when Windows NT Server Tools for Windows 95 is installed?

5. For an NT Server to service Macintosh clients, you must create an MAV, which stands for _____ _____ _____.

This chapter discusses the options the network administrator has when creating a network startup installation disk and installation disk sets. You learn about the Server Tools available for administering the Windows NT domain from a Windows NT Workstation or Windows 95 operating system. Also, you learn about Services for Macintosh.

Using Network Client Administrator

Network Client Administrator is a tool provided with Windows NT Server to enable the administrator to graphically create an installation startup disk or disk sets. You can make disks for the following clients:

- Microsoft Network Client 3.0 for MS-DOS
- LAN Manager 2.2c
- Microsoft Windows 95
- Network Client Administrator tool

Windows NT software maintains support for the Windows for Workgroups 3.11 client that was available on the Windows NT 3.51 CD-ROM. It does not ship with Windows NT 4.0. The TCP/IP-32 add-on for Windows for Workgroups does ship with the Windows NT 4.0 CD-ROM.

Microsoft Network Client 3.0 for MS-DOS

Microsoft Network Client 3.0 provides MS-DOS computers with network connectivity and resource access to Windows NT Servers. Microsoft Network Client for MS-DOS supports *Network BIOS Extended User Interface* (NetBEUI), *Internetworking Packet Exchange* (IPX)–compatible protocol, *Transmission Control Protocol/Internet Protocol* (TCP/IP), and DLC.

In addition, TCP/IP supports the *Dynamic Host Configuration Protocol* (DHCP). TCP/IP does not support *Windows Internet Name Service* (WINS) or *Domain Name System* (DNS). Network Client 3.0 for DOS supports IPX transport only. It does not support *Sequenced Packet Exchange* (SPX).

The client can be installed using either a full redirector or a basic redirector. A full redirector allows the client to log on to a network domain as a valid user, access services and resources, and run the logon scripts. By default, Microsoft Network Client for MS-DOS supports the full redirector. Basic redirector allows access to a server using a guest account. Of course, the server must have the guest account enabled. The client uses this *Remote Access Service* (RAS) version 1.1, messaging, and *interprocess communication* (IPC) mechanisms such as named pipes, *Remote Procedure Calls* (RPC), and Windows Sockets (WinSock). IPC mechanisms allow programs to communicate with each other—on the same machine or across the network.

Key Concept

MS-DOS clients are well supported by Windows NT. They can run most protocols and have their choice between a basic redirector and a full redirector.

LAN Manager 2.2c Clients

Two options exist for LAN Manager clients: LAN Manager 2.2c for MS-DOS and LAN Manager 2.2c for OS/2. LAN Manager 2.2c for MS-DOS ships with NetBEUI, Microsoft DLC, and TCP/IP. It supports DHCP, but not DNS or WINS. Also included is a NetWare connectivity disk that allows clients to connect to a NetWare server. LAN Manager 2.2c for MS-DOS supports the Remoteboot service so that MS-DOS or a Windows 95 client may be remotely started. The server in this is used as the replacement for a local active partition.

LAN Manager 2.2c for OS/2 supports OS/2 2.1 and OS/2 2.x. The protocols you can use are NetBEUI and TCP/IP. This version of TCP/IP does not support DHCP or WINS and must have its address configured manually.

Key Concept

With the DOS clients and LAN Manager clients, TCP/IP—the default protocol of Windows NT—is supported, but not all the ancillary services, such as DNS and WINS.

Microsoft Windows 95

Windows 95 is a full 32-bit operating system with a 32-bit networking interface that supports a full redirector using protected-mode and/or real-mode network drivers. Windows 95 supports NetBEUI, NWLink IPX/SPX, and TCP/IP protocols. TCP/IP supports DHCP, WINS, and DNS.

Key Concept

Windows 95 (as well as the newer Windows 98) is supported as a client to a much greater extent than older operating systems. Not only is TCP/IP supported, but also the ancillary services, such as DNS and WINS.

Network Client Administrator Tool

You use the Network Client Administrator tool to create the aforementioned client disks. It is located in the Administrative Tool's folder. After you start the Client Administrator tool, you can choose from four options:

- Installation Startup Disk
- Make Installation Disk Set
- Copy Client-Based Network Administration Tools
- View Remoteboot Client Information

The tool is designed to simplify the process of adding machines to a network and managing client access to the network. The first two options—Installation Startup Disk and Make Installation Disk Set—create disks that can be used to set up a new computer with connectivity to Windows NT.

The Installation Startup Disk option requires that the server be available to the client when the installation is to occur, and that it have the installation files shared. The client administrator automatically handles this function. You can use the Make Installation Disk Set option when you cannot immediately establish connectivity with a server.

You also can use the Client Administration tool to prepare the Windows NT Server Administration tools for Windows 95 or Windows 3.1. In addition, you can use the Client Administration tool to manage the Remoteboot settings for clients.

Installation Startup Disk

After you choose the Installation Startup Disk option, you must select the path of the shared client's folder in the Share Network Client Installation Files dialog box from the clients directory on the CD-ROM. You can choose from an existing share. Share the client folder directly from the tool itself, or copy the files to a new location and reshare them. Select the client software you want—for example, Network Client MS-DOS and Windows. Select the target computer's network adapter card type and to which floppy density this software will be sent (3 1/2-inch or 5 1/4-inch).

Now make the following selections:

1. Enter a unique name for the target computer.
2. Enter a username that identifies the user to the network and domain.
3. Enter the domain name the target needs to log on to.
4. Choose your network protocol.

5. Enable DHCP configuration if you chose TCP/IP and there is a DHCP server. If you chose TCP/IP and there is no DHCP server, enter the IP address, subnet mask, and default gateway.

6. Choose the destination path where files should be sent using the left mouse button to click choice box disk drive A or B.

Installation Disk Set

You use installation disk sets to manually install software on client computers. Installation disk sets are made for Microsoft Network Client 3.0 for MS-DOS, Microsoft LAN Manager 2.2c for MS-DOS, and Microsoft LAN Manager 2.2c for OS/2. In addition, you can make disk sets for RAS for MS-DOS and TCP/IP 32 for Windows for Workgroups 3.11. Two or more disks are required to create an installation disk set for the clients.

To create an installation disk set, use the Network Client Administration tool and follow these steps:

1. Select Make Installation Disk Set from the Network Client Administrator dialog box.

2. Select the appropriate network client or service from the list box.

3. Select the destination drive in the spin box.

4. If necessary, click Format Disks to have the Network Client Administrator format the disks for you.

5. Click OK.

Copy Client-Based Network Administration Tools

You use Copy Client-Based Network Administration Tools to administer the domain environment from a Windows 95 or Windows NT Workstation. Of course, you must have the appropriate rights to use the tools. In this section, you will examine the requirements for Windows 95 and Windows NT Workstation in order to use the tools, and what tools are available for each operating system.

These are the minimum requirements to install Windows NT Server Tools for Windows 95:

- CPU must be at least a 486DX/33.
- 8MB of RAM.

- 3MB of free disk space on the system partition, because the Srvtools folder is created here.
- You must be a client for the network you want to administer.

These are the tools available to Windows 95 for managing the Windows NT Servers:

- Event Viewer for the logs
- File Security for file and folder permissions
- Print Security
- Server Manager
- User Manager for Domains
- User Manager Extensions Services for NetWare, assuming you added on the *File and Print Services for NetWare* (FPNW) or *Domain Services Manager for NetWare* (DSMN)
- *File and Print Services for NetWare* (FPNW)

Key Concept

Noticeably absent from the Server Tools that can run on Windows 95 are the additional service managers, such as WINS Manager, DHCP Manager, and so on.

These are the minimum requirements to install Windows NT Server Tools for Windows NT Workstation:

- CPU must be at least a 486DX/33.
- 12MB of RAM.
- 2.5MB of free disk space on the system partition.
- Workstation and Server services must be running. (These services are running by default.)

Located in the Administrative Tools folder, the tools available to manage the Windows NT Servers from a Windows NT Workstation follow:

- DHCP Manager for the DHCP service running on a server
- Remote Access Administrator for the RAS on a RAS server
- Remoteboot Manager to configure the Remoteboot service

- Services for Macintosh to share Windows NT Server resources with Apple Macintosh computers
- Server Manager
- System Policy Editor
- User Manager for Domains
- WINS Manager

Working with the Macintosh Clients

Services for Macintosh enable Microsoft and Apple clients to share files and printer resources with each other. Use the Control Panel and click the Network icon to add Services for Macintosh. By adding this service, several features are installed and enabled.

Key Concept

If you have a *New Technology File System* (NTFS) partition, a *Macintosh Accessible Volume* (MAV) is created on the servers for the Mac user. This enables sharing for the Mac, and the Windows NT client still will have share access to the NTFS folder following the same Windows NT effective permission rules.

Printer Services for Macintosh also is added automatically to allow either Microsoft client to access the Mac's available printer resources. Windows NT operating systems must use a LaserWriter 5.1 or higher-level printer driver for the Mac PostScript printer. Printer Services for Macintosh also allows Macintosh clients to access any printer defined on the Windows NT Server. The PostScript is converted to the native language of the printer by the server.

You manage Mac user accounts from the Windows NT Server. AppleTalk routing is supported with zones for establishing an AppleTalk Internetwork. The AppleTalk File Protocol is added and supports 2.0 and 2.1 levels. Supported Mac clients must use version 6.07 or later.

Working with Windows NT Workstation Clients

To set up a Windows NT Workstation computer to use your Windows NT Server, you have to create a computer account for the Windows NT Workstation computer. The computer account then is used by the RPC service to make a secured communication. This service verifies when the computer is started and also can be used for monitoring services on your NT Workstation computer. To install the Windows NT Workstation computer, you first install it as a standalone system. Then, in the Network dialog box, have your NT Workstation computer join the domain. During the joining process, you can automatically create a computer account in the domain. You must have Server Operator or Administrator access to create this computer account, however. If you want to create the computer account in the Windows NT Server computer ahead of time, you can use Server Manager.

After you configure a Windows NT Workstation client, the users and the client computer can use the native Windows NT security, and all user properties apply.

Summary

Windows NT Server is made to interact with a number of clients and to provide their domain needs. The main tool for interacting with client installation/updates is the Network Client Administrator tool.

MS-DOS clients are well supported by Windows NT. They can run most protocols and have their choice between a basic redirector and a full redirector. With both the DOS clients and LAN Manager clients, TCP/IP—the default protocol of Windows NT—is supported, but not all the ancillary services, such as DNS and WINS, are supported. Windows 95 (as well as the newer Windows 98) is supported as a client to a much greater extent than older operating systems. Not only is TCP/IP supported, but also the ancillary services such as DNS and WINS.

Using Services for Macintosh, if you have an NTFS partition, a *Macintosh Accessible Volume* (MAV) is created on the servers for the Mac user. This enables sharing for the Mac, and the Windows NT client still will have share access to the NTFS folder following the same Windows NT effective permission rules.

Now that you have examined the Windows NT Network Client Administrator utility, Chapter 16 will move into the topic of clients who dial in and the Remote Access Service.

QUESTIONS AND ANSWERS

1.   What is the utility used to create client installation startup disks?

   A: Network Client Administrator

2.   What enables Microsoft and Apple clients to share files and printer resources with each other?

   A: Services for Macintosh, when installed on the NT Server

…continues

3. True or false: The minimum requirement to install Windows NT Server Tools is 8MB of RAM on Windows 95 or 12MB of RAM on NT Workstation.

A: True

4. What client tools are available when Windows NT Server Tools for Windows NT Workstation is installed that are not available when Windows NT Server Tools for Windows 95 is installed?

A: Remoteboot utilities, DHCP Manager, and WINS Manager

5. For an NT Server to service Macintosh clients, you must create an MAV, which stands for _____ _____ _____.

A: Macintosh Accessible Volume

PRACTICE TEST

1. What clients and services disks can you create with the Network Administrator tool?

a. Microsoft Windows 95

b. Microsoft Windows NT Workstation

c. Microsoft Windows for Workgroups

d. LAN Manager 2.2c clients

Answer a is correct. You can create client and service disks with the Network Administrator tool for Windows 95 clients. Answer b is incorrect. You cannot create client and service disks with the Network Administrator tool for Windows NT Workstation clients. **Answer c is correct. You can create client and service disks with the Network Administrator tool for Windows for Workgroups clients. Answer d correct. You can create client and service disks with the Network Administrator tool for LAN Manager 2.2c clients.**

2. TCP/IP and DHCP are supported for what clients?

a. LAN Manager 2.2c for MS-DOS

b. LAN Manager 2.2c for OS/2

c. Microsoft Network Client for MS-DOS

d. Microsoft Windows 95

Answer a is correct. TCP/IP and its automatic configuration through DHCP are supported for LAN Manager 2.2c for MS-DOS clients. Answer b is incorrect. TCP/IP and its automatic configuration through DHCP are not supported for LAN Manager 2.2c for OS/2 clients. **Answer c is correct. TCP/IP and its automatic**

configuration through DHCP are supported for Microsoft Network Client for MS-DOS clients. Answer d is correct. TCP/IP and its automatic configuration through DHCP (as well as DNS and WINS) are supported for Windows 95 clients.

3. What clients support Remoteboot?

a. LAN Manager 2.2c for MS-DOS
b. LAN Manager 2.2c for OS/2
c. Microsoft Network Client for MS-DOS
d. Microsoft Windows 95

Answer a is correct. LAN Manager 2.2c for MS-DOS clients support RemoteBoot. Answer b is incorrect. LAN Manager 2.2c for OS/2 clients do not support RemoteBoot. Answer c is incorrect. Microsoft Network Client for MS-DOS clients do not support RemoteBoot. Answer d is incorrect. Windows 95 clients do not support RemoteBoot.

4. Windows 95 and TCP/IP support which of the following services?

a. DHCP
b. WINS
c. DNS
d. Protected-mode drivers

Answer a is correct. TCP/IP, on Windows 95, supports DHCP. Answer b is correct. TCP/IP, on Windows 95, supports WINS. Answer c is correct. TCP/IP, on Windows 95, supports DNS. Answer d is correct. TCP/IP, on Windows 95, supports protected-mode drivers.

5. You just created a startup disk with the ne2000 interface card selected and NetBEUI. You installed the disk but cannot connect to the server. What may be the problem?

a. You have an old *network interface card* (NIC) driver.
b. DHCP server is offline.
c. Server only uses NetBEUI.
d. Server only uses TCP/IP.

Answer a is incorrect. Failure to connect to the network most likely would not be a result of an old NIC driver. Answer b is incorrect. Failure to connect to the network for a single workstation—newly installed—most likely would not be a result of a downed DHCP server. Answer c is incorrect. If the server only uses NetBEUI, and NetBEUI is what was installed on the workstation, this could never be a cause for failure to connect. **Answer d is correct. If the server and workstation do not share a common protocol, no connection can take place.**

6. Your assistant calls and wants to know why he cannot use his Server Tool User Manager for Domains from his Windows 95 client. Your answer is

    a. He does not have the correct protocol.

    b. He needs Windows NT Workstation.

    c. He is not an administrator.

    d. The server is offline.

Answer a is incorrect. With an incorrect protocol, no communication at all between the server and client is possible. Answer b is incorrect. User Manager for Domains can be run remotely on both Windows 95 and Windows NT Workstation clients. **Answer c is correct. You must have Administrator privileges to run User Manager for Domains remotely.** Answer d is incorrect. If the server were offline, there would be far greater problems than your assistant's inability to run User Manager for Domains remotely.

7. Your assistant calls and wants to know why he cannot use his Server Tools from his Windows 95 client with a 386DX/66. Your answer is

    a. He does not have the correct protocol.

    b. Insufficient hardware.

    c. He is not a backup operator.

    d. The server is offline.

Answer a is incorrect. With an incorrect protocol, no communication at all between the server and client is possible. **Answer b is correct. You must have a 486DX to be able to run Server Tools on a Windows 95 machine.** Answer c is incorrect. You do not have to be a member of the Backup Operators group. Answer d is incorrect. If the server were offline, your assistant would not even be able to access the folder, let alone run the tools.

8. To create a Macintosh Accessible Volume on the server, you must have which of the following?

    a. Pentium 166MHz processor

    b. FAT partition

    c. NTFS partition

    d. Windows NT Workstation

Answer a is incorrect. The hardware need only be a standard NT Server (486). Answer b is incorrect. An MAV must reside on an NTFS partition. **Answer c is correct. An MAV must reside on an NTFS partition.** Answer d is incorrect. Macintosh Services are available for Windows NT Server only.

CHAPTER PREREQUISITE

Before reading this chapter, you
should be familiar with network
protocols, especially the Windows
NT 4.0 protocols covered in
Chapter 15, "Network Client
Configuration and Support."

Remote Access Server

WHILE YOU READ

1. An enhancement to the *Point-to-Point Protocol* (PPP) is _____.

2. True or false: The tunneling protocol can work with NetBEUI PPP
   packets over TCP/IP.

3. The administration of the *Remote Access Service* (RAS) is done
   through _____.

4. The client component of RAS is _____.

5. True or false: You can turn on auditing of RAS features by editing
   the Registry.

The *Remote Access Service* (RAS) is one of the most powerful features of Microsoft Windows NT 4.0 Server. In this day of the virtual office, corporations are increasingly employing people who work from locations other than the office. One of the most significant features of RAS is that the caller can access corporate resources on the company's networks. Additionally, Microsoft has designed this service to work with any of the common-line protocols and any of the common transport protocols, and has optimized the code with advanced compression techniques to facilitate the interprocess communications necessary for the typical client/server applications.

An Overview of Remote Access Server

The Remote Access Server (RAS) Service has been a component of Microsoft operating systems for a long time. Windows for Workgroups 3.11 used RAS version 1.1a. Earlier versions of Microsoft Windows NT Server also used RAS. As you would expect, RAS has improved greatly over the years. Features of RAS follow:

- Support for *Point-to-Point Protocol* (PPP), *Serial Line Interface Protocol* (SLIP), and the Microsoft RAS Protocol
- Support for *Point-to-Point Tunneling Protocol* (PPTP)
- Support for various physical connections, including phone lines using modems, X.25, *Integrated Services Digital Network* (ISDN), null modem cables, and multi-link protocol connections
- Support for an array of clients, MS-DOS, Windows, Windows 95, Windows For Workgroups, Windows NT, and LAN Manager RAS

Each of these features is significant to the overall operations of RAS and should be understood. Before continuing, it will be helpful to take a closer look at each of these characteristics.

Understanding PPP, SLIP, and the Microsoft RAS Protocol

The Point-to-Point Protocol was first defined by the *Internet Engineering Task Force* (IETF). It is a protocol that encapsulates the piece of information (packet) as it goes on the line. The encapsulation process causes the addition of bits to the packet for addressing, error checking, and authentication. The addressing facilitates communications between computer to computer, computer to router, or router to router. The error checking is handled using a *checksum*, which is a method of looking at the bits in the packet to determine whether they all made it over the line. The authentication methods include *Password Authentication Protocol* (PAP), *Challenge Handshake Authentication Protocol* (CHAP), and *Shiva Password Authentication Protocol* (SPAP). These protocols are called the *PPP Control Protocols*. PPP is newer and is generally recommended over SLIP.

The Serial Line Interface Protocol is simpler and older than PPP. SLIP does not provide any error checking or authentication. SLIP also is defined by the IETF and was developed originally for use in the UNIX environment. One limitation of SLIP is that Windows NT Server can be used as a SLIP client but not a SLIP server.

The Microsoft RAS Protocol is used for the older versions of RAS. These older versions are Windows NT 3.51 and Windows for Workgroups. This protocol requires the use of *Network BIOS Extended User Interface* (NetBEUI) and uses *Network Basic Input/Output System* (NetBIOS). When the communication is made, the RAS server acts as a gateway for any other protocols that might be running on the corporate network, such as *Internetworking Packet Exchange* (IPX) or *Transmission Control Protocol/Internet Protocol* TCP/IP.

Understanding PPTP

At first glance, you might think that PPTP is just a misspelling of PPP. PPTP is *Point-to-Point Tunneling Protocol*. This is a new protocol for Windows NT Server and is particularly timely because it takes advantage of the Internet's popularity: This protocol allows access to the corporate networks through the Internet.

The Internet connection can be through an Internet provider or directly to the Internet. When either of these connections is made, the PPTP provides tunneling for the connection. The tunneling encapsulates the IP, IPX, or NetBEUI PPP packets for transmission over a TCP/IP network.

In other words, PPTP actually allows an Internet connection, and through that call, access to the corporate network. There are many advantages to PPTP, especially the reduction in phone bills. This also could be especially advantageous if the company already has established Internet connections for all its employees; therefore there is minimal setup. When PPTP is used, it is called a *virtual private network* (VPN).

PPTP provides a sophisticated level of transport protocol support and is capable of handling TCP/IP, *Internetworking Packet Exchange/Sequenced Packet Exchange* (IPX/SPX), or NetBEUI. PPTP uses data encapsulation with encryption and authentication.

Key Concept

Although the following terms usually are covered in preparation for the Networking Essentials Exam Guide, it is helpful to briefly review their definitions for this section of the Windows NT Server 4.0 Enterprise Exam Guide:

- **Data encapsulation:** A method of inserting one protocol's packet into another protocol's packet.

- **Encryption:** A method of changing data so that it is not readable for any unauthorized purpose. Typically, an algorithm is used to make the data unreadable. After the data is encrypted, it must be decrypted to be read.

- **Authentication:** A method of validation of source and accuracy.

Defining the Connections

Various methods of network communication exist—some more common than others. The most common method is connecting through phone lines using modems. These phone lines sometimes are called *Plain Old Telephone Service* (POTS) or *Public Switched Telephone Network* (PSTN). Microsoft Windows NT supports more than 200 modems, and it is strongly recommended that you choose a modem from the *hardware compatibility list* (HCL).

To assist with modem connections, Windows NT uses a `device.log` file, which is used to track modem problems. You can turn on this capability by making a Registry setting change. To use this log file, follow these steps:

1. From the Start menu, choose <u>R</u>un. Then start the Registry Editor by entering `Regedt32`.

2. From the `HKEY_LOCAL_MACHINE` subkey, access this key:

   `\SYSTEM\CurrentControlSet\Services\RasMan\Parameters`

3. Change the logging parameter to 1 so that the completed change looks like this:

   `Logging:REG_DWORD:0x1`

As with other Registry changes, it is necessary to restart the machine to have the change take effect.

If you are taking advantage of the full capabilities of Windows NT Server and are using multiple connections, you must purchase special equipment to support the 256 connections that Windows NT Server can offer. This equipment is called a *multiport I/O board*.

This board allows the addition of the 256 ports that RAS is capable of handling. As with any equipment, make sure that it is listed on the HCL. Typically, the modem standards used most often are V.32bis, which operates at 14.4Kbps, and V.34bis, which runs at 28.8Kbps. It is significant to note that RAS compression can be twice as efficient as the compression algorithms used by the V.42bis. A decrease in transmission speed may occur if both modem compression and RAS compression are enabled.

 Key Concept

> In an ideal network, it is a good rule to use the same modem model at both ends of the communications. Although this is not a requirement (and perhaps, considering the exponential growth of Internet users, can be extremely difficult), it is a good idea.

CH 16

X.25 has been around for awhile. It is a protocol that has been defined to control the connection between computers and a *packet-switched network.* A packet-switched network is a communications network that sends the data to the destination in packets, a defined groups of bits. A message may consist of many packets, each having a header. A *header* is a group of bits that contains the address of the destination. When a communication link is established in the X.25 scheme, the connection is called a *virtual circuit* because the connection is not a dedicated connection. Generally, X.25 connections experience performance problems. However, the primary advantage of this type of connection is that it is a well-established technology and is very common. X.25 uses a *packet assembler disassembler* (PAD). As the name suggests, the PAD puts the packets together and disassembles them as the communications are occurring.

ISDN is a technology with a lot of promise. The idea of ISDN is integrated communications, meaning a connection that can handle data, voice, and video. The signals that are carried on ISDN are digital as opposed to the standard analog signal that is carried on a standard phone line. The primary advantage of ISDN is speed. It is considered the communication choice of the future. ISDN connections also require special equipment and special arrangements through the phone carrier. The equipment needed is called an ISDN card. The type of card used is determined by the details of the connection. ISDN offers a *Basic Rate Interface* (BRI) and a *Primary Rate Interface* (PRI).

You can use null modem cables between two machines for a RAS connection. The null modem cable is connected at the serial port of the machines. A nine- or 25-pin cable is used with special pin definitions for each.

Multilink capabilities are possible with Windows NT 4.0. This is a new feature that allows the combining of two or more physical communication links, such as analog modems; they, in turn, act as a single channel. The purpose of multilinking is to increase the bandwidth. When it is being used, both client and server must have the capability turned on. A multilink channel can contain both digital and analog signals. This protocol is defined by the IETF in the *Request for Comment* (RFC) 1717.

Key Concept

Any clients that connect to the RAS server also must have support for the PPP Multilink standard, as described in RFC 1717.

User Security Options

One of the important implementation options is how to handle security. The most basic form of dial-in security is the username and password. Windows NT augments this with support for callback security.

Callback security is used to further verify callers by their location, or at least log their location. Windows NT defines three options for callback security:

- No Call Back Security
- Call Back to an Administrator Defined Number
- Call Back to a User Assigned Number

The highest security is to use an administrator-defined number. This ensures that users calling in will always be where the administrator expects them to be.

Unfortunately, this doesn't always work. For example, what about salespeople who travel from remote office to office? You can't establish a single callback number for them, because they move around.

In that case, you still might be able to use callback security. In this case, the client, your salesman, must provide the number where he is located.

At this point, you're not really adding security to the system, but you are building an audit trail. If you do detect a break-in, you'll have the information needed to locate the culprit.

However, there are cases when even callback security with the user setting the callback number won't work. Going back to the salespeople again, if they travel and are in hotels, you won't be able to use callback security at all, because callback security requires that the

RAS server be able to directly dial the callback number. Most hotels don't have automated attendants that allow a RAS server to call back.

Key Concept

Use callback security set to an administrator-assigned number whenever possible. This increases security. Use callback security set to a user-assigned number when the user moves around. This increases the capability to audit processes.

Most installations of RAS server do not use any kind of callback security; however, companies with security concerns certainly should consider it.

Who Can Be a RAS Server and RAS Client?

RAS communications capabilities are a Microsoft technology; therefore, RAS is not limited to Windows NT Server. MS-DOS 5.0, Windows for Workgroups, OS/2 1.31, Windows 3.1, and Windows 95 can participate in RAS communications. The difference in RAS versions is related to the RAS features. The enhancements made to RAS include support for the newer, faster modems, newer line protocols, flow control, and number of connections supported.

RAS Installation

RAS is a service and is installed as other services are. You can install RAS when you install Windows NT Server, or you can install RAS later.

Key Concept

Before you install the RAS service, you must have the appropriate network protocols installed. It is recommended that the appropriate hardware is installed.

To install RAS, follow these steps:

1. You start the RAS installation from the Network icon in the Control Panel after logging on as Administrator.

   RAS also is accessible from the Network icon on the desktop. Right-click the Network icon and choose Properties from the context menu. Figure 16.1 shows the Network dialog box that appears.

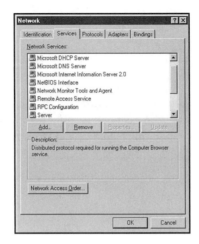

Figure 16.1
The Services tab is selected, listing the Network Services already installed.

2. After selecting the Services tab, click the Add button. Windows NT shows a selection of the services available in the Network Service list box (see Fig. 16.2). Highlight and select the Remote Access Service.

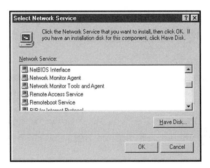

Figure 16.2
The Select Network Service dialog box lists the services available for installation.

The installation process accesses the setup files to start the installation. The typical location of these files is on the Windows NT CD in the \i386 directory. A status screen appears indicating the progress of the file access.

3. Next, you must add the RAS devices. The administrator has a choice of using the already listed RAS-capable devices or installing other devices.

   The Add RAS Device dialog box lists the RAS Capable Devices (see Fig. 16.3). The install buttons—Install Modem and Install X25 Pad—start the Installation Wizards if other devices need to be installed.

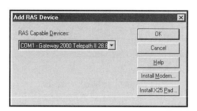

Figure 16.3
The Add RAS Device screen enables you to install RAS devices during the installation of the RAS service.

 Key Concept

A *packet assembler disassembler* (PAD) is used with X.25 public switched networks. The sending PAD accepts and buffers characters from the source machine. The sending PAD then assembles the characters into X.25 packets and transmits the packets. The receiving PAD disassembles the packet and passes the characters to the destination machine.

4. The next screen is the Remote Access Setup dialog box, shown in Figure 16.4. This screen contains the list of RAS devices and servers as the entry point for the specific configuration screen associated with each device. From this screen, you can Add a new device, Remove an existing device, and Configure a new or existing device.

   In this example, you configure the modem ports by selecting the particular modem device and then clicking Configure.

5. After you click Configure in the Remote Access Setup dialog box, the Configure Port Usage screen appears (see Fig. 16.5). Select the Dial Out Only option if the computer is going to be set up as a client. This prevents anyone from calling into the machine. Choose the Receive Calls Only option if the machine is being set up as the RAS server. The last option, Dial Out and Receive Calls, allows the most flexibility. In this case, the machine can be a RAS client or a RAS server.

CH
16

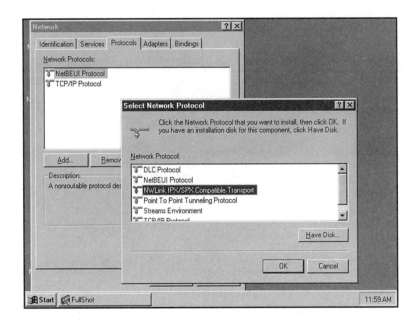

Figure 16.4
Select the modem to be configured from the Remote Access Setup screen.

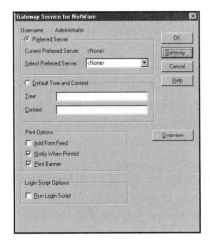

Figure 16.5
The Dial Out and Receive Calls Port Usage option is very flexible, allowing your machine to be a RAS client or server.

6. After selecting your Port Usage option and clicking OK, the Network Configuration dialog box appears (see Fig. 16.6). Table 16.1 lists the protocol and setting options from which you must choose.

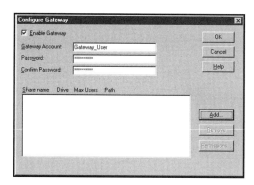

Figure 16.6

You use the Network Configuration dialog box for both RAS client and servers.

Table 16.1   Network Configuration Options

Option	Description
Dial Out Protocols	Protocols used by the machine when the machine is calling out as a client.
Server Settings	Protocols used when the machine is acting as the RAS server.
Encryption	Allow <u>A</u>ny Authentication Including Clear Text Settings indicates that the authentication method is selected by the client. Useful when different kinds of clients are calling in. The least secure of the RAS connections.
	Require <u>E</u>ncrypted Authentication permits any kind of connection with the exception of PAP. (See the following sidebar for details on PAP, MS-CHAP, and other specific protocols.)
	Require <u>M</u>icrosoft Encrypted Authentication permits authentication using the MS-CHAP method only; a very secure protocol. Require <u>D</u>ata Encryption causes all data to be encrypted during the data transfer phase and allows a high level of security by disallowing clear text authentication.
Enable Multi<u>l</u>ink	Selected if the administrator is combining communication links in order to increase bandwidth.

CH
16

More About Protocols—PAP, CHAP, and SPAP

Within the three categories of encryption settings listed in Table 16.1, you might encounter specific protocols. One of the more popular (and least secure) connections is *Password Authentication Protocol* (PAP). This method does not support encryption of the data needed for authentication.

Microsoft's encryption settings, however, revolve around a more secure protocol—Microsoft *Challenge Handshake Authentication Protocol* (CHAP). MS-CHAP uses a one-way hash function combined with a checksum procedure.

There are other encrypted authentication protocols, one of which is *Shiva Password Authentication Protocol* (SPAP). This is a proprietary methodology that was developed by SHIVA. Using SPAP provides compatibility for SHIVA clients.

The most interesting part of setting up RAS is in the configuration of the network settings (refer to Fig. 16.6). For NetBEUI configuration, enable the NetBEUI check box under Server Settings, and then click the Configure button. The RAS Server NetBEUI Configuration dialog box appears, as shown in Figure 16.7.

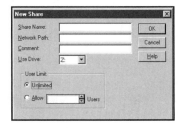

Figure 16.7
If you want to allow remote NetBEUI clients full access to the network, select the Entire Network option.

In Figure 16.7, the determination is made to use the RAS server as a NetBIOS gateway. This gateway gives NetBEUI clients the opportunity to use the corporate resources on the network. If the network is using another protocol, such as TCP/IP or IPX, the RAS server translates the packets to permit communications. One disadvantage is that if an application needs or requires the participating client to have TCP/IP or IPX on the client workstation, the application won't run.

The next possible configuration selection is TCP/IP (refer to Fig. 16.6). After enabling the TCP/IP check box and clicking Configure, the RAS Server TCP/IP Configuration dialog box appears, as shown in Figure 16.8.

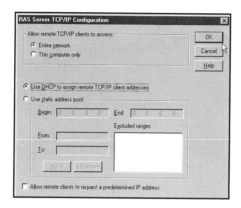

Figure 16.8
It makes sense that TCP/IP configuration is more complicated than NetBEUI configuration because of the abundance of configuration parameters in the TCP/IP scheme.

At the top of the TCP/IP configuration dialog box, the administrator indicates whether the caller can access the rest of the network or the RAS server only. This is a straightforward decision and is determined by the company's security policies.

The Use DHCP to Assign Remote TCP/IP Client Addresses option is for computing environments that have *Dynamic Host Configuration Protocol* (DHCP) servers. These are the servers that have a service running on them that allows the automatic allocation of IP addresses to the client.

The Use Static Address Pool option is for computing environments that use other methods of IP address assignment. This section permits the designation of the addresses that are set aside for RAS clients. To enter the static address pool, enter the numbers into the Begin and End boxes. Also permitted in this section is the designation of addresses that need to be excluded. In the From and To boxes, you enter the address or range of addresses that are to be excluded. Therefore, if it is necessary to exclude an address(s), type the address(s) in the From and To box and then click the Add button, which adds it to the Excluded Ranges box.

At the bottom of the TCP/IP configuration dialog box, you can enable the Allow Remote Clients to Request a Predetermined IP Address check box. The administrator should be sure that the number the client uses is a unique IP address.

To configure the third and final server setting, select the IP$\underline{\text{X}}$ check box under Server Settings and click the Con$\underline{\text{f}}$igure button (refer again to Fig. 16.6). The RAS Server IPX Configuration dialog box appears (see Fig. 16.9).

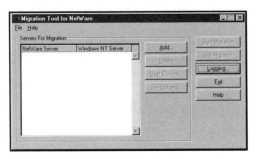

Figure 16.9
As with the other configuration screens, the top of the RAS Server IPX Configuration dialog box denotes network permissions for its clients, followed by options specific to the IPX protocol.

After deciding again to allow IPX clients access to either the Entire $\underline{\text{N}}$etwork or This $\underline{\text{C}}$omputer Only, the next configuration item enables you to specify how to allocate the network numbers.

Selecting Allocate Network Numbers $\underline{\text{A}}$utomatically causes the RAS server to use the *Router Information Protocol* (RIP) to assign a number to the client.

The next selection, Alloca$\underline{\text{t}}$e Network Numbers, is used when the administrator needs more direct control for the assignment of the numbers. For security or tracking purposes, the administrator may need to know which numbers are being used for RAS clients, and this is a convenient way to provide this information. The administrator enters into the $\underline{\text{F}}$rom box the first number of the group of available numbers.

The Assign $\underline{\text{S}}$ame Network Number to All IPX Clients option is used when the administrator wants the clients to be seen as being on the same IPX network. You can use this option whether the assignment of the numbers is automatic or manual.

The Allow Remote Clients to Request $\underline{\text{I}}$PX Node Number allows the client to select its own number. This probably is not a good idea because of security issues and the possibility of a hacker impersonating another client.

The completion of the configuration brings the installation process to an end. A final Setup Message screen appears, as shown in Figure 16.10.

Figure 16.10
This screen indicates a successful installation.

The service has been successfully installed and the machine needs to be rebooted. Because RAS is a service, the administration of RAS is the same as with other services. Verify that in fact the service is running, and start the administration of the service.

RAS Administration

The administration of RAS starts by finding the RAS Administration Manager on the menu. From the Start menu, choose Programs, Administrative Tools (Common), Remote Access Admin (see Fig. 16.11).

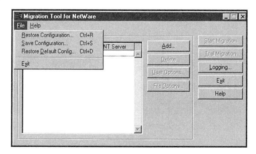

Figure 16.11
The Remote Access Admin selection is available after installation.

The administrative functions include selections for control of the service—for example, starting, stopping, and pausing. Other selections include verification of port status and, of course, the settings for the users who are going to be calling in. Figure 16.12 shows the first administration screen that appears.

CH
16

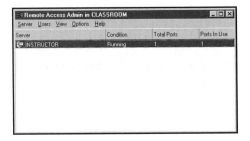

Figure 16.12
The Remote Access Admin in CLASSROOM screen shows the INSTRUCTOR machine running properly.

The first administration screen lists the RAS server that is being administered; in this case, the server is named Instructor and has one port that is available for RAS. If there is another RAS server, it would be listed here. It is also possible to access another domain.

Double-clicking the INSTRUCTOR server name displays the Communication Ports screen (see Fig. 16.13). This screen shows information related to each port.

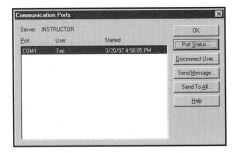

Figure 16.13
You can gather specific information on the status of a port from the Communication Ports screen.

For specific configuration information about each port, click the Port Status button. The Port Status dialog box appears (see Fig. 16.14).

The Users menu selection from the Remote Access Admin dialog box (refer to Fig. 16.12) is of particular interest, because it enables you to access the screen where you set permissions for users. You set permissions in the Remote Access Permissions dialog box shown in Figure 16.15. You access this dialog box from the Remote Access Admin dialog box by selecting Users, Permissions.

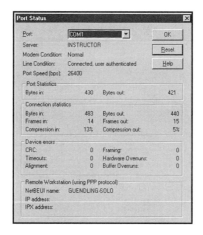

Figure 16.14
The Port Status dialog box gives you information related to the connection from the selected port.

Figure 16.15
You can set remote access permissions for each user.

Figure 16.16, the Remote Access Users dialog box, shows the activity of the users who currently are connected to the machine. This capability is available from the Remote Access Admin dialog box (refer to Fig. 16.12) by choosing Users, Active Users. If it becomes necessary to disconnect a user or send a message to a user, this is the screen that is used.

Figure 16.16
Controlling remote access users.

You can use the Remote Access Administration tool to control the configuration of the RAS server after you complete the installation process. It gives you comprehensive status information and enables you to track connections.

The Dial-Up Networking Component of RAS

The Remote Access Administration is the first administrative task after the installation is complete. Another part of the equation is from the client's side—the *Dial-Up Networking* (DUN) setup. DUN allows the connection to the RAS server and essentially converts the communication port to a network card. When the client dials in, the caller needs to be defined on the server, just as it would for any network access.

The DUN selection is available from the Start menu on Windows 95, Windows NT Workstation, and other Windows NT Server machines. It is located under the Accessories selection, as shown in Figure 16.17. The DUN Wizard walks the client through the installation of the client component, DUN.

Automatic Logon from DUN

One of the major points of interest for the DUN client installation is the automatic logon feature. This feature remembers the location of a file that was accessed previously from a DUN connection. In other words, Windows NT RAS automatically connects to the remote Windows NT RAS Server.

When the remote file is accessed, Windows NT starts the dialing procedure to get the file. This is assuming that all connecting authentication information is correct. Additionally, from the DUN Phonebook Entry dialog box, the Authenticate Using Current User Name and Password check box has been enabled.

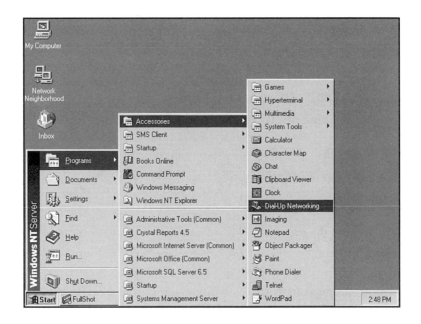

Figure 16.17
The Dial-Up Networking component is available from the Accessories selection.

This capability is in effect if the DUN client and the RAS server are both using NT 3.5x or NT 4.0 and if the Remote Access Autodial Manager service is running. You access and control this service from the Services dialog box (see Fig. 16.18). You access the Services icon from the Control Panel.

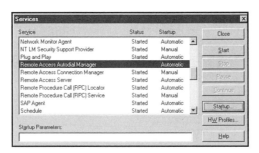

Figure 16.18
The Remote Access Autodial Manager is another Windows NT Service.

Windows 95 works in a similar manner from the Window 95 Dial Up Networking component. When a user accesses a resource that requires a connection, Windows 95 automatically activates Dial-Up Networking.

Using a RAS Server as a Router

A RAS server can act as both an IPX router and a TCP/IP router. First, the server involved needs to be configured with the protocol of interest. Additionally, it should be noted that the routing that is performed is static routing, not dynamic routing. This means that the routing tables are not updated automatically. Also, the routing is only for the networks that are connected to the RAS server. Some third-party software is involved, and the software most often used is written by SHIVA.

The IPX routing allows the passing of IPX messages from the RAS client to the IPX host. Similarly, the IP routing allows the passing of the TCP/IP messages to the associated hosts.

It is because of this routing capability that you can use a RAS server to provide routing between a network and the Internet over a dedicated PPP account from an Internet access provider.

Troubleshooting RAS

RAS is a mature, well-behaved, complex Microsoft Windows NT service. Occasionally, you might need to do some troubleshooting. The following information gives you some insights about where to look for help in the troubleshooting process.

DUN Monitor from the Client's Perspective

One of the first troubleshooting techniques for RAS is checking the status of the remote machine. You easily can do this on the Windows NT client's machine by looking at the System Tray. The System Tray is the part of the taskbar that is located in the lower-right corner. Programs and services frequently use this area to convey status information. As you can see in Figure 16.19, holding the mouse pointer over the status icon tells what the icon does.

Double-clicking the status icon for DUN displays the DUN monitor, as shown in Figure 16.20.

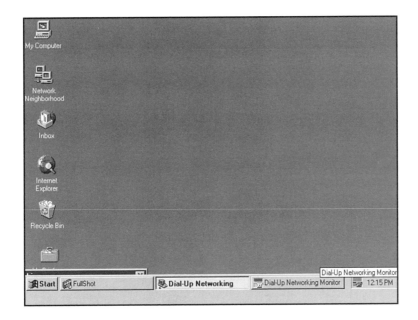

Figure 16.19
The System Tray holds the status icon for the Dial-Up Networking Monitor.

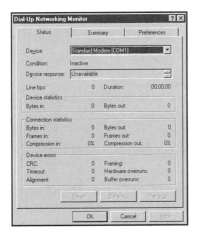

Figure 16.20
You'll find Dial-Up Networking Monitor status information on the Status Tab.

The DUN Monitor includes three tabs: Status, Summary, and Preferences. The Dial-Up Networking Monitor should be the first line of investigation for troubleshooting. The Status tab gives device information, including device statistics, connection statistics, and device errors.

The Summary tab gives information about multilink connections (see Fig. 16.21). This is the screen to check for information about remote networks and devices that are being used.

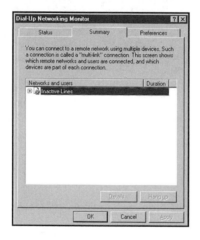

Figure 16.21
The Summary tab gives information on remote networks and devices.

The Preferences tab is the location for controlling associated sounds, the listing of DUN in the task list, and the display of status lights (see Fig. 16.22).

Hardware Considerations for Troubleshooting RAS

This troubleshooting process involves a number of hardware considerations. First, you should consider the state of the communication device (modem, PAD, or ISDN card), and view the Device Log for additional troubleshooting information. Consult the manual for detailed instructions to verify operations. As noted earlier, it is an excellent idea to make sure that the device is on the Windows NT HCL. Phone-line quality could be another issue. You easily can check the quality by using a phone and listening to the line quality. If you hear static and clicking noises, this could be the source of the problem. Line-quality problems typically cut out the connection; generally, line-quality problems do not prevent the connection from being made.

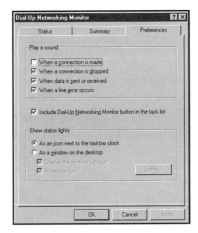

Figure 16.22
You use the Preferences tab to customize features.

Software Considerations for Troubleshooting RAS

Verifying that the RAS service is operational is the most obvious software consideration. You should check this from the Services icon in the Control Panel. All considerations that are true for other Windows NT services are true for the RAS service. Occasionally, it is necessary to stop a service and then restart it. In even worse cases, it sometimes is necessary to uninstall a service and reinstall it.

Another area of problems might be related to security issues. If a user is being denied access, it would be helpful to check the user rights and perhaps any trust relationships that might come into play. This would come under the area of typical network administration tasks. Also, consider looking at the Remote Access Administration program and checking user permissions again. The administrator should check the Event Viewer, because RAS generates audit trails of remote connections.

You also should consider protocol issues. RAS enables NetBEUI, TCP/IP, and IPX on the RAS server by default, so you might need to make an adjustment there. Binding order might be significant also; for example, if the protocol being used is NetBEUI, and the user is communicating with an application that needs Windows Sockets, you need to bring TCP/IP into the picture. Examine the applications being used to determine dependencies between the method of interprocess communication and the transport protocol.

One of the most helpful tools Windows NT provides for troubleshooting is the Event Viewer. This tool logs all system activities, including successes and failures for operations of services. The Event Viewer also can audit other RAS activities after you turn on the auditing feature. You control this with the following key:

```
HKEY_LOCAL_MACHINE\SYSTEM\CurrentControlSet\Services\RemoteAccess\Parameters
```

You need to set the data field for that key to 1 for the enhanced auditing. Extra information includes regular connections, disconnects, timed-out authentication, and line-error problems.

Summary

This chapter examined the *Remote Access Service* (RAS) from the service and client perspectives. Issues addressed included installation, administration, and troubleshooting.

On Windows NT Server, RAS can handle 256 incoming connections, whereas the same service on NT Workstation is limited to one. Line protocols supported include SLIP, PPP, and PPTP, and the networking protocols include NetBEUI, IPX/SPX-compatible, and TCP/IP.

Users added to the network must be granted dial-in permissions, and there are three settings for the callback—security used to further verify callers by their location, or at least log their location. The three options are

- No Call Back Security
- Call Back to an Administrator Defined Number
- Call Back to a User Assigned Number

QUESTIONS AND ANSWERS

1. An enhancement to the *Point-to-Point Protocol* (PPP) is _____.

   A: *Point-to-Point Tunneling Protocol* (PPTP)

2. True or false: The tunneling protocol can work with NetBEUI PPP packets over TCP/IP.

   A: True. PPTP can work with NetBEUI, IPX/SPX, or TCP/IP.

…continues

3. The administration of the *Remote Access Service* (RAS) is done through _____.

A: RAS Administration Manager. This utility appears on the Administrative Tools (Common) menu.

4. The client component of RAS is _____.

A: Dial-Up Networking (DUN)

5. True or false: You can turn on auditing of RAS features by editing the Registry.

A: True. Editing is done at

```
HKEY_LOCAL_MACHINE\SYSTEM\CurrentControlSet\Services\RemoteAccess\Parameters
```

CH
16

PRACTICE TEST

1. RAS accepts which types of inbound connections?

   a. ISDN
   b. Modem
   c. X.25
   d. PPP

Answers a, b, c, and d are correct. RAS accepts inbound ISDN, modem, X.25 connections, and PPP connections.

2. Which technology allows RAS to use two ISDN channels?

   a. PPTP
   b. PPP
   c. Multilink PPP
   d. SLIP

Answers a and b are incorrect. Multilink allows the combination of multiple connections into one—in this case, allowing RAS to use two channels. **Answer c is correct. Multilink PPP allows RAS to use the two ISDN channels. Multilink always is used to combine multiple connections into one.** Answer d is incorrect. Multilink allows the combination of multiple connections into one—in this case, allowing RAS to use two channels.

   3. The Point-to-Point Tunneling Protocol does what?

   a. Establishes a connection via the modem for the RAS server and RAS client to communicate.

   b. Establishes a connection via X.25 for the RAS server and RAS client to communicate.

   c. Enhances authentication with a longer key.

   d. Encrypts all data between the client and server.

Answers a, b, and c are incorrect. PPTP is a tunneling protocol used for the purpose of encryption. **Answer d is correct. PPTP encrypts all data between the client and server and often is used in the creation of virtual private networks.**

   4. How can you set up callback security?

   a. Not to call back.

   b. To call back to a predefined number.

   c. To call back to a user-assigned number.

   d. To call back and require a voiceprint match.

Answers a, b, and c are correct. You can configure callback to not be used, to call back to a preset number, or to call back a number the user provides when a connection is established. Answer d is incorrect. Neither the NT operating system nor the RAS service includes the capability to do voiceprint authentication.

   5. Who can install RAS on a Windows NT Server?

   a. Administrator

   b. Any member of the Administrators group

   c. Any member of the Power Users group

   d. Any member of the RAS group

Answers a and b are correct. The administrator or any member of the Administrators group can install RAS on an NT Server. Choice c is incorrect. Power users exist on NT Workstation only and not NT Server. Choice d is incorrect; by default, there is no RAS group.

   6. RAS supports what protocols?

   a. TCP/IP

   b. IPX/SPX

   c. NetBEUI

   d. DLC

Answers a, b, and c are correct. RAS supports TCP/IP, IPX/SPX, and NetBEUI. Choice d is incorrect. RAS cannot support DLC.

7. To create a log file that tracks PPP connections, turn on auditing via

    a. Network Monitor

    b. User Manager

    c. Remote Access Admin

    d. The Registry

Answers a, b, and c are incorrect. The only way to turn on auditing for PPP connections is to edit the Registry. **Answer d is correct. You must edit the Registry to turn on auditing for PPP connections.**

CH
16

Network Monitor

WHILE YOU READ

1. Messages such as `Hardware malfunction, call your hardware vendor for support` are generated by _____.

2. True or false: It is possible to have NT Server automatically reboot after a stop error.

3. The default filename for a dump file is _____.

4. The utility used to copy a dump file to floppy disks is _____.

5. What three NT Server log files can the Event Viewer look at?

This chapter introduces you to *kernel stop errors* (also known as *blue-screen errors* or *trap errors)* and describes and identifies the data areas of a stop error that are pertinent to finding the cause of the problem. This chapter also looks at the importance of pinpointing the precise time a stop error occurs—such as during installation, after installation, or during the Windows NT initialization or boot process—so that you can isolate the cause of the malfunction. You'll also examine software problems that cause stop errors.

Another topic of interest discussed in this chapter is crash dumps. You will learn how to configure the Windows NT Recovery options and how to configure the required memory resources. You'll also examine tools you can use to check, analyze, and copy a crash dump, such as dumpchk, dumpexam, and dumpflop.

Next, you'll learn about the kernel debugger programs and options, along with how to configure Windows NT systems to do live debugging procedures, both at local sites and from remote sites. Discussions include setting up and connecting the host and target computers; locating the kernel debugger programs; and locating, expanding, and using the Symbols files.

The last topic this chapter covers is the Event Viewer. You'll look at the three types of Event Logs, event details, log settings, and other pertinent Event Viewer information.

Windows NT Kernel Messages

There are three types of Windows NT kernel messages: hardware malfunction messages, status messages, and stop messages. Stop messages, also called *blue screens* or *traps,* are discussed in detail in this chapter.

Hardware Malfunction Messages

Hardware malfunction messages are caused by a hardware condition that is detected by the processor. The Windows NT Executive displays a message such as Hardware malfunction, call your hardware vender for support—the actual message is dependent on the manufacturer. Other information also is displayed indicating the nature of the problem, such as a memory parity error, a bus data error, or a specific adapter error (with slot number)—again dependent on the type of error and the manufacturer of the hardware.

Status Messages

Status messages, in most cases, are not as critical as hardware malfunction messages. A status message appears when the Windows NT Executive detects a condition within a process or application where the action required is simply clicking OK to terminate the process or application. Messages indicating the action appear in a window or dialog box.

There are three types of status messages: system information, warning, and application termination messages. System information messages could include indications of an invalid current directory, a suspended thread, or a working set range error. Warning messages indicate information such as buffer overflow, a busy device, or an out-of-paper message. Application termination messages range from access denied to a corrupt disk to a data error. Missing system files and out-of-virtual-memory messages are other examples.

Stop (Blue Screen/Trap) Messages

Stop messages are probably the most severe type of messages. These messages always require you to restart the computer, because the Windows NT Executive cannot recover from the error. A mechanism for dumping memory information into a memory dump file also is provided, if a dump file was configured prior to the error.

Stop errors can happen virtually at any time: during and after installation, during and after initialization (booting), or from a specific software condition.

Stop Messages During Installation

Stop errors that occur during installation are usually a result of incompatible hardware. Refer to the latest version of an HCL to determine whether all hardware on the computer is listed. You can find the latest HCL by doing a search on HCL from Microsoft Corporation's home Web page at www.microsoft.com.

 Key Concept

> If specific hardware is not on the HCL, contact the manufacturer for information on new hardware or updated *basic input/output system* (BIOS) and firmware revisions.

Another approach to determining the specific piece of hardware causing the problem is to configure the system to minimize requirements and try the installation again.

Stop Messages After Installation

It is very apparent that various hardware problems can happen after Windows NT is installed and operational. Also, any drivers, such as device drivers or file system drivers, can cause Windows NT Executive to generate a stop error. You can fix problems of this nature by replacing hardware or reinstalling Windows NT components.

In some cases, Microsoft NT service packs can solve various types of stop error problems. You can obtain service packs by accessing Microsoft Corporation's home Web page at www.microsoft.com.

Stop Messages Only During Windows NT Executive Initialization

A small group of stop errors can happen only during phase 4 of the boot process—when Windows NT Executive initializes. There are two parts to the initialization of Windows NT Executive: phase 0 and phase 1. During phase 0, interrupts are disabled and only a few Executive components are initialized. One of the components initialized during phase 0 is the Hardware Abstraction Layer. During phase 1, Executive is fully operational and the Windows NT subcomponents are initialized.

Key Concept

If you receive a phase 0 initialization stop message, run all the hardware diagnostic routines to try to solve the problem. If you find no hardware errors, reinstall Windows NT 4.0 and reinitialize to see whether the problem persists.

If you receive a phase 1 initialization stop message, reinstall Windows NT and reinitialize the system.

Stop Messages Caused By Software Problems

Software conditions detected by the processor in a system also can produce stop error messages. This event also is called a *software trap* and is caused by the processor executing an instruction in a process or application when it encounters an error, such as a divide by zero or a memory segment not present. All 12 software traps produce the same stop error message format:

```
*** STOP: 0X0000007F (0x0000000n, 0x00000000, 0x00000000,
0x00000000) UNEXPECTED_KERNEL_MODE_TRAP
```

How Normal Users Should React to Stop Messages

Normal users cannot be expected to diagnose the causes of stop errors. When stop errors occur, instruct users to record the first few lines of the message and then restart the system. If the stop error happens again, you can invoke a Last Known Good configuration; however, the system administrator should ensure that the Recovery option is configured properly in the system to obtain memory dump information. You then can analyze the dumps to determine the cause of the error message.

Troubleshooting Stop Messages

Microsoft recommends that you follow this procedure when you encounter a stop error:

1. Gather information about the problem.
2. Determine whether the problem is a known issue.
3. Determine whether the problem is caused by hardware.
4. Troubleshoot well-known stop codes.
5. Determine whether the problem is caused by non-HCL hardware.
6. Contact Microsoft Service Advantage.

Step 1: Gather Information About the Problem

Record, at a minimum, the following information when you experience stop errors:

- The top four lines of a stop error, including the stop error codes and other pertinent information. Here is an example of the information you should record:

    ```
    STOP: 0X0000000A(0x0000000B,0x00000002,0x00000000,0xFE34C882)

    IRQL_NOT_LESS_OR_EQUAL

    ADDRESS 0xFE34C882 has base at 0xFE000000:NTOSKRNL.EXE
    ```

- All hardware information—including system statistics, such as BIOS, *Complementary Metal-Oxide Semiconductor* (CMOS) settings, controllers/adapters installed, and their BIOS version.

- The platform and version of Windows NT installed—including any service packs, hot fixes, or third-party drivers, such as a Novell redirector.

- How often and when the stop error occurs (whether it is random or happens when a specific operation is performed, such as a certain application or process).

- Can the error be re-created?

 Key Concept

When gathering information about a problem, look at all relevant facts, including the error message obtained, the hardware installed, the current operating system build, and error frequency.

Step 2: Determine Whether the Problem Is a Known Issue

The next step is to see whether someone has been there before. Try to determine whether this error has been a common occurrence and whether an established workaround or hot fix already exists.

Search Microsoft's Knowledge Base. Go to Microsoft's home Web page, choose Support, and then choose Technical Support. Search for the word stop, followed by the stop error code, followed by the program module name. Here is an example of what you would type:

```
STOP 0x0000000A NTOSKRNL.EXE
```

If no results appear, search for just the word stop and try to locate any general stop error troubleshooting methods.

Step 3: Determine Whether the Problem Is Caused by Hardware

Stop errors are caused by hardware errors and outdated BIOS even if the hardware is on the HCL. Hardware configurations also may cause stop errors. Here are some possible situations:

- A system was working properly. However, when specific operations are performed (such as booting the system, formatting a disk, or performing a backup operation), stop errors occur. Check the specific hardware involved for that operation. A software problem usually occurs only when a certain set of conditions is present. Try to isolate exactly what conditions are present when the failure happens.

- A system was working fine until a new piece of hardware was installed; then stop errors began to occur. Check the HCL for the new piece of hardware. Check for *interrupt requests* (IRQs), I/O addresses, and *direct memory access* (DMA) conflicts. Check BIOS versions, driver versions, and configuration settings.

Step 4: Troubleshoot Well-Known Stop Codes

Some common stop errors are listed here for your information. Most of the stop error descriptions indicate the specific reason or cause of the problem.

```
STOP 0x0000000A IRQL_NOT_LESS_OR_EQUAL
STOP 0x00000019 BAD_POOL_HEADER
STOP 0x0000001E KMODE_EXCEPTION_NOT_HANDLED
STOP 0x00000024 NTFS_FILE_SYSTEM
STOP 0x0000002E DATA_BUS_ERROR
```

```
STOP 0x0000003E MULTIPROCESSOR_CONFIGURATION_NOT_SUPPORTED

STOP 0x00000051 REGISTRY_ERROR

STOP 0x00000058 FTDISK_INTERNAL_ERROR

STOP 0x00000077 KERNEL_STACK_OVERFLOW

STOP 0x00000079 MISMATCHED_HAL

STOP 0x0000007A KERNEL_DATA_INPAGE_ERROR

STOP 0x0000007B INACCESSIBLE_BOOT_DEVICE

STOP 0x0000007F UNEXPECTED_KERNEL_MODE_TRAP

STOP 0x00000080 NMI_HARDWARE_FAILURE

STOP 0x0000008B MBR_CHECKSUM_MISMATCH

STOP 0x00000218 STATUS_CANNOT_LOAD_REGISTRY_FILE

STOP 0x0000021A STATUS_SYSTEM_PROCESS_TERMINATED

STOP 0x00000221 STATUS_IMAGE_CHECKSUM_MISMATCH
```

CH

17

Step 5: Determine Whether the Problem Is Caused by Non-HCL Hardware

Microsoft, as a rule, does not totally support stop errors from hardware such as motherboards, disk drive controllers, network or video adapter cards, or multimedia devices that are not on the HCL. Because hardware that is not on the HCL has not been tested with Windows NT 4.0, diagnostic information is not available.

The first thing to do is to contact the manufacturer of the device for any information regarding Windows NT 4.0, such as device drivers.

Two articles in the Microsoft Knowledge Base on the Internet provide information concerning Microsoft's policy for supporting hardware that is not on the HCL: Q142865 and Q143244.

The first article, "Q142865 Microsoft PSS Support Policy on Hardware Not on Windows NT HCL," discusses details on troubleshooting problems with non-HCL hardware.

The second article, "Q143244 How to Check if Unsupported Hardware Allows Windows NT Install," provides troubleshooting tips on hardware that will allow Windows NT 4.0 to be installed.

Step 6: Contact Microsoft

If you do not find a solution to the stop error by performing steps 1 through 5, contact Microsoft for support. You can find the Microsoft support home page on the Internet at `http://support.microsoft.com/`.

Stop Error Screen Layout and Section Meanings

Probably one of the most intimidating errors that Windows NT can produce is a stop error. The entire screen turns blue, and a mass of numbers and letters appears, which usually causes panic and disillusion to the user. Enterprise administrators and support personnel, on the other hand, accept a stop error as a challenge and proceed to interpret the information presented to locate the cause of the error.

The first objective in diagnosing stop errors is to define the areas or sections of a stop error screen. Use Figure 17.1 and the following paragraphs to locate and define the five distinct sections:

- Debug port status indicators
- BugCheck information
- Driver information
- Kernel build number and stack dump
- Debug port information

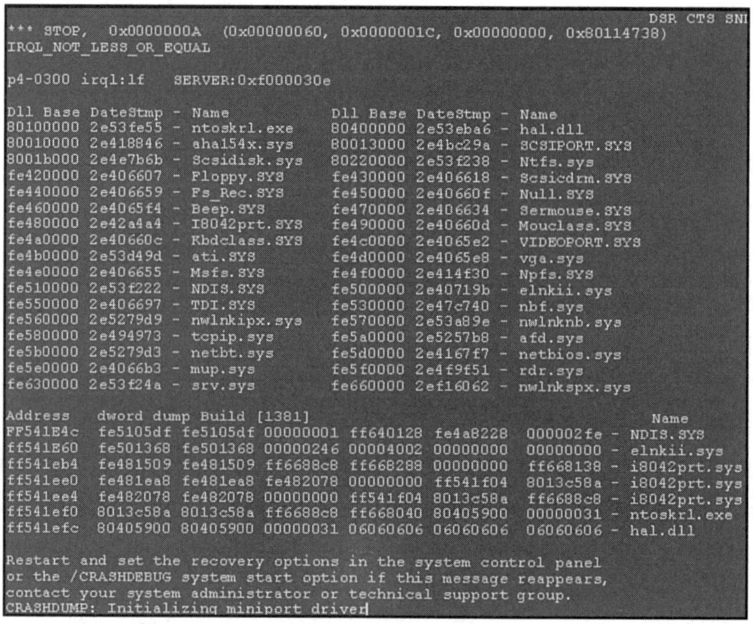

Figure 17.1
A Windows NT 4.0 stop error screen (blue screen).

Debug Port Status Indicators

If a modem or null modem cable is connected to the computer and the Kernel Debugger program is running, indicators appear in the upper right corner of the stop screen on the top line. These indicators show the serial communication port status of the communication between a host and target computer. The following is a list of the various port status indicators that can appear in this section:

Indicator	Meaning
CD	Carrier Detected
CTS	Clear to Send
DSR	Data Set Ready
FRM	Framing error
MDM	Debugger is using modem controls
OVL	Overflow
PRT	Parity error
RCV	Byte of information being received
RI	Ring Indicator
SND	Byte of information being sent

BugCheck Information

The next four lines (beginning with the line that starts with *** STOP) contain the error code (or BugCheck code) and other pertinent error code information. This information is critical to finding the cause of the error and should be recorded (as mentioned previously in the section "Troubleshooting Stop Messages"). The first line in Figure 17.1 follows:

```
*** STOP: 0x0000000A (0x0000006c, 0x0000001c, 0x00000000, 0x80114738)
IRQL_NOT_LESS_OR_EQUAL
```

- 0x0000000A indicates the stop error.
- The parameter 0x0000006c identifies the address that was not referenced correctly.
- The parameter 0x0000001c identifies the *interrupt request level* (IRQL) that was required to access memory.
- The parameter 0x00000000 indicates a read operation was in progress. (A value of 1 would indicate a write operation.)
- The parameter 0x80114738 indicates the instruction address that tried to access memory referenced in the first parameter.

Driver Information

The next section begins with the line Dll Base and continues for a number of lines, depending on the error. The example in Figure 17.1 displays an area of 17 lines and lists 34 drivers. Three columns of information are displayed on the left half of the screen, and three more columns are displayed on the right half of the screen. The first column in each half displays the base address of the driver in memory, and the second column displays the time-stamp information. The third column in each half displays the names of all drivers loaded in the system at the time of the error.

Kernel Build Number and Stack Dump

Section 4 contains the version and build level of the Windows NT 4.0 Kernel, Ntoskrnl.exe. Any service pack or third-party driver information is not displayed in this section. This section can be extremely useful, because it may indicate, depending on the stop error, the driver that failed and caused the stop error.

Debug Port Information

If Kernel Debugger is running, additional COM port information, such as what port and the speed of the port, is displayed here. Other data in this area confirms whether a memory dump has been created or gives instructions on how to further troubleshoot the problem.

Crash Dumps (Memory Dumps)

If you have analyzed the stop error and failed to determine the solution to the error, you must obtain more data and information about the problem. One of the ways to retrieve more information on a particular stop error is to have the computer dump the entire contents of memory at the time of the error. From this point, either an administrator or a support team can analyze the memory dump to determine the solution for the error.

Key Concept

The first step in initiating a memory dump if you encounter a stop error is to ensure that the Recovery option is configured correctly. You can configure this option to invoke a number of procedures; however, you should configure the option to take memory dumps if the error persists.

You configure the Recovery option from the Startup/Shutdown tab in the System Properties dialog box. Figure 17.2 shows the Recovery configuration options.

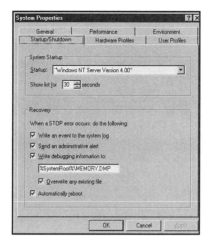

Figure 17.2
Configuring the Windows NT 4.0 Recovery option.

The following options are available on the Setup/Shutdown tab of the System Properties dialog box:

- **Write an Event to the System Log:** If selected, an event will be written to the System Log when a stop error occurs.

- **Send an Administrative Alert:** If this option is selected, and alerts have been configured in Server Manager or from the Server icon in the Control Panel, an administrative alert is sent to a designated computer on the network if a stop error occurs.

- **Write Debugging Information To:** This option, when selected, enables the entire contents of system memory to be written to a file specified in the space provided. This file will be written to %SystemRoot%\MEMORY.DMP by default. You then can use the DUMPEXAM utility to analyze the memory dump to isolate the cause of the error.

  In addition to this option being selected, four other requirements must be met to provide for a memory dump:

  - A pagefile must exist on the same partition where Windows NT 4.0 has been installed (the boot partition).

  - The pagefile must be at least 1MB larger than the physical size of RAM in the system.

- The boot partition must have at least as much free space as the size of the pagefile.
- Automatically <u>R</u>eboot should be selected.

Key Concept

The first three requirements listed in the preceding list must be met to obtain a memory dump of the system. The memory dump process puts the entire contents of RAM memory in the pagefile on the boot partition. Prior to the reboot process, the pagefile information is written to the specified .DMP file.

- **<u>O</u>verwrite Any Existing File:** If this option is selected and a MEMORY.DMP file exists in the %SystemRoot% folder, it will be overwritten.
- **Automatically <u>R</u>eboot:** This option is selected to invoke a reboot operation following a stop error. If the memory dump option also has been selected, that operation takes place prior to the reboot.

Crash Dump Analysis Utilities

The Windows NT 4.0 Server and Workstation CD-ROMs include three utilities you can use to analyze the results of a memory dump. A copy of each of these utilities is located in a platform-specific folder (Alpha, I386, MIPS, and PPC) under the Support\Debug folder. These utilities follow:

- Dumpchk.exe
- Dumpexam.exe
- Dumpflop.exe

Dumpchk.exe

You use this utility to verify the validity of a memory dump and to ensure that it can be read by a debugger application. This utility verifies all the virtual and physical memory addresses and displays basic information about the memory dump. It also displays any errors found in the memory dump. Figure 17.3 shows the command-line syntax.

You can use the information generated from this utility to determine what stop error occurred and what version of Windows NT was being used when the error occurred.

You should run this utility before analyzing a memory dump and sending it to Microsoft Support.

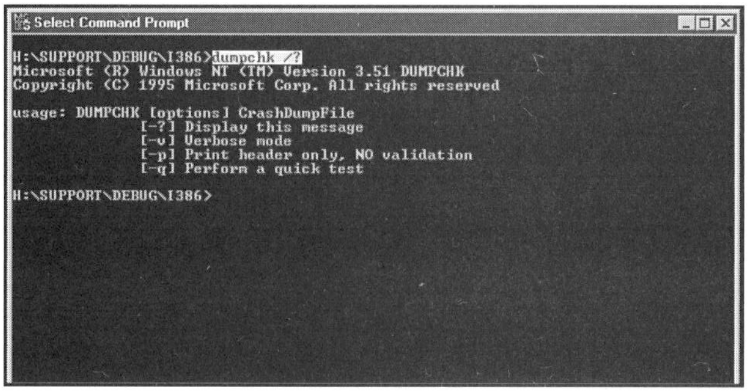

Figure 17.3
The `Dumpchk.exe` utility command-line syntax.

Dumpexam.exe

You use the DUMPEXAM utility to analyze a memory dump, extract specific information from the memory dump file, and create a text file containing specific memory dump information. This text file is considerably smaller than the raw memory dump file, `Memory.dmp` (recall that a raw memory dump file can be at least the size of physical memory). The default file DUMPEXAM creates is named `Memory.txt` and is located in the `%SystemRoot%` folder. `Memory.txt` can provide a solution to the problem in some cases.

Two other files in addition to `Dumpexam.exe` are required to analyze a memory dump. One of the files is `Imagehlp.dll`; the other file is dependent on the platform being used—`Kdextx86.dll`, `Kdextalp.dll`, `Kdextmip.dll`, or `Kdextppc.dll` for x86, Alpha, MIPS, or PowerPC computers, respectively. You can find all files on a Windows NT 4.0 Server or Workstation CD-ROM in the `Support\Debug\<platform>` folder.

Figure 17.4 shows the command-line syntax.

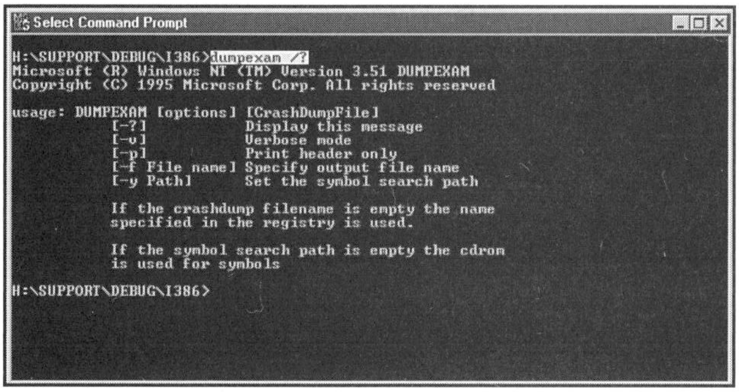

Figure 17.4
The `Dumpexam.exe` utility command-line syntax.

CH
17

Examples and Explanations of Command-Line Syntax for the Dumpexam Utility

DUMPEXAM examines a memory dump file named `Memory.dmp` located in the `%System%` folder and uses the platform-specific Symbols files located on the CD-ROM.

```
Dumpexam -y d:\sp1\symbols;f:\support\debug\i386 -f➥

d:\memdump\m1dump.txt d:\memdump\memory.dmp
```

This command will examine a memory dump file named `Memory.dmp` located in the `d:\memdump` folder and use the Symbols files located in the d:\sp1\symbols folder first, and then use the Symbols files located in the `f:\support\debug\i386` folder. It places an output file named `m1dump.txt` in the `d:\memdump` folder.

Symbols files are used in the order in which they are listed in the command-line syntax; therefore, the most recently installed service pack or hot fix Symbols files must be listed in the order in which Windows NT was updated.

Dumpflop.exe

You use the DUMPFLOP utility to copy a dump file in pieces to floppy disks to send to support personnel to analyze. This method is probably the least efficient way to send information; however, it may be the only way at a particular time because of other problems.

Compression is used when copying information to the floppy disks. A 16MB memory dump will fit on five or six floppy disks. Figure 17.5 shows the command-line syntax.

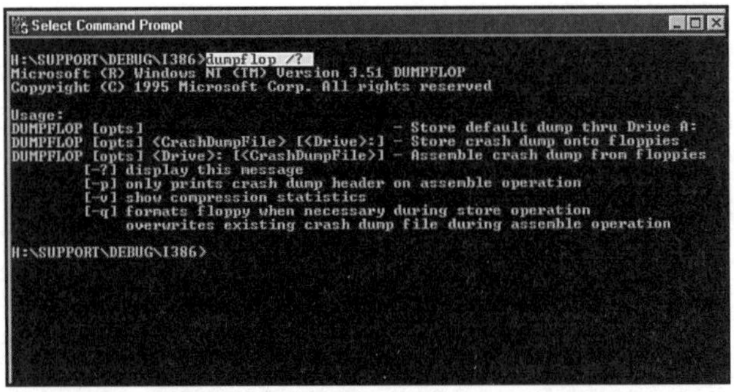

Figure 17.5
The `Dumpflop.exe` utility command-line syntax.

Kernel Debugger Sessions

If a system is continually crashing during the boot process, use the Kernel Debugger option to find the cause of the crash. However, before you dive into the process of configuring and using the Windows NT 4.0 Kernel Debugger programs, you must understand debugging terminology.

Host Computer

A *host computer* is one that is used to troubleshoot a failing computer (target computer). The host computer is the system that runs the debugger programs and has access to the Symbols files. It is physically attached to the target computer by a null modem cable or a modem connection. It also must be running at least the same version of Windows NT software as the target computer.

Target Computer

A *target computer* is the system on which stop errors are occurring. It is the system that is connected to the host computer by a null modem cable or a modem connection and configured to send information to the host computer to be analyzed. It is the system that needs to be debugged.

Symbols Files and Trees

When source code for executable programs, drivers, dynamic link libraries, and various other files is compiled for Windows NT, the resultant object code is in two forms or versions: a debug or checked version and a nondebug or free version. All files that Windows NT normally uses are much smaller versions of the object code—the nondebug version. However, each and every nondebug file has a corresponding debug version used for troubleshooting. The debug versions of the files are referred to as *Symbols files;* they contain debug codes and are used only as reference codes to debug a broken system.

Symbols files are located on the CD-ROM for both Windows NT Server and Workstation in the Support\Debug\<platform>\Symbols folder. Also note that Symbols files exist for both service packs and hot fixes, and must be obtained to troubleshoot stop errors if Windows NT updates are installed.

The Symbols folder for each platform contains a number of subfolders that contain the actual compressed Symbols (.db_) files. There is a subfolder for each type of Symbols file, such as .exe or .dll. These files must be decompressed before you use them. You decompress Symbols files by running a program called Expndsym.cmd located in the Support\Debug folder on the Windows NT 4.0 Server and Workstation CD-ROMs.

CH
17

Figure 17.6 presents the directory structure of a Windows NT 4.0 Server CD-ROM with the Support\Debug\I386\Symbols\Exe folder displayed.

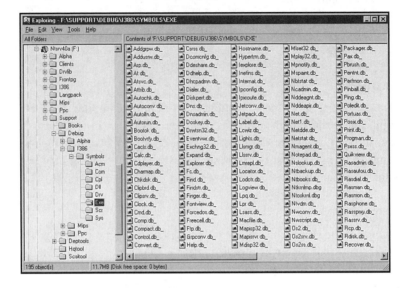

Figure 17.6
The Symbols files and the Symbols tree structure.

Kernel Debugger Programs and Files

Several executable files are necessary to perform Kernel Debugging. These programs are executed on a host computer and are used to debug the kernel on a target computer. The programs listed in Table 17.1 are located on the Windows NT Server or Workstation CD-ROM in the Support\Debug\<platform> folder (<platform> = Alpha, I386, Mips, or Ppc).

Table 17.1   Kernel Debugger Programs

Program/File	Use
Alphakd.exe	Kernel Debugger for Alpha computers
I386kd.exe	Kernel Debugger for Intel computers
Mipskd.exe	Kernel Debugger for MIPS computers
Ppckd.exe	Kernel Debugger for PowerPC computers

Configuring a Kernel Debugger Session

To configure a Kernel Debugger session, you must use a minimum of two computers: a host computer and the target computer. The two computers must be connected together, either locally with a null modem cable, or remotely with a modem connection. The host computer must be running the same platform and version of Windows NT software as the target computer.

Follow these steps to enable Kernel Debugging:

1. Connect the host computer and the target computer together.
2. Configure the host computer.
3. Configure the target computer.
4. Start the Kernel Debugger on the host computer.
5. Reboot the target computer.

CH

17

Connect the Host and Target Computers

If the host computer and the target computer are in close proximity, you can connect them with a null modem cable attached to an unused COM port in each computer.

If the computers are in remote locations from one another, you can connect them using modems. Double-click the Modem icon in the Control Panel and ensure that the following options are configured:

Auto Answer	On
Hardware Compression	Disabled
Error Detection	Disabled
Flow Control	Disabled

The default baud rate for Intel computers is 9600 baud; for *reduced instruction set computers* (RISCs), it is 19,200 baud.

Configure the Host Computer

During the debugger process, the host computer requires access to the Symbols files. You can copy these files to the host computer by using the Expndsym.cmd program located on the Windows NT 4.0 Server and Workstation CD-ROMs in the Support\Debug folder. Here is an example of the required syntax for Expndsym.cmd:

```
expndsym <Windows NT CDROM drive> <destination path>
```

As an example

`expndsym f: c:\debug` copies and expands the Symbols files from a CD-ROM f: drive to the `c:\debug\symbols` folder.

The next step in the Kernel Debugger process is to set up a batch file or run the required commands from the command prompt to start the platform-specific Kernel Debugger program. You'll look at a sample batch file later in the section "Start the Kernel Debugger."

The following list describes Kernel Debugger startup options:

Option	Description
-b	Causes the debugger to stop execution on the target computer as soon as possible by causing a debug breakpoint (INT 3).
-c	Causes the debugger to request a resync on connect.
-m	Causes the debugger to monitor modem control lines.
-n	Causes symbols to be loaded immediately instead of in a deferred mode.
-v	Verbose mode—displays more information.
-x	Causes the debugger to break in when an exception first occurs, instead of letting the application or module that caused the exception deal with it.

The most commonly used startup options are the -m and -v options.

Configure the Target Computer

If the target computer is an Intel system, you start the debugger process simply by configuring the boot.ini file to include one of the following options at the end of the specific boot.ini selection used to start the system:

Option	Description
/debug	Causes the Kernel Debugger to be loaded during the boot process and is kept in memory. Because the Kernel Debugger stays in memory, the system can be accessed remotely and debugged.
/debugport	Specifies the serial port to be used by the Kernel Debugger. Default is COM2 for Intel computers and COM1 for RISC computers.
/crashdebug	Causes the kernel debugger to be loaded during boot but swapped out to the pagefile after the boot process. Remote access and debugging cannot be done in this mode.
/baudrate	Sets the speed that the Kernel Debugger will use in bits per second. Default is 9,600bps for Intel computers and 19,200bps for RISC computers.

Key Concept

If the /baudrate option is used, the /debug option is assumed and does not have to be entered.

If the target computer is a RISC system, one line in the startup file has to be edited; however, that file is accessed differently on an Alpha system than on a MIPS or PowerPC system.

On an Alpha or PowerPC system, access the Boot Selections menu by choosing Supplementary from the System Boot menu. Then choose Setup the System from the Supplementary menu.

On a MIPS system, choose Run Setup to access the Setup menu, and then choose Manage Startup to display a Boot Options menu.

Start the Kernel Debugger

You can start the Kernel Debugger program from the command line or from a preconfigured batch file. Figure 17.7 shows a sample batch file that will configure the COM port and a path to the Symbols files, open a debug.log file, start a remote session, and execute the I386 debugger program with the v (verbose) and m (modem monitoring) options using the Remote utility, which also starts a session named "debug." Figure 17.7 shows the results of the batch file.

```
i386kd - [Remote /C WORKSTATION1 debug]

C:\debug>kd
C:\debug>REM local debug batch file named kd.bat
C:\debug>set _NT_DEBUG_PORT=com2
C:\debug>set _NT_DEBUG_BAUD_RATE=19200
C:\debug>set _NT_SYMBOL_PATH=c:\debug\symbols
C:\debug>set _NT_LOG_FILE_OPEN=c:\debug\debug.log
C:\debug>REMOTE /S "i386kd -M -v" debug
**********          REMOTE          **********
**********          SERVER          **********
**********************************************
To Connect: Remote /C WORKSTATION1 debug

Microsoft(R) Windows NT Kernel Debugger
Version 4.00
Copyright (C) Microsoft Corp. 1981-1996

Symbol search path is: c:\debug\symbols
KD: waiting to reconnect...
```

Figure 17.7
Starting a Kernel Debugger session.

After the Kernel Debugger program is running, you can enter commands to view various types of information or get a list of options. Before you can enter any of the commands shown in Table 17.2 at the host computer, you must press Ctrl+C .

Table 17.2   Kernel Debugger Commands Entered at the Host Computer

Command	Action
!reload	Reloads the Symbol files
!kb	Displays a stack trace from the last frame dumped by !trap (see below)
!errlog	If not empty, displays information about the component or process that caused the stop error
!process	Lists information about the process running on the active processor
!thread	Lists currently running threads
!kv	Verbose stack trace used to find the trap frame
!trap	Dumps the computer state when the trap<trap frame address> frame occurred
!process 0 0	Lists all processes and their headers
!drivers	Lists the drivers currently loaded
!vm	Lists the system's virtual memory use
.reboot	Restarts the target computer
g	Releases the target computer

If the Kernel Debugger is started using the Remote utility, as in the following example, other computers on the network can connect to the session "debug" and view the debugger information. The Remote utility is located on the Windows NT 4.0 Resource Kit utility CD-ROM. Figure 17.8 shows sample syntax for the Remote utility.

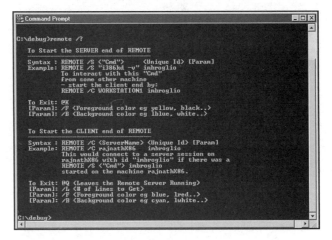

Figure 17.8
The Remote utility command-line syntax.

Reboot the Target Computer

To start recording the boot information on the host computer, simply reboot the target computer. As various drivers and dynamic link libraries load, they are displayed on the host computer. When the target computer halts with a stop error, the exact point of failure can be determined.

Remote Troubleshooting

As mentioned previously, the host computer and the target computer can be near each other and connected together using a null modem cable; however, if the systems are apart from each other, modems can be used. This type of troubleshooting scenario implies that someone from a support team is available to diagnose the error. If this is not the case, a remote session can be established with technical support, such as the Microsoft Technical Support team, through RAS.

 Key Concept

For remote troubleshooting, RAS must be configured on the host computer or some other system on the network that can access the host server; and another computer is required at some remote technical support area.

Here are the steps required to access a Kernel Debugger session from a remote location:

1. Connect the target computer to a host computer. The host computer is a RAS server or can access a RAS server.

2. Configure the host computer as mentioned previously in the section "Configure the Host Computer."

3. Configure the target computer as mentioned previously in the section "Configure the Target Computer."

4. Start the Kernel Debugger program on the host computer with the Remote utility, as mentioned previously in the section "Start the Kernel Debugger." The example given was REMOTE /S "i386kd -M -v" debug (refer to Fig. 24.7).

5. From the remote computer, establish a RAS session with the RAS server (the host computer, if it is a RAS server, or a RAS server that has access to the host computer).

6. From the remote computer, establish a connection with the Kernel Debugger session from the remote computer using the Remote utility. Here is an example:

```
REMOTE /c <host computer name> debug
```

CH
17

7. The target computer then is rebooted, as previously mentioned in the section "Reboot the Target Computer."

8. The Kernel Debugger session now can be monitored and controlled by the technical support person at the remote computer.

Events and the Event Log Viewer

An *event* is defined as a significant incident in the system, in the security of the system, or in an application that requires someone to be notified.

Some events, such as a disk drive becoming full, are considered critical events and cause a message to appear immediately to alert the user to the problem. Other events that do not need immediate attention are recorded in one of three types of Event Logs and can be viewed in the Event Viewer.

The Event Viewer is a diagnostic tool within Windows NT 4.0 that can be extremely useful in troubleshooting various types of problems encountered with the system, with security, or with applications. You also can view events of each type from other computers on the network.

Event logging is a service in Windows NT 4.0 and is, by default, started each time Windows NT is booted. As stated previously, events are logged in three categories:

Event	Description
System	The System Log contains entries logged by system components or services, such as a network adapter card or the browser service.
Security	The Security Log contains entries caused by activities such as someone accessing a resource or logging on to the system. By default, Security Log auditing is disabled. Auditing must be enabled from User Manager for Domains before a Security Log will be produced. How to enable auditing and what events are available for Security Log auditing are covered later in this chapter.
Application	An Application Log contains entries logged from various applications being run on the system. Dr. Watson and Autochk events are recorded in this log.

 Key Concept

The System and Application Logs can be viewed by everyone, including normal users; however, Security Logs can be viewed only by administrators. If a normal user tries to access the Security Log, an Access is Denied message appears.

Event Log Options

You can start the Event Viewer by choosing Start, Programs, Administrative Tools. From the Log menu, choose System, Security, or Application (see Fig. 17.9).

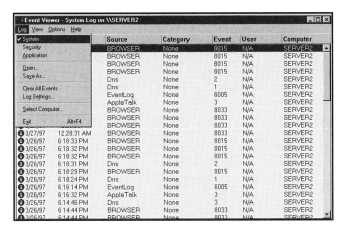

Figure 17.9
The Event Viewer Log menu.

Other options available from the Log menu follow:

Option	Description
Open	Opens and views any .evt file that was saved.
Save As	Saves a log file.
Clear All Events	Clears an Event Log. Before the log is cleared, a message asks whether you want to save the log.
Log Settings	Changes the default log settings. You can adjust settings for each log independently, including size and wrapping settings. The default maximum log size is 512KB, with a range of 64KB to 4,194,240KB in 64KB increments. Wrapping settings include Overwrite Events as Needed, Overwrite Events Older Than <days> Days, and Do Not Overwrite Events (Clear Manually). The default setting is to overwrite events older than seven days.
Select Computer	Enables you to select any Windows NT computer on the network. You also can select LAN Manager 2.x servers to view System and Security Logs only. After you choose Select Computer, a Select Computer dialog box appears. If the computer selected is available over a slow *wide-area network* (WAN) link, select Low Speed Connection in the dialog box.
Exit	Exits the Event Viewer.

CH
17

The <u>V</u>iew menu offers these options:

Option	Description
<u>A</u>ll Events	Tells Event Viewer to list all events in the selected log. (This is the default setting.)
Fi<u>l</u>ter Events	Specifies time ranges of when to display events. You also can select event types to display according to source, category, user, computer, or event ID.
<u>N</u>ewest First	Places events at the top of the list as they occur. (This is the default setting.)
<u>O</u>ldest First	Lists the oldest events first.
<u>F</u>ind	Searches for events by type, source, category, ID, computer, user, or description.
<u>D</u>etail	Displays more information about the selected event. You also can access the Event Detail dialog box by double-clicking any event in the Event Viewer.
Refresh	Refreshes the Event Viewer.

The <u>O</u>ptions menu enables you to select low-speed connections, save settings on exit (set by default), or specify a different font for the Event Viewer display. Select Low Speed Connection if you are analyzing Event Logs from other computers over a slow WAN connection. The only other menu is <u>H</u>elp.

Event Log Headings

When you display an Event Log using the Event Viewer, various headings appear across the top of the display, as shown in Figure 17.10.

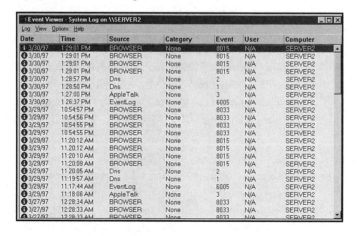

Figure 17.10
The Event Log headings.

You'll see these headings for the Event Log in the Event Viewer:

Headings	Description
Date	Displays the date the event occurred.
Time	Displays the time the event occurred.
Source	Displays the software that logged the event—an application, a network adapter driver, a service, and so on.
Category	Specifies how the event source has classified the event. This heading has meaning mostly in the Security Log but also is used in the Application Log. In the Security Log, whatever classification of event was configured in User Manager for Domains appears in this column. For example, if the logon/logoff service logged the event, `logon/logoff` appears in this column.
Event	Identifies an event type or ID. This relates back to source code and can be used by support personnel to cross check events with the source code.
User	Displays the name of the user logged on to the system or the client name if the event was caused by the Server Service when a client was accessing this computer.
Computer	Displays the name of the computer where the event occurred. This value is usually the local computer; however, if you are looking at an Event Log from another computer on the network, that computer name is displayed.

CH
17

Several types of icons are displayed in front of the events in the Event column. Table 17.3 describes the five types of icons.

Table 17.3 Event Icons

Icon	Symbol	Indicates
Error	Stop sign	Serious problem. If services did not load because of network adapter card settings, the services are displayed with this type of error.
Warning	Exclamation point	Not as serious as error events. Warnings indicate that more serious problems could occur later, however. An example of a warning is disk space getting low on a particular disk drive.
Information	Blue circle	Usually describes successful operations, such as browser, *domain name server* (DNS), and AppleTalk events. Information icons are for information only.

...continues

Table 17.3	continued	
Icon	Symbol	Indicates
Success Audit	Padlock	A security event that was successful, such as a successful logon.
Failed Audit	Key	A security event that was unsuccessful, such as an unsuccessful logon attempt.

Event Details

You can view event details in three ways:

- Select an event in the Event Viewer and press Enter.
- Double-click the selected event.
- Choose View, Detail.

In any case, an Event Detail screen appears (see Fig. 17.11). This screen, in addition to the information already displayed on the Event Viewer, includes a description window with additional information about the selected event. This information varies depending on the selected event—for example, a master browser was elected successfully, a duplicate IP address was detected on the network, an unsuccessful logon attempt was made in the Security Log, or a printer became available to the AppleTalk network in the Application Log.

The Data pane at the bottom of the Event Detail screen can contain optional data in the form of bytes or words. It is additional data created by the event source and is displayed in hexadecimal format. This data can be interpreted by support personnel familiar with the source application. Not all events display information in this area. At the bottom of the Event Detail screen are the Close, Previous, Next, and Help buttons.

Troubleshooting Problems Using the Event Viewer

To mention or display each and every possible event is impossible; however, this section can give you some general guidelines for using the Event Viewer to troubleshoot system, security, and application problems:

- Monitor the System Event log regularly on file and print servers to look for low disk space warning errors and bad sector—retry warnings.
- Monitor the Application Event Log if an application is crashing and you need to try to find out why by searching for any events concerning that application.

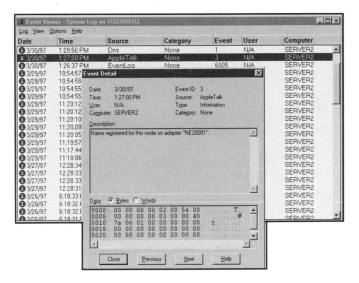

Figure 17.11
An Event Detail dialog box for an Event Log.

- Monitor the Security Event Log for any of the security event choices selected in User Manager or User Manager for Domains by choosing Policies, Audit selection.

- When analyzing events, always look for events that happened in a specific time frame. Start viewing detailed information on these events from the newest to the oldest. This information will give you a complete picture of a failure. For example, the browser did not start because the Workstation or Server Service did not start, because the network adapter card settings were detected incorrectly. In this case, the browser was not the problem; the network adapter card setting configuration was the problem.

- Through Registry editing, you can halt the computer if the Security Log is full. First of all, choose Log, Settings. Then select the default Overwrite Events Older Than x Days setting or Do Not Overwrite Events (Clear Log Manually). Next, in the

```
HKEY_LOCAL_MACHINE\System\CurrentControlSet\Control\Lsa
```

key, add the `CrashOnAuditFail` value, type `REG_WORD`, to set it to 1. If the system halts, it has to be restarted by an administrator, the auditing security events must be turned off, and the Security Log must be cleared.

■ You can save an Event Log in three ways: in an Event Log file (`.EVT`), a regular text file (`.TXT`), or a comma-delimited text file (`.TXT`). If you save a log in Event Log File format, you can view the log later with Event Viewer. If you save a log in a regular text file, you can incorporate it into a word processor application. If you save a log in a comma-delimited text file, you can incorporate it into a spreadsheet or database application. All hexadecimal data is lost if saved in any of the three types of text format.

Working with Tape Backups

Even with *redundant array of inexpensive/independent disks* (RAID), backups still must be done on a frequent basis to prevent lost data. Windows NT includes a backup utility as part of the Administrative Tools group (`NTBACKUP.EXE`).

Backing Up Files and Directories

The Backup main window shows the disk drives presently accessible to the Backup utility. Double-click on a drive to see an Explorer-type directory tree. Every directory or file has a small box beside it. Click on the box to back up the file or directory and all child files/directories below it. To start a backup, click the Backup button on the toolbar or choose Operations, Backup. The Backup Information dialog box appears, offering a number of options.

Restoring Files and Directories

To restore a file or directory using the Backup utility, open the Tapes window and select the backup set you want to restore. Like the Drives window, the Tapes window enables you to expand directories and select individual files for restoration. Select the files/directories you want to restore, and click the Restore button on the toolbar. The Restore Information dialog box appears. Select the desired restore options and click OK to restore the files/directories.

You also can run the NTBACKUP utility from the command prompt, which enables you to automate the backup process through batch files. Caution: You can back up only directories with the `ntbackup` command—not individual files.

Here is the syntax for the `ntbackup` command:

```
ntbackup operation  path
```

where `operation` is the name of the operation (backup, restore, and so on), and `path` is the path to the directory you're backing up. The NTBACKUP command includes a number of switches:

/a	Causes the backup set to be appended after the last backup set. (If you don't specify /a, overwrites existing backup sets on the tape.)
/v	Verifies the backup operation.
/d "text"	Enables you to add a description of the data in the backup set.
/t {option}	Enables you to specify the backup type (Normal, Incremental, Daily, Differential, Copy).

CH 17

Summary

This is the final chapter of the book. Here, you examined advanced troubleshooting topics in detail.

Kernel errors typically contain error messages that you can use to help identify and isolate a problem. Stop errors contain driver information as well as BugCheck information, kernel build number, and stack dump data—all of which can be useful in solving problems.

Crash dumps also are known as *memory dumps* and can be configured through the Windows NT Recover configuration parameters in the System applet. Remote troubleshooting is possible if these parameters are configured properly, and the Event Viewer utility should be one of the first places to turn to find system, security, and application errors that have been logged.

Following this chapter are a number of appendixes, including the glossary, "Certification Process," "Testing Tips," "Alternative Resources,"and "Using the CD-ROM."

Good luck on your test!

QUESTIONS AND ANSWERS

1. Messages such as `Hardware malfunction, call your hardware vendor for support` are generated by _____.

    A: Windows NT Executive

2. True or false: It is possible to have NT Server automatically reboot after a stop error.

    A: True. Enabling a check box option tells NT Server to automatically reboot after a stop error.

3. The default filename for a dump file is _____.

    A: `MEMORY.DMP`

4. The utility used to copy a dump file to floppy disks is _____.

    A: `DUMPFLOP.EXE`

5. What three NT Server log files can the Event Viewer look at?

    A: System, Security, and Application

PRACTICE TEST

1. What is the major cause of stop errors during the installation process?
   - **a.** Incompatible software.
   - **b.** Incompatible hardware.
   - **c.** Incompatible Windows NT setup program.
   - **d.** It is impossible to get stop errors during installation.

Answer a is incorrect. Incompatible software is not the major cause of stop errors during installation. **Answer b is correct. Incompatible hardware is the major cause of stop errors during installation.** Answer c is incorrect. There are only two setup programs: WINNT and WINNT32. Answer d is incorrect. It is very possible to get stop errors during installation.

2. What is the third major area of a stop screen display?
   - **a.** Debug port status indicator information
   - **b.** BugCheck information
   - **c.** Driver information
   - **d.** Kernel build number and stack dump information

Answer a is incorrect, because the third major area is BugCheck information. **Answer b is correct. The third major area of a stop screen is the Bugcheck information.** Answers c and d are incorrect, because the third major area is BugCheck information.

3. The first four lines of the _____ section are critical to finding the cause of the stop error.

   a. BugCheck information

   b. Driver information

   c. Kernel build number and stack dump

   d. Debug port information

Answer a is correct. The first four lines of the Bugcheck information section are critical to finding the cause of the stop error. Answer b is incorrect. The driver information is not as critical to finding the cause as the BugCheck information section. Answer c is incorrect. The Kernel build number and stack dump section is not as critical to finding the cause as the BugCheck information section. Answer d is incorrect. The Debug port information is not as critical to finding the cause as the BugCheck information section.

4. By default, CrashDump is placed in the _____ folder.

   a. `%systemRoot%\System32`

   b. `%systemRoot%\System32\Debug`

   c. `%SystemRoot%\System32\MemoryDump`

   d. `%systemRoot%\`

Answers a, b, and c are incorrect. These are locations other than the default location that the Dump file is written to. **Answer d is correct. `%systemRoot%\` is the default location for CrashDump.**

5. For CrashDumps to be obtained, a pagefile must exist on the

   a. system partition

   b. boot partition

   c. NTFS partition

   d. data partition

Answer a is incorrect. The pagefile *must* exist on the boot partition, not the system partition. **Answer b is correct. The only way a CrashDump is obtained is if the pagefile exists on the boot partition.** Answer c is incorrect. The pagefile *must* exist on the boot partition, not the NTFS partition. Answer d is incorrect. The pagefile *must* exist on the boot partition, not the data partition.

6. For CrashDumps to be obtained, the pagefile must be at least _____ megabytes larger than the physical size of memory.

   a. 1

   b. 2

   c. 4

   d. 8

Answer a is correct. For a CrashDump to be written, the pagefile must be equal to the size of physical memory plus 1MB. Answers b, c, and d are incorrect, because the pagefile need not be that much larger than RAM.

7. The utility to verify the validity of a CrashDump is

   a. `Dumpflop.exe`

   b. `Dumpexam.exe`

   c. `Dumpchk.exe`

   d. `Dump.exe`

Answer a is incorrect. `Dumpflop.exe` is used to dump the file to floppy disks. Answer b is incorrect. `Dumpexam.exe` is used to find the cause of the error. **Answer c is correct. `Dumpck.exe` is used to verify the validity of a CrashDump.** Answer d is incorrect; it is not a valid tool.

8. Reference to the most recently installed service pack Symbols files must be listed _____ in the DUMPEXAM utility command line.

   a. Last

   b. First after the normal Symbols files reference

   c. Second

   d. First

Answer a is incorrect. The Symbols files must be first and not last. Answer b is incorrect. The Symbols files must be first—not first after the normal Symbols files reference. Answer c is incorrect. The Symbols files must be first and not second. **Answer d is correct. Symbol files must be listed first in the DUMPEXAM utility's command line.**

9. What kind of connection can you establish between the host computer and the target computer so that the host computer can monitor the boot process on the target computer?

   a. Null modem connection using a COM port

   b. Normal network connection using a network adapter card

   c. Modem connection using a COM port

   d. Modem connection using an LPT port

Answer a is correct. You can use a null modem connection using a COM port.
Answer b is incorrect. A network connection does not give you this capability. **Answer c is correct. You can use a modem connection through a COM port.** Answer d is incorrect, because a modem through an LPT—should there be such a beast—will not give you this capability.

10. You can enter Kernel Debugger commands after you enter a _____ key sequence.

   a. Ctrl,G
   b. Ctrl,C
   c. Ctrl,K
   d. Ctrl,Q

Answer a is incorrect. Only Ctrl,C enables you to enter Kernel Debugger commands. **Answer b is correct. The Ctrl,C sequence enables you to enter Kernel Debugger commands.** Answers c and d are incorrect. Only Ctrl,C enables you to enter Kernel Debugger commands.

CH
17

Glossary

access-control entry (ACE) An entry in an access-control list that defines a set of permissions for a group or user.

access-control list (ACL) A list containing access-control entries. An ACL determines the permissions associated with an object, which can be anything in a Win32 environment.

access time The last time a file was run (if the file is executable). Otherwise, the last time the file was read from or written to.

ACE (see access-control entry)

ACK *Acknowledgment.* A control character sent to the other computer in a conversation. Usually used to indicate that transmitted information has been received correctly when using a communications protocol such as XModem.

ACL (see access-control list)

active window The window the user is currently working with. Windows identifies the active window by highlighting its title bar and border.

Advanced Program-to-Program Communications (APPC) A method of interprogram communication, usually used by applications intended for use with IBM SNA-based networks.

Advanced Research Projects Agency (ARPA) The agency responsible for the formation of the forerunner of the Internet. (see also Defense Advanced Research Projects Agency)

agent Software that runs on a client computer for use by administrative software running on a server. Agents typically are used to support administrative actions, such as detecting system information or running services.

Alerter Service A Windows NT Executive Service that notifies selected users or computers of system-generated administrative alerts.

American National Standards Institute (ANSI) A standards-making organization based in the U.S.

American Standard Code for Information Interchange (ASCII) A scheme that assigns letters, punctuation marks, and so on to specific numeric values. The standardization of ASCII enabled computers and computer programs to exchange data.

ANSI   (see American National Standards Institute)

ANSI character set   An 8-bit character set used by Microsoft Windows that enables you to represent up to 256 characters (0–255) using your keyboard. The ASCII character set is a subset of the ANSI set. (see also American National Standards Institute)

API   (see Application Programming Interface)

APPC   (see Advanced Program-to-Program Communications)

application   A computer program that is designed to do some specific type of work. An application is different from a utility, which performs some type of maintenance (such as formatting a disk).

Application Programming Interface (API)   A list of supported functions. Windows NT 4.0 supports the MS-DOS API, Windows API, and Win32 API. If a function is a member of the API, it is said to be a *supported* or *documented function*. Functions that make up Windows but are not part of the API are referred to as *undocumented functions*. An API also can be a low-level software routine that programmers can use to send requests to the operating system.

ARPA   (see Advanced Research Projects Agency)

ASCII   (see American Standard Code for Information Interchange)

ASCII character set   A 7-bit character set widely used to represent letters and symbols found on a standard U.S. keyboard. The ASCII character set is identical to the first 128 characters in the ANSI character set.

association   The process of assigning a filename extension to a particular application. When an extension is associated with an application, Windows NT 4.0 starts the application when you open the file from Windows Explorer. Associations are critical to the concept of document-centric computing.

attributes   A characteristic of a file that indicates whether it is hidden, system, read-only, archive, or compressed.

Audio Video Interleaved (AVI)   The format of the full-motion video files used by Windows NT 4.0.

Audit Policy   A definition of the types of security-related events that will be recorded by the Event Viewer.

authentication   The validation of a user's access to a computer or domain by the local computer (local validation) or a backup domain controller for the domain the user is accessing.

Autoexec.bat   A file in the root directory of the boot disk that contains a list of MS-DOS commands that are executed automatically when the system is started. Autoexec.bat can be created by the user or the operating system. Windows NT 4.0

Setup examines the `Autoexec.bat` file looking for configuration information, such as user environment variables.

auxiliary audio devices   Audio devices that generate output that is mixed with the *Musical Instrument Digital Interface* (MIDI) and waveform output devices in a multimedia computer. An example of an auxiliary audio device is the compact disc audio output from a CD-ROM drive.

AVI   (see Audio Video Interleaved)

background window   Any window created by a thread other than the thread running in the foreground.

backup domain controller (BDC)
The Windows NT controller server that performs the validation of user logon requests. The BDC obtains a copy of the master account database for the domain from the primary domain controller.

basic input/output system (BIOS)
The bootstrap code of a PC. The low-level routines that support the transfer of information between the various parts of a computer system, such as memory, disks, and the monitor. Usually built into the machine's *read-only memory* (ROM). The BIOS can have a significant effect on the performance of the computer system.

batch program   A file that contains one or more commands that are executed when you type the filename at the command prompt. Batch programs have the `.BAT` extension.

BDC   (see backup domain controller)

binding   The process that links a protocol driver with a network adapter driver.

BIOS   (see basic input/output system)

BIOS enumerator   In a plug-and-play system, the BIOS enumerator is responsible for identifying all of the hardware devices on the computer's motherboard.

bit   *Binary digit,* the smallest unit of data a computer can store. Bits are expressed as 1 or 0.

bitmap   Originally, an array of bits, but now expanded to include arrays of bytes or even 32-bit quantities, that specify the dot pattern and colors that describe an image onscreen or on printed paper.

BMP   The extension used for Windows bitmap files.

Boot Loader   Defines the location of the Windows NT boot and system files.

boot partition   The partition that contains the Windows NT system files.

Bootstrap Protocol (BOOTP)   An internetworking protocol used to configure *Transmission Control Protocol/Internet Protocol* (TCP/IP) networks across routers.

branch   A segment of the directory tree, representing a directory and any subdirectories it contains.

browse   To look through a list on a computer system. Lists include directories, files, domains, and computers.

buffer   A temporary holding place reserved in memory, where data is held while in transit to or from a storage device or another location in memory.

buffering   The process of using buffers, particularly to or from I/O devices, such as disk drives and serial ports.

bus enumerator   A driver responsible for building the hardware tree on a plug-and-play system.

byte   8 binary digits (bits) combined to represent a single character or value.

Card Services   A protected-mode VxD linked with the PCMCIA bus drivers. Card Services passes event notifications from socket services to the *Personal Computer Memory Card International Association* (PCMCIA) bus driver, provides information from the computer's cards to the PCMCIA bus driver, and sets up the configuration for cards in the adapter sockets.

cascading menu   A menu that is a submenu of a menu item. Also known as a *hierarchical menu.* The menus accessed via the Windows NT 4.0 Start button are cascading menus.

CCITT   (see International Telephone and Telegraph Consultative Committee)

CD-DA   (see Compact Disc–Digital Audio)

CD-ROM   (see compact disc–read-only memory)

CD-ROM/XA   (see Compact Disc–Read-Only Memory Extended Architecture)

CD-XA   (see Compact Disc–Extended Architecture)

CDFS   (see Compact Disc File System)

central processing unit (CPU)   The computational and control unit of a computer; the device that interprets and executes instructions. The CPU—or microprocessor, in the case of a microcomputer—can fetch, decode, and execute instructions as well as transfer information to and from other resources over the computer's main data-transfer path, the bus. The CPU is the chip that functions as the "brain" of a computer.

character   A letter, number, punctuation mark, or a control code. Usually expressed in the ANSI or ASCII character set.

character mode   A mode of displaying information onscreen, where all information is displayed using text characters (as opposed to graphical symbols). MS-DOS applications run in character mode.

check box   In the Windows NT 4.0 interface, a square box that has two or three states, and is used by the user to select an option from a set of options. A standard check box is a toggle with two states: checked and unchecked. A three-state check box has an additional state: disabled (grayed).

class   For *object linking and embedding* (OLE), a data structure and the functions that manipulate that data structure. An object is a member of a class. For hardware, a grouping of devices and buses for the purpose of installing and managing devices and device drivers, and allocating the resources used by them. The Windows NT 4.0 hardware tree is organized by device class.

clear-to-send (CTS)   A signal sent from one computer to the other in a communications conversation to indicate readiness to accept data.

client   A computer that accesses shared network resources provided by another computer, called a *server*. (see also server)

code names   A name assigned to conceal the identity or existence of something or someone. The code name for Microsoft Windows NT 4.0 was "SUR," which sometimes appears as an identifier in several places in the released product, including hardware setup files. The next major release of Windows NT is code named "Cairo."

codec   Compression/decompression technology for digital video and stereo audio.

Command.com   The command processor for MS-DOS. Windows NT 4.0 loads its version of Command.com (compatible with MS-DOS 5.0) to process commands typed in MS-DOS mode or at an MS-DOS prompt.

communications protocol   The rules that govern a conversation between two computers that are communicating via an asynchronous connection. The use of a communications protocol ensures error-free delivery of the data being communicated.

communications resource   A device that provides a bidirectional, asynchronous data stream. Examples include serial and parallel ports, and modems. Applications access the resource through a service provider.

Compact Disc–Digital Audio (CD-DA)   An optical data-storage format that provides for the storage of up to 73 minutes of high-quality digital-audio data on a compact disc. Also known as *Red Book audio* or *music CD*.

Compact Disc–Extended Architecture (CD-XA)   (see Compact Disc–Read-Only Memory Extended Architecture)

Compact Disc File System (CDFS)   Controls access to the contents of CD-ROM drivers.

compact disc–read-only memory (CD-ROM)   A form of storage characterized by high capacity (roughly 600MB) and the use of laser optics rather than magnetic means for reading data.

Compact Disc–Read-Only Memory Extended Architecture (CD-ROM/XA)   An extended CD-ROM format developed by Philips, Sony, and Microsoft. CD-ROM/XA format is consistent with the ISO 9660 (High Sierra) standard, with further specification of *adaptive differential pulse code modulation* (ADPCM) audio, images, and interleaved data.

Computer Browser Service   This Executive Service identifies Windows NT clients that have resources available for use within a workgroup or domain.

computer name   A unique name that identifies a particular computer on the network. Microsoft networking uses NetBIOS names, which can have up to 15 characters and cannot contain spaces.

config.sys An ASCII text file that contains configuration commands. Used by MS-DOS, OS/2, and Windows NT 4.0 to load real-mode device drivers.

Configuration Manager One of three central components of a plug-and-play system (one for each of the three phases of configuration management). The Configuration Managers drive the process of locating devices, setting up the hardware tree, and allocating resources.

context menu A menu that appears at the location of a submenu and is displayed after you right-click. It is called a *context menu* because the contents of the menu depend on what you're involved in at the time.

Control Panel The primary Windows NT 4.0 configuration tool. Each option you can change is represented by an icon in the Control Panel window.

controller (see domain controller)

conventional memory The first 640KB of memory in your computer, used to run real-mode MS-DOS applications.

cooperative multitasking A form of multitasking in which threads cooperate with each other by voluntarily giving up control of the processor. Contrast with preemptive multitasking.

CPU (see central processing unit)

crash A serious failure of the software being used.

CTS (see clear-to-send)

cursor A bitmap; its location onscreen is controlled by a pointing device, such as a mouse, pen, or trackball. (see also bitmap)

DARPA (see Defense Advanced Research Projects Agency)

data frame The structured packets into which data is placed by the Data Link layer.

datagram A packet of information and delivery data that is routed on a network.

default An operation or value that the system assumes, unless the user makes an explicit choice.

Defense Advanced Research Projects Agency (DARPA) An agency of the U.S. Department of Defense that sponsored the development of the protocols that became the TCP/IP suite. DARPA previously was known as ARPA, the Advanced Research Projects Agency, when ARPAnet was built.

desktop The background of your screen, on which windows, icons, and dialog boxes appear.

destination directory The directory to which you intend to copy or move one or more files.

device A generic term for a computer component, such as a printer, serial port, or disk drive. A device frequently requires its own controlling software (called a *device driver*).

device contention The method that Windows NT 4.0 uses to allocate access to peripheral devices when multiple applications are attempting to use them.

device driver   A piece of software that translates requests from one form into another. Most commonly, drivers are used to provide a device-independent way to access hardware.

device ID   A unique ASCII string created by enumerators to identify a hardware device and used to cross reference data about the device stored in the Registry.

device node   One of the data structures that make up the hardware tree, a device node is built by the Configuration Manager into memory at system startup. Device nodes contain information about a given device, such as the resources it is using.

DHCP   (see Dynamic Host Configuration Protocol)

Dial-Up Networking   Formerly known as *Remote Access Service* (RAS), it provides remote access to networks. Dial-Up Networking allows remote users to access their network. Once connected, it is as if the remote computer is logically on the network; users can do anything they could do when physically connected to the network.

dialog box   The type of window displayed by Windows NT 4.0 when user input is needed. Usually contains one or more buttons, edit controls, radio buttons, and drop-down lists.

DIP switch   *Dual in-line package switch.* Used to configure hardware options, especially on adapter cards.

direct memory access (DMA)   A technique used by hardware adapters to store and retrieve information from the computer's RAM memory without involving the computer's CPU.

directory   Part of a structure for organizing your files on a disk. A directory can contain files and other directories (called *subdirectories).*

Directory Replication Service   This service provides a means of copying a directory and file structure from a source Windows NT Server to a target Windows NT Server or Workstation.

disk caching   A method to improve performance of the file system. A section of memory is used as a temporary holding place for frequently accessed file data. Windows NT 4.0 dynamically allocates its disk cache.

disk operating system (DOS) (see Microsoft Disk Operating System)

DLL   (see dynamic link library)

DMA   (see direct memory access)

DMA channel   A channel for DMA transfers—those that occur between a device and memory directly, without involving the CPU.

DNS   (see Domain Name Service)

DNS name servers   The servers that hold the DNS name database and supply the IP address that matches a DNS name in response to a request from a DNS client. (see also Domain Name Service)

dock   To insert a portable computer into a base unit. *Cold docking* means the computer must begin from a power-off state and restart before docking. *Hot docking* means the computer can be docked while running at full power.

docking station   The base computer unit into which a user can insert a port-able computer to expand it to a desktop equivalent. Docking stations usually include drives, expansion slots, AC power, network and SCSI connections, and communication ports.

domain   For *Domain Name Service* (DNS), a group of workstations and servers that share a single group name. For Microsoft networking, a collection of computers that share a security context and account database stored on a Windows NT Server domain controller. Each domain has a unique name. (see also Domain Name Service)

domain controller   The Windows NT Server computer that authenticates domain logons and maintains a copy of the security database for the domain.

Domain Name Service (DNS)   A static, hierarchical name service for TCP/IP hosts. Do not confuse DNS domains with Windows NT domains.

DOS   (see Microsoft Disk Operating System)

DOS Protected Mode Interface (DPMI)   A technique used to allow MS-DOS–based applications to access extended memory.

dpi   *Dots per inch*—a measurement of the resolution of a monitor or printer.

DPMI   (see DOS Protected Mode Interface)

drag and drop   To selectively move or copy one or more objects between dialog boxes, using a mouse or other pointing device.

DRAM   (see dynamic random-access memory)

dynamic data exchange (DDE)   A form of *interprocess communication* (IPC) implemented in the Microsoft Windows family of operating systems. DDE uses shared memory to exchange data. Most DDE functions have been superseded by OLE.

Dynamic Host Configuration Protocol (DHCP)   A protocol for automatic TCP/IP configuration that provides static and dynamic address allocation and management.

dynamic link library (DLL)   File functions that are compiled, linked, and saved separately from the processes that use them. Functions in DLLs can be used by more than one running process. The operating system maps the DLLs into the process's address space when the process is starting up or while it is running. DLLs are stored in files with the .DLL extension.

dynamic random-access memory (DRAM)   A computer's main memory.

Eform   (see electronic mail form)

EISA (see Extended Industry Standard Architecture)

electronic mail (email) A message sent across a network between two or more store-and-forward messaging systems.

electronic mail form (Eform) A programmed form used to send email in an electronic mail system.

electronic messaging system (EMS) A system that enables users or applications to correspond using a store-and-forward system.

email (see electronic mail)

EMM (see Expanded Memory Manager)

EMS (see Expanded Memory Specification and electronic messaging system)

encapsulated PostScript (EPS) A file format used to represent graphics written in the PostScript page description language.

enumerator A plug-and-play device driver that detects devices below its own device node, creates unique device IDs, and reports to Configuration Manager during startup.

environment variable A symbolic variable that represents some element of the operating system, such as a path, a filename, or other literal data. Typically used by batch files, environment variables are created with the SET command.

EPROM (see erasable programmable read-only memory)

EPS (see encapsulated PostScript)

EPS file A file containing code written in the encapsulated PostScript printer programming language. Often used to represent graphics for use by desktop publishing applications.

erasable programmable read-only memory (EPROM) A computer chip containing nonvolatile memory. It can be erased (for reprogramming) by exposure to ultraviolet light.

event An action or occurrence to which an application might respond, such as a mouse click, key press, mouse movement, or system event. A *system event* is any significant occurrence that may require user notification or some other action by an application.

expanded memory Memory that complies with the Lotus-Intel-Microsoft Expanded Memory Specification. Used by MS-DOS–based spreadsheet applications.

Expanded Memory Manager (EMM) The device driver that controls access to expanded memory.

Expanded Memory Specification (EMS) The specification that controls and defines expanded memory. Also known as the *Lotus-Intel-Microsoft* (LIM) Specification, after the three major companies that designed it.

Extended Industry Standard Architecture (EISA) An enhancement to the bus architecture used on the IBM PC/AT that allows the use of 32-bit devices in the same type of expansion slot used by an *Industry*

Standard Architecture (ISA) adapter card. EISA slots and adapters were formerly common in server computers but have been mostly replaced with *Peripheral Component Interconnect* (PCI) slots.

extended memory   Memory that occupies physical addresses above the 1MB mark.

Extended Memory Manager (XMM) The MS-DOS device driver that provides access to *Extended Memory Specification* (XMS) memory.

Extended Memory Specification (XMS) The specification for the application program interfaces that allow an application to access and use extended memory.

family name   The name of a given font family. Windows employs five family names: Decorative, Modern, Roman, Script, and Swiss. A sixth family name, Dontcare, specifies the default font. (see also font family)

FAT   (see file allocation table)

FAT File System   A file system based on a file allocation table. Windows NT 4.0 uses a 32-bit implementation called *virtual file allocation table* (VFAT). (see also file allocation table and virtual file allocation table)

FIFO   (see first in, first out)

file   A collection of information stored on a disk and accessible using a name.

file allocation table (FAT)   A table or list maintained by some operating systems to keep track of the status of various segments of disk space used for file storage. (see also virtual file allocation table)

file attribute   A characteristic of a file that indicates whether the file is read-only, hidden, system, archived, a directory, or normal.

file sharing   The capability of a network computer to share files or directories on its local disks with remote computers.

file system   In an operating system, the overall structure in which files are named, stored, and organized.

file time   A 64-bit value representing the number of 100-nanosecond intervals that have elapsed since January 1, 1601.

File Transfer Program (FTP)   A utility defined by the TCP/IP protocol suite that is used to transfer files between dissimilar systems.

File Transfer Protocol (FTP) The standard method of transferring files using TCP/IP. FTP enables you to transfer files between dissimilar computers, with preservation of binary data, and optional translation of text file formats.

first in, first out (FIFO)   Used to describe a buffer, where data is retrieved from the buffer in the same order it went in.

floppy disk   A disk that can be inserted into and removed from a disk drive.

focus   The area of a dialog box that receives input. The focus is indicated by highlighted text or a button enclosed in dotted lines.

folder   In Windows Explorer, an object that can contain other objects (a container object). Examples include disk folders, the fonts folder, and the printers folder.

font   A collection of characters, each with a similar appearance. For example, the Arial font characters are all sans serif characters.

font family   A group of fonts that have similar characteristics.

font mapper   The routine within Windows that maps an application's request for a font with particular characteristics to the available font that best matches those characteristics.

frame   (see data frame)

free space   Unused space on a hard disk.

friendly name   A human-readable name used to give an alternative to the often cryptic computer, port, and share names. For example, `Digital 1152 Printer In The Hall` as opposed to `HALLPRT`.

FTP   (see File Transfer Program and File Transfer Protocol)

gateway   A computer connected to multiple networks and capable of moving data among networks using different transport protocols.

GDI   (see graphics device interface)

graphical user interface (GUI)   A computer system design in which the user interacts with the system using graphical symbols, tools, and events instead of text-based displays and commands, such as the normal Windows NT 4.0 user interface.

graphics device interface (GDI) The subsystem that implements graphic drawing functions.

GUI   (see graphical user interface)

handle   An interface (usually a small black square) added to an object to enable the user to move, size, reshape, or otherwise modify the object.

hardware branch   The hardware archive root key in the Registry, which is a superset of the memory-resident hardware tree. The name of this key is `Hkey_Local_Machine\Hardware`.

hardware tree   A record in RAM of the current system configuration, based on the configuration information for all devices in the hardware branch of the Registry. The hardware tree is created each time the computer is started or whenever a dynamic change occurs to the system configuration.

high-memory area (HMA)   A 64KB memory block located just above the 1MB address in a *Virtual DOS Machine* (VDM). Originally made possible by a side effect of the 80286 processor design, the memory is usable when the A20 address line is turned on.

High-Performance File System (HPFS) File system primarily used with OS/2 operating system version 1.2 or later. It supports long filenames but does not provide security. Windows NT 4.0 does not support HPFS.

hive   A discrete body of Registry information, usually stored in a single disk file.

HKEY_CLASSES_ROOT   The Registry tree that contains data relating to OLE. This key is a symbolic link to a subkey of HKEY_LOCAL_MACHINE\SOFTWARE.

HKEY_CURRENT_USER   The Registry tree that contains the currently logged-in user's preferences, including desktop settings, application settings, and network connections. This key maps to a subkey of HKEY_USERS.

HKEY_LOCAL_MACHINE   The Registry tree that contains configuration settings that apply to the hardware and software on the computer.

HKEY_USERS   The Registry tree that contains the preferences for every user that ever logged on to this computer.

HMA   (see high-memory area)

home directory   A directory that is accessible to a particular user and contains that user's files and programs on a network server.

host   Any device that is attached to the internetwork and uses TCP/IP.

host ID   The portion of the IP address that identifies a computer within a particular network ID.

host table   The HOSTS and LMHOSTS files, which contain mappings of known IP addresses mapped to hostnames.

hostname   The name of an Internet host. It may or may not be the same as the computer name. In order for a client to access resources by hostname, the name must appear in the client's HOSTS file or be resolvable by a DNS server.

HOSTS file   A local text file in the same format as the 4.3 *Berkeley Software Distribution* (BSD) UNIX/etc/hosts file. This file maps hostnames to IP addresses. In Windows NT 4.0, this file is stored in the \WINNT directory.

hotkey   Letters or combinations of keystrokes used in place of mouse clicks as shortcuts to application functions.

HPFS   (see High-Performance File System)

ICMP   (see Internet Control Message Protocol)

icon   A small bitmap (usually 16×16 pixels or 32×32 pixels) associated with an application, file type, or concept.

IEEE   (see Institute of Electrical and Electronic Engineers)

IETF   (see Internet Engineering Task Force)

IFS   (see installable file system)

IHV   (see independent hardware vendor)

I/O address   *Input/output address.* One of the critical resources used in configuring devices. I/O addresses are used to communicate with devices. Also known as *port.*

I/O bus   *Input/output bus.* The electrical connection between the CPU and the I/O devices. There are several types of I/O buses: ISA, EISA, SCSI, VL, and PCI.

I/O device   *Input/output device.* Any device in or attached to a computer that is designed to receive information from or provide information to the computer. A printer is an output-only device, for example, and a mouse is an input-only device. Other devices, such as modems, are both input and output devices, transferring data in both directions. Windows NT 4.0 must have a device driver installed in order to be able to use an I/O device.

independent hardware vendor (IHV)
A manufacturer of computer hardware. Generally used to describe the makers of add-on devices rather than makers of computer systems.

Industry Standard Architecture (ISA)
A computer system built on ISA adheres to the same design rules and constraints that the IBM PC/AT adhered to.

INF file   A file, usually provided by the manufacturer of a device, that provides the information that Windows NT 4.0 Setup needs to set up a device. INF files usually include a list of valid logical configurations for the device, the names of driver files associated with the device, and other information.

INI files   Initialization files used by Windows-based applications to store configuration information. Windows NT 4.0 incorporates INI files into its Registry when upgrading from a previous version of Windows.

installable file system (IFS)   A file system that can be installed into the operating system as needed, instead of just at startup time. Windows NT 4.0 can support multiple installable file systems at one time, including the FAT File System

and NTFS, network redirectors, and the Compact Disc File System (CDFS).

instance   A particular occurrence of an object, such as a window, module, named pipe, or DDE session. Each instance has a unique handle that distinguishes it from other instances of the same type.

Institute of Electrical and Electronic Engineers (IEEE)   An organization that issues standards for electrical and electronic devices.

Integrated Services Digital Network (ISDN)   A digital communications method that permits connections of up to 128Kbps. ISDN requires a special adapter for your computer. An ISDN connection is available in most areas of the United States at a reasonable cost.

internal command   Commands that are built into the command.com file.

International Standards Organization (ISO)   The organization that produces many of the world's standards. *Open Systems Interconnect* (OSI) is only one of many areas standardized by the ISO.

International Telephone and Telegraph Consultative Committee (CCITT)
International organization that creates and publishes telecommunications standards, including X.400. The initials CCITT actually stand for the real name of the organization, which is *Comité Consultatif International Téléphonique et Télégraphique* in French.

Internet   The worldwide interconnected wide-area network, based on the TCP/IP suite.

Internet Control Message Protocol (ICMP)   A required protocol in the TCP/IP suite. It allows two nodes on an IP network to share IP status and error information. ICMP is used by the ping utility.

Internet Engineering Task Force (IETF)   A consortium that introduces procedures for new technology on the Internet. IETF specifications are released in documents called *Requests for Comments* (RFCs).

Internet group name   A name known by a DNS server that includes a list of the specific addresses of systems that have registered the name.

Internet Protocol (IP)   The Network layer protocol of TCP/IP responsible for addressing and sending TCP packets over the network.

interprocess communications (IPC)   A set of mechanisms used by applications to communicate and share data.

interrupt   An event that disrupts normal processing by the CPU and results in the transfer of control to an interrupt handler. Both hardware devices and software can issue interrupts; software executes an INT instruction, and hardware devices signal the CPU by using one of the *interrupt request* (IRQ) lines to the processor.

interrupt request level (IRQL)   Interrupts are ranked by priority. Interrupts that have a priority lower than the processor's interrupt request level setting can be masked (ignored).

interrupt request (IRQ) lines   Hardware lines on the CPU that devices use to send signals to cause an interrupt. Normally, only one device is attached to any particular IRQ line.

IP   (see Internet Protocol)

IP address   Identifies a node on a network and specifies routing information on an internetwork. Each node on the internetwork must be assigned a unique IP address, which is made up of the network ID, plus a unique host ID assigned by the network administrator. The subnet mask is used to separate an IP address into the host ID and network ID. In Windows NT 4.0, you can assign an IP address manually or automatically by using DHCP.

IP router   A system connected to multiple physical TCP/IP networks that can route or deliver IP packets between the networks. (see also gateway)

IPC   (see interprocess communications)

IPX/SPX   *Internetworking Packet Exchange/Sequenced Packet Exchange.* Transport protocols used in Novell NetWare networks. Windows NT 4.0 includes the Microsoft IPX/SPX-compatible transport protocol (NWLINK).

IRQ   (see interrupt request (IRQ) lines)

IRQL   (see interrupt request level)

ISA   (see Industry Standard Architecture)

ISDN   (see Integrated Services Digital Network)

ISO   (see International Standards Organization)

ISO Development Environment (ISODE)   A research tool developed to study the upper layer of *Open Systems Interconnect* (OSI). Academic and some commercial ISO products are based on this framework.

ISODE   (see ISO Development Environment)

KB   Standard abbreviation for kilobyte; equals 1,024 bytes.

Kbps   Kilobits per second.

kernel   The Windows NT 4.0 core component responsible for implementing the basic operating system functions of Windows NT 4.0, including virtual memory management, thread scheduling, and file I/O services.

LAN   (see local area network)

legacy   Hardware and device cards that don't conform to the Plug and Play standard.

link   A connection at the *Logical Link Control* (LLC) layer that is uniquely defined by the adapter's address and the *destination service access point* (DSAP). Also, a connection between two objects, or a reference to an object that is linked to another object.

list box   In a dialog box, a box that lists available choices. For example, a list of all files in a directory. If all the choices do not fit in the list box, a scrollbar is provided.

LLC   (see Logical Link Control)

LMHOSTS file   A local text file that maps IP addresses to the computer names of Windows networking computers. In Windows NT 4.0, LMHOSTS is stored in the `WINNT\system32\drivers\etc` directory. (LMHOSTS stands for LAN Manager Hosts.)

local area network (LAN)   A computer network confined to a single building or campus.

local printer   A printer that is directly connected to one of the ports on your computer, as opposed to a network printer.

localization   The process of adapting software for different countries, languages, or cultures.

logical drive   A division of an extended partition on a hard drive, accessed using a drive letter.

Logical Link Control (LLC)   One of the two sublayers of the Data Link layer of the OSI Reference Model, as defined by the IEEE 802 standards.

login   The process by which a user is identified to the computer in a Novell NetWare network.

logon   The process by which a user is identified to the computer in a Microsoft network.

logon script   In Microsoft networking, a batch file that runs automatically when a user logs on to a Windows NT Server. Novell networking also uses logon scripts, but they are not batch files.

MAC   (see Media Access Control)

MAC address   The address for a device as it is identified at the Media Access Control layer in the network architecture. MAC addresses usually are stored in read-only memory on the network adapter card and are unique.

mailslot   A form of interprocess communications used to carry messages from an application on one network node to another. Mailslots are one-way.

mailslot client   A process that writes a message to a mailslot.

mailslot server   A process that creates and owns a mailslot and can read messages from it. (see also process)

management information base (MIB) A set of objects used by the *Simple Network Management Protocol* (SNMP) to manage devices. MIB objects represent various types of information about a device.

mandatory user profile   This represents a user environment profile that cannot be changed by the user. If the profile is unavailable, the user is unable to log on to the Windows NT enterprise.

map   To translate one value into another.

MAPI   (see Messaging Application Programming Interface)

mapped I/O (or mapped file I/O)   The file input/output that is performed by reading and writing to virtual memory that is backed by a file.

MB   Standard abbreviation for megabyte, or 1,024 kilobytes.

MDI   (see multiple-document interface)

Media Access Control (MAC)   The lower of the two sublayers of the Data Link layer in the IEEE 802 network model.

media control interface (MCI) High-level control software that provides a device-independent interface to multimedia devices and media files. MCI includes a command-message interface and a command-string interface.

memory   A temporary storage area for information and applications.

memory object   A number of bytes allocated from the heap.

message   A structure or set of parameters used for communicating information or a request. Every event that happens in the system causes a message to be sent. Messages can be passed between the operating system and an application, different applications, threads within an application, and windows within an application.

message loop   A program loop that retrieves messages from a thread's message queue and dispatches them.

Messaging Application Programming Interface (MAPI)   A set of calls used to add mail-enabled features to other Windows-based applications. It is one of the *Windows Open Systems Architecture* (WOSA) technologies.

metafile   A collection of structures that store a picture in a device-independent format. (There are two metafile formats: the enhanced format and the Windows format.)

MIB   (see management information base)

Microsoft Disk Operating System (MS-DOS)   The dominant operating system for personal computers from the introduction of the IBM personal computer until the introduction of Windows 95 and Windows NT 4.0.

MIDI   (see Musical Instrument Digital Interface)

minidriver   The part of the device driver that is written by the hardware manufacturer and provides device-specific functionality.

MS-DOS   (see Microsoft Disk Operating System)

MS-DOS–based application   An application designed to run under MS-DOS. Windows NT 4.0 supports most MS-DOS–based applications except those that communicate directly to hardware devices.

multiple-document interface (MDI) A specification that defines the standard user interface for Windows-based applications. An MDI application enables the user to work with more than one document at the same time. Microsoft Word is an example of an MDI application. Each of the documents is displayed in a separate window inside the application's main window.

multitasking   The process by which an operating system creates the illusion that many tasks are executing simultaneously on a single processor. (see also cooperative multitasking and preemptive multitasking)

multithreading   The capability of a process to have multiple, simultaneous paths of execution (threads).

Musical Instrument Digital Interface (MIDI)   A standard protocol for communication between musical instruments and computers.

mutex   A MUTually EXclusive flag used to prevent reentry. For example, when you open a copy of Word, a mutex flag is set that prevents you from opening another. Any attempt to open another iteration of Word simply brings to the forefront the copy you already have running.

name registration   The way a computer registers its unique name with a name server on the network, such as a *Windows Internet Name Service* (WINS) server.

name resolution   The process used on the network to determine the address of a computer by using its name.

named pipe   A one-way or two-way pipe used for communications between a server process and one or more client processes. A server process specifies a name when it creates one or more instances of a named pipe. Each instance of the pipe can be connected to a client. Microsoft SQL Server clients use named pipes to communicate with the SQL Server.

NBF Transport Protocol   *NetBEUI Frame Protocol.* A descendant of the NetBEUI Protocol, which is a Transport Layer Protocol, not the programming interface NetBIOS.

NCB (see network control block)

NDIS (see Network Device Interface Specification)

NetBEUI transport NetBIOS (Network Basic Input/Output System) Extended User Interface A transport protocol designed for use on small subnets. It is not routable, but it is fast.

NetBIOS Interface A programming interface that allows I/O requests to be sent to and received from a remote computer. It hides networking hardware from applications.

NetBIOS Over TCP/IP The networking module that provides the functionality to support NetBIOS name registration and resolution across a TCP/IP network.

network A group of computers and other devices that can interact by means of a shared communications link.

network adapter driver Software that implements the lower layers of a network, providing a standard interface to the network card.

Network Basic Input/Output System (NetBIOS) A software interface for network communication. (see NetBIOS Interface)

network control block (NCB) A memory structure used to communicate with the NetBIOS Interface.

Network DDE DSDM Service The Network *Dynamic Data Exchange* (DDE) *DDE Share Database Manager* (DSDM)

Service manages shared DDE conversations. It is used by the Network DDE Service.

Network DDE Service The Network *Dynamic Data Exchange* (DDE) Service provides network transport and security for DDE conversations. Network DDE is supported in Windows NT 4.0 for backward compatibility, because most of its functions are superseded by OLE.

network device driver Software that coordinates communication between the network adapter card and the computer's hardware and other software, controlling the physical functioning of the network adapter cards.

Network Device Interface Specification (NDIS) In Windows networking, the interface for network adapter drivers. All transport drivers call the NDIS Interface to access network adapter cards.

network directory (see shared directory)

Network File System (NFS) A service for distributed computing systems that provides a distributed file system, eliminating the need for keeping multiple copies of files on separate computers. Usually used with UNIX computers.

network ID The portion of the IP address that identifies a group of computers and devices located on the same logical network. Separated from the host ID using the subnet mask.

Network Information Service (NIS) A service for distributed computing systems that provides a distributed database system for common configuration files.

network interface card (NIC)   An adapter card that connects a computer to a network.

network interface printers   Printers with built-in network cards, such as Hewlett-Packard laser printers equipped with Jet Direct cards. The advantage of network interface printers is that they can be located anywhere on the network.

network operating system (NOS)   The operating system used on network servers, such as Windows NT Server or Novell NetWare.

network provider   The Windows NT 4.0 component that allows Windows NT 4.0 to communicate with the network. Windows NT 4.0 includes providers for Microsoft networks and for Novell NetWare networks. Other network vendors may supply providers for their networks.

network transport   This can be a particular layer of the OSI Reference Model between the Network layer and the Session layer, or the protocol used between this layer on two different computers on a network.

New Technology File System (NTFS)   The native file system used by Windows NT 4.0, which supplies file and directory security, sector sparing, compression, and other performance characteristics.

NIC   (see network interface card)

NIS   (see Network Information Service)

NOS   (see network operating system)

NTFS   (see Windows NT File System)

object   A particular instance of a class. Most of the internal data structures in Windows NT 4.0 are objects.

object linking and embedding (OLE)   The specification that details the implementation of Windows objects, and the interprocess communication that supports them.

OCR   (see Optical Character Recognition)

OEM   (see original equipment manufacturer)

OLE   (see object linking and embedding)

Open Systems Interconnect (OSI)   The networking architecture reference model created by the ISO.

operating system (OS)   The software that provides an interface between a user or application and the computer hardware. Operating system services usually include memory and resource management, I/O services, and file handling. Examples include Windows NT 4.0, Windows NT, and UNIX.

Optical Character Recognition (OCR)   A technology used to generate editable text from a graphic image.

original equipment manufacturer (OEM)   A company that manufactures hardware that needs an operating system. Software that is sold by Microsoft to OEMs includes only the operating system versions that are preloaded on computers before they are sold.

OS   (see operating system)

OSI   (see Open Systems Interconnect)

PAB   (see Personal Address Book)

packet   A transmission unit of fixed maximum size that consists of binary information representing data, addressing information, and error-correction information, created by the Data Link layer.

page   A unit of memory used by the system to manage memory. The size of a page is computer dependent (the Intel 486 computer, and therefore Windows NT 4.0, uses 4KB pages).

page map   An internal data structure used by the system to keep track of the mapping between the pages in a process's virtual address space and the corresponding pages in physical memory.

paged pool   The portion of system memory that can be paged to disk.

paging file   A storage file (`pagefile.sys`) the system uses to hold pages of memory swapped out of RAM. Also known as a *swap file.*

parity   Refers to an error-checking procedure in which the number of 1s must always be the same (either even or odd) for each group of bits transmitted without error. Also used in the main RAM system of a computer to verify the validity of data contained in RAM.

partition   A portion of a physical disk that functions as though it were a physically separate unit. (see also system partition)

partition table   Contains entries showing the start and end points of each of the primary partitions on the disk. The partition table can hold four entries.

password   A security measure used to restrict access to computer systems. A password is a unique string of characters that must be provided before a logon or an access is authorized.

path   The location of a file or directory. The path describes the location in relation to the root directory or the current directory—for example, `C:\WINNT\System32`. A path is also a graphic object that represents one or more shapes.

PCI   (see Peripheral Component Interconnect)

PCMCIA   (see Personal Computer Memory Card International Association)

performance monitoring   The process of determining the system resources an application uses, such as processor time and memory. Done with the Windows NT 4.0 Performance Monitor.

Peripheral Component Interconnect (PCI)   The local bus being promoted as the successor to VL. This type of device is used in most Intel Pentium computers and in the Apple PowerPC Macintosh.

persistent connection   A network connection that is restored automatically when the user logs on. In Windows NT 4.0, persistent connections are created by enabling the Reconnect at Logon check box.

Personal Address Book (PAB)   One of the information services provided with the Microsoft Exchange client included with Windows NT 4.0. The PAB is used to store the names and email addresses of people you correspond with.

Personal Computer Memory Card International Association (PCMCIA) The industry association of manufacturers of credit card–sized adapter cards (PC cards).

PIF   (see program information file)

pixel   *Picture element.* A dot that represents the smallest graphic unit of measurement on a screen. The actual size of a pixel is screen dependent and varies according to the size of the screen and the resolution being used. (Also known as *pel.)*

platform   The hardware and software required for an application to run.

Plug and Play   A computer industry specification intended to ease the process of configuring hardware.

Plug and Play BIOS   A BIOS with responsibility for configuring plug-and-play cards and system board devices during system powerup. Provides runtime configuration services for system board devices after startup.

p-node   A NetBIOS implementation that uses point-to-point communications with a name server to resolve names as IP addresses.

Point-to-Point Protocol (PPP)   The industry standard that is implemented in

Dial-Up Networking. PPP is a line protocol used to connect to remote networking services, including Internet service providers. Prior to the introduction of PPP, another line protocol, *Serial Line Internet Protocol* (SLIP), was used.

pointer   The arrow-shaped cursor onscreen that follows the movement of a mouse (or other pointing device) and indicates which area of the screen will be affected after you press the mouse button. The pointer may change shape during certain tasks.

port   The socket to which you connect the cable for a peripheral device. (see also I/O address)

port ID   The method *Transmission Control Protocol* (TCP) and *User Datagram Protocol* (UDP) use to specify which application running on the system is sending or receiving the data.

Postoffice   The message store used by Microsoft Mail to hold the mail messages. It exists only as a structure of directories on disk and does not contain any active components.

PostScript   A page-description language, developed by Adobe Systems, Inc., that offers flexible font capability and high-quality graphics. PostScript uses English-like commands to control page layout and to load and scale fonts.

PPP   (see Point-to-Point Protocol)

preemptive multitasking   A multitasking technique that breaks time up into time slices, during which the operating system allows a particular program thread to run. The operating system can interrupt any running thread at any time. Preemptive multitasking usually results in the best use of CPU time and overall better perceived throughput. (see also cooperative multitasking)

primary partition   A portion of a physical disk that can be marked for use by an operating system. Each physical disk can have up to four primary partitions (or up to three, if an extended partition is present). A primary partition cannot be subpartitioned.

print device   The actual hardware device that produces printed output.

print monitor   Keeps track of printers and print devices. Responsible for transferring information from the print driver to the printing device, including any necessary flow control.

print provider   A software component that allows the client to print to a network printer. Windows NT 4.0 includes print providers for Microsoft networks and Novell networks.

printer driver   The component that translates *graphics device interface* (GDI) objects into printer commands.

printer fonts   Fonts that are built into your printer.

priority class   A process priority category (high, normal, or idle) used to determine the scheduling priorities of a process's

threads. Each priority class has five levels. (see also thread)

private memory   Memory owned by a process and not accessible by other processes.

privileged instruction   Processor-privileged instructions have access to system memory and the hardware. Privileged instructions can be executed only by Ring 0 components.

process   The virtual address space, code, data, and other operating system resources (such as files, pipes, and synchronization objects) that make up an executing application. In addition to resources, a process contains at least one thread that executes the process's code.

profile   A set of data describing a particular configuration of a computer. This information can describe a user's preferences (user profile) or the hardware configuration. Profiles usually are stored in the Registry; for example, the key HKEY_USERS contains the profiles for the various users of the computer.

program file   A file that starts an application or program. A program file has an .EXE, .PIF, .COM, or .BAT filename extension.

program information file (PIF) Windows NT 4.0 stores information about how to configure the virtual machine for running MS-DOS applications in PIF files.

programmable read-only memory (PROM)   A type of integrated circuit generally used to store a computer's BIOS.

PROM chips, once programmed, can only be read from, not written to.

PROM (see programmable read-only memory)

properties In Windows NT 4.0, the dialog boxes that are used to configure a particular object.

protocol A set of rules and conventions by which two computers pass messages across a network. Protocols are used between instances of a particular layer on each computer. Windows NT 4.0 includes NetBEUI, TCP/IP, and IPX/SPX–compatible protocols. (see also communications protocol)

provider The component that enables Windows NT 4.0 to communicate with the network. Windows NT 4.0 includes providers for Microsoft and Novell networks.

RAM (see random-access memory)

random-access memory (RAM)
The RAM memory in a computer is the computer's main memory, where programs and data are stored while the program is running. Information stored in RAM is lost when the computer is turned off.

read-only A device, document, or file is read-only if you are able to view it but are not permitted to make changes to it.

read-write A device, document, or file is read-write if you can view it and make changes to it.

reboot You reboot to restart a computer. To reboot a Windows NT 4.0 computer,

click the Start button, choose Shut Down, and then choose Restart the Computer.

redirector The networking component that intercepts file I/O requests and translates them into network requests. Redirectors (also called *network clients)* are implemented as installable file system drivers in Windows NT 4.0.

REG_BINARY A data type for Registry value entries that designates binary data.

REG_DWORD A data type for Registry value entries that designates data represented by a number that is 4 bytes long.

REG_SZ A data type for Registry value entries that designates a data string that usually represents human-readable text.

Registry Windows NT 4.0's and Windows NT's binary system configuration database.

Registry Editor (REGEDT32.EXE) A utility supplied with Windows NT 4.0 that enables users to view and edit Registry keys and values.

Registry key A Registry entry that can contain other Registry entries.

Remote Access Service (RAS)
A Windows NT Executive Service that provides remote networking access to the Windows NT Enterprise for telecommuters, remote users, system administrators, and home users. (see also Dial-Up Networking)

remote administration The process of administrating one computer from another computer across a network.

remote initiation program load (RIPL)
A technique that enables a workstation to boot by using an image file on a network server instead of a disk.

Remote Procedure Call (RPC)   An industry-standard method of interprocess communication across a network. Used by many administration tools.

Requests for Comments (RFCs)
The official documents of the Internet Engineering Task Force that specify the details for protocols included in the TCP/IP family.

requirements   The conceptual design and functional description of a software product and any associated materials. Requirements describe the features, user interface, documentation, and other functions the product will provide.

resource   Windows resources include icons, cursors, menus, dialog boxes, bitmaps, fonts, keyboard-accelerator tables, message-table entries, string-table entries, version data, and user-defined data. The resources used by an application are part of the system or private resources stored in the application's program file. A resource also is a part of a computer system that can be assigned to a running process, such as a disk drive or memory segment.

RFCs   (see Requests for Comments)

RIP   (see Routing Information Protocol)

RIPL   (see remote initiation program load)

ROM   (see read-only)

router   A computer with two or more network adapters, each attached to a different subnet. The router forwards packets on a subnet to the subnet to which those packets are addressed.

routing   The process of forwarding packets until they reach their destination.

Routing Information Protocol (RIP)
A protocol that supports dynamic routing. Used between routers.

RPC   (see Remote Procedure Call)

RPC server   The program or computer that processes Remote Procedure Calls from a client.

SAM Database   The Registry database that contains the user and group account information, as well as user account policies. It is managed by the User Manager or User Manager for Domains utility.

screen buffer   A memory buffer that holds a representation of an MS-DOS virtual machine's logical screen.

screen saver   Pictures or patterns that appear on your screen when your computer has not been used for a certain amount of time. Originally intended to protect the monitor from damage, modern screen savers are used mostly for their entertainment value.

scroll   To move through text or graphics (up, down, left, or right) to see parts of the file that cannot fit onscreen.

scroll arrow   An arrow on either end of a scrollbar that you use to scroll through the contents of the window or list box.

scroll box   In a scrollbar, a small box that shows where the information currently visible is relative to the contents of the entire window.

scrollbar   A bar that appears at the right and bottom edge of a window or list box in which the contents are not completely visible. The scrollbar consists of two scroll arrows and a scroll box, which you use to scroll through the contents.

SCSI   (see small computer system interface)

security ID (SID)   The unique, randomly generated, alphanumeric identifier assigned by Windows NT when a new user, group, trust, or other security object is created.

sequence number   Sequence numbers are used by a receiving node to properly order packets.

Serial Line Internet Protocol (SLIP)
The predecessor to *Point-to-Point Protocol* (PPP), SLIP is a line protocol supporting TCP/IP over a modem connection. SLIP support is provided for Windows NT 4.0. (see also Point-to-Point Protocol)

server   A computer or application that provides shared resources to clients across a network. Resources include files and directories, printers, fax modems, and network database services. (see also client)

server message block (SMB)   A block of data that contains a work request from a workstation to a server, or that contains the response from the server to the

workstation. SMBs are used for all network communications in a Microsoft network.

Server Service   An Executive Service that makes resources available to the workgroup or domain for file, print, and other Remote Procedure Call services.

service   A process that performs a specific system function and often provides an *Application Programming Interface* (API) for other processes to call. Windows NT 4.0 services Computer Browser, Server, and Workstation.

session   A layer of the OSI Reference Model that performs name recognition and the functions needed to enable two applications to communicate over the network. A session is also a communications channel established by the Session layer.

share   In Microsoft networking, the process of making resources, such as directories and printers, available for network users.

share name   The name that a shared resource is accessed by on the network.

shared directory   A directory that has been shared so that network users can connect to it.

shared memory   Memory that two or more processes can read from and write to.

shared network directory   (see shared directory)

shared resource   Any device, data, or program used by more than one other device or program. Windows NT 4.0 can share directories and printers.

sharepoint A shared network resource, or the name that one is known by.

shell The part of an operating system that the user interacts with. The Windows NT 4.0 shell is Windows Explorer.

shortcut key A combination of keys that results in the execution of a program or the selection of an option, without going through a menu.

shut down The process of properly terminating all running programs, flushing caches, and preparing the system to be powered off.

signaled One of the possible states of a mutex.

SIMM (see Single In-Line Memory Module)

Simple Mail Transfer Protocol (SMTP) The Application layer protocol that supports messaging functions over the Internet.

Simple Network Management Protocol (SNMP) A standard protocol for the management of network components. Windows NT 4.0 includes an SNMP agent.

Single In-Line Memory Module (SIMM) One of the types of RAM chips.

SLIP (see Serial Line Internet Protocol)

small computer system interface (SCSI) Pronounced "scuzzy," a standard for connecting multiple devices to a computer system. SCSI devices are connected in a daisy chain, which can have up to seven devices (plus a controller) on it.

SMB (see server message block)

SMTP (see Simple Mail Transfer Protocol)

SNMP (see Simple Network Management Protocol)

socket A channel used for incoming and outgoing data defined by the Windows Sockets API. Usually used with TCP/IP.

socket services The protected-mode VxD that manages PCMCIA sockets adapter hardware. It provides a protected-mode PCMCIA Socket Services 2.x interface for use by Card Services. A socket services driver is required for each socket adapter.

source directory The directory where files in a copy or move operation start out in.

spooler A scheduler for the printing process. It coordinates activity among other components of the print model and schedules all print jobs arriving at the print server.

static VxD A *virtual device driver* (VxD) that is loaded at system startup.

string A sequence of characters representing human-readable text.

subdirectory A directory within a directory.

subkey A Registry key contained within another Registry key. All Registry keys are subkeys, except for the six top-level keys.

subnet On the Internet, any lower network that is part of the logical network identified by the network ID.

subnet mask A 32-bit value used to distinguish the network ID portion of the IP address from the host ID.

swap file   A special file on your hard disk used to hold memory pages that are swapped out of RAM. Also called a *paging file.*

syntax   The order in which you must type a command and the elements that follow the command.

system directory   The directory that contains the Windows DLLs and drivers. Usually `c:windows\system`.

system disk   A disk that contains the files necessary to start an operating system.

system partition   The volume that contains the hardware-specific files needed to load Windows NT 4.0.

TAPI   (see Telephony Application Programming Interface)

TCP   (see Transmission Control Protocol)

TCP/IP transport   *Transmission Control Protocol/Internet Protocol.* The primary *wide-area network* (WAN) transport protocol used on the worldwide Internet, which is a worldwide internetwork of universities, research laboratories, government and military installations, organizations, and corporations. TCP/IP includes standards for how computers communicate and conventions for connecting networks and routing traffic, as well as specifications for utilities.

TDI   (see Transport Driver Interface)

Telephony Application Programming Interface (TAPI)   An API that enables applications to control modems and telephony equipment in a device-independent manner. TAPI routes application function calls to the appropriate service provider DLL for a modem.

Telnet   The Application layer protocol that provides virtual terminal service on TCP/IP networks.

terminate-and-stay-resident (TSR)   A technique used by MS-DOS applications that allows more than one program to be loaded at a time.

text file   A file containing only ASCII letters, numbers, and symbols, without any formatting information except for carriage return/linefeeds.

thread   The basic entity to which the operating system allocates CPU time. A thread can execute any part of the application's code, including a part currently being executed by another thread (reentrancy). Threads cannot own resources; instead, they use the resources of the process they belong to.

thread local storage   A storage method in which an index can be used by multiple threads of the same process to store and retrieve a different value for each thread. (see also thread)

thunking   The transformation between 16-bit and 32-bit formats, which is carried out by a separate layer in the virtual DOS machine.

timeout   If a device is not performing a task, the amount of time the computer should wait before detecting it as an error.

toolbar   A frame containing a series of shortcut buttons providing quick access to commands. Usually located below the menu bar, although many applications provide *dockable* toolbars, which may be moved to different locations onscreen.

Transmission Control Protocol (TCP)
A connection-based protocol responsible for breaking data into packets, which the *Internet Protocol* (IP) sends over the network. TCP provides a reliable, sequenced communication stream for internetwork communication.

Transmission Control Protocol/Internet Protocol (TCP/IP)   The primary WAN used on the worldwide Internet, which is a worldwide internetwork of universities, research laboratories, military installations, organizations, and corporations. TCP/IP includes standards for how computers communicate and conventions for connecting networks and routing traffic, as well as specifications for utilities.

Transport Driver Interface (TDI)
The interface between the Session layer and the Network layer, used by network redirectors and servers to send network-bound requests to network transport drivers.

transport protocol   Defines how data should be presented to the next receiving layer in the networking model and packages the data accordingly. It passes data to the network adapter card driver through the NDIS Interface, and to the redirector through the Transport Driver Interface.

TrueType fonts   Fonts that are scalable and sometimes generated as bitmaps or soft fonts, depending on the capabilities of your printer. TrueType fonts can be sized to any height, and they print exactly as they appear onscreen. TrueType fonts are stored as a collection of line and curve commands, along with a collection of hints that are used to adjust the shapes when the font is scaled.

trust relationship   A security relationship between two domains in which the resource domain "trusts" the user of a trusted account domain to use its resources. Users and groups from a trusted domain can be given access permissions to resources in a trusting domain.

TSR   (see terminate-and-stay-resident)

UDP   (see User Datagram Protocol)

UNC   (see Universal Naming Convention)

Unimodem   The universal modem driver used by TAPI to communicate with modems. It uses modem description files to control its interaction with VCOMM.

uninterruptible power supply (UPS)
A battery-operated power supply connected to a computer to keep the system running during a power failure.

Universal Naming Convention (UNC)
A naming convention, including a server name and share name, used to give a unique name to files on a network. The format follows:

```
\\servername\sharename\path\filename
```

UPS   (see uninterruptible power supply)

UPS Service   A software component that monitors an uninterruptible power supply and shuts down the computer gracefully when the line power fails and the UPS battery is running down.

usability   A determination of how well users can accomplish tasks using a software product. Usability considers the characteristics of a product, such as software, manuals, tutorials, help, and so on.

user account   Refers to all the information that identifies a user to Windows NT 4.0, including username and password, group membership, and rights and permissions.

User Datagram Protocol (UDP)
The Transport layer protocol offering a connectionless mode transport service in the Internet suite of protocols. (see also Transmission Control Protocol)

username   A unique name identifying a user account in Windows NT 4.0. Usernames must be unique and cannot be the same as another username, workgroup, or domain name.

value entry   A parameter under a key or subkey in the Registry. A value entry has three components: name, type, and value. The value component can be a string, binary data, or a DWORD.

VDM   (see virtual DOS machine)

VFAT   (see virtual file allocation table)

virtual DOS machine (VDM)   Provides a complete MS-DOS environment and a character-based window in which to run an MS-DOS–based application. Every MS-DOS application runs in its own VDM.

virtual file allocation table (VFAT)
(see file allocation table)

virtual machine (VM)   An environment created by the operating system in memory. By using virtual machines, the application developer can write programs that behave as though they own the entire computer. For example, this leaves the job of sorting out which application is receiving keyboard input at the moment to Windows NT 4.0.

virtual memory   The technique by which Windows NT 4.0 uses hard drive space to increase the amount of memory available for running programs.

visual editing   The capability to edit an embedded object in place, without opening it in its own window. Implemented by OLE.

VL VESA   Local bus standard for a bus that allows high-speed connections to peripherals. Preceded the PCI specification. Because of limitations in the specification, generally used only to connect video adapters to the system.

VM   (see virtual machine)

volume   A partition that has been formatted for use by the file system.

VxD   *Virtual device driver.* The x represents the type of device—for example, a virtual device driver for a display is a VDD, and a virtual device driver for a printer is a VPD.

wildcard   A character that represents one or more characters, such as in a file specification. You can use the question mark (?) wildcard to represent any single character, and the asterisk (*) wildcard to represent any character or group of characters that might match that position in other filenames.

Win32 API   The 32-bit Application Programming Interface used to write 32-bit Windows-based applications. Provides access to the operating system and other functions.

window handle   A 32-bit value that uniquely identifies a window to Windows NT 4.0.

window name   A text string that identifies a window for the user.

Windows Internet Name Service (WINS) A name-resolution service that resolves Windows networking computer names to IP addresses in a routed environment. A WINS server handles name registrations, queries, and releases.

Windows NT   The portable, secure, 32-bit preemptive multitasking member of the Microsoft Windows operating system family. Windows NT Server provides centralized management and security, advanced fault tolerance, and additional connectivity. Windows NT Workstation provides operating system and networking functionality for computers without centralized management.

Windows NT File System (NTFS) The native file system used by Windows NT. The only other usable file system is FAT. Windows NT 4.0 can detect, but not use, HPFS partitions.

WINS   (see Windows Internet Name Service)

wizard   A Windows NT 4.0 tool that asks you questions and performs a system action according to your answers. You can use the Add Printer Wizard, for example, to add new printer drivers or connect to an existing network printer.

workgroup   A collection of computers that are grouped for viewing purposes or resource sharing, but do not share security information. Each workgroup is identified by a unique name. (see also domain)

Workstation Service   The Windows NT computer's redirector. It redirects requests for network resources to the appropriate protocol and network card for access to the server computer.

WYSIWYG   *What You See Is What You Get.*

X.25   A connection-oriented network facility.

x86-based computer   A computer using a microprocessor equivalent to an Intel 80386 or higher chip. Only x86-based computers can run Windows NT 4.0.

X.121   The addressing format used by X.25 base networks.

X.400   An international messaging standard used in electronic mail systems.

XModem/CRC   A communications protocol for transmitting binary files that uses a *cyclic redundancy check* (CRC) to detect any transmission errors. Both computers must be set to transmit and receive 8 data bits per character.

Certification Process

In addition to a resource like this book, this list of tasks tells you what you need to know to get on with the certification process.

Getting Started

After you decide to start the certification process, you should use this list as a guideline for getting started:

1. Get the latest Microsoft Certification track information and requirements from http://www.microsoft.com/train_cert.

2. Use the certification track information to determine your certification path. Be careful to avoid basing your MCSE status on exams that will retire soon.

3. Take the Assessment Exam located on the CD-ROM that accompanies this book to determine your competency level. Run through the test engine as many times as possible until you know the material backward and forward.

Getting Prepared

Getting started is one thing, but getting prepared to take the certification exam is a rather difficult process. The following guidelines will help you prepare for the exam:

1. Gain experience with Windows NT 4.0. No matter how much studying you do, nothing can prepare you as well as hands-on experience with the product.

2. Review the section "Testing Tips" in Appendix C.

3. Practice with as many test engines as you can find. Many vendors offer samples on their Web sites.

4. Search the Web for braindumps and other sites where others in the process of certification share their knowledge. *Braindumps* are files that are written by people as soon as they finish an exam—in other words, they dump what is in the brain after seeing the exam. These are useful pointers to what you need to study.

Getting Certified

Call Sylvan Prometric at 800-755-EXAM or visit its Web site at `www.2test.com` to schedule your exam at a location near you. When you register, you can find out how much time currently is allotted for the exam as well as center availability. In most cases, you just need to schedule one day before the exam. At busy testing sites, however, you will want to register a week or so before you expect to take the exam to block off the time.

Getting Benefits

Microsoft will send your certification kit approximately two to four weeks after you pass the exam. This kit qualifies you to become a Microsoft Certified Professional. You can find the latest benefits at `http://www.microsoft.com/mcp`. The benefits differ per certification but currently consist of the following:

	MCP	MCSE	MCSD
Certificate	X	X	X
Wallet Card	X	X	X
Lapel Pin	X	X	X
Subscription to `Microsoft Certified Professional Magazine`	X	X	X
Access to secure portion of Web site	X	X	X

	MCP	MCSE	MCSD
One-year subscription to TechNet Plus		X	X
Subscription to MSDN Online	X	X	
One-year subscription to MSDN CDs			X

To quote from Microsoft, every certification also includes "invitations to Microsoft conferences, technical training sessions, and special events."

Testing Tips

You've mastered the required tasks to take the exam. After reviewing and re-reviewing the exam objectives, you're confident that you have the skills specified in the exam objectives. You're ready to perform at the highest cognitive level. And it's time to head for the testing center. This appendix covers some tips and tricks to remember.

Before the Test

Make sure you take care of the following items:

- Wear comfortable clothing. You want to focus on the exam, not on a tight shirt collar or a pinching pair of shoes.

- Allow plenty of travel time. Get to the testing center 10 or 15 minutes early; nothing's worse than rushing in at the last minute. Give yourself time to relax.

- If you've never been to the testing center before, make a trial run a few days before to make sure that you know the route to the center.

- Carry with you at least two forms of identification, including one photo ID (such as a driver's license or company security ID). You will have to show these IDs before you can take the exam.

Remember that the exams are closed book. The use of laptop computers, notes, or other printed materials is not permitted during the exam session.

At the test center, you'll be asked to sign in. The test administrator will give you a Testing Center Regulations form that explains the rules that govern the examination. You will be asked to sign the form to indicate that you understand and will comply with its stipulations.

When the administrator shows you to your test computer, make sure that

■ The testing tool starts up and displays the correct exam. If a tutorial for using the instrument is available, you should be allowed the time to take it.

Key Concept

If you have any special needs, such as reconfiguring the mouse buttons for a left-handed user, you should inquire about them when you register for the exam with Sylvan Prometric. Special configurations are not possible at all sites, so you should not assume that you will be permitted to make any modifications to the equipment setup and configuration. **Site administrators are *not* permitted to make modifications without prior instructions from Sylvan.**

■ You have a supply of scratch paper for use during the exam. (The administrator collects all scratch paper and notes made during the exam before you leave the center.) Some centers now provide wipe-off boards and magic markers to use instead of paper. Always ask for paper and a pencil—wipe-off boards and markers have a tendency to smear and become unreadable. You are not permitted to make any kind of notes to take with you, due to exam security.

■ Find out whether your exam includes additional materials or exhibits. If any exhibits are required for your exam, the test administrator provides you with them before you begin the exam and collects them from you at the end of the exam.

■ The administrator tells you what to do when you complete the exam.

■ You get answers to any and all of your questions or concerns before the exam begins.

■ Write down all you can remember for the test as soon as you sit down at your station and before you begin. The time does not start for the test until you actually log on and walk through a few screens. Sitting at the desk itself does not start the time.

As a Microsoft Certification examination candidate, you are entitled to the best support and environment possible for your exam. If you experience any problems on the day of the exam, inform the Sylvan Prometric test administrator immediately.

During the Test

The testing software lets you move forward and backward through the items, so you can implement a strategic approach to the test:

1. Go through all the items, answering the easy questions first. Then go back and spend time on the harder questions. Microsoft guarantees that there are no trick questions. The correct answer is always among the list of choices. Also, test questions can be marked and returned to later. If you encounter a question that you are not sure about, mark it and go back to it later. Chances are that you may gain some insight into how to answer the marked question from another subsequent question.

2. Eliminate the obviously incorrect answer first to clear away the clutter and simplify your choices.

3. Answer all the questions. You aren't penalized for guessing, so it can't hurt.

4. Don't rush. Haste makes waste (or substitute the cliché of your choice).

After the Test

After you complete an exam,

- The testing tool gives you immediate online notification of your pass or fail status, except for beta exams. Because of the beta process, your results for a beta exam are mailed to you approximately six to eight weeks after the exam.

- The administrator gives you a printed Examination Score Report indicating your pass or fail status and your exam results by section.

- Your test scores are forwarded to Microsoft within five working days after you take the test. If you pass the exam, you receive confirmation from Microsoft within two to four weeks.

- Make a copy of the test results; never give the original to anyone. The original has an official stamp from the testing center and is the only proof you have of your score, should you need to correct anything.

If you don't pass a certification exam,

- Review your individual section scores, if they are available, noting areas where you must improve your score. The section titles in your exam report generally correspond to specific groups of exam objectives. This section does not appear on adaptive-format exams but is present on all others.

- Review the exam information in this book; then get the latest Exam Preparation Guide and focus on the topic areas that need strengthening.

- Intensify your efforts to get real-world, hands-on experience and practice with Windows NT 4.0.

- Try taking one or more of the approved training courses through a *Certified Training and Educational Center* (CTEC).

- Review the suggested readings listed in Appendix D.

- Call Sylvan Prometric to register for, pay for, and schedule the exam again. You may make your second attempt at any time. If you fail your second attempt, however, you must wait 14 days between all successive attempts. This regulation prevents you from passing merely by seeing the questions enough times to memorize them.

Alternate Resources

Que Corporation and Macmillan Computer Publishing (MCP) offer a wide variety of technical books for all levels of users. The following are some recommended titles, in alphabetical order, that can provide you with additional information on many of the exam topics and objectives.

To order any books from Que Corporation or other imprints of Macmillan Computer Publishing (Sams, Ziff-Davis Press, and others), call 800-428-5331, visit Macmillan's Information SuperLibrary on the World Wide Web (http://www.mcp.com), or check your local bookseller.

MCSE Fast Track: Networking Essentials

Author: Emmett Dulaney

ISBN: 1-56205-939-4

MCSE Fast Track: Windows NT Server 4

Author: Emmett Dulaney

ISBN: 1-56205-935-1

MCSE Fast Track: Windows NT Server 4 Enterprise

Author: Emmett Dulaney

ISBN: 1-56205-940-8

MCSE Fast Track: Windows NT Workstation 4
Author: Emmett Dulaney

ISBN: 1-56205-938-6

Platinum Edition Using Windows NT Server 4
Author: Jerry Honeycutt

ISBN: 0-7897-1436-1

Special Edition Using Windows NT Server 4.0
Author: Roger Jennings

ISBN: 0-7897-1388-8

Windows NT 4.0 Installation and Configuration Handbook
Author: Jim Boyce

ISBN: 0-7897-0818-3

Windows NT Server 4 Administrator's Desk Reference
Author: John Enck

ISBN: 0-7897-1271-7

Windows NT Server 4 Advanced Technical Reference
Author: John Enck

ISBN: 0-7897-1167-2

Windows NT Workstation 4 Advanced Technical Reference
Author: Paul Sanna

ISBN: 0-7897-0863-9

Using the CD-ROM

The tests on this CD-ROM consist of performance-based questions. This means that instead of asking you what function an item would fulfill (a knowledge-based question), you are presented with a situation and asked for an answer that shows your ability to solve the problem.

Using the Self-Test Software

The program consists of three main test structures:

- **Non-randomized test:** This test is useful when you first begin study and want to run through sections that you have read to make certain you understand them thoroughly before continuing on.

- **Adaptive test:** This test emulates an adaptive exam and randomly pulls questions from the database. You are asked 15 questions of varying difficulty. If you successfully answer a question, the next question you are asked is of a higher difficulty, as it tries to "adapt" to your skill level. If you miss a question, the next one asked is easier, as it, again, tries to "adapt" to your skill level. This tool is useful for becoming familiar with the adaptive format, but not for actual study, because the number of questions presented is so few.

- **Random/mastery test:** This is the big one. This test is different from the two others in the sense that questions are pulled from all objective areas. You are asked 50 questions, and the test simulates the exam situation. At the conclusion of the exam, you get your overall score and the chance to view all wrong answers. You also can print a report card featuring your test results.

All test questions are of the type currently in use by Microsoft on this exam. In some cases, that consists solely of multiple-choice questions offering four possible answers. In other cases, there are exhibits, scenarios, and other question types.

Equipment Requirements

To run the self-test software, you must have at least the following equipment:

- IBM-compatible Pentium
- Microsoft Windows 95, 98, or NT 4.0 (Workstation or Server)
- 16MB of RAM
- 256-color display adapter, configured as an 800×600 display or larger
- Double-speed CD-ROM drive
- Approximately 5MB free disk space

Running the Self-Test Software

Access the SETUP.EXE file, and the self-test software installs on your hard drive from the CD-ROM and runs directly from there. After you follow the simple installation steps, you will find the software very intuitive and self-explanatory.

Lab Exercises

Getting Started

The best way to become familiar with the installation process is to install Windows NT 4.0 Server a few times and pay close attention to what is happening. Later in these exercises, you will need at least two computers running Windows NT 4.0 Server to understand the way NT handles access security. If you have two computers available, install one using the Custom option and the other using Typical. The following preparation checklist will help you double-check your hardware configuration before beginning setup. Then follow the process outlined in Chapter 2, "Understanding Microsoft Windows NT 4.0." You'll get specific instructions in the steps that follow. As you proceed with installation, be sure to read each screen for your own edification.

Preparation Checklist

- Read all NT documentation files.
- Assess system requirements.
- Assess hardware compatibility. Refer to the hardware compatibility list.
- Assess necessary drivers and configuration data:

    Video   Display type, adapter, and chipset type

    Network   Card type, *interrupt request* (IRQ), I/O address, *direct memory access* (DMA), connector, and so on

SCSI controller   Adapter and chipset type, IRQ, bus type

Sound/Media   IRQ, I/O Address, DMA

I/O ports   IRQ, I/O address, DMA

Modems   Port, IRQ, I/O address, modem type

Before installing, back up your current configuration and data files. Make sure you have the answers to all these questions:

- What type of initial setup will you perform? (You may need three blank, formatted disks before running setup.)
- Where are the installation files located?
- On what partition will NT system files be installed?
- What file system will you install?
- Will you create an *Emergency Repair Disk* (ERD)? (If so, you need one blank disk available before running setup.)
- What is your installation CD key?
- What is the unique computer name?
- What is the workgroup or domain name the computer joins?
- What is the network connection data: IP addresses, *Internetworking Packet Exchange* (IPX) card numbers, and so on?
- In what time zone is the computer located?

Recommended Computer Configuration

- At least two 486/66 or higher computers with 32MB of RAM.
- Working network connection between these computers.
- If you are part of a larger network, try to have your computer isolated on its own network. If this is not possible, be sure to inform your network administrator of what you intend to do so that both of you can take all necessary precautions to preserve security on the network.
- *File allocation table* (FAT) formatted C: drive primary partition.
- At least 300MB free space on same or other drive.
- Two or more physical disk drives to demonstrate disk striping.
- CD-ROM drive for installation.
- Optional: Four, blank formatted disks—three for startup disks and one for an ERD.
- One printer attached to either computer.

Exercise 1: Setting Up Your Computers for This Book's Labs

1. If you have your own installation CD-ROM and a compatible CD-ROM, run setup from the CD-ROM. If you are accessing the installation files over the network, you first must make a connection to the installation directory. Connect as you normally would on your network, or consult with your network administrator for appropriate access.

2. If you have four formatted, blank, 3 1/2-inch disks available (three for startup disks and one for an ERD), run WINNT.EXE from the installation directory and follow the directions onscreen. If you choose not to create the startup disks, run WINNT /B.

Key Concept

If you are installing NT on a *reduced instruction set computer* (RISC)–based system, be sure to create a minimum 2MB FAT partition and a large enough system partition for NT before starting setup. Then follow the RISC-installation guidelines outlined in Chapter 3, "Windows NT Server 4.0 Setup."

3. Press Enter to install NT.

4. If you have any additional storage devices other than what NT detects, add them.

5. Verify that your basic hardware settings are correct and press Enter.

6. Create a 250MB partition out of the free space during installation, format it as FAT, and install the NT system partition there in a directory called WINNT40.

7. Let NT do an exhaustive scan of your disk drive, and then reboot the computer.

8. For your first installation, choose Custom. For your second installation, choose Typical. Read all screens as you go along. Explore all buttons. It is impossible to create an exercise for all possible permutations that you might encounter, so it is up to you to explore.

9. When prompted for the username and company name, enter your own.

10. When prompted for a computer name, use COMPUTER1 for the first installation and COMPUTER2 for the second (and so on for additional installations). Of course, you may name the computers anything you want. Future labs refer to these suggested names, however, so remember to substitute your own. If you are part of a larger network, be sure that your computer names are unique.

11. Enter student as your password just as it appears—in lowercase. Again, you may choose your own password. Just don't forget it!

12. If you receive a message regarding the floating-point error, do not choose the workaround.

13. If you have a formatted disk handy, create the ERD. Remember that you can create it later.

14. Look at all the Optional Component lists and sublists to understand your choices. Install as many additional options as you want. Install at least the recommended options that NT displays. If you are low on disk space, deselect games and other unessential accessories.

15. Let NT detect your network card, or if you have an *original equipment manufacturer* (OEM) driver disk, install your card from the disk.

16. Deselect *Transmission Control Protocol/Internet Protocol* (TCP/IP) and select *Network BIOS Extended User Interface* (NetBEUI) as your protocol. Also keep the default network services and bindings.

17. You will create a workgroup called STUDYGROUP. As before, you can call the workgroup anything you want, but you must remember what you called it for future exercises and make sure that it does not conflict with any other workgroups on your network.

18. Enter the appropriate date and time zone values.

19. Select the appropriate settings for your monitor.

20. Complete the installation, and let NT restart the system.

Exercise 2 (Optional)

Follow the instructions in the "Troubleshooting Installation and Setup" section of Chapter 3, "Windows NT Server 4.0 Setup," and run the NTHQ utility to see how it works. Log and print a report.

Chapter 4: Configuring Windows NT Server 4.0

There is no better way to get acquainted with the new NT 4.0 interface than by trying out the new features, exploring *all* object properties sheets, and having fun. Here is an exercise that uses the more significant features of the interface. You will need one blank, formatted disk.

Exercise 1: Navigating the Interface Taskbar, Explorer, Shortcuts, and Briefcase

1. Start Windows Help and select the Contents tab.

2. From the topic list, choose How To, Change Windows Settings, Change Taskbar Settings. Indicate that you do not want the taskbar to appear on top of all other windows.

3. Open My Computer. Choose View, Options and choose the option that replaces previous windows.

4. Right-click the A: drive icon and drag it to the desktop. Choose Create Shortcut from the pop-up menu.

5. Double-click the C: drive icon. Choose File, New and create a new folder called LAB2.

6. Choose Start, Programs, Accessories and start the WordPad program.

7. Create a file called MEMO.DOC with the following text:

   This is the first draft of my memo.

8. Choose File, Save As. Use the browse feature to find the LAB2 directory and save the MEMO.DOC file there. Minimize WordPad.

9. Open Windows Explorer and select the LAB2 directory. Right-click the file and drag it to the Briefcase icon on the desktop. Choose Create Synch Copy from the pop-up menu.

10. Insert the formatted, blank disk into the A: drive.

11. Drag the Briefcase from the desktop to the A: drive shortcut icon.

12. Move your mouse to the bottom of the screen until the taskbar appears. Select WordPad. Open the MEMO.DOC file in the Briefcase on the A: drive. Add the text

    This is the second draft of my memo.

    and save the file.

13. Open the A: drive shortcut icon and drag the Briefcase back to the desktop.

14. Open the Briefcase and choose Briefcase, Update. Notice that the window displays the documents that have changed and suggests that you update the older document.

15. Choose Update All. Close the Briefcase.

16. Start WordPad and open the MEMO.DOC file in the LAB2 directory. Verify that the file has been updated.

17. Start the Find program. On the Advanced tab, search for all files on the C: drive containing the text "first draft." In the results window, verify that both copies appear.

Exercise 2: Using the Control Panel to Configure Windows NT

1. Use the Control Panel to modify the wallpaper on your computer to LEAVES.BMP, and change your WAIT mouse pointer to the animated cursor BANANA.ANI. Note that these changes take effect immediately.

APP
F

2. Close the Control Panel and open the Registry Editor by choosing Start, <u>R</u>un and entering REGEDT32.EXE.

3. Click in the HKEY_CURRENT_USER subtree window to make it active.

4. Choose <u>V</u>iew, <u>F</u>ind Key and search for "cursors." When the Cursors key is found, close the Find dialog box and select the Cursors key. Notice that the WAIT cursor parameter on the right side of the window shows that BANANA.ANI has been selected.

5. Change the WAIT value from BANANA.ANI to HORSE.ANI by double-clicking the WAIT value and typing HORSE.ANI (using the appropriate path).

6. Choose <u>E</u>dit, Add <u>V</u>alue and enter the value name APPSTARTING with a data type of REG_SZ. Choose OK and enter the filename and path to DINOSAUR.ANI.

7. Choose <u>V</u>iew, <u>F</u>ind Key again to find the WALLPAPER key. Were you able to? Recall that wallpaper is a feature of the desktop. Search for "DESKTOP."

8. Select the DESKTOP key and view the right side of the window for entries related to wallpaper. You should find two: WALLPAPER and TILEWALLPAPER.

9. Modify the WALLPAPER entry (currently leaves.bmp) to WINNT40\FURRYD~1.BMP. Check the path for this file before making the change. Hint: Use FIND.

10. Modify the TileWallpaper entry to the value 1.

11. Close the Registry. When do these changes take effect? Log off and then log back on and see whether the changes have taken effect. If not, shut down and restart.

Exercise 3: Using the Registry—Part 1

1. Open the Registry Editor.

2. Click in the HKEY_LOCAL_MACHINE subtree window to make it active.

3. Expand through the SOFTWARE hive to find the WINLOGON key:

    SOFTWARE\Microsoft\Windows NT\Current Version\Winlogon

4. Double-click the parameter Legal Notice Caption on the right side of the window and enter the caption Legal Notice.

5. Double-click the parameter Legal Notice Text and enter the following:

    Unauthorized access will be punished!

6. Choose <u>E</u>dit, Add <u>V</u>alue and enter the value name DontDisplayLastUserName with a data type of REG_SZ. Click OK and enter the value 1 for Yes.

7. Close the Registry. When do these changes take effect? Log off and then log back on and see whether the changes have taken effect. If not, shut down and restart.

Exercise 4: Using the Registry—Part 2

1. Open the Registry Editor and make the HKEY_USERS subtree window active.

2. Expand through the .DEFAULT key to find DESKTOP: .DEFAULT\Control Panel\Desktop.

3. Modify the Wallpaper entry with the value LEAVES.BMP and change the TileWallpaper entry to 1. This changes the default wallpaper that appears after booting NT.

4. Close the Registry. When do these changes take effect? Log off and then log back on and see whether the changes have taken effect. If not, shut down and restart.

Exercise 5: System Policy Editor

1. Log on to the server as Administrator.

2. Start the System Policy Editor by choosing Start, Programs, Administrative Tools, System Policy Editor.

3. If an existing NTCONFIG.POL file exists in WINNT40\SYSTEM32\REPL\IMPORT\SCRIPTS, open it. Otherwise, choose File, New Profile.

4. Choose Edit, Add User and enter your valid user account.

5. Double-click your new user icon to display the policies.

6. Select Desktop, enable the Wallpaper check box, and enter the path and filename to your favorite wallpaper in the lower part of the window (WINNT40\leaves.bmp, for example).

7. Choose System, Restrictions and enable the Disable Registry Editing Tools check box.

8. Choose Shell, Restrictions and enable the Remove Run Command from Start Menu check box and the Don't Save Settings at Exit check box.

9. Close the policy and save it as NTCONFIG.POL in the WINNT40\SYSTEM32\REPL\IMPORT\SCRIPTS subdirectory.

10. Log off and log back on as the user account whose policy you modified. Note the changes that have taken effect: The wallpaper now should be LEAVES, you should be unable to run REGEDT32, you should not have Run as a Start menu option, and any changes you make to the environment (for example, colors, cursors) will not be saved.

11. Log back on as Administrator and experiment by making further changes; or delete the policy.

APP
F

Chapter 5: Managing Users and Groups

These exercises are most helpful if you have two computers available.

Exercise 1: Creating Users and Groups

If you have two workstations, complete this exercise on both of them.

1. Using Notepad, create the following logon script called `KITE.BAT` and save it in the `WINNT40\SYSTEM32\REPL\IMPORT\SCRIPTS` subdirectory:

   ```
   @echo Welcome to the Kite Flyers network!
   @echo off
   Pause
   ```

2. Use User Manager to create the following user accounts on both workstations. Require both users to change their password when they log on (enable the User Must Change Password at Next Logon check box). In Profiles for each, enter the `KITE.BAT` logon script you created in Step 1, and enter the following home directory: `c:\users\%USERNAME%` using the drive in which you installed NT and that contains the `USERS` directory.

   New Users

Username	Full Name	Description	Password
BrownC	Chris Brown	Chairperson	password
KreskeL	Lois Kreske	Secretary General	password
BarnesD	David Barnes	Marketing Manager	password
Donovan	Donovan	MIS Manager	password

3. Create the following local group accounts:

Group Name	Description	Members	
Managers	Kite Flyers	BrownC	
Management Team	KreskeL		
		BarnesD	Donovan
Marketing	Marketing Team	BarnesD	
MIS	MIS Team	Donovan	

4. Create the following template accounts. Require users to change their passwords at the next logon. Click the Groups button, remove the users group for each, and add the corresponding group you created in Step 3 (`Sales` for `SalesTemp`, `Marketing` for `MarketingTemp`, `MIS` for `MISTemp`). Click the Profile button for each and enter the

logon script you created (kite.bat) and the following home directory:
c:\users\%USERNAME% using the drive in which you installed NT that contains the
USERS directory (use Windows Explorer to confirm it).

Username	Full Name	Description	Password
SalesTemp	Sales Template	Sales Representative	stemplate
MarketingTemp	Marketing Template	Account Manager	mtemplate
MIStemp	MIS Template	System Analyst	itemplate

5. Create the following accounts by copying the appropriate template you created in
Step 4. Notice which elements of the template account are copied (description,
password options, group and profile information) and for which you need to fill in
the username, full name, and password.

Sales

FlagL, Lois Flag, password

BarnesD, David Barnes, password

Marketing

Doggie, Doggie, password

MIS

GatesB, William Gates, password

BaileyG, George Bailey, password

6. Use Windows Explorer to confirm that the home directories for each account were
created.

Exercise 2: Managing User Profiles—Part 1

Complete this exercise from Computer1.

1. Log on as GatesB. Change the password as instructed. Modify your environment
settings by changing the screen colors, adding a wallpaper, and creating a shortcut
to Solitaire on the desktop.

2. Log off and log on again as Administrator.

3. Use Windows Explorer to find the WINNT40\PROFILES directory. Notice the new subdirectory structure for GatesB with the file NTUSER.DAT in the GATESB subdirectory.
Expand GATESB to find the Desktop subdirectory and notice the shortcut to Solitaire
located there.

APP
F

4. Find the `WINNT40\PROFILES\Default User` subdirectory. Expand it to display the `Desktop` subdirectory. Create a shortcut here for Solitaire (right-click and drag the Solitaire icon from `WINNT40\SYSTEM32`). Also, rename the `NTUSER.DAT` file in `Default User` to `NTUSER.OLD` and copy the `NTUSER.DAT` file from `GATESB`.

5. Create a new user called `PAT` with no password and no password options selected.

6. Log on as `PAT`. Notice that the Solitaire shortcut and the environment settings became part of `PAT`'s profile. This will be true not only for each new user you create, but also for any previous users who have not yet logged on for the first time and thus created their own profiles.

7. Log back on as Administrator. Use Windows Explorer to delete the `NTUSER.DAT` file from `WINNT40\PROFILES\Default User` and rename `NTUSER.OLD` back to `NTUSER.DAT`.

Exercise 3: Managing User Profiles—Part 2

1. Use Windows Explorer to create a new directory called `Profiles` in the root directory of `Computer2`. Right-click it and choose Sharing, Shared As. Then click OK. (If you do not have two computers installed, complete this exercise from the same computer and adjust the directions accordingly.)

2. On the first computer, start User Manager. Delete the account `PAT`. Create a new user account called `MEG` with no password and no password options selected. Click Profile, and in User Profile Path dialog box, enter the following: `\\Computer2\profiles\ntuser.dat`.

3. Start the System applet from the Control Panel and select the User Profiles tab. You will note an `Account Deleted` entry. This was `PAT`, which you deleted in Step 2. Select this entry, and click Delete and then Yes.

4. In the list, select the entry for `GATESB` and click Copy To.

5. In the Copy Profile To text box, enter `\\computer2\profiles`, or click Browse to find the directory in Network Neighborhood. In Permitted to Use, select Change and choose `MEG` from the list (be sure to select Show Users). Choose OK and exit from System.

6. Log on as `MEG`. Notice that `MEG` received her profile from the second computer and that her environment settings match `GATESB`.

7. On the first computer, log off and log back on again as Administrator. Open the properties for `MEG` in User Manager and change the profile file reference from `NTUSER.DAT` to `NTUSER.MAN`.

8. Try to log on as `MEG`. Notice that you are unable to log on, because you have referenced a mandatory profile that does not exist.

9. Log back in as Administrator. Delete the account `MEG`.

Chapter 6: Security and Permissions

This set of labs will be most effective if you use both computers, and if you have one *New Technology File System* (NTFS) partition created on each computer.

If you do not currently have an NTFS partition, but you have an existing FAT partition that you can convert to NTFS (other than the boot partition), use the following steps to convert it to NTFS:

1. Open a DOS prompt window.
2. At the prompt, type `CONVERT D: /FS:NTFS`, where `D:` represents the letter of the partition that you are converting.
3. Press Enter. If there are any files in use by NT on that partition, such as the pagefile, you see a message telling you that you must reboot for the conversion to take effect. Do so. Otherwise, NT converts the partition after you press Enter.

If you do not have a partition that you can convert, but you do have at least 50MB of free disk space available, you can use Disk Administrator to create an NTFS partition. Follow these steps:

1. Start Disk Administrator. If this is the first time you are starting this utility, click OK in response to the startup message.
2. Click the free disk space available in the graphic provided.
3. Choose Partition, Create.
4. Specify the total size of the partition and click OK. The partition should be at least 50MB but can be no smaller than 10MB.
5. Choose Partition, Commit Changes Now.
6. Choose Tools, Format, and NTFS.
7. When format is complete, exit Disk Administrator.

Exercise 1: Using Shares—Part 1

Log on as Administrator. Then follow these steps:

1. Using Windows Explorer, create the following folders and files on both computers in the NTFS partition. Place a few lines of text in each file (you don't need to get fancy, now).

`\TOOLS`	`DOOM.TXT` (Create new text file.)
	`BUDGET97.DOC` (Create new Wordpad file.)
`\TOOLS\DATA`	`MEMO.DOC`
	`WELCOME.TXT`

2. Share `TOOLS` as `TOOLS`.

3. Remove Everyone from the *access control list* (ACL) for the share. Add the Managers group with Change and the Sales group with Read.

4. Create a new user called SimmonsB on Computer1. Add this user to the Sales group on Computer1.

5. Log on as SimmonsB on Computer1.

6. Using Network Neighborhood, access the TOOLS share on Computer2. Can you access it? NT should tell you that you do not have a valid account or password on Computer2. Recall that in a workgroup environment, you must either create a valid account for every user who needs access to shared resources on a computer or be able to connect as a valid user.

7. Create the account SimmonsB on Computer2 using the same password as you did on Computer1. Make this account a member of the Sales group on Computer2.

8. On Computer1, access the TOOLS share again. Your access now should be successful, because you have a valid account on Computer2 that matches the username and password of the account on Computer1. Disconnect from the share.

9. On Computer2, change SimmonsB's password to something else.

10. On Computer1, right-click Network Neighborhood and choose Map Network Drive.

11. Choose the TOOLS share from the list displayed, or type in the path \\Computer2\TOOLS.

12. In the Connect As box, enter SimmonsB and click OK. NT requests the password for SimmonsB on Computer2. Enter it to gain access to the share. If you know the name and password of a valid user account on another computer, you can access the share on that computer.

Exercise 2: Using Shares—Part 2

1. On Computer1, log on as BrownC.

2. Connect to the TOOLS share on Computer2.

3. Open the file DOOM.TXT, make a change to the file, and close it.

4. Log off, and log on as BarnesD.

5. Connect to the TOOLS share on Computer2.

6. Open the file DOOM.TXT and make a change to the file. Can you save the file? Note that NT does not let you save changes made to the file, because BarnesD is a member of the Sales group, which has been given Read access to the file. Do not close the file.

7. On `Computer2`, make `BarnesD` a member of the Managers group.

8. On `Computer1`, try to access the file and save changes again. Can you do it? Note that you are not able to save your changes, because `BarnesD`'s access token for the file still reflects the old group membership.

9. Close the file, and try to access it again and save changes. Could you do it? Disconnect from the share and reconnect, modify the file, and save the changes. Were you successful? Note at which point after group membership changes the change took effect.

Exercise 3: Hidden Shares

1. Share the `DATA` folder on `Computer2` as `DATA$`. Give only Managers Change permission to the share.

2. Log on as `BrownC` on `Computer1`.

3. Using Network Neighborhood, look for the `DATA` share in the list of shares for `Computer2`. You should not see it, because the $ makes it a hidden share.

4. Right-click Network Neighborhood and choose Map Network Drive. In the Path box, type `\\Computer2\DATA$` and click OK. You should be able to access the share.

5. Modify the file `MEMO.DOC` and save your changes.

6. Disconnect from the share and log off.

Exercise 4: File and Folder Permissions—Part 1

Log on to both computers as Administrator and make the following changes:

- Modify the NTFS permissions for the `TOOLS` folder. Remove Everyone, and add Managers with Read and Administrators with Full Control.

- Modify the NTFS permissions for the `DATA` folder. Remove Everyone, and add Sales with Change and MIS with Add.

1. Log on to `Computer1` as `BrownC`.

2. Use Windows Explorer to expand the NTFS partition. Open the file `BUDGET97.DOC` in `TOOLS` and modify it.

3. Can you save your changes? Note that the NTFS permission for Managers is Read. Because `BrownC` is a member of Managers, that user also gets Read access to the file and therefore cannot save changes.

4. Log off and log back on as `Donovan`, a member of the MIS and Managers group.

APP
F

5. Use Windows Explorer to access the DATA folder. Because MIS has only Add permission, you cannot access the DATA folder.

6. Use Notepad to create a document called DONOVAN.TXT. Try to save it in the DATA folder. *Access is denied.* Try to save it in the TOOLS folder. *You only have Read access, so you can't write a file to this folder.* Save the document in the root directory of the NTFS partition.

7. Open a DOS prompt window. At the prompt, copy the file DONOVAN.TXT from the root of the NTFS partition to the TOOLS\DATA directory. Note that you can do this because you have Add permission to the DATA folder.

8. Log off.

Exercise 5: File and Folder Permissions—Part 2

1. Log on as BrownC.

2. Access the TOOLS share on Computer2.

3. Open the file DOOM.TXT and modify it.

4. Save your changes. Can you do it? Not this time. The share permission is Change for Managers, and the NTFS permission is Read for Managers. When accessing a resource through a share, the more restrictive of the permissions become the effective permissions. Thus, your effective permission is Read and you cannot save changes.

5. Log on as Administrator on Computer2.

6. Change the NTFS permission for Managers on TOOLS to Full Control.

7. On Computer1, reconnect to the share and try to modify and save the file again. This time, you can because the effective permission is Change (the more restrictive of the share permission—Change—and the NTFS permission—Full Control).

8. As BrownC, create a new file called BrownC.TXT in the TOOLS directory on Computer2.

9. Log off.

10. As Administrator on Computer2, change the NTFS permission for Managers on TOOLS to Change.

Exercise 6: File and Folder Permissions—Part 3

1. Log on as Donovan on Computer2.

2. Locate the TOOLS folder on Computer2.

3. Locate the file BrownC.TXT and display its security properties (right-click, Properties, Security).

4. Choose Ownership to see that `BrownC` is the owner.

5. Can you take ownership of the file? No, because you only have Change permission.

6. Log off and log back on as Administrator.

7. Add `Donovan` to the ACL for the file `BrownC.TXT` with the NTFS Special Access Take Ownership permission.

8. Log on as Donovan again, and try to take ownership of the file. This time you can, because you have the permission to do so. Verify that `Donovan` is now the owner of `BrownC.TXT`.

Chapter 8: Performance Monitor

Exercise 1: Using the Performance Monitor

1. At a command prompt, type `DISKPERF -Y`.

2. If your computer has more than 16MB of RAM installed, modify the `boot.ini` file so that you boot only with 16MB of RAM:

   Add the switch `/MAXMEM:16` to the line under `[Operating Systems]` that contains the location of the NT 4.0 Workstation system files. (Remember, `boot.ini` is a read-only file.)

3. Shut down and restart NT to enable the Performance Monitor disk objects and their counters.

4. Start the Windows Explorer utility and Pinball.

5. Start the Performance Monitor from the Administrative Tools group and add the following objects and counters to a new chart:

Object	Counter	Instance
Processor	%Processor Time	0
Process	%Processor Time	Perfmon, Explorer, Pinball
Process	Working Set	Perfmon, Explorer, Pinball
Memory	Commit Limit	default
Memory	Pages/Sec	default
Logical Disk	Avg. Disk Sec/Transfer	pagefile drive
Logical Disk	%Disk Time	pagefile drive

APP
F

6. Track the values of each of the counters you added to the chart, especially noting the working set values for Performance Monitor, Windows Explorer, and Pinball (about 2.2MB, 175KB, and 184KB, respectively). Note also the commit limit for the pagefile (this will vary). Hint: Press Ctrl+H to highlight each line graph.

7. Switch to Explorer and create a new folder called PERFMON. Switch to Pinball and start the demo game.

8. Track the activity of the chart again and note the average values for each of the counters in the chart. Note any significant changes. In particular, you should have noticed a spike for %Processor Time for the processor and each of the three processes driven proportionately as each one performed its activity (creating the folder, running the demo game, updating the chart with the new statistics). Notice the flurry in disk counter activity initially, and then how it settles after the actions are performed. Notice, too, the increased amount of memory required by Pinball and Performance Monitor to correspond with their activities. Multiply Pages/Sec and Avg. Disk Sec/Transfer to obtain the percent of disk I/O related to pagefile activity. It will be well below Microsoft's suggested 10 percent threshold.

9. Switch to Windows Explorer. Copy the files only from the WINNT40 directory into the Perfmon folder. While the copy is taking place, switch to the Performance Monitor and note the Pages/Sec and Avg. Disk Sec/Transfer counters. These have peaked at or near the top of the scale. Multiply the average value for each together to obtain a percentage. This should be a little more than 10 percent and indicates that for this activity, the percentage of disk I/O related to pagefile activity was greater than Microsoft's recommended 10 percent. If this is consistently more than 10 percent, you might consider adding more RAM.

10. Open the BOOT.INI file and remove the /MAXMEM:16 switch. Restart NT.

11. If you have more than 16MB of RAM installed, repeat Steps 4 through 9 and note the differences (all disk values and %processor times should be less, although they will vary depending on the amount of additional RAM you have).

12. Close Windows Explorer and Pinball.

Exercise 2: Performance Monitor Logs

1. With Performance Monitor still running, choose View, Log, Add to Log. Add each of the following objects to the log:

   Logical Disk, Memory, Process, Processor

   Then click Done.

2. Choose Options, Log. Enter PERF1.LOG for the log name and save it in the PERFMON folder. Set the interval to 1 second and click Start Log.

3. Start Pinball and run the demo. Start Windows Explorer and create a new folder called `PERFMON2`. Copy everything from `Perfmon` into `Perfmon2`.

4. Switch to Performance Monitor. Wait another minute, and then choose Options, Log, Stop Log. Then save the log file.

5. Choose File, New Chart to clear and reset the Chart view for new values.

6. Choose Options, Data From. In the Log File list box, find and select the `PERF1.LOG` file you just created. Click OK.

7. Choose Edit, Add to Chart. Note that the entries listed represent those you collected during the log process. Add the following objects and counters to the chart as you did before. This time, the chart represents static data collected from the log.

Object	Processor	Instance
Processor	%Processor Time	0
Process	%Processor Time	Perfmon, Explorer, Pinball
Process	Working Set	Perfmon, Explorer, Pinball
Memory	Commit Limit	N/A
Memory	Pages/Sec	N/A
Logical Disk Drive	Avg. Disk Sec/ Transfer	pagefile
Logical Disk Drive	%Disk Time	pagefile

8. Note the average values for each during the log period.

9. Choose Edit, Time Window to change the time range to show only the period of peak activity. Note how the average values change.

10. Close Performance Monitor.

11. Use Windows Explorer to delete the folders `Perfmon` and `Perfmon2`.

Chapter 9: Disk Management and Fault Tolerance

These exercises are designed for computers that have two physical disk drives and at least 100MB of free space outside of an extended partition on one or more drives. If you have less, or if the free space includes an area of an extended partition, you will need to modify the exercise according to your configuration.

Exercise 1: Using Disk Administrator

1. Start Disk Administrator.
2. Select an area of free space.
3. Choose Partition, Create and create a new primary partition of 20MB.
4. Create another primary partition of 50MB.
5. Commit the changes.
6. Change the drive letter for the 50MB partition to x and the 20MB partition to y by using Tools, Assign Drive Letter.
7. Format the Y: drive as FAT and the X: drive as NTFS.
8. Close Disk Administrator and save your changes.

Exercise 2: Using Compression

1. Start Windows Explorer.
2. Select the Y: drive and create a new folder called TRUMP.
3. Copy WINNT256.BMP from the WINNT40 directory into TRUMP.
4. Look at the properties sheet for the file. Is there a Security tab? Is there a Compress attribute on the General tab? *No! It's a FAT partition!*
5. Copy the folder and its file from the Y: drive to the X: drive.
6. Look at the file's properties sheet again. Is there a Security tab and Compress attribute option? *Yes! It's an NTFS partition!*
7. Enable the Compress attribute for the file and click Apply. What is the file's compressed size?
8. Close Windows Explorer.
9. Open a DOS prompt window by choosing Start, Programs, DOS Prompt.
10. At the prompt, type CONVERT Y: /FS:NTFS and press Enter. NT converts the partition from FAT to NTFS. (If it tells you to restart, do so.)
11. Start Windows Explorer.
12. Select the Y: drive and look at the properties of the file in TRUMP. You now should see the Security tab and Compress attribute option because the partition is now NTFS.

Exercise 3: Using Volume Sets

1. Start Disk Administrator.

2. Select the Y: drive and delete it. Note the confirmation message.

3. Select that area of free space (20MB) and the remaining free space on the drive.

4. Choose Partition, Create Volume Set. Note the change in legend information indicating the new volume set.

5. Commit your changes, assign the volume set to drive letter y, and format the volume set as FAT.

6. Close Disk Administrator.

7. Start Windows Explorer and select the Y: drive. Can you tell that it is a volume set? *No! Not even through properties!* NT treats the volume set as a single drive.

8. Copy X:\TRUMP to the Y: drive.

9. Close Windows Explorer and start Disk Administrator.

10. Select the second member of y and choose Partition, Delete. Note the confirmation message, and delete it. What did you delete? *The entire volume set.*

11. Close Disk Administrator and start Windows Explorer.

12. Confirm that the Y: drive is gone.

Exercise 4: Extended Volume Sets

1. Start Disk Administrator.

2. Select any FAT partition on your computer and an area of free space on the same or another drive.

3. Choose Partition, Extend Volume Set. Can you do it? *No! You cannot extend FAT partitions!*

4. Select the NTFS partition X: drive and an area of free space on the same drive or another drive.

5. Choose Partition, Extend Volume set. Can you do it? *Yes! You can extend NTFS partitions!* What else do you notice? *The extended set is automatically formatted as NTFS.*

6. Delete the X: drive. Notice that if you delete any member of the extended volume set, you delete the entire volume set.

APP
F

Exercise 5: Using Stripe Sets

Only if you have at least two physical disks with free space on each

1. Start Disk Administrator.
2. Select an area of free space on one disk, and an area of free space on another. (If you have additional disks, select free space on these as well.)
3. Choose Partition, Create Stripe Set.
4. Create the largest stripe set you are allowed to create.
5. Notice in Disk Administrator how the stripe set is evenly distributed across the free space on the disks.
6. Delete the stripe set.

Exercise 6: Backup and Restore

Only if you have a working tape drive attached to your computer

1. Use Disk Administrator to create a 50MB NTFS partition (the Z: drive).
2. Use Windows Explorer to create a folder called BITMAPS and copy the bitmap files from the WINNT40 directory to BITMAPS.
3. Insert a new tape into the tape backup device.
4. Start Backup by choosing Start, Programs, Administrative Tools, Backup.
5. Select the Z: drive and enable the check box in front of it to select all its contents. Double-click it to verify that the bitmap folder and all its files are selected.
6. Choose Backup. Enter a tape name, select Verify Files, keep all other defaults, and proceed.
7. When the backup is complete, exit the utility.
8. Use Notepad to view the BACKUP.LOG file created in the WINNT40 directory.
9. Start Windows Explorer.
10. Select the Z: drive and delete the BITMAPS folder.
11. Start Backup. The existing tape appears in the window with the backup set you created.
12. If you appended to an existing tape, choose Operations, Catalog to find and load the backup set for the BITMAPS files and folder. Otherwise, double-click the backup set in the tapes window to load the catalog for the backup set.
13. Select all files from the backup set, including the BITMAPS folder.

14. Choose Restore and keep all defaults. Be sure the restore path is pointing to the Z: drive.

15. After the restore completes, exit the utility.

16. Start Windows Explorer and verify that the files and folder have been restored.

Chapter 10: Managing Printers in the Domain

This lab requires that you have one printer attached to one of your computers and assumes that it is connected to `Computer1`. Installing Windows 95 print drivers is also an option if you have the Windows 95 CD-ROM handy.

Exercise 1: Creating a Printer

Even if you already have installed your printer, complete this exercise on `Computer1`. Pay close attention to the screens, messages, and options available to you. Refer back to Chapter 10 for explanations of the screens.

1. Start the Add Printer Wizard by double-clicking My Computer, double-clicking Printers, and double-clicking Add Printer.

2. You will install the printer on your local computer. Select My Computer.

3. Select the port to which your print device is attached.

4. Select the manufacturer and model of the print device connected to your computer.

5. Set your Step 4 specifications to be your print default.

6. Call this configuration Managers Printer and share the printer as `NTPRINT`. If you have the Windows 95 source CD-ROM, select Windows 95 from the list of additional print drivers to support.

7. Print a test page to verify that your configuration works.

8. If necessary, enter the appropriate path to the NT source files to complete installation.

Exercise 1A (Optional)

If you have a network TCP/IP printer available that you can use and are allowed to manage, be sure to add the TCP/IP protocol to your computer and repeat Exercise 1. For Step 3, choose Add Port and select local port. Enter the IP address of the network printer.

Exercise 2: Connecting to a Network Printer

1. On Computer2, start the Add Printer Wizard.

2. This time, choose Network Printer Server to connect to the printer you just created on Computer1.

3. From the Connect to Printer browse screen, expand through the Microsoft Windows Network entries to find the printer you created on Computer1 called NTPRINT and select it.

   or

   Type this *Universal Naming Convention* (UNC) path to the printer: \\COMPUTER1\NTPRINT.

4. Make the printer you just specified the default printer on Computer2.

5. Complete the installation. A network printer icon appears in the Printers folder.

6. Use Notepad to create and save a short text document called PRINT.TXT. Suggested content:

   If you can read this, printing was successful.

7. Print PRINT.TXT to the network printer to which you just connected. Was printing successful? Yes.

8. On Computer1, open the NTPRINT print manager window and pause the shared printer.

9. Resubmit PRINT.TXT on Computer2.

10. In the NTPRINT window, select the PRINT.TXT print job and explore the document properties. Schedule the job to print at the next half-hour.

11. Resume the printer and wait until the next half-hour to see your print job print.

Exercise 3: Managing Printer Properties

1. On Computer1, open the NTPRINT Properties dialog box and select the Scheduling tab.

2. Set the priority to the highest setting (99).

3. On the Security tab, choose Permissions.

4. Remove Everyone and add Managers with Print permission.

5. Close the NTPRINT Properties dialog box.

6. Create another printer for the same print device on the same port. Call it Staff Printer and share it as STAFFPRT.

7. After you create the printer, open its Properties dialog box and select the Scheduling tab.

8. Set the priority to the lowest setting (1).

9. On the Security tab, choose Permissions.

10. Remove Everyone and add MIS with Print permission.

11. Close the STAFFPRT Properties dialog box.

12. Make Donovan a member of the Power Users group on Computer1.

13. Log on to Computer1 as a Manager account—Donovan.

14. Open both NTPRINT and STAFFPRT windows. Pause NTPRINT and STAFFPRT.

15. Create a text document called TESTP1.TXT with the text

```
This is a test print - 1
```

and print to NTPRINT. You should see the document queued up in the NTPRINT window.

16. On Computer2, log on as GatesB.

17. Connect to STAFFPRT and make it the default.

18. Create a text document called Staffp1.TXT with the text

```
This is a staff test print - 1
```

and print to STAFFPRT. You should see the document queued up in the STAFFPRT window on Computer1.

19. Create two more documents on Computer1 (TESTP2.TXT and TESTP3.TXT with similar text) and on Computer2 (Staffp2.TXT and Staffp3.TXT with similar text) and print them to their respective printers. You will see them queued up.

20. Resume STAFFPRT then NTPRINT. In what order did the print jobs print? Chances are that because STAFFPRT resumed first, its low priority STAFFp1.TXT job was sent to the print device ahead of TESTP1.TXT. Nevertheless, before any other staff jobs print, the Managers' jobs will print first, because their print queue associated with the same printer has a higher priority than staff print jobs.

If your computer had a previous printer setup, restore it as your default now if you like.

Chapter 11: Windows NT 4.0 Architecture and Boot Sequence

Portions of this lab require that you have installed at least two 16-bit Windows 3.1 applications. These might be earlier versions of Microsoft Office, or even your favorite Windows games.

APP
F

Exercise 1: Running DOS and Windows 16-Bit Applications

1. Right-click the taskbar and start the Task Manager. Choose View, Select Columns, Base Priority. Resize the Task Manager window so that you can see the Base Priorities column.

2. Select the Processes tab. Unless you started a Windows 16-bit application earlier, you will see no entries for NTVDM.

3. Choose Start, Run and start the MS-DOS application EDIT.COM. This is the 16-bit MS-DOS Editor that comes with NT in the WINN40\SYSTEM32 directory.

4. Switch back to Task Manager and notice the addition of a new NTVDM entry. Notice the amount of memory allocated for it and its priority.

5. Start one of your Windows 16-bit applications.

6. Switch back to Task Manager and notice a new NTVDM entry with subentries for the application and the WOWEXEC.EXE. Notice also its memory use and CPU use and priority.

7. Start another Windows 16-bit application. Make a mental note of the speed with which it loaded. Because it is being loaded into an existing WOW NTVDM, it loads rather quickly.

8. Switch back to Task Manager and notice its subentry in the WOW NTVDM, as well as the memory and CPU changes.

9. Close the DOS application and both of the Windows 16-bit applications and note the changes in Task Manager. The WOW NTVDM remains loaded in case there will be a new Windows 16-bit application starting, but the closed application entries have been removed.

10. Leave Task Manager running.

Exercise 2: Running 16-Bit Windows Applications in Their Own Memory Space

1. Start both of the Win 16 applications.

2. Switch to Task Manager and notice the WOW NTVDM subentries. On the Performance tab, note the total physical RAM in use.

3. Close one of the Win 16 applications and notice the change in physical RAM.

4. Create a shortcut on your desktop for the Win 16 application you closed. Right-click it and display its properties. On the Shortcut tab, select Run in Separate Memory Space.

5. Start the Win 16 application from its shortcut. Notice that it takes a little longer to load than in the last exercise, because NT must create a new WOW NTVDM for this application.

6. Switch back to Task Manager and confirm that a new WOW NTVDM has been created. Note its memory, CPU, and priority statistics.

7. Select the Task Manager Performance tab and note the total physical RAM in use. It is noticeably higher than when both applications ran in the same WOW NTVDM.

8. Close each Win 16 application and monitor the decrease in physical RAM used. How many WOW NTVDM entries remain on the Processes tab? *One.*

Exercise 3: Managing Process Priorities

1. Start Pinball by choosing Start, Programs, Accessories, Games. If Pinball is not available, load it through the Add Programs applet in the Control Panel. (A quick way to activate a Pinball game and to notice changes in this exercise is to run a demo game from the Game menu.)

2. Switch to Task Manager and find its entry. Notice that its priority is set to Normal.

3. Close Pinball. Open a DOS command prompt window.

4. Start Pinball with a low priority by typing

   ```
   START /LOW PINBALL
   ```

5. Switch to Task Manager and verify that Pinball is running with low priority. Pinball itself should appear to be running a bit sluggishly, although on fast Pentium systems, the change may not be noticeable.

6. On the Processes tab in Task Manager, right-click the Pinball entry and choose Set Priority. Change the priority to Normal. Select the Performance tab and arrange Pinball so that you can see part of the Performance charts in the background. Notice that the charts continue to record data while you play Pinball.

7. Switch to Task Manager. On the Processes tab, right-click Pinball and change its priority to High. Select the Performance tab and arrange the screens as before. Notice that the chart ceases to record or records very slowly while you play Pinball in the foreground.

8. Close Pinball and Task Manager.

APP
F

Chapter 12: Windows NT Networking Services

Exercise 1: Managing Network Properties

Complete this exercise from both `Computer1` and `Computer2`.

1. Start the Network applet from the Control Panel (or right-click Network Neighborhood and choose Properties).

2. Select the Adapters tab to view your installed network adapter card.

3. Select the adapter card from the list and choose Properties. Note the properties of your adapter.

4. Close the Adapter Properties dialog box and select the Bindings tab. Record the bindings for NetBEUI under NetBIOS *(Network Basic Input/Output System),* Workstation, and Server.

5. Select the Protocols tab and note that only NetBEUI is installed (unless you did something you weren't told to do in another lab).

6. Choose Add, and select TCP/IP from the Network Protocols list. Be sure to have the source CD-ROM available. When prompted, enter the drive and path to the source files.

7. After the protocol is installed, click OK. NT prompts you for TCP/IP settings. For `Computer1`, enter `121.132.4.1` with subnet mask `255.255.255.0`, and for `Computer2`, enter `121.132.4.2` with subnet mask `255.255.255.0`. If you are connected to your company network and are using TCP/IP, use your company's recommended IP address and subnet mask, if appropriate. If you have a *Dynamic Host Configuration Protocol* (DHCP) server available and can use it, configure the computers to obtain their IP addresses from the DHCP server.

8. Restart NT when prompted. After NT reboots, open the Network applet again.

9. On the Bindings tab, note the additional bindings for TCP/IP. Record these and compare them against the NetBEUI bindings. Notice that both bindings are bound to the Workstation and Server Service. This means that you can connect to network resources on any server using NetBEUI or TCP/IP, and that your computer can service requests from any computer using NetBEUI or TCP/IP.

10. At a command prompt, enter the command `IPCONFIG`. What information is displayed? *IP address, subnet mask, and default gateway.* Record the information.

11. Now enter the command `IPCONFIG /ALL`. What additional information is displayed? *Host, DNS, node, and other NT IP configuration parameters; and the description and physical address of the adapter card.* Record the adapter information.

12. At the command prompt, PING the other computer's address. For example, on Computer1, type `PING 121.132.4.1`. You should receive four `Reply from...` messages indicating that communication is established between the computers.

13. Through Windows Explorer, map a network drive to a resource on Computer2. You should be successful. Disconnect the mapping.

14. In the Network applet on Computer1, select the Protocols tab and remove NetBEUI. Restart NT when prompted.

15. After NT reboots, use Windows Explorer to map a drive to the same resource on Computer2. You should be successful. Why? *NT used TCP/IP to establish the connection.* Computer2 *has both NetBEUI and TCP/IP installed.* Disconnect the mapping.

16. In the Network applet on Computer2, select the Protocols tab and display the properties for TCP/IP.

17. Change the subnet mask to `255.255.0.0`. Restart NT when prompted.

18. After Computer2 reboots, use Windows Explorer on Computer1 to map a drive to the same resource on Computer2. You should be unsuccessful this time. Why? *Even though both computers are using TCP/IP and are on the same subnet, they have different subnet masks and so are treated as though they were on different subnets. Therefore, they cannot communicate with each other.*

19. At a command prompt, try the `PING` command again. You should be unsuccessful *(for the same reason as in Step 18).*

20. Change the subnet mask on Computer2 back to `255.255.255.0`. After the computer reboots, verify that communications can be established between the computers. (Use PING and Windows Explorer.)

21. Reinstall NetBEUI on Computer1. Restart NT when prompted.

Exercise 2: Workstation Bindings

1. In the Network applet on Computer1, select the Bindings tab and expand the Workstation bindings. Highlight Workstation in the list and choose Disable to disable its bindings. Click OK and restart NT when prompted.

2. When Computer1 reboots, you probably will receive a service message error. Use the Event Viewer to note which service failed to start (Workstation), and what other services dependent on it also failed to start (Computer Browser, Messenger).

3. Use Network Neighborhood to locate Computer2. Were you successful? *No, because the Workstation Service is used to perform this network request, and its bindings have been disabled.*

APP
F

4. Use Network Neighborhood to locate Computer1. Were you successful? *Yes.* Connect to a shared folder on Computer1 and copy a file to your desktop. Were you successful? *Yes.* Why? *The Server Service on Computer1 handles requests for resources from other computers. These bindings still are enabled, so Computer1 can't browse the network, but it still can share its own resources. You can use this tactic to optimize bindings and improve network performance for NT computers that only need to make their resources available to other computers but not establish connections of their own.*

5. Re-enable the Workstation bindings on Computer1 and restart NT when prompted.

Chapter 13: TCP/IP and Windows NT

Exercise 1: Manually Configuring an IP Address

This exercise asks you to install TCP/IP and to manually configure an IP address and subnet mask. The exercise assumes that only the NetBEUI protocol is installed and the source files are located on your computer in the ntsrv folder on your C: drive.

1. Log on to your domain controller as the administrator and open the Network application by choosing Start, Settings, Control Panel, Network Icon.

2. Select the Protocols tab in the Network Properties dialog box and click the Add button.

3. From the list of available protocols in the Select Network Protocol dialog box, select TCP/IP and click OK.

4. A TCP/IP Setup dialog box appears asking whether you want to use a DHCP server. Click No to continue.

5. After the Windows NT Setup dialog box appears, type the location of the source file in the space provided (c:\ntsrv) and click Continue.

Files are copied and TCP/IP and related services are installed. Notice that TCP/IP appears in the Network Protocols list box on the Network Properties dialog box.

6. Click Close. (Bindings will be reviewed and configured.)

7. A Microsoft TCP/IP Properties dialog box appears so that you can manually configure an IP address, subnet mask, and default gateway. Enter an IP address of 131.107.2.x, where x is a unique assigned number. Change the default subnet mask from 255.255.0.0 to 255.255.255.0. Leave the Default Gateway entry blank.

Key Concept

You may require a different IP address and subnet mask because of your local network characteristics. Make sure that you supply a unique IP address, or error messages indicating a duplicate IP address on the network will result.

8. The Networks Settings Change confirmation box appears asking whether you want to shut down and restart your computer. Click Yes.

Exercise 2: Installing DHCP

This exercise asks you to install the DHCP service to become a DHCP server and to configure a scope of address. You also will designate a group of addresses to be excluded from the scope and add an address reservation. This exercise assumes that NetBEUI and TCP/IP are installed and that the source files are located on your computer in the ntsrv folder on your C: drive.

1. Log on to your domain controller as the administrator and open the Network application by choosing Start, Settings, Control Panel, Network Icon.

2. Select the Services tab in the Network properties dialog box and click the Add button.

3. From the list of available services in the Select Network Services dialog box, select Microsoft DHCP Server and click OK.

4. After the Windows NT Setup dialog box appears, type the location of the source file in the space provided (c:\ntsrv) and click Continue.

Files are copied and the DHCP server service is installed.

An information box appears stating that if any adapters are using DHCP to obtain an IP address, they now are required to use a static IP address.

5. Click OK.

Notice that the DHCP server appears in the Network Services list box on the Network Properties dialog box.

6. Click Close on the Network Properties dialog box. (Bindings will be reviewed and configured.)

7. The Networks Settings Change confirmation box appears asking whether you want to shut down and restart your computer. Click Yes.

8. After your computer restarts, log on to your domain controller as the administrator and open the DHCP Manager application by choosing Start, Programs, Administrative Tools, DHCP Manager. The DHCP Manager dialog box appears.

9. Choose Scope, Create. A Create Scope (Local) configuration dialog box appears.

10. In the IP Address Pool Start Address text box, enter 131.107.2.150, and in the IP Address Pool Stop Address text box, enter 131.107.2.199. In the IP Address Pool Subnet Mask text box, enter 255.255.255.0.

11. In the Exclusion Range Start Address text box, enter 131.107.2.170, and in the Exclusion Range Start Address text box, enter 131.107.2.180 and click Add. The range of address appears in the Exclusion Addresses list box.

12. In the Lease Duration area, make sure that the Limited To radio button is selected and change the lease duration from the default value of 3 days to 1 day. Click OK.

13. A DHCP Manager message box appears telling you the scope was created successfully but is not activated yet. It then asks whether you would like to activate the scope now. Click Yes.

14. The new scope appears under the Local Machine entry on the DHCP Manager dialog box with the light bulb on (this means the scope is active). If the new scope does not appear automatically, double-click the Local Machine entry.

15. In the DHCP Manager dialog box, select the newly created scope. Choose Scope, Add Reservations. The Add Reserved Clients information screen appears.

16. Review the required information for this screen. Notice that the network number appears in the IP Address portion of the screen. Why did this happen? *The starting address and subnet mask values were entered when the scope was created.*

17. In the IP Address text box, enter the value of your IP address used in Exercise 1, Step 7.

    For the next step, a unique identifier is required to associate a specific network card with this reservation. To obtain a network card unique *Media Access Control* (MAC) address, follow these steps:

    1. Start up a command prompt.
    2. Type ipconfig /all.
    3. Record the physical address (this is the unique identifier).

18. In the Unique Identifier text box, enter your 12-digit MAC address.

19. Enter your computer name in the Client Name text box and click Add, Close.

20. In the DHCP Manager, choose Scope, Active Leases. Ensure that the reservation you added is present. Remove the reservation by clicking Delete, and then click Close.

Exercise 3: Becoming a WINS Server

This exercise asks you to install the *Windows Internet Naming Service* (WINS) on your computer to become a WINS server. The exercise assumes that NetBEUI and TCP/IP are installed and that the source files are located on your computer in the ntsrv folder on your C: drive.

1. Log on to your domain controller as the administrator and open the Network application by choosing Start, Settings, Control Panel, Network Icon.

2. Select the Services tab in the Network Properties dialog box and click the Add button.

3. From the list of available services in the Select Network Services dialog box, select Windows Internet Name Service and click OK.

4. After the Windows NT Setup dialog box appears, type the location of the source file in the space provided (C:\ntsrv) and click Continue.

   Files are copied and the WINS server service is installed.

5. Click Close in the Network Properties dialog box. (Bindings will be reviewed and configured.)

6. The Networks Settings Change confirmation box appears asking whether you want to shut down and restart your computer. Click Yes.

7. After your computer restarts, log on to your domain controller as the administrator and open the WINS Manager application by choosing Start, Programs, Administrative Tools, WINS Manager. The WINS Manager dialog box appears.

8. Your IP address should appear in the WINS Server list box. Double-click your IP address. The statistics area on the right side of the dialog box should refresh.

9. Choose Mappings, Show Database. View the Show Database [Local] Mappings dialog box. How many entries are in the database pertaining to your computer? List the entries in the database for your computer in the spaces below.

   _____   _____   _____
   _____   _____   _____

   Answers will vary; however, at least two entries should be registered in the database pertaining to the local computer. There may be a browser entry, a domain entry, a computer entry, and a user entry.

10. Click Close and then exit WINS Manager.

APP
F

Exercise 4: Installing DNS Service

This exercise asks you to install the *domain name server* (DNS) service and to manually configure an alias computer name. You then will PING the alias to ensure proper configuration. The exercise assumes that NetBEUI and TCP/IP are installed, and that the source files are located on your computer in the ntsrv folder on your C: drive.

1. Log on to your domain controller as the administrator and open the Network application by choosing Start, Settings, Control Panel. Then double-click the Network icon.
2. Select the Services tab in the Network Properties dialog box and click the Add button.
3. From the list of available services in the Select Network Services dialog box, select Microsoft DNS Server and click OK.
4. After the Windows NT Setup dialog box appears, type the location of the source file in the space provided (C:\ntsrv) and click Continue.

   Files are copied and the DNS server service is installed.
5. In the Network Properties dialog box, click Close. (Bindings will be reviewed and configured.)
6. The Networks Settings Change confirmation box appears asking whether you want to shut down and restart your computer. Click Yes.
7. After your computer starts, log on to your domain controller as the administrator and open the Network application by choosing Start, Settings, Control Panel. Then double-click the Network icon.
8. Select the Protocols tab in the Network Properties dialog box, choose TCP/IP, and choose Properties.
9. In the Microsoft TCP/IP Properties dialog box, select DNS.
10. In the Domain box, type <your first name>.com. Your computer name appears in the Host Name box; do not alter your computer name.
11. Click the Add button below the DNS Service Search Order list box and enter your IP address in the TCP/IP DNS Server dialog box. Then click Add.
12. Click OK to close the Microsoft TCP/IP Properties dialog box and click OK again to close the Network application.
13. Open the DNS Manager application by choosing Start, Programs, Administrative Tools, DNS Manager. The DNS Manager dialog box appears.

14. Choose DNS, New Server. The Add DNS Server dialog box appears. Enter your computer name or your IP address in the space provided and click OK. Your DNS server should appear in the Server list, and Cache should appear below your DNS Server name or IP address.

15. Choose DNS, New Zone. The Creating New Zone for <computer name> dialog box appears. Select the Primary option button and click Next.

16. In the Creating New Zone for <computer name> dialog box, type the same name you entered in Step 10 (<your first name>.com) and press the Tab key. Verify that <your first name>.com.dns appears in the Zone File box. Then click Next, Finish.

    Verify that your new zone name appears below your server name on the left pane of the dialog box, and that an NS record and an SOA record appear under Zone Info in the right pane of the dialog box.

17. Right-click your zone name in the left pane and choose New Record. In the Record Type list box, select ARecord. Enter your hostname and your host IP address, and disable the Create Associated PTR Record check box. Click OK.

18. Right-click your zone name in the left pane and choose New Record. In the Record Type list box, select the CNAME Record. Enter an alias name of your choice in the Alias Name box and click OK.

19. In the For Host DNS box, type your computer name and your DNS domain name separated by a period. (Example: <computer name>.<your first name>.com.) Then click OK.

20. Close the DNS Manager.

21. Start a command prompt window.

22. Type Ping <alias name>.

Chapter 14: Novell NetWare Connectivity Tools

Exercise 1: NetWare Connectivity

Complete this exercise if you have access to a NetWare server. Create an account on your NT Workstation that matches your account and password on the NetWare server. Make this account a member of the Administrators local group on your NT Workstation.

1. Start the Network applet on Computer1. On the Protocols tab, click Add and choose NWLink from the list. Be sure to have the source files available. On the Services tab, click Add and choose Client Services for NetWare from the list. Click OK and restart NT when prompted.

2. After NT restarts, log on as the NT account you created to match the account on the NetWare server. You are prompted for a preferred NetWare server. Select the NetWare server that you have access to and click OK. You are logged in to the NetWare server.

3. Start the newly added *Gateway Service for NetWare* (GSNW) applet in the Control Panel. Review the options that are available. If your NetWare server is version 4.x, enter any appropriate *NetWare Directory Services* (NDS) information.

4. From Windows Explorer, choose Tools, Map Network Drive. Notice the new entry for NetWare or Compatible Network. Expand this entry and find your server in the list.

5. Expand the server entry and select a directory to which you have access. Connect to it. If there is another server on which you have an account, select it from the list, choose a folder, and in the Connect As box, enter the logon ID for that NetWare server. *Client Services for NetWare* (CSNW) completes the connection, no doubt asking you for a password for that server.

6. Disconnect from both NetWare servers.

7. In the CSNW applet, set the preferred server to <NONE>.

Chapter 15: Network Client Configuration and Support

The first exercise of this lab assumes that at least one Windows NT Server installation is available to use Network Client Administrator to create a shared folder to be used to install Server Tools on client computers on the network.

If a Windows NT 4.0 Workstation is available, Exercise 2 has you install Server Tools on that platform. If a Windows 95 platform is available, Exercise 3 has you install Server Tools on that platform.

Exercise 1: Install Server Tools Using Windows NT Server

Complete this exercise from your domain controller.

1. Log on to your *primary domain controller* (PDC) and start the Network Client Administrator utility by choosing Start, Programs, Administrative Tools, Network Client Administrator.

2. When the Network Client Administrator selection box appears, select Copy Client-Based Network Administration Tools and click Continue.

3. In the Share Client-Based Network Administration Tools dialog box that appears, enter the path where the Server Tools source files are located. (Example: `F:\Clients`.) Accept the default destination path and share name and click OK.

4. When the files are copied to the selected folder, a Network Client Administrator information box appears. Read the message and click OK.

5. Another Network Client Administrator information box appears stating that the Network Administration Tools are now available. Click OK.

6. In the Network Client Administrator selection box, click Exit.

Exercise 2: Install Server Tools Using Windows NT Workstation

Complete this exercise from a Windows NT Workstation computer if one is available on the network.

1. Log on to a Windows NT 4.0 Workstation on the network with the Administrator account.

2. Map to the network share created in Exercise 1.

3. Double-click the `Winnt` folder.

4. Double-click `Setup.bat`.

5. An MS-DOS prompt starts, and the Server Tools files are copied to your computer. In the following spaces, record the Server Tools `.exe` files that are copied:

_____, _____, _____, _____, _____, _____, and _____.

Dhcpadmin.exe, Poledit.exe, Rasadmin.exe, Rplmgr.exe, Srvmgr.exe, Usrmgr.exe, and Winsmgr.exe

6. Press any key to continue.

7. Right-click the Start button and choose Open.

8. Choose Start, File, New, Folder, and type Server Tools.

9. Open Explorer and locate the `<winntroot>\System32` folder.

10. Locate the Server Tools `.exe` files one at a time as recorded in Step 5. Click and drag each file to the Server Tools folder created in Step 9.

Hint: Position the Explorer window and the Start menu window so that you can view each.

11. Choose Start, Server Tools, Shortcut to Usrmgr.exe.

12. Choose User, Select Domain. From the Select Domain window, select Domain A.

13. View the user and group accounts from that domain.

14. Close User Manager.

APP
F

Exercise 3: Install Server Tools Using Windows 95

Complete this exercise from a Windows 95 computer if one is available on the network.

1. Start Windows 95, open the Control Panel, and double-click the Add/Remove Programs icon.

2. Select the Windows Setup tab in the Add/Remove Programs Properties dialog box and click the Have Disk button.

3. In the Install from Disk dialog box that appears, enter the path to the Server Tools source files created in Exercise 1. (Example: <computername>\SetupAdm\Win95.)

4. In the Have Disk Properties dialog box, enable the check box next to the Windows NT Server Tools item and click Install.

5. After the Server Tools are installed, choose Start, Programs, Windows NT Server Tools. Then select User Manager for Domains.

6. Choose User, Select Domain. From the Select Domain dialog box, select Domain A.

7. View the user and group accounts from that domain.

8. Close User Manager.

Chapter 16: Remote Access Server

Exercise 1: Using RAS

To complete this exercise, you must have either a null modem cable to connect to the COM1 port on both computers, or modems installed in both computers and a separate working phone line and number for each.

Perform these steps on both computers. Log on as Administrator.

1. Start the Network Applet and select the Services tab.

2. Click Add and select Remote Access Service from the list. Be sure to have the source files ready, and provide NT with the installation path when prompted.

3. The New Modem Wizard appears. If you are using a modem, let NT detect it. Otherwise, choose to select it yourself, and select Dial-Up Networking Serial Cables Between 2 PCs. As you continue through the wizard, choose COM1, specify your country and area code, and finish the modem installation.

4. Next you need to configure the COM port. In the RAS Setup dialog box, choose the COM port from the list and select Configure. On Computer1, choose Dial Out Only; on Computer2, select Dial Out and Receive Calls. Then click OK.

5. Click the Network button and verify that all protocols are selected for both computers. For each protocol on `Computer2` in the Server Settings area, be sure that the Entire Network option is selected. For TCP/IP, select Use Static Address Pool and enter 121.132.4.100 and 121.132.4.110 as the begin and end addresses.

6. Click OK and complete the RAS installation. Click No when asked whether you want to enable NetBIOS Broadcast Propagation. Restart NT when prompted.

7. After NT reboots, start the Remote Access Admin program on `Computer2` (from the Administrative Tools folder).

8. Choose Users, Permissions, Grant All to grant permission to all users.

9. On `Computer1`, start the Dial-Up Networking program from Accessories. Create a phonebook entry for `Computer2` (be creative). Leave the phone number blank if using a null modem cable, or the actual phone number if you are configured with modems and separate phone lines.

10. Disconnect `Computer1`'s network cable connection.

11. Connect the null modem cable to the COM1 port on both computers.

12. Restart NT on `Computer1`. In the Logon dialog box that appears, select Logon Using Dial-Up Networking. Select the phonebook entry you created for `Computer2` as your dial-up number and choose Dial. If prompted for a password, enter the appropriate password for your account. RAS connects you to `Computer2`.

13. Use Windows Explorer to connect to a resource on `Computer2`. Were you successful? *Yes. You are connected using RAS.*

14. Note the connection statistics recorded in the Remote Access Admin utility on `Computer2`.

15. Start the Dial-Up Networking program again and choose Hang Up.

16. Remove RAS from both computers by starting the Network Applet, selecting Remote Access Service from the Services tab, choosing Remove, and answering Yes to the warning message. Restart NT when prompted.

17. Reconnect `Computer1` to the network, and remove the null modem cable from both computers.

Chapter 17: Network Monitor

Exercise 1: Using Event Viewer to Troubleshoot

1. Use the Services applet in the Control Panel to change the startup value for the Messenger Service to Manual.

2. Restart NT. You should receive this message:

```
At least one service or driver failed to start.
```

APP
F

3. Start the Event Viewer and look for the first Event Log entry for the approximate time you restarted NT. Look at the message for the first stop error right above it. This entry probably will say that some service that depends on the Messenger failed to start.

4. Use Services in the Control Panel to set the Messenger Service startup value back to Automatic, and restart the computer.

5. The error message now should not occur.

Exercise 2: Viewing Audit Events

1. If you haven't already, start User Manager. Choose Policy, Audit, and enable auditing for successful and failed logons and logoffs.

2. Log on to the workstation as BrownC with an incorrect password.

3. Try again with the correct password.

4. Log off and log back on as Administrator.

5. Start the Event Viewer and switch to the Security Log.

6. Locate—or, if you prefer, filter—logon/logoff entries.

7. Find the entry for the incorrect password. (Hint: Look for the lock icon). What information does it give you? *Reason for the failure, the user account involved, and the workstation on which the logon attempt took place, among other things.*

8. Review the entries for the successful logons.

9. Close the Event Viewer.

The following lab exercises require you to have a null modem connection between your two computers. One computer will be configured as a host computer, the other as a target computer. If a null modem cable is not available, you cannot accomplish Exercise 3.

Exercise 3: Connecting via a Null Modem Adapter

Complete this exercise from both domain controllers.

1. Verify that the COM port settings on each computer match by checking the settings from the Ports applet in the Control Panel. Use these settings on both computers:

   Baud Rate: 19,200 or 9,600
   Auto Answer: OnHardware
   Compression: Disabled
   Error Detection: Disabled

2. Using a null modem cable, connect the two domain controllers together using any available COM port.

Exercise 4: Copying the Debug Utilities

Complete this exercise from the host computer.

1. Create a folder named Debug on the C: drive (use another drive if less than 100MB of free space is available on C:).

2. Insert the Windows NT 4.0 Server CD-ROM into the CD-ROM drive.

3. Copy the file Expndsym.cmd from the <cdrom>:\Support\Debug folder to C:\Debug.

4. Copy the contents of the <cdrom>:\Support\Debug\I386 folder to C:\Debug (excluding the Symbols folder).

5. From a command prompt window, display the C:\Debug folder and run the Expand Symbols Files program by typing expndsym <cdrom>: c:\debug.

6. After the Symbols files are copied to the host computer, enter the following commands in the command prompt window:

   ```
   set _nt_debug_port=com<port number>set _nt_debug_baud_rate=<baud rate>set
   _nt_symbol_path=c:\debug\symbolsi386kd -m -v
   ```

7. Verify that the command prompt window reads KD: waiting to reconnect...

Exercise 5: Editing the BOOT.INI File

Complete this exercise from the target computer.

1. From Explorer, right-click the boot.ini file in the c:\ folder and choose Properties.

2. If selected, clear the Hidden and Read-Only attributes and click OK to close the boot.ini Properties dialog box.

3. From Explorer, double-click the boot.ini file and add /debug to the first line of the [operating systems] section of the file.

4. Reboot the target computer by selecting the [debugger enabled] selection.

Exercise 6: Working with the Kernel Debugger

Complete this exercise from the host computer.

1. Verify communications between the two computers when the blue screen appears.

2. From the host computer screen, press Ctrl+C to stop the Kernel Debugger. In the spaces below, list the first five software modules loaded. (Answers may vary depending on the hardware used.)

   _____, _____, _____, _____, and _____.

   ntoskrnl.exe, hal.dll, atapi.sys, scsiport.sys, and disk.sys

APP
F

3. Press the G key and then Enter to continue the boot process.

4. When the boot process completes, type `@k` to exit the Kernel Debugger.

Exercise 7 (Optional): Examining a Memory Dump

If a file called `Memory.dmp` is available in the `%SystemRoot%` folder, complete this exercise.

1. From the command prompt window, display the `c:\debug` folder.

2. Enter the command `dumpchk -v`.

3. View the results. (Hint: You may want to make the command prompt window larger by adjusting the height of the window from the Command Prompt Layout tab in the Properties dialog box.)

4. Enter the command `dumpexam -v`.

5. View the result by opening the `Memory.txt` file in the `%SystemRoot%` folder.

Objectives Index

APP
G

APP
G

Get **FREE** books and more...when you register this book online for our Personal Bookshelf Program

http://register.quecorp.com/

 Register online and you can sign up for our *FREE Personal Bookshelf Program...*unlimited access to the electronic version of more than 200 complete computer books—immediately! That means you'll have 100,000 pages of valuable information onscreen, at your fingertips!

 Plus, you can access product support, including complimentary downloads, technical support files, book-focused links, companion Web sites, author sites, and more!

 And you'll be automatically registered to receive a *FREE subscription to a weekly email newsletter* to help you stay current with news, announcements, sample book chapters, and special events, including sweepstakes, contests, and various product giveaways!

 We value your comments! Best of all, the entire registration process takes only a few minutes to complete, so go online and get the greatest value going—absolutely FREE!

Don't Miss Out On This Great Opportunity!

QUE® is a brand of Macmillan Computer Publishing USA.

For more information, please visit *www.mcp.com*

Exam Guide

MCSE Networking Essentials Exam Guide
Dan York
0789722658
12/99
U.S. price: $39.99
Canadian price: $57.95

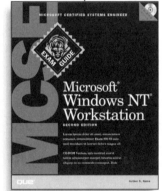

MCSE Windows NT 4.0 Workstation Exam Guide
Emmett Dulaney
0789722623
12/99
U.S. price: $39.99
Canadian price: $57.95

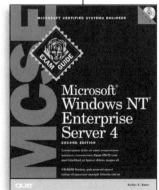

MCSE Windows NT 4.0 Server in the Enterprise Exam Guide
Emmett Dulaney
0789722631
12/99
U.S. price: $39.99
Canadian price: $57.95

www.quecorp.com

All prices are subject to change.

What's on the Disc

The companion CD-ROM contains Que's new TestPro test engine as well as MCSE Microsoft Windows NT Server Exam Guide, Second Edition in Adobe PDF format.

Windows 95 Installation Instructions

1. Insert the CD-ROM disc into your CD-ROM drive.
2. From the Windows 95 desktop, double-click on the My Computer icon.
3. Double-click on the icon representing your CD-ROM drive.
4. Double-click on the icon titled START.EXE to run the installation program.

 NOTE

If Windows 95 is installed on your computer, and you have the AutoPlay feature enabled, the START.EXE program starts automatically whenever you insert the disc into your CD-ROM drive.

Windows NT Installation Instructions

1. Insert the CD-ROM disc into your CD-ROM drive.
2. From File Manager or Program Manager, choose Run from the File menu.
3. Type <*drive*>\START.EXE and press Enter, where <*drive*> corresponds to the drive letter of your CD-ROM. For example, if your CD-ROM is drive D:, type D:\START.EXE and press Enter.

Technical Support from Macmillan

We can't help you with Windows or Macintosh problems or software from third parties, but we can assist you if a problem arises with the CD-ROM itself.

Email Support: Send email to http://www.mcp.com/support

Telephone: (317) 581-3833

Fax: (317) 581-4773

Mail: Macmillan USA
               Attention: Support Department
               201 West 103rd Street
               Indianapolis, IN 46290-1093

Here's how to reach us on the Internet:

World Wide Web: http://www.quecorp.com